the *Washington* Almanac™

Facts About Washington

1st Edition

Andrea Jarvela

WestWinds Press™

First edition published 1999

ISBN 1-55868-473-5
ISSN 1526-288X

Key title: The Washington Almanac

WestWinds Press™
An imprint of Graphic Arts Center Publishing Company
P.O. Box 10306, Portland, Oregon 97296-0306, 503-226-2402
www.gacpc.com

President: Charles M. Hopkins
Editorial Staff: Douglas A. Pfeiffer, Ellen Harkins Wheat, Timothy W. Frew, Jean Andrews, Alicia I. Paulson, Deborah J. Loop, Julia Warren
Editor: Kris Fulsaas
Production Staff: Richard L. Owsiany, Susan Dupere
Cover and interior design: Michelle Taverniti
Cover illustration: Cheri O'Brien
Maps: Gray Mouse Graphics

Printed on acid-free recycled paper in the United States of America.

Contents

Acknowledgments

This edition of The Washington Almanac *was compiled from information gleaned from a variety of sources, including publications, information posted on organization Web sites, and personal interviews with local, state, and federal government agencies, and other organizations and individuals, including (but not limited to) the following:*

Aviation & Aerospace Almanac
Bonneville Power Administration
Forest Products Association
Hydroplane and Raceboat Museum
Microsoft Corporation
Museum of Flight, Seattle
National Academy of Television Arts & Sciences, Pacific Northwest
National Audubon Society of Washington State
National Oceanic and Atmospheric Administration (National Weather Service, Western Regional Climate Center, National Marine Fisheries, Marine Sanctuaries Office)
National Register of Historic Places
Newspaper Publishers Association of Washington
Northwest Intertribal Court System
Northwest Weather and Avalanche Center
Pacific 10 Conference
Pacific Coast Oyster Growers Association
Pacific Northwest Seismograph Network
Professional Golfers Association
Rail-Trail Resource Center
Seattle Mariners
Seattle Seahawks
Seattle Supersonics
Tacoma Public Library, Northwest Room
The Technology Alliance, Seattle
The Boeing Company
The Foundation Center, New York
U.S. Air Force
U.S. Army Corps of Engineers
U.S. Army, Fort Lewis
U.S. Border Patrol
U.S. Bureau of the Census (Statistical Abstracts of the United States)
U.S. Coast Guard, 13th Coast Guard District
U.S. Customs Service
U.S. Department of Agriculture, Forest Service
U.S. Department of Energy, Hanford
U.S. Department of the Interior; National Parks Service, Bureau of Indian Affairs
U.S. Department of Transportation
U.S. Fish and Wildlife Service
U.S. Geological Survey
U.S. Navy, Seattle
University of Washington (Athletics Department, Libraries Special Collections, Manuscripts & University Archives Division, Center for the Study of the Pacific Northwest)
Washington Apple Commission
Washington Association of Museums
Washington Council on International Trade
Washington Department of Corrections
Washington Library Association
Washington Office of Archaeology and Historic Preservation
Washington Office of Management and Budget
Washington Office of Superintendent of Public Instruction
Washington Ornithology Society
Washington Public Ports Association
Washington Secretary of State
Washington State Arts Commission
Washington State Association of Counties
Washington State Community, Trade, and Economic Development Department
Washington State Department of Agriculture
Washington State Department of Fish & Wildlife
Washington State Department of Health
Washington State Department of Labor and Industries
Washington State Department of Licensing
Washington State Department of Natural Resources
Washington State Department of Revenue
Washington State Department of Tourism
Washington State Department of Transportation; State Ferries
Washington State Gambling Commission
Washington State History Museum
Washington State Legislature
Washington State Parks and Recreation
Washington State Patrol
Washington State Wine Commission

Permissions/Credits for Photos and Illustrations

Miscellaneous Facts About Washington

Motto: Al-ki, or Alki, an Indian word meaning "by and by."

Nickname: "The Evergreen State."

State capital: Olympia. The capitol building was first occupied by the Legislature in March 1927.

Entered the Union: November 11, 1889, the 42nd state to enter the Union.

Governor: Gary Locke, elected 1996, the first Chinese-American governor in the contiguous United States.

Total area: 70,637 square miles.

Land area: 66,581 square miles.

Water area: 4,055 square miles; 1,545 square miles of inland waters, 2,511 square miles of coastal waters.

State population: Total population (1998 figures) 5,685,300; 2,415,539 in unincorporated areas and 3,269,761 in incorporated cities and towns. Seventh-fastest-growing state in population growth, 1990-97 (15.3 percent increase).

Largest city in population: Seattle, 539,700 people.

Largest city in area: Seattle, 83.64 square miles.

Largest county in population: King, 1,665,800 people.

Largest county in area: Okanogan, 5,301 square miles.

Personal income per capita: $27,718 (1997), 12th highest nationally.

Population density: 84.3 people per square mile of land area.

Highest temperature: 118°F, August 5, 1961, Ice Harbor Dam.

Lowest temperature: –48°F, December 30, 1968, Mazama.

Record Snowfall: 1,124 inches, winter of 1998-99, Mount Baker.

Record 24-hour precipitation: 14.26 inches, November 23-24, 1986, Mount Mitchell No. 2 Weather Station.

Record annual maximum precipitation: 184.56 inches, 1931, Wynoochee-Oxbow Weather Station.

Record annual minimum precipitation: 2.61 inches, 1980, Upper Tract Weather Station.

Rain forest: The Hoh Rain Forest on the Olympic Peninsula is the only temperate rain forest in the continental United States.

Highest point: Mount Rainier, 14,410 feet, 15th-tallest mountain in North America.

Lowest point: Sea level, Pacific Ocean.

Mean elevation: 1,700 feet.

Worst volcanic eruption in continental United States: eruption of Mount St. Helens, May 18, 1980.

Westernmost point in contiguous United States: Cape Alava.

Busiest airport: Sea-Tac, 18th busiest in the nation in passengers served, 24,324,596 (1998).

Largest newspaper: Seattle Times.

Country's largest producer of apples: The 1998 apple crop was 100.3 million boxes, a record crop.

World's largest aircraft manufacturer: Boeing.

World's largest software company: Microsoft.

World's richest man: Bill Gates, personal wealth estimated at about $100 billion (1999).

Most glaciers in the United States outside of Alaska: More than 500; 300 in the North Cascades alone, and 60 in the Olympic Mountains.

Largest bivalve: The geoduck, largest clam in North America, can weigh up to 40 pounds.

North America's largest concrete dam: Grand Coulee Dam; total concrete 11,975,521 cubic yards.

World's longest floating bridge: Albert D. Rosellini Bridge (State Route 520) across Lake Washington, 12,596 feet; floating section, 7,518 feet. ✷

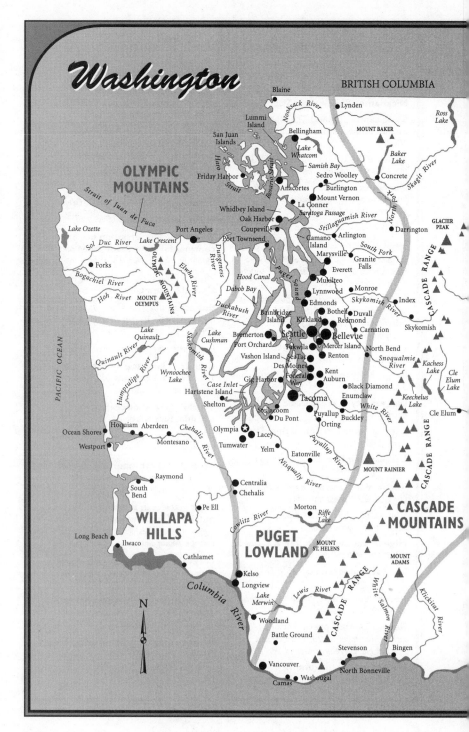

Washington

BRITISH COLUMBIA

Blaine
Lynden
Nooksack River
Lummi Island
Bellingham
MOUNT BAKER
San Juan Islands
Lake Whatcom
Baker Lake
Friday Harbor
Haro Strait
Resurio Strait
Samish Bay
Sedro Woolley
Concrete
Skagit River
Ross Lake

OLYMPIC MOUNTAINS

Strait of Juan de Fuca
Anacortes
Burlington
Mount Vernon
La Conner
Whidbey Island
Saratoga Passage
Stillaguamish River
Darrington
GLACIER PEAK

Lake Ozette
Port Angeles
Oak Harbor
Coupeville
Sol Duc River
Lake Crescent
Port Townsend
Camano Island
Arlington
South Fork
CASCADE RANGE

Forks
OLYMPIC MOUNTAINS
Dungeness River
Marysville
Granite Falls

Bogachiel River
Elwha River
Everett
Hoh River
MOUNT OLYMPUS
Hood Canal
Dabob Bay
Mukilteo
Lynnwood
Monroe
Index
Skykomish River

Duckabush River
Edmonds
Bothell
Duvall
Skykomish

Lake Quinault
Lake Cushman
Bainbridge Island
Kirkland
Redmond
Carnation

Quinault River
Bremerton
Port Orchard
Seattle
Bellevue
Mercer Island
North Bend
Snoqualmie River
Kachess Lake

PACIFIC OCEAN
Skokomish River
Vashon Island
Tukwila
SeaTac
Renton
Cle Elum Lake

Wynoochee Lake
Des Moines
Kent
Auburn
Keechelus Lake
Cle Elum

Humptulips River
Case Inlet
Gig Harbor
Federal Way
Black Diamond
Enumclaw

Hartstene Island
Shelton
Tacoma
Puyallup
White River

Hoquiam
Aberdeen
Chehalis River
Steilacoom
Du Pont
Orting
Buckley

Ocean Shores
Montesano
Olympia
Lacey
Puyallup River
MOUNT RAINIER
CASCADE RANGE

Westport
Tumwater
Yelm
Eatonville

Raymond
Nisqually River

South Bend
Pe Ell
Centralia
Chehalis

WILLAPA HILLS
Cowlitz River
Morton
Riffe Lake
CASCADE MOUNTAINS

Long Beach
Ilwaco
Cathlamet
PUGET LOWLAND
MOUNT ST. HELENS
MOUNT ADAMS

Kelso
Longview
Lake Merwin
Lewis River
White Salmon River

N

Woodland
Battle Ground
CASCADE RANGE
Klickitat River

Columbia River
Vancouver
Camas
Washougal
Stevenson
North Bonneville
Bingen

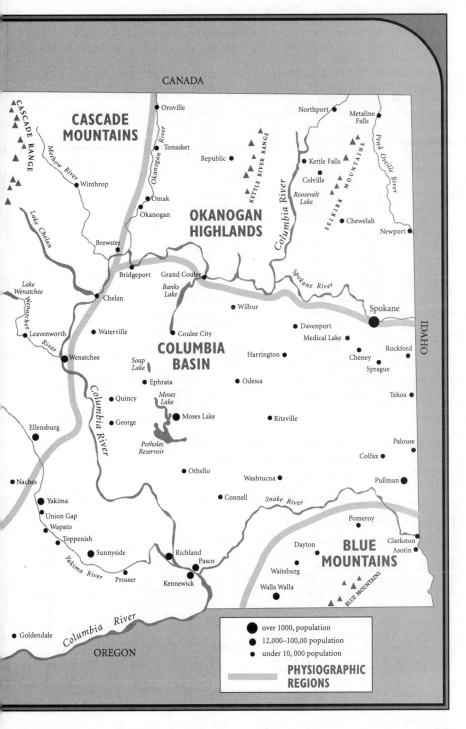

CANADA

CASCADE
MOUNTAINS

CASCADE RANGE

Methow River

Winthrop

Lake Chelan

Brewster

Oroville

Tonasket

Omak

Okanogan

Bridgeport

Chelan

Okanogan River

Republic

KETTLE RIVER RANGE

OKANOGAN
HIGHLANDS

Northport

Metaline
Falls

Kettle Falls

Colville

Roosevelt
Lake

Chewelah

Newport

SELKIRK MOUNTAINS

Pend Oreille River

Columbia River

Spokane River

Grand Coulee

Banks
Lake

Wilbur

Spokane

Lake
Wenatchee

Wenatchee River

Leavenworth

Wenatchee

Waterville

Coulee City

COLUMBIA
BASIN

Soap
Lake

Ephrata

Quincy

Moses
Lake

George

Moses Lake

Potholes
Reservoir

Columbia River

Ellensburg

Naches

Yakima

Union Gap

Wapato

Toppenish

Sunnyside

Yakima River

Prosser

Othello

Connell

Richland

Pasco

Kennewick

Davenport

Medical Lake

Harrington

Odessa

Ritzville

Washtucna

Snake River

Columbia River

Goldendale

OREGON

Cheney

Rockford

Sprague

Tekoa

Palouse

Colfax

Pullman

Pomeroy

Dayton

Clarkston
Asotin

BLUE
MOUNTAINS

Waitsburg

Walla Walla

BLUE MOUNTAINS

IDAHO

● over 1000, population

● 12,000–100,00 population

• under 10, 000 population

PHYSIOGRAPHIC
REGIONS

African Americans

Washington's African-American community can be traced back to the state's earliest explorers and settlers. A black man named York was a member of the Lewis and Clark Corps of Discovery in 1805. In the winter of 1844-45, among one of the first groups of settlers to land in the Puget Sound country was George Washington Bush. His party, which settled near what is now Tumwater, had intended to homestead in Oregon but continued north across the Columbia River because Oregon law forbade blacks to settle or own land. Those who followed, like most settlers of all races, had headed west in search of opportunities. While they fared somewhat better in the West, they did not escape discrimination.

During the 1880s the Northern Pacific Railroad recruited African Americans to work the coal mines near Roslyn, in the Cascade Mountains; others arrived aboard ships and trains or while serving in the military, and more and more were moving to Washington's towns and cities. By 1900 there were 400 African Americans in Seattle; by 1940 there were 3,800. During World War II, thousands more came to work in the shipyards and airplane factories.

By 1950 the state's African-American population had grown to about 30,000, more than four times the figure from 10 years before. New or larger African-American communities could be found in Tacoma, Bremerton, Spokane, Pasco, and other towns. They were the state's largest urban minority group, and they were becoming more active in state politics. African Americans have held the top jobs in the state's largest city and county, and have contributed much to the state's arts and culture.

Nationally known performers have been entertaining here since the turn of the century, when Seattle was a major stop on the vaudeville circuit, and a local music scene developed around the jazz clubs of Seattle's Central District. Musicians who began their careers here went on to make national reputations—Ernestine Anderson, Quincy Jones, and Ray Charles all started in Seattle's nightclubs, and Seattle's Jimi Hendrix and Tacoma's Robert Cray became major stars. The Northwest cultural landscape has been further enriched by the presence of renowned painter Jacob Lawrence, celebrated playwright August Wilson, and novelist Charles Johnson, winner of a National Book Award for fiction.

Organizations and Events of Interest.

African-American Museum of Washington, 925 Court C, Tacoma, WA 98402; (253) 274-1278.

Black Pioneer Picnic, August, Roslyn; (509) 674-2431.

Festival Sundiata, February, annual celebration of African-American art, history, and culture, Seattle Center,

Jimi Hendrix

James Marshall "Jimi" Hendrix was the leading practitioner of psychedelic rock in the 1960s. His blazing guitar riffs, voodoo voice, and suggestive stage presence made him an instant sensation. His meteoric national presence began in 1967 with a European tour and a gig at the Monterey Pop Festival. In 1968, he and his band, The Jimi Hendrix Experience, played a shatteringly electric version of "The Star-Spangled Banner" at the Woodstock Festival, which galvanized the free love/free spirit/anti-war yearnings of his generation. Jimi Hendrix was born in Seattle in 1942. He graduated from Garfield High School, where he had his first band, The Rocking Kings. He died in 1970 from a drug overdose. Opening in 2000 at the Seattle Center will be Seattle billionaire Paul Allen's tribute to Jimi Hendrix, an interactive music museum called the Experience Music Project. The concept for the museum echoes Jimi Hendrix's idea of Sky Church, a place where artists could exchange ideas, write, and make music. ✳

Seattle; (206) 296-8638.

Juneteenth Festival, June, Seattle; (206) 322-8296.

Langston Hughes Cultural Arts Center, 104 17th Ave. S., Seattle, WA 98144; (206) 684-4757.

NAACP, 105 14th Ave., Seattle, WA 98122; (206) 324-6600.

Urban League of Metropolitan Seattle, 105 14th Ave., Seattle, WA 98122; (206) 461-3792.

Agriculture (SEE ALSO

APPLES) Washington State's agricultural output is important to the state's economy, and to the nation's as well. Washington not only ranks among the top 10 producing states, but is the leading producer of a number of crops, including apples, pears, and hops. Agriculture employs more than 84,000 people, only 1,700 fewer than aerospace—the state's largest manufacturing industry—and agricultural commodities generate more than $5.6 billion in gross sales.

Farm Size. Farms cover 15.7 million acres of the state, or 36.8 percent of the state's total land area. In western Washington, farms tend to be smaller than in eastern Washington. As of 1997, there were 36,000 farms in the state; the average acreage for farms was 436 acres. Only a fifth of the farms in Washington State typically achieve $100,000 or more in annual sales of farm commodities. These "commercial farms," with an average of 1,388 acres, account for more than 70 percent of all the farmland in the state. At the other extreme, 56 percent of the state's farms generate commodity sales of less than $10,000 annually. Most of these farms, which average less than 50 acres in size, are part-time or hobby farms. In between these extremes lies a mix of commercial and part-time farms that average 468 acres in size and have annual sales of between $10,000 and $99,999.

Types of Crops.

Field crops. The dominant category of crops is field crops, which account for 35 percent of the state's value of agricultural

Vast fields of wheat blanket the rolling farm lands of the Palouse. Wheat is the state's most valuable field crop. Photo by John Marshall.

production. Wheat and hay are the most extensively planted crops in the state, though many other interesting and specialized crops are grown as well. For example, Washington is a leading producer of mint, hops, and lentils. The total value of field crops is $1.94 billion.

Field Crop Production, 1997

	Amount Produced (1,000 units)	Value ($1,000s)
Wheat (all)	168,080 bu.	602,692
Potatoes	88,160 cwt.	431,984
Hay (all)	3,270 tons	394,980
Hops	55,816 pounds	87,631
Barley	37,240 bu.	87,514
Corn grain	18,050 bu.	55,955
Corn silage	1,540 tons	45,430
Peppermint	3,347 pounds	37,152
Sugar beets	595 tons	25,526
Spearmint	1,782 pounds	20,671
Dry peas	2,587 cwt.	20,179
Dry beans	850 cwt.	18,445
Lentils	1,124 cwt.	14,612
Oats	1,360 bu.	2,380
Other		77,351
Total		1,941,432

Fruits and berries. Washington is the fruit basket of the Pacific Rim and of much of North America. While apples are the main crop, pears, cherries, apricots, peaches, and other stone fruits are also important. The Yakima Valley and Wenatchee are the largest fruit-producing regions in the state. Fruit crops contributed $1.23 billion to Washington's value of agricultural production in 1997. Apples ranked No. 1 in the nation, with a total value of $823 million; sweet cherries ranked No. 9. Washington is the nation's No. 1-ranking producer of apples and red raspberries.

Fruit Crop Production, 1997

	Total (1,000 tons)	Value ($1,000s)
Apples	2,500	822,800
Sweet cherries	92	128,975
Winter pears	250	69,900
Grapes, Concord	242.5	60,521
Grapes, wine	62	60,264
Bartlett pears	205	53,770
Peaches	22.5	19,297
Apricots	6	4,949
Grapes, Niagara	14.5	3,625
Prunes	6.5	1,193
Tart cherries	2	1,100
Hazelnuts	0.15	134
Other fruits	8.05	6,000
Total fruits	3,412.7	1,922,502

Berries Crop Production, 1997

	Value ($1,000s)
Red raspberries	28,020
Cranberries	10,148
Blueberries	7,769
Strawberries	4,882

Vegetables. The value of production for the 1997 vegetable crop was $344 million. Onions, the No. 12-ranking vegetable crop, contributed $93 million to Washington's farm income; sweet corn contributed $62 million. Nationally, Washington was the No. 1 producer of asparagus and processed sweet corn.

Vegetables Crop Production, 1997

	Amount (1,000 cwt)	Value ($1,000s)
Onions, storage	8,580	87,120
Asparagus	828	64,204
Sweet corn, processing	15,575.6	58,175
Green peas	2,094.4	25,342
Carrots, fresh	903	12,642
Carrots, processing	3,840	12,288
Onions, non-storage	333	5,794
Sweet corn, fresh	336	3,730
Lettuce	180	2,718
Other, fresh	2,000	58,600
Other, processing	1,050	13,700
Total	35,720	344,313

Livestock. Livestock, poultry, and their associated products are the agricultural products second-highest in value. In 1997 milk production yielded $732 million; cattle and calves, $466 million; eggs, $76 million.

Animal Inventory

Chicken broilers (production) (1996)	40,100,000
Cattle (1997)	1,200,000
Sheep and lambs (1997)	56,400
Swine (1996)	39,000

Employment. Agriculture is a major source of jobs in Washington State, providing employment to some 84,300 workers. Total employment in agriculture includes seasonal workers (defined as those who work fewer than 150 days on any one farm), regular hired workers, unpaid family workers, and farm operators. Four-fifths of the state's agricultural employment is located east of the Cascade Mountains, with the largest concentration in the south-central part of the state, which includes Yakima and Klickitat Counties. This region accounted for nearly 21,000 agricultural jobs in 1996, about one-fourth of all farm jobs in the state.

In addition, many of the nonfarm jobs in the area are dependent on agriculture.

Food processing is the largest manufacturing industry, and fruit and vegetable packing houses dominate local wholesale and retail trade. Among the crops that require the most seasonal farm labor are apples, potatoes, nursery products, pears, sweet cherries, hops, grapes, and asparagus.

Agricultural Employment

	Total Workers	Agricultural Workers	%
Eastern Washington	583,610	67,660	11.6
Western Washington	2,115,730	16,690	0.8
Statewide	2,699,300	84,350	3.1

Source: Washington Agricultural Statistics Service

Agricultural Organizations.

Agriculture statistics are compiled by the **Washington Agricultural Statistics Service** in Olympia, and are available on the World Wide Web at http://www.nass.usda.gov/wa/ homepage. The site also has names, addresses, and phone numbers of county extension agents and USDA Farm Service Agency offices in all 39 counties (www. nass.usda.gov/wa/annual98/exten298.htm).

Individual commodities commissions work to promote and market the state's various agricultural products. Commissions are established for alfalfa seed, apples, asparagus, barley, beef, blueberries, (flower) bulbs, cranberries, dairy products, dry peas and lentils, eggs, fruit, fryers, hops, mint, potatoes, red raspberries, seed potatoes, strawberries, tree fruit research, wheat, and wine.

American Hop Museum, P.O. Box 230, 22 S. B St., Toppenish, WA 98948; (509) 865-4677.

Broadview Dairy Museum, 411 W. Cataldo, Spokane, WA 99201; (509) 324-0910.

Central Washington Agricultural Museum, 4508 Main St., Union Gap, WA 98903; (509) 457-8735.

USDA Farm Service Agency, State Executive Director's Office, 316 W. Boone

Ave., Suite 568, Spokane, WA 99201-2350; (509) 323-3001.

Washington State University Cooperative Extension Service County Agents, State Executive Director's Office, College of Agriculture and Home Economics, 421 Hulbert Hall, Pullman, WA 99163; (509) 335-4561.

Washington's Fruit Place Visitor Center, 105 S. 18th St., Yakima, WA 98901; (509) 576-3090.

Events of Interest.

County fairs. County and community fairs showcase Washington's agricultural communities throughout the year.

For a complete list of activities, contact the **Washington State Fairs Association,** P.O. Box 744, Conway, WA 98238, (360) 445-3413, http://www.wastatefairs.org; for dates for the current year, call the numbers listed below.

Apricot orchard. From *Washington II* by John Marshall.

In addition to fairs held by individual counties, there are several regional fairs:

North Central Washington District Fair (Waterville), August

Northwest Washington Fair (Lynden), August

Southwest Washington Fair (Centralia-Chehalis), August

Evergreen State Fair (Monroe), August–September

Central Washington State Fair (Yakima), September

Northeast Washington Fair (Colville), September

Palouse Empire Fair (Colfax), September

Spokane Interstate Fair (Spokane), September

Washington State 4-H Fair (Puyallup), September

Western Washington Fair (Puyallup), September

Farmers markets. There are more than 50 farmers markets across the state. For a guide, contact Washington State Farmers Market Association, 11910-C Meridian E., Suite 29, Puyallup, WA 98573; (253) 304-1063.

Cherry Festival, May, Granger, (509) 854-2448.

Herb Festival, May, Yacolt, (360) 686-3537.

Spring Dairy Show, May, Enumclaw, (360) 825-7666.

Antique Farm Fair, June, Ferndale, (360) 384-3444.

Farmers' Day Parade, June, Lynden, (360) 354-5995.

Draft Horse Show, July, Republic, (509) 634-4388.

Sweet Onion Harvest Fest, July, Walla Walla (509) 525-0850.

Annual Threshing Bee and Tractor Show, August, Lynden, (360) 354-3754.

Blackberry Festival, August, Bremerton, (360) 377-3041.

Cowlitz Prairie Grange Threshing Bee, August, Toledo, (360) 864-4917.

National Lentil Festival, August, Pullman (800) 365-6948.

Washington State Pioneer Power Show, August, Union Gap, (509) 453-2395.

Draft Horse & Mule Extravaganza, September, Monroe, (360) 805-6700.

Farmer-Consumer Awareness Days, September, Quincy, (509) 787-2140.

Huckleberry Festival, September, Bingen, (509) 493-2293.

Apple Days, October, Cashmere, (509) 782-7404.

Cranberry Festival, October, Ilwaco, (360) 642-3446.

Cranberry Harvest Festival, October, Grayland (800) 473-6018.

Old Apple Tree Celebration, October, Vancouver, (360) 696-8031.

Country Lighted Farm Implement Parade, December, Sunnyside (800) 457-8089.

Airports (SEE ALSO AVIATION AND AEROSPACE)

There are 437 public and private airports in the state. Of these, 13 are commercial airports with scheduled passenger service:

Anacortes
Bellingham
East Wenatchee
Friday Harbor
Grant/Moses Lake
Paine Field (Everett)
Pullman/Moscow Regional
Seattle-Tacoma International Airport
Spokane International Airport
Tri-Cities
Walla Walla City-County
William R. Fairchild International
(Port Angeles)
Yakima Air Terminal

The State Department of Transportation manages 16 airports across the state, which serve as staging areas for search and rescue operations and provide emergency landing sites for aircraft in distress. These airports are also used extensively by recreational pilots.

The state hub, Sea-Tac International Airport, operated by the Port of Seattle, dominates air carrier service offered at all the state's airports, with Spokane the second-largest airport. According to the *1998 Aviation & Aerospace Almanac,* the state's two largest airports rank worldwide-and nationally as follows:

Seaplanes at Kenmore Air Harbor, the largest floatplane base in the world, located at the north end of Lake Washington. Photo courtesy of Kenmore Air Harbor.

Sea-Tac International Airport

		World Rank	U.S. Rank
No. of operations	395,216	25	22
Total passengers	24,324,596	30	18
Cargo (metric tons)	388,218	35	19

Spokane International Airport

		World Rank	U.S. Rank
No. of operations	113,131	161	104
Total passengers	3,258,762	178	72
Cargo (metric tons)	44,005	163	68

Source: Aviation & Aerospace Almanac

Of the commercial air traffic flowing through the state, Alaska Airlines, the only large commercial air carrier headquartered in the state, accounts for the largest share of the market at 31 percent.

The top 10 major carriers (and their market share) are Alaska Airlines, United Airlines, Horizon Air, Southwest, Delta, Northwest, American, Reno, America West, and Continental.

The Federal Aviation Administration estimates that there are about 24,000 registered pilots in the state. There are almost 7,000 general aviation aircraft, and almost 4 million general aviation operations flight plans filed per year. **FAA Field Office, Northwest Mountain Region,** 1601 Lind Ave. SW, Renton, WA 98055; (206) 431-2001.

Events of Interest.
Fly in Days, July, Forks, (360) 374-5412.
Elma Fly-In (with Wild Blackberry Festival), September, Elma, (360) 482-2228.

American Indians

(*SEE ALSO* ARCHAEOLOGY) American Indian tribes in Washington are often distinguished as two distinctive types of cultures: the coastal and Puget Sound tribes of western Washington, and the plateau tribes of eastern Washington. Anthropologists believe the coastal tribes of the Pacific Northwest were traditionally the richest indigenous peoples of North America because of the local abundance of fish, game, and edible plants. This wealth gave rise to a unique cultural tradition of the potlatch, a great feast during which accumulated wealth was given away.

Washington Indian Reservations and Trust Lands

Reservation and Trust Lands
County Borders

Like all other indigenous peoples of the United States, Washington's tribes by the mid-1800s had reluctantly signed away their land in a flurry of treaty agreements, here engineered by the first territorial governor, Isaac Stevens. The treaties that formed the basis for most of Washington's current Indian reservations were signed in 1854 and 1855: the Medicine Creek Treaty of 1854 (Nisqually, Puyallup, Squaxin, and other tribes); the Point Elliott Treaty of 1855 (Duwamish, Suquamish, and other tribes), the Point No Point Treaty (S'Klallam, Skokomish, and other tribes); the Makah Treaty of 1855; the 1855 treaties with the Walla Walla, Cayuse, and Umatilla tribes; the 1855 treaty with the Yakima Nation; and the 1855 treaty with the Quinaults and Quileute.

Under these treaties, the United States claimed title to 64 million acres of land. In exchange for land, the treaties assured the tribes of their right to fish and hunt in their "usual and accustomed places," yet they had to take the state to court more than 100 years later to exercise that right. In 1979 the Supreme Court upheld the decision handed down in 1974 by Tacoma Judge George Boldt, which reaffirmed those treaties and gave Indians the right to take up to half of the annual salmon harvest.

More recently, Indians have returned to court to claim a share of shellfish and hunting rights as well.

Not all of Washington's tribes are recognized by the federal government. Some tribes have petitioned for official status; others were combined when the reservations were established. There are currently 26 Indian reservations in Washington State. The largest reservations are the Colville Reservation outside of Spokane and the Yakama Reservation south of Yakima. The most populous reservations are the Puyallup Reservation outside of Tacoma and the Yakama Reservation.

The following tribes have petitioned for official status: Chinook Indian Tribe/Chinook Nation, Cowlitz Tribe of Indians, Duwamish Tribe, Samish Tribe of Indians, Snohomish Tribe of Indians, Snoqualmie Tribal Council, Snoqualmoo Tribe of Whidbey Island, and Steilacoom Tribe.

Population and Area of Indian Reservations

	Population*	Land Area (in Acres**)
Chehalis Reservation	871	4,215
Colville Reservation	4,929	1.4 million
Hoh Reservation	97	443
Jamestown S'Klallam Tribe	641	210
Kalispel Reservation	170	4,600
Lower Elwha Klallam Tribe	1,149	443
Lummi Reservation	4,648	13,500
Makah Reservation (plus Ozette Village Site)	1,753	44 square miles
Muckleshoot Reservation	3,521	3,600
Nisqually Reservation	2,905	5,000
Nooksack Tribe	820	2,062
Port Gamble Reservation	753	1,301
Puyallup Reservation	14,282	18,061.5
Quileute Reservation	785	1 square mile
Quinault Reservation	2,975	196,645
Sauk-Suiattle Reservation	120	23
Shoalwater Bay Reservation	74	1 square mile plus tidelands
Skokomish Reservation	1,33	4,987
Spokane Reservation	1,416	155,000
Squaxin Island Reservation	515	2,175
Stillaguamish Reservation	1,476	60
Suquamish Tribal Council (Port Madison)	1,032	7,800
Swinomish Reservation	959	10 square miles
Tulalip Reservation	4,549	22,000
Upper Skagit Tribe	610	130
Yakama Reservation	15,968	1.4 million

Salmon, by Marvin Oliver.

* Local estimates of resident Indian population, male/female Indians living on and adjacent to reservations.
** Unless otherwise noted. Source: Bureau of Indian Affairs, 1995.

Tribal Casinos. Washington Indian tribes have agreements with the state that allow them to operate gambling casinos; most, though not all, currently operate some form of gambling enterprise on their reservations (SEE GAMBLING).

Confederated Tribe and Bands of the Yakama Indian Nation ·
Confederated Tribes of the Chehalis Reservation
Jamestown S'Klallam Tribe of Washington
Lower Elwha Klallam Tribe
Lummi Nation
Muckleshoot Indian Tribe
Nisqually Indian
Nooksack Indian Tribe of Washington
Port Gamble S'Klallam

Puyallup Tribe of Indians
Quileute Tribal Council
Quinault Tribe of the Quinault Reservation
Skokomish Indian Tribe
Squaxin Island Indian Tribe
Suquamish Tribe
Swinomish Indian Tribal Community
Tulalip Tribes of Washington

Organizations and Events of Interest.

Alex Sherwood Memorial Center Museum, Spokane Reservation, P.O. Box 100, Wellpinit, WA 99040; (509) 258-4581.

Colville Confederated Tribes Museum, Meade Way, P.O. Box 233, Coulee Dam, WA 99116; (509) 633-0751.

Daybreak Star Arts Center, Discovery

Park, P.O. Box 99100, Seattle, WA 98199; (206) 285-4425.

Lelooska Foundation Museum and Gallery, 165 Merwin Village Rd., Ariel, WA 98674; (360) 225-9735.

Makah Museum and Research Center, Bayview Ave., P.O. Box 160, Neah Bay, WA 98357; (360) 645-2711.

Museum of Quileute, P.O. Box 279, La Push, WA 98350; (360) 374-6163.

Puyallup Tribal Museum, 2002 E. 28th St., Tacoma, WA 98404; (253) 597-6200, ext 308.

Quinault Indian Nation Museum, P.O. Box 189, Taholah, WA 98587; (360) 276-8211.

Skokomish Tribal Center, N. 80 Tribal Center Rd., Shelton, WA 98584; (360) 426-4232.

Steilacoom Tribal Cultural Center and Museum, 1515 Lafayette St., P.O. Box 88419, Steilacoom, WA 98388; (253) 584-6308.

Suquamish Museum, 15838 Sandy Hook Rd., P.O. Box 498, Suquamish, WA 98392; (360) 598-3311, ext 422.

Tulalip Hebolb Museum, 6410 23rd Ave. NE, Marysville, WA 98270; (360) 651-3300.

Yakama Indian Nation Cultural Center and Museum, 100 Spilwi Loop, P.O. Box 151, Toppenish, WA 98948; (509) 865-2800.

Eagle Plume Society Powwow, February, Nespelem, (509) 634-4711.

Washington's Birthday Powwow, February, Yakama Reservation, Toppenish, (509) 865-2800.

Shoalwater Bay Nation Pow-Wow, April, Westport, (360) 267-6766.

Chief Taholah Days, July, Taholah, (360) 276-8211.

Fourth of July Powwow and Open Rodeo, July, Nespelem, (509) 634-4711.

Seafair Indian Days Pow Wow, July, Seattle, (206) 285-4425.

Chief Seattle Days, August, Suquamish, (206) 598-3311.

Kalispel Powwow, August, Usk, (509) 445-1147.

Spokane Indian Days Encampment/ Pow Wow, August, Spokane Reservation, (509) 258-4581.

Puyallup Tribal Powwow and Salmon Bake, September, Puyallup, (206) 597-6200.

Northwest Coast Indians compete at canoe races during a tribal gathering in Tacoma. From Washington II *by John Marshall.*

Amphibians and Reptiles

Washington's wildlife resources include several dozen amphibian and reptile species, including salamanders, frogs and toads, lizards, and snakes. The damp forest environments of western Washington are the favored habitat of most of the salamander species, while the dryer, rocky hills of eastern Washington are home to the state's only venomous reptile, the western rattlesnake. The following species occur in the state:

Salamanders and newts: Northwestern salamander, tiger salamander, long-toed salamander, Cope's giant salamander, Pacific giant salamander, Olympic or Olympic torrent salamander, Columbia torrent salamander, Cascade torrent salamander, roughskin or rough-skinned newt, Dunn's salamander, Larch Mountain salamander, Van Dyke's salamander, Ensatina.

Frogs and toads: tailed frog, Great Basin spadefoot, western toad, Woodhouse's toad, Pacific treefrog, red-legged frog, Cascades frog—west Cascades, spotted frog, northern leopard frog, bullfrog, green frog.

Turtles: western pond turtle, painted turtle, green turtle, loggerhead turtle, leatherback turtle.

Lizards: sagebrush lizard, western fence lizard, side-blotched lizard, western skink, northern alligator lizard, southern alligator lizard.

Snakes: rubber boa, ringneck snake, sharpland snake, racer, striped whipsnake, gopher snake, California mountain king snake, common garter snake, western terrestrial garter snake, northwestern garter snake, night snake, western rattlesnake.

Apples

The apple is far from forbidden fruit in Washington; it is officially "The State Fruit," and it is lauded. To honor the power of the pomme, Wenatchee holds the annual Washington State Apple Blossom Festival (the oldest major festival in the state of Washington), Yakima hosts the Washington Apple Festival, Cashmere has its Apple Days, Pateros holds the Apple Pie Jamboree, and Vancouver celebrates the state's first apple

Vacillating Vertebrates

We have 32 species of amphibians in the Northwest: 18 salamanders, 10 frogs, and 4 toads. South Prairie marsh in the Gifford Pinchot National Forest is a perfect place for the vacillating vertebrates. In the 15-acre pond and nearby creeks and puddles, amphibians can easily trade back and forth between the water and an amphibian-friendly forest floor littered with decaying leaves and rotting logs. Pacific chorus frogs (known until recently as Pacific treefrogs), red-legged frogs, and Northwestern salamanders and Pacific giant salamanders are among the species you can turn up there.—Susan Ewing, Going Wild ✸

tree. The winner of the cross-state college football rivalry between the Washington State University Cougars and University of Washington Huskies takes home the Apple Cup, and the 17th hole of the Apple Tree Golf Course in Yakima is on an apple-shaped island.

Apples are big business—nearly a billion dollars' worth—and the state's highest-value cash crop. The first apple tree was planted in Washington in 1826 at Fort Vancouver, and the first orchard was begun near Oroville in 1854. By 1910 the state had become the nation's leading apple producer, a distinction it has held ever since, producing more than half of all fresh apples grown in the United States. There are 172,000 acres of apple orchards in the state, with approximately 45 million apple trees. A new tree requires at least two to three years after planting before it bears fruit, and can produce efficiently for 20 to 30 years. A fully producing tree can produce up to 20 boxes per year.

During harvest season, which runs from August through October, approximately 35,000 to 45,000 workers handpick the crop—more than 12 billion apples in an average year. Eastern Washington has enough warehouse storage for 181 million boxes of apples.

Apple Country

Today, Washington produces close to 100 million boxes of fresh, packed apples each year, more than half the nation's total apple supply. Stacked side by side, that is enough apples to reach to the moon and halfway back, or to build a road from Seattle to New York 65 apples wide.

—John Marshall, Washington Apple Country ❧

Approximately 75 percent of the apples are sold to the fresh market, and the other 25 percent are processed into juice, sauce, or dehydrated products.

Apple Production, 1997-98

Red Delicious	42.8 million
Golden Delicious	14.6 million
Granny Smith	7.2 million
Fuji	6.4 million
Gala	4.2 million
Braeburn	1.6 million
Total fresh apple crop	78,545,000 boxes

Red delicious apples growing in the Wenatchee Valley. From Washington II by John Marshall.

Major Apple Producing Areas

Yakima Valley	78,000 acres
Wenatchee	56,000 acres
Columbia Basin	31,000 acres
Other Areas	7,000 acres
Total	172,000 acres

Top Ten Export Markets (1996)

1.	Mexico	5,512,532 boxes
2.	Taiwan	4,195,661 boxes
3.	Indonesia	4,119,839 boxes
4.	Canada	3,306,769 boxes
5.	Hong Kong	2,286,974 boxes
6.	Thailand	1,637,356 boxes
7.	Philippines	1,499,172 boxes
8.	Dubai	1,382,298 boxes
9.	Malaysia	1,300,786 boxes
10.	Saudi Arabia	1,258,760 boxes

Source: Washington Apple Commission

Apple Crop Value (1996)

Fresh	Processed
$836 million	$108 million

Organizations and Events of Interest.

Apple Commission, 2900 Euclid Ave., Wenatchee, WA 98807-0018; (509) 633-9600; http://www.bestapples.com.

Apple Industry Tour, Wenatchee, (509) 663-9600.

Washington's Fruit Place Visitor Center, Yakima, (509) 576-3090.

Washington State Apple Blossom Festival, April, Wenatchee, (509) 662-3616 (the oldest major festival in the state of Washington).

Apple Pie Jamboree, July, Pateros, (509) 923-2571.

Top Ten Domestic Markets (1996)

1.	Los Angeles	5,674,182 boxes
2.	Chicago	2,339,447 boxes
3.	New York	2,068,367 boxes
4.	Seattle area	1,539,772 boxes
5.	Sacramento/Stockton	1,530,100 boxes
6.	Atlanta	1,370,863 boxes
7.	San Francisco	1,364,895 boxes
8.	Boston	1,278,301 boxes
9.	Dallas/Fort Worth	1,228,618 boxes
10.	Philadelphia	1,189,256 boxes

Apple Days, October, Cashmere, (509) 782-7404.

Old Apple Tree Celebration, October, Vancouver, (360) 696-8031.

Aquaculture (SEE ALSO FISH HATCHERIES)

Aquaculture is the cultivation or "farming" of fish and shellfish. In Washington, aquaculture is carried out in an extensive system of state and national salmon hatcheries, commercial farming of salmon in saltwater pens, and the culture of shellfish in Puget Sound and Willapa Bay.

Legislation passed in the late 1800s allowed private ownership of tidelands, which encouraged the development of the state's shellfish industry. Prior to that time, tidelands were public property and anyone could dig for clams or collect oysters for their personal use or for sale. The shellfish industry that developed began with culture of the native Olympia oysters, which were once plentiful in the inland waters. In the 1940s, the oyster industry introduced cultivation methods for nonnative species, such as Japanese and European oysters. A later development was the introduction of rope and raft culture of mussels. Shellfish culti-vation is a $40 million industry, with more than 300 licensed, certified shellstock shipper firms and 30 shellfish processing firms.

Salmon farmers grow more than 11 million pounds of Atlantic salmon in saltwater pens in Puget Sound and other state waters.

Organizations of Interest.

Farmed Salmon Commission, P.O. Box 5305, Bellingham, WA 98227; (360) 671-1997.

Pacific Coast Oyster Growers Association, 120 State Ave. NE, Suite 142, Olympia, WA 98501-8212; (360) 754-2744.

West Coast Clam Growers Association, SE 1042 Bloomfield Rd., Shelton, WA 98584; (360) 426-3354.

Archaeology (SEE ALSO PETROGLYPHS AND PICTOGRAPHS)

Washington's human prehistory is believed to date back as far as 12,000 years ago. Evidence of this early presence was found in 1977 at the Manis mastodon site near Sequim on the Olympic Peninsula, where a mastodon rib was dug up that had a remnant of a spearpoint still in it. This is only one of more than 5,000 archaeological

Oystermen have been farming shellfish on Washington tidelands since the nineteenth century. Courtesy of University of Washington Libraries.

sites around the state, only a handful of which have been examined in any detail. Among these are the Marmes Rock Shelter, where archaeologists uncovered numerous artifacts and partial skeletons of people known collectively as "Marmes Man" in a cave overlooking the Palouse River, and Ozette Village, a Makah Indian village site on the Olympic Peninsula.

A more recent archaeological discovery caused a political uproar. Scientists named the skeletal remains "Kennewick Man" and carbon-dated it to 9,000 years old. Local Native American tribes called him one of theirs and initiated a custody battle with scientists to bury the remains. Scientists, who want to be able to study the bones for clues about Washington's past, won the first round: Kennewick Man is currently interred in the basement of the Burke Museum of Natural History and Culture on the University of Washington campus.

Organizations and Events of Interest.

Burke Museum, NE 45th St. and 17th Ave. NE, University of Washington campus, Seattle, WA 98105; (206) 543-5590.

Museum of Anthropology, College Hall, Washington State University, Pullman, WA 99164-4910; (509) 335-3936.

Office of Archaeology and Historic Preservation, 111 21st Ave. SW, P.O. Box 48343, Olympia, WA 98504-8343; (360) 407-0752.

Washington State Archaeology Month, October; (206) 324-7278.

Archives **State Regional Archives System.** The Secretary of State's office operates Regional Archives facilities that maintain records of personal and community history. The regional archives may be used by private citizens as well as public officials to settle legal claims, research family history, write local or state history, or analyze government programs. The archives' collections include records from legislators, government agencies, courts, and school districts. They also offer microfilm editions of larger collections, such as territorial census rolls and court

records. Appointments for consultation and research must be scheduled at least one day in advance.

Southwest Region (Clark, Cowlitz, Grays Harbor, Lewis, Mason, Pacific, Skamania, Thurston, and Wahkiakum Counties), 1120 Washington St. SE, P.O. Box 40238, Olympia, WA 98504-0238; (360) 753-1684.

Puget Sound Region (King, Kitsap, and Pierce Counties), Bellevue Community College, Pritchard-Fleming Bldg., 3000 Landerholm Circle SE, MS-N100, Bellevue, WA 98007-6484; (425) 373-3940.

Northwest Region (Clallam, Island, Jefferson, San Juan, Skagit, Snohomish, and Whatcom Counties), Western Washington University, Goltz-Murray Archives Bldg., Bellingham, WA 98225-9123; (360) 650-3125.

Central Region (Benton, Chelan, Douglas, Franklin, Grant, Kittitas, Klickitat, Okanogan, and Yakima Counties), Central Washington University, Bledsoe-Washington Archives Bldg., Ellensburg, WA 98926-7547; (509) 963-2136.

Eastern Region (Adams, Asotin, Columbia, Ferry, Garfield, Lincoln, Pend Oreille, Spokane, Stevens, Walla Walla, and Whitman Counties), Eastern Washington University, Cheney, WA 99004-2423; (509) 359-6900.

National Archives. One of the National Archives and Records Administration's nine regional offices across the country, the Pacific Northwest collection is held in Seattle. The Seattle Federal Records Center maintains records of federal agencies for Washington, Oregon, and Alaska generated by federal agencies during the past century and a half. **National Archives and Records Administration,** Pacific Alaska Region, 6125 Sand Point Way NE, Seattle, WA 98115; (206) 526-6501.

Private and Specialized Archives. Colleges and universities, historical societies, museums, and libraries throughout the state maintain various archives. Of these, the most comprehensive ones are those at the University of *(Continued on page 24)*

State Area Codes

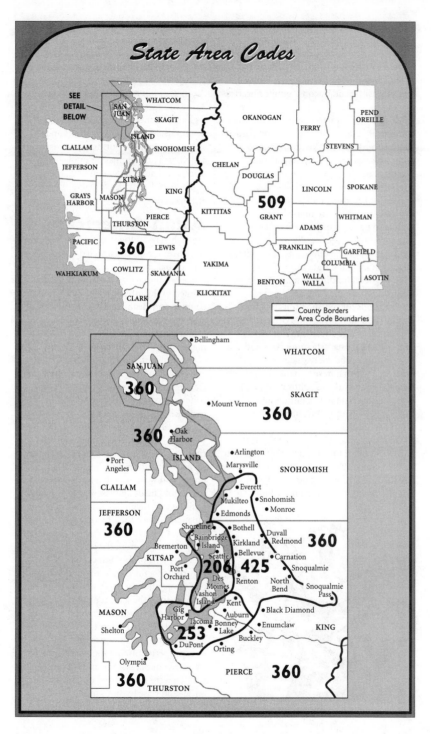

SEE DETAIL BELOW

| County Borders |
| Area Code Boundaries |

Top map (state):

SAN JUAN, WHATCOM, SKAGIT, ISLAND, CLALLAM, SNOHOMISH, JEFFERSON, KITSAP, CHELAN, OKANOGAN, FERRY, PEND OREILLE, STEVENS, DOUGLAS, LINCOLN, SPOKANE, GRAYS HARBOR, MASON, KING, KITTITAS, **509**, GRANT, WHITMAN, THURSTON, PIERCE, ADAMS, PACIFIC, **360**, LEWIS, FRANKLIN, GARFIELD, COLUMBIA, WAHKIAKUM, COWLITZ, SKAMANIA, YAKIMA, BENTON, WALLA WALLA, ASOTIN, CLARK, KLICKITAT

Detail map (Puget Sound):

- Bellingham
- WHATCOM
- SAN JUAN **360**
- SKAGIT **360**
- Mount Vernon
- **360** Oak Harbor
- ISLAND
- Port Angeles
- Arlington
- Marysville
- SNOHOMISH
- Everett
- Mukilteo
- Snohomish
- Monroe
- Edmonds
- CLALLAM
- JEFFERSON **360**
- Shoreline
- Bothell
- Bainbridge Island
- Kirkland
- Duvall
- Redmond **360**
- Bremerton
- Seattle
- Bellevue
- Carnation
- KITSAP
- Port Orchard
- **206** **425**
- Des Moines
- Renton
- North Bend
- Snoqualmie
- Snoqualmie Pass
- Vashon Island
- Kent
- MASON
- Gig Harbor
- **253**
- Tacoma
- Auburn
- Black Diamond
- Shelton
- Bonney Lake
- Enumclaw
- KING
- DuPont
- Buckley
- Orting
- Olympia
- PIERCE **360**
- **360** THURSTON

23

Washington in Seattle, Washington State University in Pullman, the Washington State Historical Society in Tacoma, the Eastern Washington State Historical Society in Spokane, the State Library in Olympia, and the Seattle and Tacoma public libraries.

Arts Washington has a vibrant arts community that includes dance companies, opera companies, jazz venues, symphony orchestras, art museums and galleries, theater, and film. The Washington State Arts Commission is the primary state-level agency for the visual and performing arts in the state, and there are myriad regional, local, and national organizations as well. The commission receives biennial general-fund state appropriations, a 0.5 percent art allocation from the state capital budget, an annual federal funding from the National Endowment for the Arts, and limited private funds for specific projects. The commission administers the Governor's Arts and Heritage Awards to honor outstanding artists, arts supporters and organizations, and individuals and organizations that have enhanced our state's rich and diverse cultural heritage. **Washington State Arts Commission,** P.O. Box 42675, Olympia, WA 98504-2675; (360) 586-2421.

The state spent $1,367,567 to purchase 467 works of art for the State Art Collection in 1997. Since 1975, the State Art Collection has accumulated more than 4,000 works of art, purchased for more than $12 million.

The Washington State Arts Commission awarded grants and services to 786 organizations and individuals, funding 40,093 events, with 26,174 artists, attended by 10,401,919 individuals.

In addition to the Washington State Arts Commission, numerous statewide, regional, countywide, municipal, and neighborhood arts organizations and centers promote performing and visual arts activities. The commission publishes a directory that includes contact names, budgets, and activities for 80 of these local arts agencies.

Asian Americans

In the early days of the Washington Territory, Asian Americans constructed the railroads, mined coal and gold, tilled the fields, harvested the crops, canned the salmon, worked in the forests, and did much of the cooking and cleaning. They rebuilt Seattle after the great fire of 1889. Yet these same immigrants who contributed so much in so many ways to building the modern Northwest suffered grave discrimination and hardships, the result of ignorance and fear. Forced into social isolation, Asian-American communities developed their own rich history.

The Chinese began to come to the western United States in the mid-19th century. They fled governmental collapse, social exploitation, flooding, and famine at home, and were attracted by tales of riches in the gold fields and elsewhere. Similar pullings and tuggings caused numbers of Japanese to seek their fortunes in the western United States; Japanese immigrants arrived in force from the late 1880s through the early part of the 20th century. Filipinos constituted a third wave of emigration, beginning after the Spanish American War at the turn of the 20th century.

Asian immigrants encountered harsh laws in the United States that denied them citizenship and sometimes even the right to own property. Immigration was controlled by a strict quota system, and for years Asian women were not allowed into the country. Social and class tensions in the West occasionally erupted into mob violence

An old newspaper illustration depicting the Anti-Chinese riots in Tacoma and Seattle. Courtesy of University of Washington Libraries.

targeting Asian Americans. During the 1880s, for example, when Asian Americans were building and operating sawmills and canneries, other working-class people sought to run Asians out of the region, forcing brief exoduses of Asian Americans from Tacoma and Seattle.

Many Asian immigrants came to make their fortune in America and expected to return to their Asian homeland to retire. Laws that denied them citizenship, social unrest akin to class warfare, and discriminatory immigration policies all contributed to this mindset. Yet over the decades, temporary immigrants survived the hardships, developed their own communities, and became part of the American cultural pastiche. The Chinese predominated in the mines and in railroad construction. By 1920, Filipinos had replaced the Chinese as the dominant workers in the fish canning industry. The Japanese became associated with farming, supplying the cities with produce from truck farms. Before the Second World War, the Japanese grew 75 percent of all the vegetables in the state. Their stalls dominated Seattle's Pike Place Market.

Within weeks of the bombing of Pearl Harbor in December 1941, all persons of Japanese descent were remanded, by Executive Order, to concentration camps. Most Washington residents were relocated to Minidoka, near Hunt, Idaho. Those who were relocated lost houses and property, much of it never regained. Not until 1988

did the federal government apologize and compensate the survivors and their families for this denial of their civil liberties. Many American-born Japanese men volunteered for combat duty in Europe. Many Japanese-American Washingtonians served in the 100th Battalion and the 442nd Regimental Combat, both highly decorated units.

After the war, and coincident with the rise of the civil rights movement in the United States, many of the historic wrongs against Asian Americans began to be redressed. Harsh immigration laws were relaxed, and Asian Americans, educated in integrated schools, joined the mainstream of American society. Asian Americans rose to prominence in every walk of life, including politics. The first Asian American elected to a citywide office in Seattle was Wing Luke, in 1960. Gary Locke, an Asian American, was elected governor of Washington in 1996.

A new wave of immigration from Asia has occurred in the last 20 years. Some immigrants have fled civil war and strife in their homeland; for example, the Vietnamese, Laotians, and Cambodians. Recently, many Asians from Korea, China, and elsewhere have come to the United States. These latest arrivals are in the main skilled professionals and managers, who have started out much higher on the economic ladder than their forebears. Moreover, they have come with their (Continued on page 30)

Arts Calendar

The events listed here include only a sampling of the multitude of fine arts shows, music festivals, arts and crafts fairs, and heritage fairs that occur in the state throughout the year. Many other venues also feature performing and visual arts events, including most county and local community fairs. Check local papers for specific dates and for other events in your area of interest or check the events calendar on the Washington Tourism Web site at http://198.239.32.88/pubs/events/events.htm.

January
Auburn-Symphony Orchestra (253) 939-8509.
Wenatchee—A Joyful Noise (509) 664-3340

February
Olympia-Ethnic Celebration (360) 753-8380.
Tacoma—February Fling—Celtic Dance (253) 939-8413; Wintergrass winter bluegrass festival (253) 926-4164.

March
Fife—RAGS '99 Wearable Art Show (253) 272-4181.
Goldendale—Maryhill Museum of Art Gala Opening (509) 773-3733.
Langley—Spring Art Walk (800) 250-7522.
Lynden—A Country Collection Craft & Antique (360) 966-5573.
Pasco—Columbia Annual Quilt Show (509) 582-3257.

Seattle—Irish Week Festival (206) 684-7200.
Sequim—Elegant Flea antiques and collectibles show and sale (360) 683-8110.
Spokane—Spring Arts & Crafts Show (509) 924-0588. Tenino-Old-time Music Festival (360) 273-5360.
Whidbey—Dance Theatre (800) 638-7631.

April
Bellingham—Children's Theatre (360)

734-5468 April through December; Northwest Guitar Festival (360) 650-7712
Elma—Antique/Collectible Show & Gem Show (360) 482-2650.
Mount Vernon—Street Fair/Tulip Festival (360) 336-9277.
Odessa—Spring Fling and Quilt Show (509) 982-0049.
Olympia—Arts Walk (360) 753-8380.
Puyallup—Jordan Family Circus (253) 841-5045.
Seattle—Annual Worldfest (206) 443-1410; Cherry Blossom/ Japanese Cultural Festival (206) 684-7200.
Sequim—23rd Annual Bonsai Show (360) 683-7712.
Shelton—Old Time Fiddlers Fest (800) 576-2021.
Spokane—Spring Antique & Collectors Show (509) 924-0588.
Tonasket—Grand Ol' Opry (509) 486-1239.
Tri-Cities—Ala Carte Festival (800) 254-5824.
Yakima—Artistry in Wood Show and Sale (509) 697-4143

May
Blaine—International Sculpture Exhibition (360) 332-7165 May through September.
Ellensburg—National Western Art Show & Auction (509) 962-2934.
Grand Coulee—Sunbanks Spring Blues Festival (509) 633-3786
Hoodsport—Oyster Bite (360) 877-9474.
Klickitat—Klick.Klickitat Photo Shoot (509) 493-3630
Lakewood—Civil War Battle & Re-enactment (253) 756-3928.
Matlock—Old Timers' Historical Fair & Exhibition (800) 576-2021.

More Arts Calendar

Pomeroy—Civic Theatre (509) 843-1211 May through September.

Puyallup—Art @ the Market (253) 840-6015.

Seattle—Seattle International Children's Festival (206) 684-7200; Seattle International Film Festival; Northwest Folklife Festival (206) 684-7200.

Sedro-Woolley—Woodfest wood carvers exhibit. (888) 225-8365.

Shelton—Bronze Works Art Fair (800) 576-2021.

Tukwila—Annual World Music and Dance Festival (206) 443-1410.

June

Anatone—Anatone Days BBQ, country music, dancing. (509) 256-3331.

Bremerton—Medieval Faire (360) 297-4751.

Chelan—Classic Car Show (800) 424-3526.

Colville—Alpine Square Dance Festival (509) 684-2408

Edmonds—Edmonds Arts Festival (425) 771-6412.

Ferndale—Scottish Highland Games (360) 384-3444

Graham—Tacoma Highland Games (253) 535-0887.

Ocean Shores—Associated Arts Photography & Fine Arts Shows (800) 762-3224; Sand & Sawdust at the Shore, sand sculpture and chainsaw carvers (800) 762-3224

Omak—Art in the Park (509) 826-4218.

Pacific—Pacific Days Arts & Music Festival (253) 929-1100.

Port Townsend—Centrum's Port Townsend Country Blues Festival (360) 385-3102.

Puyallup—Meeker Days Hoe-down & Bluegrass Festival (253) 840-2631.

Shoreline—Shoreline Arts Festival (206) 361-7133.

Skamokawa—Classic Car/Motorcycle Show and BBQ (360) 795-8107.

Spokane—Annual ArtFest (509) 456-3931; Dixieland Jazz Festival (509) 235-4401; IMAX Film Festival & Summer Celebration (509) 625-6624.

Tacoma—Music & Murals in the Park (253) 627-7031.

Toppenish—Mural-in-a-Day, Arts, Crafts, Food Fair (800) 569-3982.

Wenatchee—Wenatchee Youth Circus (performs statewide) (509) 662-2849 June through September; Square & Round Dance Festival (800) 842-0977.

July

Anacortes—Shipwreck Day & Flea Market, collectibles, antiques (360) 293-7911.

Bainbridge Island—Island Days & Street Dance (206) 842-2982.

Bellevue—Annual Pacific Northwest Arts Fair (425) 454-3322.

Brewster—Backyard Blues Picnic (360) 945-4545.

Centralia—Antique Festival (360) 736-8730.

Darrington—Bluegrass Festival (888) 338-0976.

Enumclaw—Pacific Northwest Scottish Highland Games (206) 522-2541.

Everett—Nubian Jam Community Festival (425) 356-8082.

Friday Harbor—San Juan Island Jazz Festival (360) 378-5509.

Gig Harbor—Renaissance Faire & Gothic Fantasy (800) 359-5948.

Kalama—Blues Festival Benefit (360) 673-3209.

More Arts Calendar

Klickitat—Canyon Days (509) 369-2322.
Lake Chelan—Bach Feste (800) 424-3526.
Leavenworth—Icicle Creek Music Center Summer Music Festival (509) 548-5807.
Longview—Theatre Fest (360) 575-8499.
Port Gamble—North Kitsap Arts & Crafts Festival (360) 697-2735.
Port Townsend—Centrum's Airtouch Jazz Port Townsend (360) 385-3102; Centrum's Festival of American Fiddle Tunes (360) 385-3102.
Redmond—Heritage Festival (206) 296-4232.
Richland—Allied Arts Sidewalk Show (509) 943-9815.
Ritzville—Blues Festival (509) 659-1936.
Seattle—Chinese Culture & Arts Festival (206) 684-7200.
Skamania—Columbia Gorge Bluegrass Festival (509) 427-8928.
Spokane—American Music Festival (509) 921-5579; Royal Fireworks Festival & Baroque Period Arts Festival (509) 455-6865.

Stanwood—Old-Time Fiddlers Stage Show & Campout (360) 435-5848.
Trout Lake—Festival of the Arts (509) 493-2294.
Winthrop—Rhythm & Blues Festival (509) 997-2541.
Yakima—Folklife Festival (509) 248-0747; Vintiques Northwest Nationals (509) 575-6626.

August

Anacortes—Annual Arts Festival (360) 293-6211.
Bainbridge Island—Filipino-American Day (206) 780-2313.

Bellingham—Festival of Music (360) 676-5997.
Ferndale—Hot Air Balloon/Folk Festival-Civil War Reenactment (360) 384-3042.
Grayland—International Nautical Chainsaw Carving (800) 572-0177.
Kent—Canterbury Faire (253) 859-3991.
Monroe—Art in the Park (360) 794-0364.
Olalla—Bluegrass Festival (253) 857-5285.
Olympia—Renaissance Faire (360) 943-9492; Washington Shakespeare Festival (360) 943-9492.
Omak—Native & Western Arts Show (509) 826-1880.
Oysterville—Jazz and Oysters (800) 451-2542.
Republic—NE Washington Fiddle Contest (509) 775-3819. Tacoma—Proctor Summer Arts Festival (253) 272-5767.
Toppenish—Cowboy Poetry Performance (800) 569-3982; Western Art Show (800) 569-3982.
Tumwater—Heritage Art Festival (360) 943-1805.

Usk—Traditional Salish Fair (509) 445-1147.
Whidbey Island—Folk Festival (360) 678-1912.
Winthrop—Methow Music Festival (800) 340-1458.
Yakima—A Case of the Blues and All That

More Arts Calendar

Jazz (509) 453-8280, Allied Arts Festival of the Arts (509) 966-0930.

September
Cashmere—Western Art Show (509) 782-3230.
Kingston—Bluegrass Festival (360) 297-3813.
Metaline Falls—An Affair on Main Street (509) 446-2429.
Mountlake Terrace—Arts of the Terrace (425) 776-9173.
Ocean Shores—Arts & Craft Show (800) 762-3224.
Pacific Beach—Sand Castle & Sculpture Contest (360) 276-4525.
Port Angeles—Blue Grass Festival (360) 417-8878.
Port Angeles—Forest Storytelling Festival (360) 457-3169.
Richland—Tumbleweed Music Festival (509) 943-2787.

Seattle—Bumbershoot (206) 684-7200; Fiestas Patrias, Hispanic Cultural Festival (206) 684-7200.
Vancouver—Wine & Jazz Festival (360) 892-6233.
Walla Walla—Celebration of Regional Art Action (509) 525-2570.
Whidbey Island—Artichokes and Arts (360) 675-3535.

October
Ilwaco—Cranberrian Fair (800) 451-2542.
Langley—Kaleidoscope of

Dance (800) 638-7631.
Leavenworth—Oktoberfest (509) 548-5807.
Long Beach—Peninsula Water Music Festival (800) 451-2542.
Moses Lake—Mennonite Country Auction (509) 765-8683.
Port Townsend—Great Kinetic Sculpture Race (888) 365-6978.

Seattle—Northwest Bookfest (206) 378-1883.
Skamania—Artists in the Gorge Series (509) 427-5471.
Spokane—Annual Craft Fair (509) 327-1584.
Walla Walla—Holiday Art in Action (509) 529-8755 November through December.
Yakima—Annual Central Washington Artists Exhibition (509) 574-4875 November and December.

November
Ocean Shores—Dixieland Jazz Festival (800) 762-3224.
Pasco—Christmas Arts & Crafts Show (509) 924-0588.
Walla Walla—Blue Mountain Chorus of Sweet Adelines (509) 525-0709.

December
Chelan—Caroling Cruise (800) 424-3526.
Sequim—Community Christmas Concert (360) 683-6197.
Spokane—Annual Christmas Juried Arts & Crafts Sale (509) 625-6677.
Toppenish—Christmas Bazaar & All-Indian Talent Show (509) 865-5121.

families, also a departure from the past. These latest immigrants have entered the mainstream of American life almost instantaneously.

Organizations and Events of Interest.

Cambodian Community of Tacoma, P.O. Box 8558, Tacoma, WA 98418; (206) 596-2824.

Filipino-American Association of Yakima Valley, P.O. Box 298, Wapato, WA 98951; (509) 575-8643.

Japan-American Society of the State of Washington, 1800 Ninth Ave., Suite 1550, Seattle, WA 98101-1322; (206) 623-7900.

Music and Cultural Society of India, 4505 NE 86th St., Seattle, WA 98115; (206) 525-5380.

Seattle Asian Art Museum, 1400 E. Prospect St., Seattle, WA 98112; (206) 654-3100.

Tacoma Buddhist Temple, 1717 S. Fawcett Ave., Tacoma, WA 98402; (253) 627-1417.

Tibetan Association of Washington, P.O. Box 27334, Seattle, WA 98125; (206) 526-5296.

Tibetan Cultural Center, 5042 18th Ave. NE, Seattle, WA 98105; (206) 522-6967.

Vietnamese Friendship Association, E. 412804 Skyview, Spokane, WA 99216; (509) 926-6129.

Washington State Commission on Asian Pacific Affairs, 701 S. Jackson St., Suite 301, Seattle, WA 98104; (206) 464-5820.

Wing Luke Asian Museum, 407 Seventh Ave. S., Seattle, WA 98104; (206) 623-5124.

Cherry Blossom & Japanese Cultural Festival, April, Seattle, (206) 684-7200.

Philippine Festival, June, Seattle, (206) 684-7200.

Seattle Chinatown Parade, July, Seattle, (206) 236-0657 (popular Seafair parade).

Bon Odori Japanese Festival, July, Olympia, (360) 754-6833.

Hmong New Year Celebration, November, Seattle, (206) 684-7200.

Avalanches
Avalanches are an annual fact of life in the Cascade Mountains, the site of one of the worst snowslide disasters in the United States. It happened March 1, 1910, when a Great Northern passenger train bound for Puget Sound from Spokane was buried under a mass of snow near the small town of Wellington in Stevens Pass. Ninety-six people died. Avalanches have also claimed the lives of those climbing on Mount Baker and Mount Rainier.

Outdoor recreationists who venture into the backcountry during winter can learn to recognize avalanche danger by looking for certain conditions. Anywhere there is a combination of heavy or sticky snow and steep slopes (especially any slope that appears to have experienced a recent slide), hollow drumming or *whomp*ing sounds coming from the snow underneath may signal that the snow may be ready to release. Rime ice on trees is a sign of high winds during a storm, which may have overloaded leeward slopes with snow.

State Department of Transportation avalanche control units monitor and control avalanches on the mountain passes, using explosives to set off controlled preventive avalanches. To learn more about avalanches or to check on avalanche danger in specific areas, contact the **Northwest Avalanche Institute** on-line at http://www.avalanche.org or call (360) 825-9261; call the **Northwest Avalanche Hotline** at (206) 526-6677; or check the **Northwest Weather and Avalanche Center** Web site at http://www.nwac.noaa.gov/nwac1.htm.

Aviation and Aerospace (SEE ALSO BOEING)
Washington became one of the pioneering centers of aviation when William Boeing

Aviation buffs can view a variety of vintage and historical aircraft, including the original presidential jet, Air Force One, at Seattle's Museum of Flight. Courtesy of Museum of Flight.

established the Boeing Airplane Company in 1916 in Seattle. Boeing is now the largest aerospace company in the world, and the cornerstone of the aviation and aerospace industry in Washington State.

The Boeing Company accounted for more than 90 percent of the total 1996 employment of 86,100 people within the state aerospace industry. Other major companies include such well-known names as BF Goodrich, Allied Signal, and Northrop Grumman. In addition to Boeing, there are 110 other companies in the Washington Manufacturers Register identified as manufacturers of aircraft, aircraft parts, or space systems equipment, instruments, and other materials. An estimated one out of every four manufacturing jobs in Washington is directly engaged in the aerospace industry. When both direct and indirect jobs are considered, aerospace supports one out of every six jobs in the state.

Periodically the aerospace industry goes through serious cyclical downturns, most notably in 1968-71, 1975-77, the early 1980s, and the early 1990s. However, a Boeing downturn no longer means statewide disaster because the state's economy has become more diversified and less dependent upon the aerospace industry. This does not diminish the overall importance of aerospace on the state's economy, which is based on several factors, as noted below.

High wages and a skilled workforce. The high wage structure of aerospace is directly related to the industry's occupational profile. More than two-fifths of the aerospace workforce are professional and technical workers, with such occupations as engineers, engineering technicians, system analysts, and computer programmers. Product assembly and material handlers' occupations (e.g., precision inspectors and testers, aircraft mechanics, tool and die makers, machinists, aircraft structure assemblers, electrical assemblers, machine tool operators, and general assemblers) garner a significant share of the aerospace workforce.

Purchases in other industrial sectors. In 1995, Boeing spent more than $2.9 billion on goods and services in the state. Such spending supports a significant number of jobs within the state's economy.

Aerospace is a leading export. In 1995, aerospace foreign exports amounted to $9.5 billion, or one out of every three dollars of foreign sales.

Over the next two decades, Boeing predicts that the demand for new passenger jets will grow 5.3 percent per year on average, a significant portion of which is expected to come from replacement aircraft due to fuel inefficiency, excessive noise, or obsolescence. The remaining three-fourths will be generated by new growth in air travel, particularly in the Asia-Pacific region. Among the limiting factors to growth of aerospace employment in Washington, the most significant is foreign competition, particularly from the European consortium Airbus.

Organizations and Events of Interest.

Jack Murdock Aviation Center and Historic Pearson Field, 1115 E. Fifth St., Vancouver, WA 98661; (360) 694-7026. Aviation history and hands-on demonstrations of the science and mechanics of flight are featured. Pearson Field is the oldest continuously operating airfield in the United States.

Museum of Flight, 9404 E. Marginal Way, Boeing Field, Seattle, WA 98108; (206) 764-5700. The museum tells the story of flight from the dawn of aviation to the Space Age. It features vintage aircraft—bombers, fighters, the Blackbird spy plane, the original Air Force One, an air traffic control tower exhibit, and the restored "Red Barn," birthplace of The Boeing Company.

Yakima International Air Fair, July,
Yakima, (509) 248-4282. This air show and displays feature warbirds, experimental aircraft, antique aircraft, and military aircraft.

Three Rivers Air Show, August (biannual), Kelso, (360) 425-3688. Historical/military aircraft are displayed, and aerobatics and military fly-bys are performed.

Basalt (SEE ALSO VOLCANOES AND VOLCANISM)

Basalt is a dark, fine-grained rock formed by lava flowing from volcanoes or volcanic fissures. Thick layers of basalt underlie the Columbia Plateau, in some areas thousands of feet deep. When solidified, it sometimes forms large, four-, five-, or six-sided columns. Extensive cliffs formed of columnar basalt can be found in many parts of Washington, especially along the Columbia and Snake Rivers, and along the Grand Coulee.

Beacon Rock

Beacon Rock, the second-largest rock in the world (second only to the Rock of Gibraltar) rises 848 feet above the great gorge of the Columbia River, near Skamania, Washington, just 5 miles west of Bonneville Dam. The rock, technically known as a monolith—a single rock formation detached from bedrock—is the core of a 9-million-year-old volcano that was active during the uplift of the Cascade Mountains. Erosion of the outer surface of ejected material left only the hardened plug standing.

Charles Ladd, a Portland, Oregon, banker, bought Beacon Rock in the early 1900s to save it from being quarried. A narrow, ¾-mile trail to the summit zigzags along 52 switchbacks and crosses 22 wooden bridges spanning fissures in the huge rock. The summit offers impressive views of Mount Hood, Mount Adams, and the Columbia River.

Looking Back

1926

Bertha Landes was elected mayor of Seattle, becoming the first woman to lead a major American city. Earlier, she had been one of the first two women on the Seattle City Council. Her administration was known for cleaning up city police corruption and pressing for tough economizing efforts.

Beer Given that Washington produces 75 percent of the hops grown in the United States, it is not surprising that the state's specialty beers are many and of high quality. Not all of Washington's "craft" beer producers are still considered "microbreweries" (since they produce more than 15,000 barrels a year). Bert Grant of Yakima was the first of many entrants in Washington's now crowded microbrew industry. He started making Grant's Scottish Ale in Yakima in 1982 and was the first modern brewer to serve cask-conditioned ales in North America. Some of the better-known microbreweries are among the state's largest breweries, including Redhook (No. 3), Pyramid (No. 4), Bert Grant's (No. 5), Hale's (No. 6), Pike Brewing (No. 7), Maritime Pacific (No. 8), and Birkebeiner Brewing (No. 10). They are just the top layer of the foam, however. For those still looking for the perfect brewski, try some of these (and remember, the microbrewery biz is very fluid; some of these may have disappeared or changed names, and new ones may have come onto the scene that we haven't heard of yet).

Bert Grant at his renowned Yakima microbrewery.
Courtesy of Yakima Brewing & Malting Co.

Anacortes Brewhouse, Anacortes
Atomic Ales and Rattesnake Mountain
    Brewery, Richland
Bayou Brewery, Spokane
Big Time Brewery, Seattle
Birkebeiner Brewing Company, Spokane
Bingen Brewing Co., Bingen
Boundary Bay Brewing, Bellingham
Buchanan Brewing Co., Oroville
California & Alaska Street Brewery, Seattle
Captains City Brewery, Coupeville
Caveman Brewing, Spokane
Cedar River Brewing, Redmond
Cirque Brewery, Prosser
CJ's Brew Pub, Vancouver
Crown Point Brewing, Vancouver
Diamond Knot Brewery, Mukilteo
Eagle Brewing, Mukilteo
Eagle River Brewing Co. & Issaquah
    Brewhouse, Issaquah
Elysian Brewing, Seattle

Engine House Brewery, Tacoma
Fish Brewing, Olympia
Flying Pig Brewery, Everett
Fort Spokane Brewing Co., Spokane
Bert Grant's (Yakima Brewing & Malting
    Company), Yakima
Hale's Ales, Seattle
Hart Brewery & Pub, Seattle
Hazel Dell Brewpub, Vancouver
Hood Canal Brewery, Poulsbo
Ice Harbor Brewing Co., Pasco
Kelley Creek Brewing Co., Bonney Lake
La Conner Brewing, La Conner
Mac & Jack Brewing, Redmond
Maritime Pacific Brewing, Seattle
McMenamins, Seattle
Moon Ales, Seattle
Northern Lights Brewing Co., Airway
    Heights (Spokane area)
Orchard Street Brewery, Bellingham
Pacific Crest Brewing, Tukwila
Pacific Northwest Brewing, Seattle
Pike Brewing Company, Seattle
Port Angeles Brewery, Port Angeles
Port Townsend Brewing Co., Port
    Townsend
Powerhouse Restaurant & Brewery,
    Puyallup
Pyramid/Hart Brewing, Seattle
Ram Big Horn Brewing, Spokane
Red Dawg Brew Pub, Young's Brewing Co.,
    Chehalis and Centralia
Redhook, Seattle
Redmond Brewing, Redmond

Rock Bottom Brewery & Restaurant,
 Seattle
Roslyn Brewing Co., Roslyn
Salmon Creek Brewery, Woodland
San Juan Brewing & Front Street Alehouse,
 Friday Harbor
Scuttlebutt Brewing, Everett
Seattle Brewers, Seattle
Silver City Brewing Co., Silverdale
Skagit River Brewing Co., Mount Vernon
Snoqualmie Falls Brewing Co., Snoqualmie
Sweetwater Brewing Co., Spokane
Tapps Brewing Co., Sumner
The Leavenworth Brewery, Leavenworth
The Ridge Brewpub & Grill, Seattle
Titanic Brewing Co., Olympia
Twin Rivers Brewing Co., Monroe
Vancouver Brewing Co., Vancouver
Vashon Brewing Co., Vashon Island
Western Ale, SeaTac
Whatcom Brewery, Ferndale
Whidbey Island Brewing Co., Langley
Whitstran Brewery, Prosser
Winthrop Brewing Co., Winthrop
Yakima Brewing & Malting Co., Yakima

Events of Interest.
 Northwest Microbrewery Festival, June,
The Herbfarm, 32804 Issaquah-Fall City
Rd., Fall City, WA 98024; (206) 784-2222.

Bellingham
Bellingham is the
largest town in the state's northwest corner,
with a population of 61,980. Nestled between
Bellingham Bay and the Nooksack Valley,
Bellingham, like most western Washington
towns, was founded with the notion of
extracting trees and floating them to the
water for transport. The town's founders,
Henry Roeder and Russell Peabody, built a
mill where Whatcom Creek poured into
Bellingham Bay. What is now Bellingham
was originally several small towns—
Bellingham, Whatcom, Fairhaven, and
Sehome. All were situated along Bellingham
Bay, and all derived their economic base
from natural resources—most notably
trees, coal, and fish—and agriculture.
 Bellingham's working-class roots now
mix with a college-town atmosphere. Western Washington University's 224-acre
campus overlooks the downtown area and

*Bellingham's historical former city hall is now a
centerpiece cultural museum.* Courtesy of
Whatcom Museum of History & Art.

its working waterfront. The campus features a renowned outdoor sculpture garden.
The neighborhood that is the site of the old
town of Fairhaven, with its Victorian
homes, restaurants, and galleries, is a
favorite destination for visitors, many of
whom come through Bellingham to catch
the ferry to Alaska. Among its other attractions are scenic Chuckanut Drive, Lake
Whatcom, and nearby Mount Baker.

Birds
Washington's bird life, or
avifauna, includes more than 400 species of
resident and migratory birds that rely on a
wide range of feeding, nesting, and resting
habitat. A critical part of the Pacific Flyway,
the state's coastal estuaries, offshore islands,
freshwater rivers and lakes, prairies, and
mountains are home to marine birds,
waterfowl, shorebirds, wading birds,
songbirds, and raptors. Among these are
endangered and threatened species, such as
the northern spotted owl, sandhill crane,
bald eagle, and marbled murrelet, that rely
on shrinking habitat (*see also* Endangered
Species). Below are some places to view
Washington's rich avifauna.
 Along the Pacific coast, Willapa Bay and
Grays Harbor's Bowerman Basin (the Grays

Harbor National Wildlife Refuge) are major spring and fall feeding and resting areas for migrating shorebirds. At times, congregating shorebirds have been estimated at more than 1 million at Grays Harbor's Bowerman Basin. The old-growth habitat of the Olympic Peninsula is home to northern spotted owls and marbled murrelets.

The Puget Sound and San Juan Islands regions are home to numerous river estuaries and eelgrass beds that provide nesting and feeding habitat for eagles, waterfowl, and wading birds. Dungeness Spit and Dungeness Bay, with its eelgrass beds, attract harlequin ducks, black brant, and nearly every other species of waterfowl found in western Washington. Protection Island in the Strait of Juan de Fuca is home to nesting colonies of gulls, Wilson's snipe, and tufted puffins. While its nesting areas are a mystery, the marbled murrelet can be seen feeding along the Strait of Juan de Fuca. The Skagit River is home to more than 300 nesting pairs of bald eagles (the largest congregation of nesting eagles in the Lower 48). Snow geese congregate in large numbers in the Skagit estuary, while waterfowl, herons, falcons, and shorebirds fill Padilla Bay and, farther south, the Nisqually River estuary.

The subalpine and alpine areas of the Cascade Mountains and the Selkirk Mountains of northeastern Washington are home to numerous songbirds, jays, woodpeckers, grouse, red-tailed hawks, goshawks, and bald and golden eagles.

The Columbia Basin has both shrub-steppe habitat and a vast system of ponds and marshes that attract migratory waterfowl and wading birds. Along the Channeled Scablands, chukar partridge, valley quail, desert songbirds, prairie falcons, ferruginous hawks, and great horned owls can be seen. A wide variety of waterfowl, songbirds, and wading birds, such as avocets, black-necked stilts, Wilson's phalaropes, egrets, and even white pelicans, can be seen in the areas around Moses Lake and the Potholes Reservoir. In the Columbia National Wildlife Refuge south of the Potholes, sandhill cranes feed and rest in March and April.

Mystery of the Marbled Murrelet

Where does it nest? Although adult murrelets (Brachyramphus marmoratus) were often seen as winter residents of waters along Washington's Strait of Juan de Fuca, the San Juan Islands, and Puget Sound, for decades the birds kept their nests secret... until in 1990 wildlife researchers finally found five nests in Oregon and Washington, located 20 to 26 miles inland, 100 to 140 feet high in old-growth western hemlock and Douglas fir forest.... Flying at speeds of up to 60 miles an hour, the parents made a round trip of 50 miles to feed their chicks in the safety of the forest. Mystery solved.—Ann Saling, The Great Northwest Nature Factbook

Organizations and Events of Interest. There are 27 Audubon chapters throughout Washington State. To find the one nearest to you, contact the state office. **National Audubon of Washington State,** P. O. Box 462, 1063 Capitol Way S., Suite 201, Olympia, WA 98501; (360) 786-8020; http://wa.audubon.org/.

Upper Skagit Bald Eagle Festival, January, Concrete, (360) 853-7009.

Sandhill Crane Festival, March, Othello, (800) 684-2556.

Grays Harbor Shorebird Festival, April, Grays Harbor, (360) 495-3289 or (800) 321-1924.

Audubon Wenas Creek Campout, May, Wenas Creek, (509) 697-8144.

Audubon Christmas Bird Count, December, statewide, (360) 786-8020.

Boeing (SEE ALSO AVIATION AND AEROSPACE) The Boeing Company, headquartered in Seattle, is the largest aerospace company in the world (measured by total sales) and the nation's leading exporter. In 1996, Boeing announced two major acquisitions: the buyout of Rockwell International's aerospace and defense operations, and the $13 billion acquisition of McDonnell Douglas. The acquisitions

made Boeing the world's largest manufacturer of commercial jetliners and military aircraft, and the nation's largest contractor to the National Aeronautics and Space Administration. The company has an extensive global reach, with customers in 145 countries and operations in 27 states. Worldwide, Boeing and its subsidiaries employ more than 238,000 people. The company's capabilities in aerospace also include helicopters, electronic and defense systems, missiles, rocket engines, launch vehicles, and advanced information and communication systems.

The company is organized into four major business segments: Boeing Commercial Airplane Group; Space and Communications Group; Military Aircraft and Missile Systems Group; and Shared Services Group. Below are its main commercial products.

Jet aircraft: 717 (formerly MD-95), 737, 747, 757, 767, and 777; MD-80, MD-90, and MD-11. More than 9,000 Boeing commercial jetliners are in service worldwide.

Military-aircraft and defense-system products and programs: Fighters (F/A-18E/F Super Hornet, F/A-18 Hornet, F-15 Eagle, F-22 Raptor, AV-8B Harrier, and Joint Strike Fighter), C-17, T-45 Goshawk, 767 AWACS, and Airborne Laser.

Military rotorcraft: RAH-Comanche, CH-47 Chinook, AH-64D Apache Long-bow, and V-22 Osprey.

Missiles: Harpoon anti-ship missile, Standoff Land Attack Missile (SLAM) ER, and Joint Direct Attack Munition (JDAM).

Space: International Space Station, the largest international science and technology venture in history; Space Shuttle orbiters; satellites and launch vehicles.

Aviation buffs can tour Boeing's Everett factory, the world's largest building by volume (472,000,000 cubic feet). Information: (206) 764-5720.

Bonneville Power Administration

(*SEE ALSO* DAMS) The Bonneville Power Administration (BPA), a division of the U.S. Department of the Interior, is the agency that markets the electrical power produced by federal dams on the Columbia River and its tributaries. BPA's power transmission grid—the "highway system" over which the products of electrical generation flow—provides about three-fourths of the Northwest's power transmission. The agency's 363 substations and 15,012 circuit miles of transmission lines provide service to an area encompassing 300,000 square miles.

BPA supplies on average 40 percent of the power sold in the Northwest, and controls more than half the region's high-voltage transmission. More than 80 percent of the power BPA sells is hydroelectric, and about 60 percent of the Northwest's electricity comes from hydropower.

BPA sells its power directly to federal agencies such as the Department of Energy and the Navy, to certain non-aluminum industries, and to utility companies, which in turn sell it to their retail customers. Bonneville markets about 40 percent of its "firm power" (this is calculated as the power that can be produced even under poor water conditions) at cost to public agency customers.

The West Coast power market is quickly becoming a commodities market. New power trading hubs have been established at the California-Oregon border and at Palo Verde, Arizona; power prices at these hubs are listed daily in *The Wall Street Journal*. BPA sells much of its surplus power in this open market. BPA power traders sell surplus hydropower on the open market and buy to meet short-term gaps in supply. The agency first offers surplus and excess federal power to buyers in the Northwest. Northwest publicly owned utilities (PUDs) are BPA's largest customer group; traditionally they have accounted for about half of BPA's total revenues.

The federal power system in the Pacific Northwest has conferred significant benefits on the region for more than 50 years, both as a source of inexpensive electricity and for irrigation, flood control, and navigation. In recent years, however, BPA has had to adjust to operating within a much more competitive electricity industry. BPA's power has lost its price advantage due to low natural gas prices, surplus generating capacity on the West Coast, and the opening of the competitive wholesale electricity market, which resulted in lower electricity prices. BPA also had to cope with its high operating costs, which included such items as paying for salmon recovery efforts, payment of its debt to the U.S. government for construction of dam and transmission systems, and its share of three Washington Public Power Supply System nuclear power plants.

BPA is one reason Washington has enjoyed low-cost electricity. The average residential rate in the Northwest is 5.4 cents per kilowatt-hour, compared to the U.S. average residential rate of 8.4 cents per kilowatt-hour (1995 figures).

Bridges
Washington has many bridges that stand out, but the best-known may be those that have fallen down. The most notorious of all was Galloping Gertie, which once spanned the Tacoma Narrows. She earned her name from her habit of undulating during strong winds, a characteristic caused by the design of her deck sections. On November 7, 1940, just 130 days after she was formally opened to traffic, the right combination of wind speed and gusts got her swaying and twisting so violently that she broke apart and fell 190 feet into the Narrows.

Four of the world's eight floating highway bridges are found in this state—two side-by-side bridges that make up the I-90 bridge, the Albert D. Rosellini Bridge—also known as the (Highway) 520 or Evergreen Point floating bridge—and the Hood Canal Bridge. Both the original I-90 bridge (its formal name is the Lacey V. Murrow Bridge) and the Hood Canal Bridge have sections that are replacements for parts that sank. In both instances, compartments of the floating pontoons were swamped by storm-driven waves. The Albert D. Rosellini Bridge is also the longest bridge located completely inside the state.

The Washington Department of Transportation, which keeps track of bridges, maintains a list of more than 4,700 bridges, viaducts, highway overpasses, tunnels, and major culverts (defined as those whose failure would compromise the road—in other words, a simple bridge). Some are distinctive—78 Washington bridges are on the National Register of Historic Places

The Albert D. Rosellini bridge (Highway 520) crosses Lake Washington, connecting Seattle and Bellevue. Photo by Andrea Jarvela.

and a number of bridges have been recognized for their outstanding design and engineering.

The Cicero Bridge spanning the North Fork of the Stillaguamish River, the Cowlitz River Bridge east of Mossyrock on U.S. Highway 12, and the Selah Creek twin bridges on Interstate 82 north of Yakima are among the state's design award winners.

Fred Redmon Memorial Bridge, on I-82 north of Yakima, is the longest single concrete arch bridge in North America, 13th longest in the world (total span 1366.6 feet, arch span 549.5 feet).

The 2,503-foot Ed Hendler Bridge crossing the Columbia River between Pasco and Kennewick is the second-longest cable-stayed bridge in the world.

The 4.1-mile Astoria-Megler Bridge across the mouth of the Columbia River is the longest continuous steel span truss bridge in the world. It joins Washington to Oregon.

Grays River Covered Bridge on Highway 4 in Grays Harbor County is the state's only existing covered bridge, and is on the National Register of Historic Places.

Cascade Mountains

(SEE ALSO MOUNT RAINIER, MOUNT ST. HELENS, VOLCANOES AND VOLCANISM) The Cascades, Washington's largest mountain range, run north to south the length of the state—and beyond. The five highest peaks

are great volcanoes, Mount Rainier (14,410 feet), Mount Adams (12,276 feet), Mount Baker (10,778 feet), Glacier Peak (10,568 feet), and Mount St. Helens (8,365 feet). The Cascade Mountains are about 25 million years old, but the volcanoes are much younger; indeed, the major volcanoes remain geologically active. Mount St. Helens erupted violently in 1980. Mount Baker has recently heated up, causing its glaciers to melt and recede. The dramatic Cascade volcanoes exist because the floor of the Pacific Ocean sinks beneath the West Coast of the North American continent. The major active volcanoes lie along a remarkably smooth and continuous line that marks where the sinking slab beneath the continent gets hot enough to start the steamy action.

The Cascades bifurcate the state into two distinct climate regions: wet and evergreen western Washington, and the drier, sunnier inland empire of eastern Washington. In addition to creating climatic differences, the Cascades serve as a political and psychological demarcation between east and west, sometimes called the Cascade Curtain. Western Washington is more urban and industrial, while eastern Washington is mainly rural and agricultural.

The only natural break in the Cascades is the Columbia River Gorge, the southern boundary of the state. Other crossings are the high mountain passes used by the railroads and the major east-west highways (see also Roads and Highways). Geologists distinguish the North Cascades from the South Cascades, with the dividing line at Snoqualmie Pass. Average elevations at the northern end are roughly twice as high as at the southern end—8,000 feet in the north versus 4,000 feet in the south. Smaller mountain groups that are part of the Cascades include the Twin Sister, Stuart, and Tatoosh Ranges, and the Chelan, Chiwaukum, Cleman, Cultus, Entiat, Saddle, Simcoe, and Wenatchee Mountains.

Replete with jagged peaks, large recreational lakes, and abundant forests and wildlife, the Cascades are a recreation mecca. Recreational lands and activities are centered in North Cascades National Park and Mount Rainier National Park (*see also* National Parks), in three national forests, and in other publicly owned lands.

Mount Adams. Washington's second-highest peak and volcano (12,307 feet) rises 50 miles east of Mount St. Helens in northeast Skamania and southwest Yakima Counties. This volcano's broad base and irregular shape are clues to its geological history: A series of basalt eruptions built a broad base, followed by subsequent eruptions of several coalescing cones and then scouring by glaciers. Eight glaciers still cling to the mountain and feed its glacial streams. Although Mount Adams has been active since the last ice age and there are steam vents near the summit, geologists don't believe this volcano presents a hazard of a potentially cataclysmic eruption like that of its neighbor, Mount St. Helens. Mudflows caused by rapid subterranean heating and steam venting are a more likely hazard. In a recent display of its dangerous nature, in 1997 a series of avalanches sent millions of cubic yards of snow and debris crashing down the mountain, leaving some 5 miles of scarred slope on different sides of the mountain.

The Mount Adams Wilderness borders the mountain's west slope. The wilderness area offers 56 miles of hiking trails with views of glaciers, alpine forests, lava flows, and rimrock. The eastern side of the mountain is part of the Yakama Indian Reservation.

The Indian name for the mountain was *Pah-too*, which means "high sloping mountain." Its Anglo namesake is the second president of the United States, John Adams; the name was bestowed by an eager patriot who wanted to name all the Cascade volcanoes for U.S. presidents. He thought he was naming Mount St. Helens at the time, but he missed.

From the 1930s through the 1950s, sulfur was mined from the mountain, but the necessity of hauling supplies and workers up the mountain by mule, and hauling the sulfur back down the same way, made the venture unprofitable.

Mount Baker. The northernmost of Washington's Cascade volcanoes, Mount Baker (10,778 feet) is named for Lt. Joseph Baker, an officer who accompanied Capt. George Vancouver on the official British expedition that explored Puget Sound in 1792. The mountain's icy covering inspired the Native American and early explorers' names for the mountain, most of which are variations of the word white—"white, steep mountain," "white mountain," "white friar," and "great white watcher."

The mountain's summit area has two peaks and a large crater that was probably created by an eruption after the last ice age. The crater has been belching steam and hydrogen sulfide gas since the mid-19th century. Mount Baker sports a dozen glaciers that cover about 20 square miles. Snowfields cover another 44 square miles.

With its extensive ice and snow cover and steamy activity, Mount Baker poses the threat of potentially dangerous mudflows. The Nooksack River, which drains Mount Baker, shows indications of catastrophic mudflows in prehistoric times. The mountain has been heating up in recent years, and as a result, its glaciers are receding and snowfields are melting back. An ash fall on the east side of the mountain has been radiocarbon-dated to less than 500 years old.

Glacier Peak. This ice-clad mountain is the least visible, least accessible, and probably least known of the Washington volcanoes. Glacier Peak has experienced

large, explosive eruptions in its past—in fact, more of them than any other Washington volcano except Mount St. Helens—the most recent in the 1700s. Before that, Glacier Peak's largest series of eruptions began some 13,000 years ago and lasted about 600 years, the largest one expelling more than three times as much ash as the 1980 Mount St. Helens blast. Despite its apparent lack of activity in recorded time, however, the three hot springs on its flanks are a reminder that there is still molten magma deep beneath its icy cover.

Caves

Washington has a number of fascinating caves, especially the lava tube caves that are found only in the West. Lava tube caves are formed when flowing basalt lava cools rapidly enough on the top and bottom to solidify, while molten lava continues to flow within the cooling crust. Washington has the longest unbroken lava tube cave in the Western Hemisphere, 12,810-foot Ape Cave on the south flank of Mount St. Helens. Other lava tube caves in the Mount Adams-Mount St. Helens lava flows include 3,775-foot-long Lake Cave, which features unique brick-red lava; Ole's Cave (5,800 feet), created in the most recent ropy lava flow in the 48 contiguous states; and Cheese Cave (1,814 feet), where pioneers once stored potatoes. Another lava tube cave was known for its ice—it actually was a source of ice for human consumption

in pioneer days. Ice Cave's four distinct sections trap cold winter air, forming a floor of ice, while dripping water is frozen into huge drip masses.

A more spectacular type of ice cave was once found on Mount Rainier. The Paradise ice caves, formed at the terminus of the Paradise Glacier, once comprised the largest known glacier cave system in the world. They were a popular attraction at Mount Rainier National Park for visitors who marveled at the eerily beautiful blue light. Unfortunately, as the glacier retreated uphill, the ice caves shrank, until they became too dangerous for visitors and were closed to the public in 1971. In the fall of 1991, the last cave disappeared.

Gardner Cave (850 feet), located in Crawford State Park in Pend Oreille County (*see also* State Parks), contains the state's most spectacular limestone cavern. The cave is lighted and park staff conduct guided tours.

Channeled Scablands

In eastern Washington, ancient massive floods eroded soil and exposed the black lava underneath in the 2,500-square-mile Channeled Scablands. The landscape was a puzzle to scientists until Washington geologist J. Harlen Bretz, who began studying the area in the 1920s, concluded that only a major catastrophic flood could have caused such erosion. It was a number of years before he could combine his theory of what he named the Spokane Floods with the work of a geologist who discovered the remains of ancient Glacial Lake Missoula in Montana. When a dam of ice broke in Idaho some 15,000 years ago, all the water of Glacial Lake Missoula washed onto eastern Washington in what was the most catastrophic flood known—a 2,000-foot-tall wall of water backed by 500 cubic miles of water rushing headlong across Washington. The scene was repeated numerous times, a mountain of water scooping up the soil and dumping it downstream, leaving behind ripple marks, potholes, and stream channels etched in the exposed basalt.

Charities

Washington State has a number of large charitable foundations supporting a broad range of causes. According to the Urban Institute, a national think tank, there are more than 3,000 public charities in the state.

Distribution of Charitable Funds

Human Services	39.6%
Health	15.5%
Education	13.7%
Arts and Culture	11.9%
Public Benefit	5.8%
Religion Related	4.2%
Environment and Animals	3.2%
International	1.3%
Unknown	4.9%

A review by the national Foundation Center of the many "Top 25" and "Top 100" lists of charitable organizations, ranked according to assets and total giving, turned up only two Washington organizations in three categories. The Seattle Foundation ranked 25th among the "Top 25 Community Foundations by Total Giving," with grants of $10,055,727. Vancouver's M. J. Murdock Charitable Trust, established by Tektronix co-founder Melvin J. (Jack) Murdock, was ranked 97th among the "Top 100 U.S. Grant-Making Foundations by Value of Total Giving ($18,075,566), and 99th among the top 100 by value of assets ($360,998,408). The William H. Gates Foundation, which had assets in excess of $312 million when these rankings were compiled, will likely make the next such listing, since Bill and Melinda Gates added billions of dollars to their foundation's endowment in 1998 and 1999.

While a 1994 study by the *Chronicle of Philanthropy* ranked Washington in the lower half of states in charitable giving—32nd in the nation—as the fortunes of the high-tech and Internet companies swelled the ranks of millionaires in the state, individual large-scale charitable donations also increased and are expected to continue to do so. A number of big-ticket philanthropists are included among the ranks of the state's major donors besides Bill Gates. Among them are Paul Allen, a co-founder of Microsoft, and telecommunications magnate Craig McCaw. Paul Allen has created four charitable foundations and given away more than $100 million to libraries, AIDS research, theaters, museums, parks, and the search for extraterrestrial life. His gifts have included $10 million to the University of Washington. Craig McCaw gave $1 million to the Seattle public school system through the district's charitable foundation, the Alliance for Education.

Individuals and organizations that hold assets in trust for charitable purposes are registered by the Secretary of State's Charitable Trust Program, which makes the information available upon request. **Office of the Secretary of State,** Charities Program, 505 E. Union Ave., P.O. Box 40234, Olympia, WA 98504-0234; charities hotline: 1-800-332-GIVE, TDD: 1-888-658-1485; E-mail: charities@secstate.wa.gov.

Looking Back

May 12, 1792

American Robert Gray sailed into "a large river of fresh water" and named it after his ship, *Columbia.* Five months later, Englishman George Vancouver explored the lower river, but Gray's journey gave the United States a basis to claim territory on the Northwest Coast.

Cities and Towns

More than half the population of Washington State resides in its 277 incorporated municipalities, primarily in the state's 25 largest cities. The earliest towns were established along the Columbia River in the 1850s. Seattle, Spokane, and other major centers of population were established in the 1860s-1880s. The number of municipalities has remained relatively stable since the 1950s, though several rural communities

have disincorporated, some municipalities have consolidated, and a few new suburban areas, especially around Puget Sound, have incorporated.

A number of Washington's cities and towns have been honored as great places to live. *Money* magazine has consistently ranked Seattle as one of its "Best Places to Live" in the United States, using 37 "Quality of Life" factors such as housing cost, cultural opportunities, schools, and crime. For 1998, the magazine ranked cities by region. In the West, Seattle was ranked as the best large city to live in; Tacoma and Spokane were ranked 2nd and 7th, respectively, among medium-size cities; and the best small cities included Olympia (3rd), Bellingham (5th), Bremerton (8th), Yakima (11th), and the Tri-Cities of Richland-Kennewick-Pasco (16th).

In another ranking of great places to live, *National Demographics* magazine extolled the virtues of small cities, which it calls "micropolitan" areas. The highly regarded small municipalities were noted for such factors as high per capita income, spectacular locations, climate, and growth. In Washington, Wenatchee, Port Angeles, Mount Vernon, Olympia, Bremerton, and Bellingham were cited as attractive small cities.

The All-America City Award, sponsored by the National Civic League and Allstate Insurance, recognizes community involvement and problem solving. Over the past years, the following Washington cities have won this honor: Anacortes (1961), Bellevue (1955), Bellingham (1979-80), Chewelah (1972), Leavenworth (1967), Olympia (1986-87), Port Angeles (1953), Richland (1960), Seattle (1966), Spokane (1974-75), Tacoma (1983-84), Vancouver (1986-87), and Yakima (1994).

Organizations of Interest.
Association of Washington Cities, 1076 SE Franklin, Olympia, WA 98501; (360) 753-4137.

City Management Association, Washington, 1200 Fifth Ave., Suite 1300, Seattle, WA 98202; (206) 625-1300.

Ten Largest Cities by Population (1998)

City	Population
1. Seattle	539,670
2. Spokane	188,300
3. Tacoma	186,000
4. Vancouver	132,000
5. Bellevue	105,700
6. Everett	84,330
7. Federal Way	76,820
8. Kent	71,610
9. Yakima	64,290
10. Lakewood	62,540

Ten Largest Cities by Land Area (1998)

Municipality	Land Area (in sq. mi.)
1. Seattle	83.64
2. Spokane	54.38
3. Tacoma	48.96
4. Vancouver	43.75
5. Richland	33.71
6. Bainbridge Island	32.02
7. Bellevue	28.38
8. Kent	25.74
9. Bellingham	25.21
10. Everett	25.13

Ten Smallest Towns (1998)

Town	Population
1. Krupp	51
2. Lamont	88
3. Waverly	115
4. Hatton	120
5. Index	140
6. Marcus	155
7. Farmington	158
8. Starbuck	165
9. Metaline	180
10. Hartline	185

Selected Cities and Towns (1998) (Continued on P. 44)

Municipality	Population	Land Area (in sq. mi.)
Aberdeen	16,610	11.73
Anacortes	13,900	8.39
Arlington	6,635	8.67
Asotin	1,095	1.31
Auburn	33,650	20.1
Bainbridge Island	19,080	32.02
Battle Ground	8,460	2.87
Bellevue	86,872	28.4
Bellingham	61,980	26.92
Bingen	698	1
Black Diamond	1,422	5.11
Blaine	3,595	5.68
Bothell	12,345	10.86
Bremerton	37,260	19.45
Brewster	2,050	5.11
Bridgeport	2,100	0.64
Buckley	3,950	3.75
Burlington	5,525	3.64
Camas	10,300	4.89
Carnation	1,243	4.65
Cathlamet	545	2
Centralia	13,340	5.83
Chehalis	6,965	3.73
Chelan	3,365	4.9
Cheney	8,495	3.56
Chewelah	2,405	2.32
Clarkston	6,890	2.01
Cle Elum	1,800	1.36
Colfax	2,880	1.49
Colville	4,750	2
Concrete	785	1.18
Connell	2,780	3.47
Coulee City	630	5.43
Coupeville	1,630	1.02
Darrington	1,235	1.01
Davenport	1,772	1.33
Dayton	2,553	1.28
Des Moines	27,200	4.52
Du Pont	1,370	5.86
Duvall	4,120	1.55
Eatonville	1,905	1.47
Edmonds	38,610	8.79
Ellensburg	13,440	6.19
Enumclaw	10,550	3.11
Ephrata	6,065	4.81
Everett	84,330	27.11
Federal Way	76,820	1.09
Forks	3,450	2.58
Friday Harbor	1,890	1.89

Municipality	Population	Land Area (in sq. mi.)
George	465	0.58
Gig Harbor	6,350	4.09
Goldendale	3,550	2.36
Grand Coulee	1,215	1.08
Granite Falls	1,985	1.65
Harrington	479	0.40
Hoquiam	8,995	7.3
Ilwaco	876	1.24
Index	140	0.19
Kelso	12,100	7.16
Kennewick	50,390	17.39
Kent	71,610	28.04
Kettle Falls	1,505	0.86
Kirkland	44,220	6.21
La Conner	775	1.52
Lacey	28,240	13.5
Leavenworth	2,250	0.96
Long Beach	1,420	1.63
Longview	34,060	14.32
Lynden	8,510	3.93
Lynnwood	33,110	9.15
Marysville	19,740	7.53
Medical Lake	3,830	3.46
Mercer Island	21,690	6.2
Metaline Falls	230	0.19
Monroe	10,690	3.67
Montesano	3,555	10.04
Morton	1,265	0.79
Moses Lake	13,710	8.04
Mount Vernon	22,540	9.46
Mukilteo	16,810	4.56
Naches	715	0.34
Newport	1,955	0.97
North Bend	3,675	2.3
North Bonneville	532	2.13
Northport	348	0.54
Oak Harbor	20,510	8.71
Ocean Shores	3,220	9.3
Odessa	975	1
Okanogan	2,415	1.81
Olympia	39,070	17.74
Omak	4,435	3.24
Oroville	1,595	1.28
Orting	3,575	2.58
Othello	5,415	2.5
Palouse	975	1
Pasco	26,090	20.65
Pe Ell	693	0.62

Coffee

Washington may be the only state where every child knows he or she can someday grow up to be a barista. And many do—the state is littered with coffee bars, outdoor espresso stands, indoor espresso stands (check out the lobby of many large office buildings and airports), and drive-through espresso stands for those on the go. It is not unheard of to see a Starbucks, SBC, and Tully's occupying three corners of a single intersection in Seattle.

It all began in the 1970s, so the story goes, when some Seattle entrepreneurs who were just passionate about a good cup of coffee started opening up small specialty coffee stores that sold perfectly roasted whole beans with exotic names. From those modest beginnings, within a quarter of a century Washington's specialty coffee pushers set out to put a quality cuppa joe on every breakfast table in America and the world. Those great beans are now sold not only in supermarkets, but even major fast-food outlets and airlines are serving local upscale coffee brands.

Seattle's Starbucks Coffee Company is the nation's leading specialty coffee purveyor, with 2,030 retail locations in North America, the United Kingdom, and the Pacific Rim, and total net revenues of more than $400 million in 1998. While Starbucks is the best known of the coffee purveyors worldwide, there are a good many smaller coffee roasters and retailers headquartered in the state, including SBC, Seattle's Finest Coffee, Caffe Appassionato, Caffe D'Arte, Tully's, Torrefazione Italia, Brothers, and others.

Don't forget—National Specialty Coffee Week is in February.

Coffee & Cuisine Magazine, 1218 Third Ave., Suite 1315, Seattle, WA 98101; www.coffeetalk.com.

Columbia Plateau

The Columbia Plateau is one of the world's most spectacular volcanic regions. It extends from the middle of eastern Washington into Idaho, through most of eastern Oregon, and all the way into the northeastern corner of California. The Columbia River forms the northwesternmost border of the Columbia Plateau. The area is actually a basin between the Rocky Mountains and the Cascades that was covered by hundreds of lava flows over some 4 million years. In some areas, these lava flows are thousands of feet deep.

Columbia River (SEE ALSO RIVERS)

The Columbia River is the largest river in the western United States. From its headwaters in British Columbia, it flows some 1,240 miles to the Pacific Ocean. Its drainage area covers parts of seven states and British Columbia, an area of some 258,000 square miles. Its principal tributaries in Washington include the Snake, Spokane, Pend Oreille, Wenatchee, Okanogan, Methow, and Yakima Rivers in eastern Washington and the Lewis and Cowlitz Rivers in southwestern Washington. It is the fourth-largest river in the conterminous 48 states in volume of discharge, pouring some 265,000 cubic feet per second into the Pacific Ocean at its mouth, which is 6 miles wide.

The huge volume of fresh water from the Columbia dilutes the ocean salt water for several hundred miles, and the sediment carried by the river creates a sandy-colored plume that is noticeable to ships sailing past and can be seen from space. The mouth of the Columbia is treacherous to navigators. It has been nicknamed the "Graveyard of the Pacific" because its shifting sandbars, erratic currents, and high winds have resulted in more than 2,000 shipwrecks and 1,500 deaths. The river mouth is so dangerous, the state's first lighthouse was built at nearby Cape Disappointment to aid mariners. Treacherous waves at the mouth can slam even a large ship onto the bottom.

The American explorer Robert Gray, while not the first explorer to sail past the river, was the first to sail up the river and explore it, in 1792. He named it for his ship. The Lewis and Clark expedition explored the lower Columbia from 1805 to 1806, and David Thompson, a Canadian explorer, followed the river from its source to its mouth in 1811. Today, oceangoing vessels can navigate upriver as far as Vancouver, and barges and smaller vessels can venture even farther using the series of locks at the various dams built as part of the Columbia Basin Reclamation Project. Begun in the 1930s as part of Franklin Roosevelt's New Deal, the dams were constructed not only to generate hydroelectricity, but to irrigate the semiarid Columbia Plateau. The dams include Bonneville, The Dalles, John Day, McNary, Grand Coulee (the largest), Chief Joseph, Priest Rapids, and Rocky Reach.

The Columbia once had great numbers of salmon, but the fish stocks were severely depleted after the 1930s as the result of dam construction and other factors. Recently, major efforts have been directed to protecting and restoring salmon habitat and the salmon stocks. The plans generally involve rebuilding salmon stock by increasing the water flow through the dams and by developing habitat protection standards.

The raw material for the Columbia bar and for Pacific beaches and sand spits comes from huge amounts of sediment the river carries and dumps at its mouth. The Columbia used to dump more sediment into the Pacific than any other Western

Windsurfers flock to the Columbia River Gorge to enjoy its strong, steady winds. From Washington II by John Marshall.

Hemisphere river—7.5 million tons a year—gouged from Cascade volcanoes by glaciers and carried into the Columbia by its tributaries. Now, more due to the extensive network of dams on the river and its tributaries, most of the silt remains behind.

In 1986, Congress declared 85 miles of the Columbia River Gorge as a National Scenic Area. This portion of the river marks the only sea-level break in the Cascade Mountain Range.

Organizations of Interest.
Center for Columbia River History, 802 "C" Officers Row, Vancouver, WA 98661; (360) 737-2044. The center's projects focus on the interaction between the environment of the Columbia River Basin and its inhabitants from prehistory to the present.

Columbia Gorge Interpretive Center, 990 SW Rock Creek Dr., Stevenson, WA 98648; (509) 427-8211. Opened in 1995, this new center features cultural and natural history exhibits about the Columbia River area and its inhabitants.

Congressional Delegation

Washington's congressional delegation consists of two senators and nine members of the House of Representatives. In the last decade, the delegation has reflected the major shifts in party representation that occurred nationwide. As the Republicans swept the 1992 elections and gained the majority of the U.S. House of Representatives, Washington's delegation shifted from predominantly Democratic to a Republican majority, then back again in the 1998 elections, again reflecting the national trend. 106th Congress: www.senate.gov and www.house.gov.

Senators.
Slade Gorton (R). First elected 1980 (served one term, 1981-86), regained Senate seat in 1988. Committee assignments: Committee on Appropriations, Subcommittees on Interior (Chair); Labor, Health and Human Services; Education; Agriculture; Energy and Water; Transportation. Committee on Commerce, Science and Transportation, Subcommittees on

Columbia River Sturgeon

The Columbia and Snake Rivers also have the largest population of white sturgeon left in North America. These ancient, paleozoic fish can grow to a very large size and live as long as 200 years. One caught in 1811 measured 13 feet, 9 inches and weighed 1,130 pounds. In 1888, a New York firm that established a sturgeon camp at Oneonta below the Cascades shipped 85 tons the first year. Some of the sturgeon they raised in ponds reached 1,800 pounds. Although the numbers of sturgeon have been dramatically reduced, they still provide commercial as well as recreational fishing. A good place to see them up close is in the sturgeon pool at the Bonneville Fish Hatchery. —James Holloway, Columbia River Gorge ✂

Aviation (Chair); Consumer Affairs; Communications; National Ocean Policy Study. Committee on Energy and Natural Resources. Committee on the Budget. Select Committee on Indian Affairs. http://www.senate.gov/~gorton. 730 Hart Senate Office Bldg., Washington, DC 20510; (202) 224-3441, fax (202) 224-9393.

State offices: 10900 NE Fourth St., Suite 2110, Bellevue, WA 98004; (425) 451-0103, fax (425) 451-0234.

11120 Gravelly Lake Dr. SW, Suite 8, Lakewood, WA 98499; (253) 581-1646, fax (253) 581-0861.

697 U.S. Courthouse, W. 920 Riverside, Spokane, WA 99201; (509) 353-2507, fax (509) 353-2547.

1523 Country Club Dr., East Wenatchee, WA 98802; (509) 884-3447, phone/fax modem (509) 884-3447.

402 E. Yakima Ave., Box 4083, Yakima, WA 98901; (509) 248-8084, (509) 248-8167.

8915 W. Grandridge Blvd., Suite M, Kennewick, WA 99336; (509) 783-0640, fax (509) 735-7559.

1340 Federal Office Bldg., 500 W. 12th St., Vancouver, WA 98660; (360) 696-7838, fax (360) 696-7844.

Patty Murray (D). First elected in 1992. Committee assignments: Committee on Labor and Human Resources, Subcommittees on Children and Families; Aging. Committee on Appropriations, Subcommittees on Transportation; Foreign Operations; Energy and Water Development; Labor, Health and Human Resources; Military Construction. Committee on the Budget. Committee on Veterans' Affairs. Select Committee on Ethics. http://www.senate.gov/~murray.

111 Russell Senate Office Bldg., Washington, DC 20510; (202) 224-2621, fax (202) 224-0238.

State offices: 2988 Jackson Federal Bldg., 915 Second Ave., Seattle, WA 98174; (206) 553-5545, fax (206) 553-0891.

402 E. Yakima Ave., Suite 390, Yakima, WA 98901; (509) 453-7462, fax (509) 453-7731.

W. 601 First Ave., Spokane, WA 99201; (509) 624-9515, fax (509) 624-9561.

140 Federal Bldg., 500 W. 12th, Vancouver, WA 98660; (360) 696-7797, fax (360) 696-7798.

2930 Wetmore Ave., Suite 903, Everett, WA 98201; (425) 259-6515, fax (425) 259-7152.

House of Representatives.

1st Congressional District (parts of King, Kitsap, and Snohomish Counties). Jay Inslee (D). Elected 1992 (served one term, 1993-94) and 1998. Committee assignments: Resources Committee, Subcommittees on National Parks and Public Lands, Energy and Minerals. Banking and Financial Services Committee, Subcommittee on Domestic and International Monetary Policy. http://www.house.gov/inslee/.

308 Cannon House Office Bldg., Washington, DC 20515; (202) 225-6311.

District offices: 21905 64th Ave. W., Suite 101, Montlake Terrace, WA 98043; (425) 642-0233.

17791 Fjord Dr. NE, Door 112, Poulsbo, WA 98370; (360) 598-2342.

2nd Congressional District (Island, San Juan, Skagit, and Whatcom Counties, and part of Snohomish County). Jack Metcalf

(R). Elected 1994. Committee assignments: Banking and Financial Services Committee, Subcommittees on Housing and Community Opportunities, Financial Institutions and Consumer Credit, Domestic and Internet, and Monetary Policy. Transportation and Infrastructure Committee, Subcommittees on Aviation and Ground Transportation. http://www.house.gov/metcalf/.

1501 Longworth House Office Bldg., Washington, DC 20515; (202) 225-2605.

District offices: 2930 Wetmore Ave., Suite 9-E, Everett, WA 98201; (425) 252-3188.

322 N. Commercial, Suite 203, Bellingham, WA 98225; (360)733-4500.

3rd Congressional District (Clark, Cowlitz, Lewis, Pacific, Skamania, and Wahkiakum Counties, and parts of Grays Harbor, Klickitat, and Thurston Counties). Brian Baird (D). Elected 1998. Committee assignments: Transportation and Infrastructure Committee, Subcommittees on Coast Guard and Marine Transportation, Water Resources and the Environment.

1721 Longworth House Office Bldg., Washington, DC 20515; (202) 225-3536.

District office: 1220 Main St., Suite 360, Vancouver, WA 98660; (360) 695-6292, fax (360) 695-6197; E-mail: brian.baird@ mail.house.gov.

4th Congressional District (Benton, Chelan, Douglas, Franklin, Grant, Kittitas, Okanogan, and Yakima Counties, and parts of Adams and Klickitat Counties). Richard "Doc" Hastings (R). Elected 1994. Committee assignments: House Committee on Rules, Subcommittee on the Legislative and Budget Process. http://www.house.gov/hastings/.

1323 Longworth House Office Bldg., Washington, DC 20515; (202) 225-5816.

Scoop, Maggie, and Tom

In the early 1960s, a new generation of politicians shook up the political landscape and changed the face of the state's congressional delegation from Republican to Democratic and decidedly young. The freshmen crew included Representatives Brock Adams (who would later serve as Secretary of Transportation under Jimmy Carter and as Senator) and Tom Foley, who would eventually rise to the most powerful position in the U.S. House of Representatives, Speaker of the House. The state's senators were increasing in seniority and power; Warren G. Magnuson had been in the senate since 1945 and Henry M. Jackson since 1952. By the late 1970s, the state's congressional delegation was considered to be the most powerful in Congress and one that was very effective in bringing home the pork and protecting the state's interests. Those heady days were numbered, however. In 1980, the 75-year-old Magnuson lost his Senate seat to a much younger Slade Gorton, and in 1983 Jackson died suddenly of a heart attack. The state's House seats, too, were changing, as several retired in the early to mid-1980s, and others lost their seats to another new generation, this time of young Reagan Republicans. ❈

District offices: 2715 St. Andrews Loop, Suite D, Pasco, WA 99302; (509) 783-0310.

302 E. Chestnut, Yakima, WA 98901; (509) 452-3243.

5th Congressional District (Asotin, Columbia, Ferry, Garfield, Lincoln, Pend Oreille, Spokane, Stevens, Whitman, and Walla Walla Counties, and most of Adams County). George Nethercutt (R). Elected 1994. Committee assignments: House Appropriations Committee, Subcommittees on Agriculture, Rural Development, Food and Drug Administration, and Related Agencies; and Defense. http://www. house.gov/nethercutt/.

1527 Longworth House Office Bldg., Washington, DC 20515; (202) 225-2006.

District office: W. 920 Riverside, Suite 594, Spokane, WA 99201; (509) 353-2374.

6th Congressional District (Clallam, Jefferson, and Mason Counties, and parts of Grays Harbor, Kitsap, and Pierce Counties). Norman D. Dicks (D). Elected 1976. Committee assignments: House Appropriations Committee, Subcommittees on Defense and Military Construction. House Permanent Select Committee on Intelligence (ranking minority). http://www.house.gov/dicks/.

2467 Rayburn House Office Bldg., Washington, DC 20515; (202) 225-5916.

District offices: 1717 Pacific Ave S.,

Former senators Warren G. Magnuson (right) and Henry M. Jackson (left). Courtesy of University of Washington Libraries.

Suite 2244, Tacoma, WA 98402-3234; (253) 593-6536.

500 Pacific Ave., Suite 301, Bremerton, WA 98337; (360) 479-4011.

7th Congressional District (part of King County). Jim McDermott (D). Elected 1988. Committee assignments: Committee on Ways and Means, Subcommittee on Oversight and Health. http://www.house.gov/mcdermott/.

1035 Longworth House Office Bldg., Washington, DC 20515; (202) 225-3106.

District office: 1809 Seventh Ave., Suite 1212, Seattle, WA 98101-1313; (206) 553-7170.

8th Congressional District (parts of King and Pierce Counties). Jennifer Dunn (R). Elected 1992. Committee assignments: Committee on Ways and Means, Subcommittees on Trade and Oversight. http:// www.house.gov/dunn/.

(Continued on page 50)

State Congressional Districts

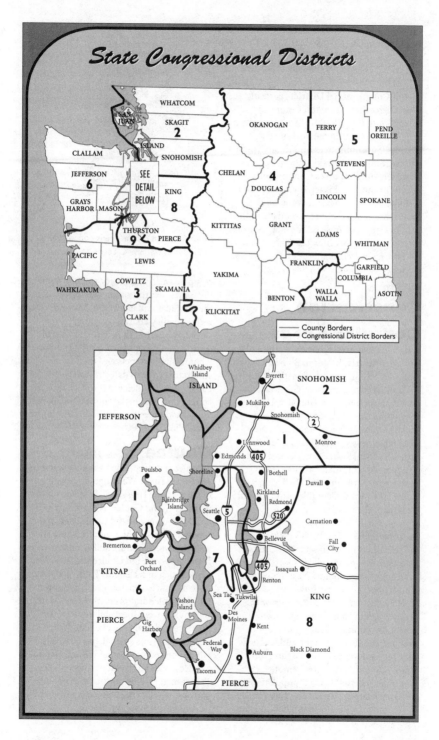

County Borders
Congressional District Borders

432 Cannon House Office Bldg., Washington, DC 20515; (202) 225-7761.

District office: 2737 78th Ave. SE, Suite 202, Mercer Island, WA 98040; (206) 275-3438.

9th Congressional District (parts of King, Pierce, and Thurston Counties). Adam Smith (D). Elected 1996. Committee assignments: Committee on Armed Services, Subcommittees on Military Installations and Facilities and Military Procurement. Resources Committee, Subcommittees on Fisheries Conservation, Wildlife, and Oceans; and Water and Power. http://www.house.gov/adamsmith/.

116 Cannon House Office Bldg., Washington, DC 20515; (202) 225-8901.

District office: 3600 Port of Tacoma Rd. E., Suite 38, Tacoma, WA 98424; (253) 926-6683.

Constitution (See Laws)

Consular Corps

There are 35 consulates of foreign governments in the state: Austria, Belgium, Bolivia, Canada, Chile, Cyprus, Denmark, Ecuador, Estonia, Finland, France, Germany, Great Britain, Guatemala, Honduras, Hungary, Iceland, Italy, Jamaica, Japan, Korea, Luxembourg, Malawi, Mexico, The Netherlands, New Zealand, Norway, Peru, Russia, Seychelles, Spain, Sweden, Switzerland, Taipei, and Uruguay. All consulates are located in the Seattle metropolitan area. The Dean of Consular Corps is Georgi Vlaskin, Consul General of the Russian Federation.

Cougar

The West's great wild cat, the cougar is known in scientific circles as *Felis concolor* and in college sports circles as a "Coug," the symbol of Washington State University. The cougar is the largest of the North American cats. Cougars grow to nearly 8 feet in length and can weigh in at nearly 200 pounds. Cougar populations declined greatly early in the 20th century, with remnant populations of these loner animals found in the most remote mountain recesses. Cougar populations came back late in the 20th century. Today in Washington State, about 2,000 cougars

North American cougar. (Felis concolor). Illustration by Marjorie C. Leggitt.

compete with humans for space in some of the toniest exurbs, on the western slopes of the Cascades and elsewhere. Shy and reclusive, they are rarely sighted by the casual walker, but they may occasionally prowl around populated outlying areas, where household pets and even small children may be in danger. If stalked by a cougar, the best defense is to face the cougar squarely, make yourself look large (by extending your arms, for example), and make a lot of noise.

Coulee (See also Dry Falls)

A coulee is a steep-sided gulch or water channel. Eastern Washington has a number of coulees, the largest and best known of which is Grand Coulee. It is actually two coulees—Upper Grand Coulee and Lower Grand Coulee—which run for some 50 miles between Ephrata and Grand Coulee Dam. Upper Grand Coulee has sheer walls along much of its length. To the west is Moses Coulee, which is nearly as long as Grand Coulee and probably older. Many of the coulees were spectacular waterfalls during the glacial Spokane Floods, and are now dry canyons and valleys. Dry Falls, which connects Upper and Lower Grand Coulees, was the largest of these. Frenchman Coulee northeast of Vantage was another area of cataracts and waterfalls during the great ice-age floods.

Counties

Counties were the first units of local government established in Washington, the first created when it was still a territory. In 1845, the Oregon Territory was divided into several administrative districts and the area that would become Washington was formed into three large counties—Clark, Lewis, and Clackamas. Washington Territory was created in 1853; when its first legislature convened in 1854, there were eight counties—Island, Pierce, Jefferson, King, Thurston, Clark, Pacific, and Lewis—and by the time the territory became a state, its counties numbered more than 30. The total number of 39 was established by 1911, when Pend Oreille County was created, but that hasn't been the end of further attempts to carve out new counties from existing ones. The authority to do this rests with the State Legislature, which has not done so, although it has approved at least one transfer of land area from one county to another, in 1970. In 1984, an effort to slice off the western ends of Clallam and Jefferson Counties to form Olympic County passed the State Senate, but died in the House. In the 1990s, there have been movements to create new counties from parts of Whatcom, Snohomish, and King Counties.

The land area and population of Washington's counties vary widely. The largest, Okanogan, is 5,000 square miles; the smallest is San Juan County, with less than 200 square miles. King County, the most populated, has 1.6 million people, versus Garfield, with only 2,400.

Largest Counties by Area (in sq. mi.)

1.	Okanogan	5,301
2.	Yakima	4,268
3.	Chelan	2,918
4.	Grant	2,675
5.	Stevens	2,481
6.	Lewis	2,423
7.	Kittitas	2,317
8.	Lincoln	2,306
9.	Ferry	2,202
10.	Whitman	2,153

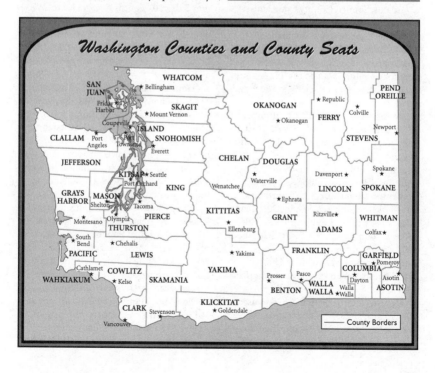

Washington Counties and County Seats

1.	King	1,665,800
2.	Pierce	686,800
3.	Snohomish	568,100
4.	Spokane	410,900
5.	Clark	328,000
6.	Kitsap	229,000
7.	Yakima	210,500
8.	Thurston	199,700
9.	Whatcom	157,500
10.	Benton	137,500

Source: Washington Office of Financial Management

Most of Washington's counties are governed by three-member boards of county commissioners, elected to four-year terms, although several larger counties have adopted home rule charters and are governed by a county council and a county executive or manager. Other elected county officials include the assessor, auditor, clerk, treasurer, sheriff, and prosecuting attorney.

County Profiles.

Adams County. County Courthouse: 210 W. Broadway, Ritzville, WA 99169. Area: 1,894 square miles. Population: 15,900. Miles of county road: 1,764. Year established: 1883, created from a portion of Whitman County. Named for John Adams, first vice president of the United States and the second president.

Asotin County. County Courthouse: 135 Second St., Asotin, WA 99402. Area: 633 square miles. Population: 20,000. Miles of county road: 393. Year established: 1883. Asotin county's name comes from the Nez Perce Indian word meaning "eel creek."

Benton County. County Courthouse: 620 Market St., Prosser, WA 99350. Area: 1,722 square miles. Population: 137,500. Miles of county road: 878. Year established: 1905, created from portions of Yakima and Klickitat Counties. Named for Thomas Hart Benton, senator from Missouri (1820-1851).

Chelan County. County Courthouse: Washington and Orondo Sts., Wenatchee, WA 98801. Area: 2,918 square miles. Population: 62,600. Miles of county road: 658.

Year established: 1899. The original plan was to call the county Wenatchee but legislators decided on the present name, which comes from an Indian word meaning "deep water."

Clallam County. County Courthouse: 223 E. Fourth, Port Angeles, WA 98362. Area: 1,753 square miles. Population: 66,700. Miles of county road: 488. Year established: 1854. Clallam County's name comes from an Indian word meaning "brave people."

Clark County. County Courthouse: 1200 Franklin St., Vancouver, WA 98666-5000. Area: 627 square miles. Population: 328,000. Miles of county road: 1,252. Year established: 1844. Clark County is named after Capt. William Clark, of the Lewis and Clark expedition.

Columbia County. County Courthouse: 341 E. Main St., Dayton, WA 99328. Area: 853 square miles. Population: 4,200. Miles of county road: 504. Year established: 1874, from part of Walla Walla County. Named after the Columbia River.

Cowlitz County. County Administration Bldg., 207 Fourth Ave. N., Kelso, WA 98626. Area: 1,144 square miles. Population: 93,100. Miles of county road: 537. Year established: 1854. Named after a local Indian tribe, the Cow-e-lis-kee or Cow-e-lis-ke.

Douglas County. County Courthouse: 213 S. Rainier, Waterville, WA 98858. Area: 1,831 square miles. Population: 31,400. Miles of county road: 1,636. Year established: 1883, created from a portion of Lincoln County. Named for Stephen A. Douglas, U.S. senator from Illinois between 1847 and 1861, and twice a candidate for the presidency of the United States.

Ferry County. County Courthouse: 350 E. Delaware, Republic, WA 99166. Area: 2,202 square miles. Population: 7,300. Miles of county road: 726. Year established: 1899. Named for Elisha P. Ferry, territorial governor of Washington (1872-1880) and the first governor of the state (1889-1893).

Franklin County. County Courthouse: 1016 N. Fourth Ave., Pasco, WA 99301. Area: 1,253 square miles. Population: 44,400. Miles of county road: 1,018. Year established: 1883. Named for the American patriot Benjamin Franklin.

Garfield County. County Courthouse: P. O. Box 278, Pomeroy, WA 99347. Area: 709 square miles. Population: 2,400. Miles of county road: 457. Year established: 1881, created from part of Columbia County. Named for President James A. Garfield.

Grant County. County Courthouse: 35 C St. NW, Ephrata, WA 98823. Area: 2,675 square miles. Population: 69,400. Miles of county road: 2,503. Year established: 1909. Named for Ulysses S. Grant, 18th president of the United States and leader of Union forces in the Civil War who had served at Fort Vancouver in the 1850s.

Grays Harbor County. County Courthouse: 100 W. Broadway, Montesano, WA 98563. Area: 1,910 square miles. Population: 67,900. Miles of county road: 563. Year established: 1854. Named after the early explorer Capt. Robert Gray.

Island County. County Courthouse: NE Sixth and Main St., Coupeville, WA 98239-5000. Area: 212 square miles. Population: 72,500. Miles of county road: 592. Year established: 1853. So named because it is composed entirely of islands.

Jefferson County. County Courthouse: 1820 Jefferson St., Port Townsend, WA 98368. Area: 1,805 square miles. Population: 26,500. Miles of county road: 389. Year established: 1852. Named after President Thomas Jefferson.

King County. County Courthouse: 516 Third Ave., Seattle, WA 98104. Area: 2,128 square miles. Population: 1,665,800. Miles of county road: 2,361. Year established: 1852, created from a portion of Thurston County. Originally named after U.S. Vice President-elect William R. King; in 1985 the King County Council changed the name origin to honor Dr. Martin Luther King Jr., a prominent civil rights leader of the 1960s.

Looking Back

March 16, 1999

The federal government placed nine Northwest salmon population groups on the endangered species list. The listings cover nearly every corner of Washington State and include Puget Sound chinook.

Kitsap County. County Courthouse: 614 Division St., Port Orchard, WA 98366. Area: 393 square miles. Population: 229,000. Miles of county road: 965. Year established: 1857, created from portions of King and Jefferson Counties. Named after an Indian chief.

Kittitas County. County Courthouse: 205 W. Fifth Ave., Ellensburg, WA 98926. Area: 2,317 square miles. Population: 31,400. Miles of county road: 565. Year established: 1883. Name is derived from an Indian word meaning "gray gravel bank," which refers to an extensive gravel bank on a river shoal near Ellensburg.

Klickitat County. County Courthouse: 205 S. Columbus, Goldendale, WA 98620. Area: 1,908 square miles. Population: 19,100. Miles of county road: 1,082. Year established: 1859. Named after an Indian tribe.

Lewis County. County Courthouse: 351 NW North St., Chehalis, WA 98532-1900. Area: 2,423 square miles. Population: 68,600. Miles of county road: 1,056. Year established: 1845. Named after Capt. Meriwether Lewis of the Lewis and Clark expedition.

Lincoln County. County Courthouse: 450 Logan St., Davenport, WA 99122. Area: 2,306 square miles. Population: 10,000. Miles of county road: 2,046. Year established: 1883. Named after President Abraham Lincoln.

Mason County. County Courthouse: 411 N. Fifth, Shelton, WA 98584. Area: 926 square miles. Population: 48,300. Miles of county road: 620. Year established: 1854. Named after Charles H. Mason, the first secretary of the Washington Territory.

Okanogan County. County Courthouse: 149 Third N., Okanogan, WA 98840. Area: 5,301 square miles. Population: 38,400. Miles of county road: 1,389. Year established: 1888. The name comes from an Indian word meaning "rendezvous."

Pacific County. County Courthouse: 300 Memorial Ave., South Bend, WA 98586. Area: 908 square miles. Population: 21,500. Miles of county road: 353. Year established: 1851. Named after the Pacific Ocean, which forms the county's western boundary.

Pend Oreille County. County Courthouse: 625 W. Fourth, Newport, WA 99156. Area: 1,402 square miles. Population: 11,200. Miles of county road: 546. Year established: 1911. Name was derived from a French description of an Indian tribe.

Pierce County. County Courthouse: 930 Tacoma Ave. S., Tacoma, WA 98402. Area: 1,676 square miles. Population: 686,800. Miles of county road: 1,855. Year established: 1852. Named after President Franklin Pierce.

San Juan County. County Courthouse: 350 Court St., Friday Harbor, WA 98250. Area: 179 square miles. Population: 12,600. Miles of county road: 272. Year established: 1873. Named after the principal island in this all-island county.

Skagit County. County Courthouse: 700 S. Second St., Mount Vernon, WA 98273. Area: 1,735 square miles. Population: 98,700. Miles of county road: 805. Year established: 1883. Named was derived from an Indian tribe.

Skamania County. County Courthouse: 240 NW Vancouver St., Stevenson, WA 98648-0790. Area: 1,672 square miles. Population: 9,900. Miles of county road: 249. Year established: 1854. Name comes from an Indian word meaning "swift waters."

Snohomish County. County Courthouse: 3000 Rockefeller Ave., Everett, WA 98201. Area: 2,098 square miles. Population: 568,100. Miles of county road: 1,604. Year established: 1861. Named after an Indian tribe.

Spokane County. County Courthouse: W. 1116 Broadway, Spokane, WA 99260. Area: 1,758 square miles. Population: 410,900. Miles of county road: 2,958. Year established: 1858. Name comes from an Indian word meaning "chief of the sun."

Stevens County. County Courthouse: 215 S. Oak St., Colville, WA 99114. Area: 2,481 square miles. Population: 37,600.

Miles of county road: 1,503. Year established: 1863. Named after the first territorial governor, Isaac I. Stevens.

Thurston County. County Courthouse: 2000 Lakeridge Dr. SW, Olympia, WA 98502. Area: 714 square miles. Population: 199,700. Miles of county road: 995. Year established: 1852. Named after Samuel R. Thurston, the first delegate to Congress from the Oregon Territory.

Wahkiakum County. County Courthouse: 64 Main St., Cathlamet, WA 98612. Area: 261 square miles. Population: 3,900. Miles of county road: 143. Year established: 1854. Named after an Indian chief.

Walla Walla County. County Courthouse: 315 W. Main St., Walla Walla, WA 99362. Area: 1,262 square miles. Population: 54,600. Miles of county road: 967. Year established: 1854. Name is an Indian word meaning "many waters."

Whatcom County. County Courthouse: 311 Grand Ave., Bellingham, WA 98225. Area: 2,126 square miles. Population: 157,500. Miles of county road: 971. Year established: 1854. Name was derived from an Indian word meaning "noisy waters."

Whitman County. County Courthouse: N. 404 Main St., Colfax, WA 99111. Area: 2,153 square miles. Population: 41,400. Miles of county road: 1,930. Year established: 1871, created from a portion of Stevens County. Named after Marcus Whitman, a pioneer missionary.

Yakima County. County Courthouse: 128 N. Second St., Yakima, WA 98901. Area: 4,268 square miles. Population: 210,500. Miles of county road: 1,753. Year established: 1865. Named after an Indian tribe.

Organizations of Interest.
Washington State Association of Counties, 206 10th Ave. SE, Olympia, WA 98501; (360) 753-1886.

Washington State Association of County Officials, 206 10th Ave. SE, Olympia, WA 98501; (360) 753-7319.

Crabs Washington's waters are
home to a great variety of crabs, delectable spiders of the sea. As crabs grow, they molt, shedding the old shell and passing through

a soft-shell stage, then growing a new, larger, hard carapace. Crab catches in Washington State run about 20 million pounds a year, and are valued at about $20 million. Largest and best known is the succulent Dungeness crab (Cancer magister), which grows to 10-12 inches across over a five-year life span. The red crab (C. productus) and the red rock crab (C. antennarius) are almost as large as the Dungeness, are more abundant locally, and are generally found closer to shore. Other edible crabs in Washington State include the stone crab, the Puget Sound king crab, and the box crab.

Decorative (inedible) crabs found in the region include spider crabs and hermit crabs. Hermit crabs are not true crabs (they belong to the genus Pagurus). Since they lack protective armor, they occupy empty shells of other species. The most ubiquitous crab on the beach is the inch-long sand crab (Emerita analoga), which darts around the surf zone and buries itself in sand up to its eyes and antennae.

Abandoned Shells

All those empty, intact Dungeness crab (Cancer magister) shells that lie scattered on the beach are not evidence of mass suicide.... The Dungeness crab molts twice a year during its first two years, and then once a year until age six. During very low tides, the deep-water bottom-dweller comes into shallow water to shed its segmented, bluish-brown shell. Highly vulnerable until its new shell hardens, the crab hides for two days without eating.—Ann Saling, The Great Northwest Nature Factbook ✦

Crime

In addition to being the land of the free and home of the brave, Washington State can lay claim to a cast of cattle rustlers, log poachers, rum runners, kidnappers, bank robbers, and serial killers throughout its history. These days, property crimes account for the largest number of reported crimes, according to the FBI's most recent statistics (1996).

The state has a "three strikes, you're out" law, and in its first four years, 39 murderers and sex offenders and 74 other criminals were sent to prison for life. Of these, the overwhelming majority were male (98 percent) and white (58 percent).

Crime Rate in Washington (offenses known to police)

	(per 100,000 population)
Violent Crimes	
Murder	4.6
Forcible rape	51.1
Robbery	119
Aggravated assault	256
Total	431
Property Crimes	
Burglary	1,058
Larceny-theft	3,899
Motor vehicle theft	522
Total	5,478
Hate Crimes Reported	
Incidents reported	198
Number of reporting agencies	62
Child Abuse and Neglect Cases Reported and Investigated	
Number of reports	33,913
Number of children subject of a report	47,631
Number of children substantiated	20,033
Population under 18 years old	1,436,804

Source: U.S. Federal Bureau of Investigation, 1996

Criminal History Records. The Washington State Patrol maintains fingerprint-based criminal history records for felonies and gross misdemeanors. The information is made available to criminal justice agencies (which may receive unrestricted information), and conviction information is available to the general public. Any state agency or government entity that educates, trains, treats, supervises, houses, or provides recreation to developmentally disabled persons, vulnerable adults, or children under 16 years of age may also obtain criminal history information. **Identification and Criminal History Section,** Washington State Patrol, P.O. Box 42633, Olympia, WA 98504-2633.

Dams

There are nearly a thousand dams in Washington State, which serve a variety of purposes. Nearly 9 percent generate hydropower, 24 percent are used for irrigation, 27 percent were built for recreation purposes, 6.4 percent are for flood control, still others contain water supplies or aid in maintaining water quality, and a small number contain mine tailings. More than half of the dams in the state are privately owned. Local governments comprise the next largest group of dam owners (18.8 percent), with ownership rounded out by the public utilities (10.5 percent), federal government (9 percent), and state government (6.9 percent). Both private and public utility companies operate large hydroelectric projects.

Among nonfederal power projects are those owned by Public Utility Districts (Chelan, Cowlitz, Douglas, Franklin, Grant, Okanogan, Pend Oreille, and Snohomish PUDs all own dams); the cities of Aberdeen, Kennewick, Spokane, Tacoma, and Seattle; and Energy Northwest, (formerly the Washington Public Power Supply System) and Washington Water Power Company, among others. (In the list below, statistics vary because type of ownership and, thus, information available varies.)

The majority of dams (520) are those categorized as small (6-14 feet high), and the next greatest number (341) are intermediate in size (15-49 feet high). There are 91 large dams, those 50 feet or higher. The big dams are all located on the Columbia River, and the biggest of the big is the Grand Coulee Dam. When it was constructed in the 1930s, Grand Coulee became the largest concrete structure in the United States (it still ranks among the largest concrete dams)

and created a 130-mile-long lake behind it. Altogether, in the mid-1990s, the state had 260 hydroelectric generators, with a capacity of about 21.1 million kilowatts; the Grand Coulee Dam alone accounted for 6.5 million kilowatts.

While the Northwest's dams were originally heralded as public works projects that benefited the state and its people, in recent years the focus on dams has been their lethal impact on native salmon runs. For salmon fry headed toward the ocean, passing through a dam at certain times was akin to swimming through a Cuisinart. The mortality rate could range from 15 percent to 35 percent per dam, depending on the rate of river flow. Solutions such as trucking salmon fry around the dams or spilling more water over them may help somewhat, but the salmon runs have been seriously depleted. A more drastic approach—taking out dams—has been proposed and may actually come to pass in some places, such as the Elwha River on the Olympic Peninsula, where the dams have outlived their original purpose. Dams that are essential to the local or regional economies, such as those on the Columbia, are unlikely to come tumbling down.

Washington's Major Dams.

Bonneville Dam. Columbia River, river mile 146.1 Constructed: 1938 (second powerhouse completed in 1982). Owner: U.S. Army Corps of Engineers, Portland District. First powerhouse capacity: 518-574 megawatts (MW) total. Second powerhouse capacity: 532-612 MW total. Fishway units capacity: two at 13.1 MW, 26.2 MW total. Spillway 1: 1,450 feet, 18 gates.

Brownlee Dam. Snake River, river mile 285.0. Constructed: 1959 (units 1-4), 1980 (unit 5). Owner: Idaho Power Company. Powerhouse capacity: 585.4 MW total. Spillway 2: 1,097 feet, 4 gates.

Chief Joseph Dam. Columbia River, river mile 545.1. Constructed: 1961 (units 1-16), 1979 (units 17-27). Owner: U.S. Army Corps of Engineers, Seattle District. Powerhouse capacity: 2,069-2,614 MW total. Spillway: 980 feet, 19 gates.

The Dalles Dam. Columbia River, river

Water cascades over the spillway at Grand Coulee Dam on the Columbia River, one of the largest concrete dams in the world. From *Washington II* by John Marshall.

mile 191.5. Constructed: 1960 (units 1-14); additional units 15-22 completed in 1973. Powerhouse capacity: 1,780-2,038 MW. Spillway: 1,380 feet, 23 gates.

Grand Coulee Dam. Columbia River, river mile 596.6. Constructed: 1942; modified in 1974, 1982, and 1984. Owner: U.S. Bureau of Reclamation. Powerhouse capacity: 6,494-7,416 MW total. Hydraulic capacity: 280 kilo cubic feet per second. Spillway: crest elevation 1,311 feet, 11 drum gates, 40 outlet tubes (two gates each outlet).

Ice Harbor Dam. Snake River, river mile 9.7. Constructed: 1962 (units 1-3), 1976 (units 4-6). Owner: U.S. Army Corps of Engineers, Walla Walla District. Powerhouse capacity: 603-693 MW total. Spillway 2: 590 feet, 10 gates.

John Day Dam. Columbia River, river mile 215.6. Constructed: 1971. Owner: U.S. Army Corps of Engineers, Portland District. Powerhouse capacity: 2,160-2,485 MW. Spillway: 1,228 feet, 20 gates.

Little Goose Dam. Snake River, river mile 70.3. Constructed: 1970 (units 1-3);

additional units 4-6 completed in 1978. Owner: U.S. Army Corps of Engineers, Walla Walla District. Powerhouse capacity: 810-932 MW. Spillway: 512 feet, eight gates.

Lower Granite Dam. Snake River, river mile 107.5. Constructed: 1975 (units 1-3); additional units 4-6 completed in 1978. Owner: U.S. Army Corps of Engineers, Walla Walla District. Powerhouse capacity: 810-932 MW. Spillway: 512 feet, eight gates.

Lower Monumental Dam. Snake River, river mile 41.6. Constructed: 1969 (units 1-3); additional units 4-6 completed in 1981. Owner: U.S. Army Corps of Engineers, Walla Walla District. Powerhouse capacity: 810-930 MW. Spillway 1: 572 feet, eight gates.

McNary Dam. Columbia River, river mile 292.0. Constructed: 1957; second powerhouse de-authorized 1991. Owner: U.S. Army Corps of Engineers, Walla Walla District. Powerhouse capacity: 980-1,127 MW. Spillway: 1,310 feet, 22 gates.

Priest Rapids Dam. Columbia River, river mile 397.1. Constructed: 1961. Owner:

Grant County PUD No. 2. Powerhouse capacity: 907.15-910 MW.

Rock Island Dam. Columbia River, river mile 453.4. Constructed: 1933, 6 additional units completed 1953, second powerhouse completed 1979. Owner: Chelan County PUD No. 1. Powerhouse capacity: 622.5-660 MW total. Spillway 1: 1,184 feet, 31 gates.

Rocky Reach Dam. Columbia River, river mile 473.7. Constructed: 1961 (units 1-4); additional units completed 1971. Owner: Chelan County PUD No. 1. Powerhouse capacity: 1,347-1,287 MW total. Spillway: 12 gates.

Wanapum Dam. Columbia River, river mile 415.8. Constructed: 1964. Owner: Grant County PUD No. 2. Powerhouse capacity: 1,038 MW total. Spillway: 12 gates.

Wells Dam. Columbia River, river mile 515.8. Constructed: 1967. Owner: Douglas County PUD No. 1. Powerhouse capacity: 774.3-840 MW total.

Dry Falls (SEE ALSO GLACIERS AND GLACIATION)

This immense gash in the earth near modern-day Coulee City is an extinct waterfall created by huge floods in the Columbia River Basin. The floods occurred during the melting of the glaciers of the last ice age, more than 10,000 years ago.

The remains of the largest cataract, which was many times greater than Niagara Falls, is called Grand Coulee, a 3½-mile-wide horseshoe-shaped ledge over which water once plunged 417 feet. Fossilized trees and leaves may be found in the rocks.

Eagles

Washington has more bald eagles (*Haliaetus leucocephalus*) than any other state except Alaska. The population has been estimated at about 3,000, with as many as 150 mating pairs. An adult bald eagle may grow to 3 feet tall, weigh up to 15 pounds, and have a wingspread of 6-7 feet. Bald eagles, birds of prey, occasionally can be seen chasing and wearing down their prey; for example, other birds, salmon, and

Bald eagles (Haliaetus leucocephalus) *feeding.* From *Going Wild in Washington and Oregon* by Susan Ewing.

snakes. One of the best places to watch bald eagles, inhabitants of coastal regions, is at the Skagit River Bald Eagle Natural Area outside of Mount Vernon. Bald eagle nests are unmistakable, as their nests are the largest of any bird. Constructed of large sticks and debris, some eagle nests grow to be more than 10 feet across and as deep as 20 feet. The largest nests have been known to break the branches of the trees that they are built in. Golden eagles are also found throughout the state.

Earthquakes
More than 1,000 earthquakes are recorded in the state each year, a dozen or more of which produce significant shaking or damage. However, major destructive earthquakes occur much less often. While magnitude-5.0+ quakes shook the Puget Sound region two years running in 1995 and 1996, the last earthquake to cause widespread damage in Washington occurred more than 30 years ago. It was a magnitude-6.5 quake centered around Seattle-Tacoma in 1965. Another significant 20th-century quake occurred in 1949 around Olympia; it registered 7.0 in magnitude.

The largest earthquake now considered a possibility in the Pacific Northwest is a shallow subduction-style earthquake similar to recent destructive earthquakes in Alaska and Mexico, which had magnitudes greater than 8. An earthquake this large would be expected to occur along the coast. A magnitude-8 subduction earthquake would not only cause widespread, dangerous ground shaking, but would also likely produce water waves capable of inundating coastal areas in a matter of minutes. A 1975 study of six counties in the Puget Sound area, now considered by some to be too conservative and also out of date in terms of recent population growth in the state, projects as many as 2,200 deaths and 8,700 injuries in the next magnitude-7.5 earthquake.

Earthquake Geology. Earthquakes occur because pressure builds where sections of the earth's crust, called plates, eventually drift together and slide or grind against each other. In Washington, the small Juan de Fuca plate off the coast of Washington, Oregon, and northern California is slowly moving eastward and being forced down beneath the much larger North American continent plate. Plate movement in the Pacific Northwest results in shallow earthquakes distributed over Washington, and deep earthquakes in the western parts of Washington and Oregon.

While scientists cannot predict precisely where, when, and how large the next destructive earthquake will be in Washington, the best possibility is along the "Cascadia" or "Benioff" fault zones of the subducting Juan de Fuca plate and North America plate. The most recent and best documented of this type of earthquake were the 1949 Olympia earthquake and the 1965 Seattle-Tacoma earthquake, both of which caused millions of dollars in damage. Large earthquakes similar to these are likely to occur several times a century. The largest earthquake recorded in the state did not occur in the Puget Sound or coastal region but, rather, at a shallow depth under the North Cascades, in 1872. However, the really Big One, geologists believe, occurred in about A.D. 900 on the Seattle Fault, which raised Restoration Point on one side of Puget Sound about 21 feet, and Alki Point on the other side at least 12 feet. The time between earthquakes of such great force may be hundreds or even thousands of years.

Living with Earthquakes. Earthquake damage is primarily caused by ground shaking, which displaces and distorts nonstructural features of buildings, such as windows, doorways, ceiling tiles, and partitions. Other hazards from earthquakes include ground liquefaction, landslides on slopes and bluffs, and flooding in coastal areas, the result of tsunamis, which are large waves produced by undersea earthquakes. The Long Beach Peninsula in southwestern Washington is considered particularly vulnerable to overflooding from a tsunami, even one originating far off in the Pacific Ocean.

A major earthquake in Washington could occur tomorrow, or not for another 25 years, say the experts. Yet preparing for

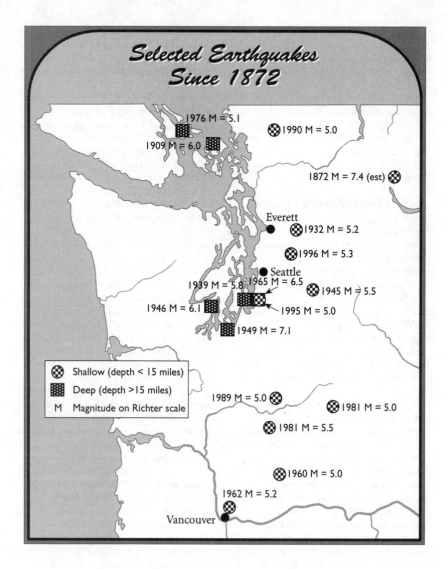

Selected Earthquakes
Since 1872

1976 M = 5.1
1909 M = 6.0
1990 M = 5.0
1872 M = 7.4 (est)
Everett
1932 M = 5.2
1996 M = 5.3
Seattle
1939 M = 5.8
1965 M = 6.5
1945 M = 5.5
1946 M = 6.1
1995 M = 5.0
1949 M = 7.1

Shallow (depth < 15 miles)
Deep (depth >15 miles)
M   Magnitude on Richter scale

1989 M = 5.0
1981 M = 5.0
1981 M = 5.5
1960 M = 5.0
1962 M = 5.2
Vancouver

such an event is something everyone—especially businesses—can do. Here are some prevention measures suggested by emergency planning experts:

• Have a plan, and post instructions for actions to take during and after an earthquake.

• Hold earthquake drills. For those working with or caring for children, make sure they know what to do during an earthquake.

• Instruct personnel to give instructions to customers during an earthquake and to direct evacuation of buildings.

• Securely store hazardous materials.

• Keep a flashlight at sales counters, in desk drawers, and in other areas that would be difficult to evacuate or inspect in the dark.

• Securely store files essential to business operations.

• Maintain an inventory and location list

of valuable items that may need to be moved to a temporary site following an earthquake.

• Protect computer systems against damage and loss of data as a result of ground shaking and power outage.

Eastern Washington's lower population and sparser settlement somewhat limit the earthquake risk there. One concern, however, is the impact of an earthquake on the storage of hazardous and radioactive materials near the Columbia River in central Washington, at Hanford.

The Pacific Northwest Seismograph Network, based at the University of Washington, operates seismograph stations and locates earthquakes in Washington and Oregon. On its Web site, you can check the latest seismograph data, view maps of area fault zones, and read more about earthquake preparedness. **Pacific Northwest Seismograph Network,** www.geophys.washington.edu/SEIS.

Education (SEE ALSO
UNIVERSITIES AND COLLEGES) Washington's first school, at Fort Vancouver, opened in 1832, but it wasn't until 1881 that the government established a school system for the whole territory. Another 14 years passed before the now-State Legislature passed a bill providing funds for a statewide public education system. The Office of the State Superintendent of Public Instruction is the administrative department of education for the state, and is responsible for supervising the state's public school system, which consists of more than 2,000 schools in 298 public school districts and universities and colleges.

In the mid-1990s, Washington spent $5,540 per student on education versus $5,310 on average for the United States. The state has created a K-20 telecommunications Internet system to bring Internet capability to every school district and college.

In 1993, the Legislature passed a bill establishing academic standards in reading, writing, mathematics, and listening, and requiring testing to assess student performance. The *Washington Assessment of Student Learning,* or WASL, tests are given to fourth-, seventh-, and 10th-graders. WASL assesses students based on four levels of achievement: level 4 is superior performance that exceeds the essential skills standard, level 3 is *solid* academic performance in essential learning skills, level 2 is below the standard and means the student demonstrated *partial* accomplishment of knowledge and skills, and level 1 indicates the student demonstrated little or no knowledge and skills. In the first year of testing, 47 percent of fourth-graders met or exceeded the standard in reading, 21.1 percent met the math standard, 62.3 percent met the listening standard, and 41.7 percent met the writing standard.

The second year of testing showed overall improvement: 55.6 percent met or exceeded the reading standard, 31.2 percent met or exceeded the math standard, a 9.8 percent increase; and 71.3 percent met or exceeded the standard in listening, a 9.1 percentage point gain. Writing scores, however, dipped to 36.7 percent, down by 6 percentage points.

Still, there is room for improvement, and Gov. Gary Locke has proclaimed education as his administration's highest priority. Washington's classrooms are more crowded than the national average, 20.2 students for every teacher in Washington versus 17.3 nationally. Teacher salaries per student are also below national average: While the top 10 states spend $3,056 per student in teacher salaries, Washington

spends significantly less, $1,865 per student. A beginning teacher in Washington makes $22,950 a year, $1,720 below the poverty level, and more than 30 percent of new teachers in the state leave in their first five years.

Home Schooling. State law allows children to be taught at home by a parent who has been qualified to do so and under the supervision of a certificated person. To be qualified, a parent must have earned 45 college credits, have completed a course in home-based instructions, or be deemed qualified by the superintendent of the local school district. The home-based instruction must consist of planned and supervised activities and curriculum in the basic skills—science, mathematics, language, social studies, history, health, reading, writing, spelling, art, and music.

Organizations of Interest.

Office of the Superintendent of Public Instruction, Old Capitol Bldg., P.O. Box 47200, Olympia 98504-7200; (360) 753-6738.

State Board of Education, P.O. Box 47206, Olympia, WA 98504-7206; (360) 753-6715.

Washington Education Association, 33434 Eighth Ave. S., Federal Way, WA 98003-6397; (253) 941-6700, (253) 946-4690.

Washington State Parent Teachers Association (PTA), 2003 65th Ave. W., Tacoma, WA 98466-6215; (253) 565-2153, (800) 562-3804. http://wastatepta.org.

Washington Homeschool Organization, 6632 S. 191st Pl., Suite E100, Kent, WA 98032-2117; (425) 251-0439.

Family Learning Organization, P.O. Box 7247, Spokane, WA 99207-0247; (509) 467-2552.

Elected Officials (*See*

Also Governor) Washington State government's executive branch is headed by the governor and eight other statewide-elected officials who serve as the senior executives. All elected officials serve four-year terms; the next election of these officials is November 2000.

Governor: Gary Locke. The governor is the chief executive officer of the state. The governor prepares the state budget and appoints the directors of the administrative departments of the state government and members of the numerous state boards and commissions. The governor may veto legislation and individual items of appropriations bills passed by the State Legislature. Office of the Governor, Legislative Bldg., P.O. Box 40002l, Olympia, WA 98504-0002; (360) 902-4111. E-mail: Governor.Locke@Governor.wa.gov.

Washington Governor Gary Locke. Courtesy of the Office of the Governor.

Lieutenant Governor: Brad Owen. The lieutenant governor serves as acting governor during the governor's absence and is the presiding officer of the State Senate. The lieutenant governor also is the chair of numerous statewide committees and commissions. Office of Lieutenant Governor, 304 Legislative Bldg., P.O. Box 04482, Olympia, WA 98504-0482; (360) 786-7700. E-mail: owen_br@leg.wa.gov.

Secretary of State: Ralph Munro. The secretary of state is the chief elections officer, chief corporations officer, and supervisor of the state archives. The secretary's office registers and licenses corporations and nonprofit organizations; conducts and verifies the results of elections, initiatives, and referendums; and collects and maintains state records and documents. Office of the Secretary of State, Legislative Bldg., P.O. Box 40220, Olympia, WA 98504-0220; (360) 902-4151. http://www.secstate.wa.gov.

State Treasurer: Michael J. Murphy. The state treasurer is the government's chief fiscal officer, managing the state's finances—disbursing funds, managing investments and bonds, and collecting revenue. State Treasurer, Legislative Bldg., P.O. Box 40200, Olympia, WA 98504-0200; (360) 902-9000. E-mail: michaelj@tre.wa.gov. http://www.wa.gov/tre/home/html.

State Auditor: Brian Sonntag. The office of the state auditor conducts financial and legal audits of state agencies and local governments. The auditor also administers the state's "whistleblower" law. Office of State Auditor, Legislative Bldg., P.O. Box 40021, Olympia, WA 98504-0021; (360) 902-0360.

Attorney General: Christine O. Gregoire. The attorney general, the state's top legal officer, serves as legal counsel to other elected officials, the Legislature, state agencies and offices, and higher education institutions; and provides information to the public on consumer protection. Office of the Attorney General, 1125 Washington St. SE, P.O. Box 40100, Olympia, WA 98504-0100; (360) 753-6200.

Superintendent of Public Instruction: Teresa Bergeson. The superintendent of public instruction is the top school supervisor in the state. The superintendent's office certifies teachers and accredits education programs. Office of the Superintendent of Public Instruction, Old Capitol Bldg., P.O. Box 47200, Olympia, WA 98504-7200; (360) 586-6738.

Commissioner of Public Lands: Jennifer Belcher. The commissioner of public lands is the top official of the Department of Natural Resources, which oversees state forest, agricultural, range, tidal, and shore lands. Office of the Commissioner of Public Lands, 1111 Washington St. SE, P.O.

Box 47001, Olympia, WA 98504-7001; (360) 902-1004.

Insurance Commissioner: Deborah Senn. The insurance commissioner regulates all insurance companies doing business in the state, licensing agents and brokers, approving rates, and handling complaints from the public. Office of the Insurance Commissioner, Insurance Bldg., P.O. Box 40255, Olympia, WA 98504-0255; (360) 753-7301, consumer hotline (800) 562-6900. http://www.wa.gov/ins.

Elk Elk are nearly as large as horses and look like deer. The only larger member of the deer family is the moose, which is found in the far northeastern corner of Washington State. Large elk measure 5 feet at the shoulder and weigh more than 600 pounds. Coastal elk populations, most numerous in the Olympic Mountains, are called Roosevelt elk, named after Theodore

Returning Wildlife
The first large mammals to return to Mount St. Helens after the 1980 eruption were Roosevelt elk. Herds browsed on newly planted tree seedlings, leaving behind hoofprints that broke up the ashy crust and helped seed germination. —Ann Saling, *The Great Northwest Nature Factbook* ❋

A bull Roosevelt elk, bugling during the rut. From *Going Wild in Washington and Oregon* by Susan Ewing,

Roosevelt, the great conservationist and hunter. About 5,000 Roosevelt elk are estimated to live in Olympic National Park. They can also be spotted in the Cascade Mountains. During the fall, in elk country, listen for the unmistakable bugling call of the male elk looking for a mate.

Endangered Species

In addition to the federal Endangered Species Act, which protects plants and animals that face the possibility of becoming extinct, Washington State has a state endangered wildlife law. The state law provides protection for wildlife species that are endangered or likely to become endangered (threatened) throughout "all or a significant portion of their range within the state." Both the federal and the state laws protect both a species in general or distinct populations of species. The federal endangered species program lists 19 endangered or threatened species—13 animals and six plants—within Washington. The state law lists 35 endangered or threatened animals.

Endangered Animals. (Federal status in parentheses: E = Endangered, T = Threatened, C = Candidate, SC = Species of Concern)

American white pelican, *Pelecanus erythrorhynchos*
Black right whale, *Balaena glacialis* (E)
Blue whale, *Balaenoptera musculus* (E)
Brown pelican, *Pelecanus occidentalis* (E)
Columbian white-tailed deer, *Odocoileus virginianus leucurus* (E)
Fin whale, *Baleonoptera physalus* (E)
Fisher, *Martes pennanti* (SC)
Gray wolf, *Canis lupus* (E)
Grizzly bear, *Ursus arctos* (T)
Humpback whale, *Megaptera novaeangliae* (E)
Leatherback sea turtle, *Dermochelys coriacea* (E)
Oregon silverspot butterfly, *Speyeria zerene hippolyta* (T)
Oregon spotted frog, *Rana pretiosa*
Peregrine falcon, *Falco peregrinus* (E)
Pygmy rabbit, *Brachylagus idahoensis* (SC)

Sandhill crane, *Grus canadensis*
Sea otter, *Enhydra lutris*
Sei whale, *Balaenoptera borealis* (E)
Snowy plover, *Charadrius alexandrinus* (T)
Sperm whale, *Physeter macrocephalus* (E)
Spotted owl, *Strix occidentalis* (T)
Upland sandpiper, *Bartramia longicauda*
Western pond turtle, *Clemmys marmorata* (SC)
Woodland caribou, *Rangifer tarandus* (E)

Threatened Animals.

Aleutian Canada goose, *Branta canadensis leucopareia* (T)
Bald eagle, *Haliaetus leucocephalus* (T)
Ferruginous hawk, *Buteo regalis* (SC)
Green sea turtle, *Chelonia mydas* (T)
Loggerhead sea turtle, *Caretta caretta* (T)
Lynx, *Lynx canadensis* (C)
Marbled murrelet, *Brachyramphus marmoratus* (T)
Sage grouse, *Centrocercus urophasianus* (SC)
Sharp-tailed grouse, *Tympanuchus phasianellus* (SC)
Steller sea lion, *Eumetopias jubatus* (T)
Western gray squirrel, *Sciurus griseus* (SC)

Source: Washington Department of Fish and Wildlife

Erratics

Driving through eastern Washington, you can see huge rocks that appear to have been plopped down in the middle of a field. These are erratics, giant boulders that were transported and deposited by glacial ice from the last ice ages. There are hundreds of these geologic anomalies scattered across the Columbia Plateau, but they can also be seen in the glacial till exposed along road cuts. The large haystack-shaped rocks that litter the wheat fields of eastern Washington are among the most dramatic erratics. They exist because the glacial ice picked them up from the northern rim of the Columbia Plateau, carried them along, then dropped them farther south, near the moraine, the ice sheet's receding edge. Erratics also appear high in the Olympic Mountains, carried there by glaciers from mountains in British Columbia and deposited at elevations as high as 3,000 feet.

Exports and Imports

Washington State has unique advantages that make it a leader in international trade: It is equidistant by air from Asia and Europe, closer to Asia by water than other West Coast states, and blessed by deep-water harbors. According to the Washington Council on International Trade, trade represents more than 23 percent of the gross state product. In 1997, $110.8 billion worth of exports and imports moved through the state, $36 billion of which originated in the state (or about 36 percent of the state's overall trade). Other significant facts about Washington State's role in international trade:

Export-related jobs represent 31 percent of the total increase in jobs from 1963 to 1995. Export-related jobs expanded twice as fast as non trade employment.

International trade supports one-fourth of Washington State's workforce, nearly 740,000 wage and salary workers and proprietors. Jobs producing exports pay on average 46 percent more than the overall state average.

By 2005, foreign markets are expected to account for 42 percent of Washington's external sales. As a result, one out of every three jobs will be directly or indirectly supported by sales abroad. Washington is now the fourth-largest exporting state in the United States, after California, Texas, and New York.

Service exports are the state's second-largest export. They comprised one-fourth of total exports in 1995. Exports of services grew faster than merchandise exports: 9.6 percent for services and 6.9 percent for manufactured goods from 1963 to 1995. If software were counted as part of merchandise trade for 1996, Washington-originated exports would be $2.5 billion higher than the $6.9 billion total.

Agricultural exports were more than $5 billion in 1997. Not only are wheat and apples primary commodities, but hops, barley, peas, lentils, mint, and other crops are also important and provide employment, revenues, and diversity to the state's export base.

A container ship arriving at the Port of Seattle. From *Washington II* by John Marshall.

Washington State Trade by Major World Regions (1997)

	Value ($US millions)
Asia-Pacific Economic Community (APEC), 17 nations	83,231.5
European Union, 15 nations	11,965.1
North America, 2 nations	16,825.3

Two-Way Trade (1986-1996)

Value ($US billions 1992)

	Exports	Imports	Balance
1986	46.3	17.3	29.0
1988	58.4	23.7	34.7
1990	71.5	34.9	36.6
1992	78.7	37.8	40.9
1994	81.2	34.7	46.5
1995	80.3	33.5	46.8
1996	103.4	47.8	55.6

Top Exports and Imports in Value (1997)

Top Exports	Value ($US millions)
Airplanes	18,114.9
Forest products	3,304.4
High-technology equipment	3,178.2
Maize	1,320.3
Tobacco products	548.2
Soybeans	544.5
Motor vehicle parts	519.4
Animal hides	442.8
Other	19,712.2
Total Top Exports	47,684.9

Top Imports	Value ($US millions)
High-technology equipment	8,571.2
Forest products	3,599.0
Motor vehicles	3,214.6
Motor vehicle parts	2,321.8
Games	1,875.0
Aircraft parts	1,644.2
Petroleum gases	1,641.7
Airplane engines	1,402.6
Office machine parts	1,062.5
Toys	1,020.4
Total Top Imports	53,193.4

Top Trading Partners for Selected Exports (1996)

	Value ($US millions)
Airplanes	18,114.9
United Kingdom	3,790.0
Japan	2,965.2
China	1,458.0
South Korea	1,377.6
Singapore	1,025.1
Others	9,810.9
Forest Products	3,304.4
Canada	639.2
Japan	563.0
South Korea	201.9
Hong Kong	108.6
Taiwan	105.2
Others	1,686.2
High Technology	3,178.2
Canada	838.7
Japan	377.4
Hong Kong	166.5
Holland	139.8
Taiwan	137.2
Others	1,518.0
Wheat	877.6
Japan	327.4
Philippines	139.2
Pakistan	119.9
South Korea	103.8
Taiwan	89.1
Others	97.9
Seafood*	556.9
Japan	297.6
Canada	140.0
South Korea	19.2
France	10.9
Hong Kong	7.9
Others	81.3

*Note: The actual impact of seafood trade is greater than the $556.9 million documented figure because many of Alaska's and Oregon's seafood companies are headquartered in Washington State, while some of their products are exported out of other states. Also, due to the rounding of value, totals may not be precisely equal the sum of the individual items listed here.

Top Trading Partners for Selected Exports (1996) *(continued)*
Value ($US millions)

Apples	$465.6
Mexico	$77.2
Taiwan	$58.2
Indonesia	$57.7
Canada	$47.1
Hong Kong	$32.2
Others	$193.2

Top Trading Partners (1997)

	Value ($US millions)
Japan	30,703.6
Exports: aircraft, forest products, radioactive elements	9,870.5
Imports: high tech, motor vehicles, motor vehicle parts	20,833.1
Canada	16,794.1
Exports: high tech, automatic data process machines, forest products	7,131.2
Imports: forest products, petroleum gases, crude oil	9,662.9
European Union	11,965.1
Exports: airplanes, automatic data process machines, office machine parts	9,107.6
Imports: aircraft engines, aircraft parts, high tech	2,857.5
China	9,885.2
Exports: aircraft, aluminum plates, aircraft parts	2,272.9
Imports: toys, high tech, footwear	7,612.3
South Korea	6,643.6
Exports: aircraft, corn, animal skins	4,289.8
Imports: motor vehicles, high tech, automatic data process machines	2,353.8
Taiwan	5,463.4
Exports: corn, aircraft, soybeans	2,246.2
Imports: high tech, automatic data process machines, and screws, nuts, and bolts	3,217.2
Hong Kong	2,710.9
Exports: poultry, forest products, automatic data process machines	1,330.8
Imports: sweaters, women's suits, high tech	1,380.1
Thailand	2,525.8
Exports: aircraft, high tech, soybeans	1,347.2
Imports: high tech, automatic data process machines, footwear	1,178.6
Singapore	2,205.5
Exports: aircraft, high tech, tobacco	1,968.3
Imports: office machine parts, automatic data process machines, high tech	237.2
Malaysia	1,953.8
Exports: aircraft, soybeans, high tech	1,354.4
Imports: high tech, rubber, office machine parts	599.4

Source: Washington Council on International Trade, 2615 Fourth Ave., Suite 350, Seattle, WA 98121-1253; (206) 443-3826.

Ferries (*SEE ALSO* TRANSPORTATION)

Washington State Ferries (WSF) began in 1951, taking over from private ferry operators. It is the nation's largest ferry system and Washington's number-one tourist attraction (tourists and vacationers account for about one-third of the passengers). Ferry ridership is growing at about 5 percent per year. WSF operates 27 vessels over 10 routes (see below). These include 23 auto-passenger vessels and four passenger-only vessels. Twenty terminals are located in eight counties and British Columbia. More than 25.5 million passengers were carried in 1997 over the Puget Sound ferry routes; that is an average of more than 70,000 passengers per day. **Washington State Ferries,** http://www.wsdot.wa.gov/ferries.

Washington State Ferries, Puget Sound Routes.

Anacortes-Sidney, BC, via San Juan Islands
Edmonds-Kingston
Fauntleroy-Southworth
Mukilteo-Clinton
Point Defiance-Tahlequah
Port Orchard-Bremerton
Port Townsend-Keystone
Seattle-Bainbridge
Seattle-Bremerton

In addition to the busy Puget Sound ferries, WSF runs the Keller ferry in eastern Washington, which crosses the Columbia River where it meets the Sanpoil River. A number of private and small public ferries cross rivers and waterways throughout the state; (800) 843-3779 or (206) 464-6400, http://www.wsdot.wa.gov/ferries/. The Colville Confederated Tribes operate a ferry upstream from the confluence of the Columbia and Spokane Rivers; (509) 324-6000. On the lower Columbia, you can ride the Wahkiakum County Ferry between Cathlamet, Washington, Puget Island, and Westport, Oregon; (360) 795-3301.

Privately Operated Ferries.

Alaska Marine Highway, Bellingham to Juneau, (800) 642-0066.

Anderson Island and Ketron Island from Steilacoom, Pierce County, (253) 798-2766.

Black Ball Transport, Port Angeles to

The ferry Kalakala, shown here in 1935 during her glory days, originally sailed for the Puget Sound Navigational Company, a private ferry company that was purchased by the state to become today's state-owned ferry system. Courtesy of the Museum of History and Industry.

Victoria, BC, daily auto service, (360) 457-4491.

Horluck Transportation Co., Bremerton to Port Orchard to Annapolis, passenger-only service, (360) 876-2300.

Lady of the Lake, Chelan to Stehekin, (509) 682-2224.

Lummi Island Ferry, Bellingham to Lummi Island, hourly car ferry, (360) 676-6692.

Princess Marguerite III, Seattle to Victoria, BC, daily auto/passenger service, (206) 441-4460.

P.S. Express, Port Townsend to Friday Harbor, (360) 385-5288.

San Juan Island Shuttle Express, Bellingham to San Juan Islands, summer only, passenger-only service, (360) 671-1137.

Victoria Clipper, Seattle to Victoria, BC, daily passenger-only service, (206) 448-5000.

Victoria Rapid Transit, Port Angeles to Victoria, BC, daily passenger-only service, (360) 452-8088.

Victoria-San Juan Cruises, Bellingham to Victoria, BC, and San Juan Islands, (800) 443-4552.

Fire Lookouts In the early

1900s, when the nation's national forests were created, the new Forest Service began erecting the first fire lookouts in the Pacific Northwest. The first of these structures were little more than a crude platform constructed in a tree with a few of its branches removed and a ladder nailed to the tree trunk for access. Gradually, the structures became more permanent and the designs were standardized to make them easier to build and maintain. What they had in common, however, was mountaintop location and windows all around to accommodate a 360-degree view.

Some of the fire lookouts can now be rented from the Forest Service for those who really like roughing it. Most of the fire lookouts and cabins are in remote areas and with few to no amenities. Often there is no plumbing or heat, and you must in most cases bring your own cooking utensils, drinking water, bedding, and other supplies. So if the call of the wild is calling you, call the **Forest Service Regional Office,**

Nature of the Northwest, 800 NE Oregon St., Suite 177, Portland, OR 97232; (503) 872-2750; http://www.naturenw.org (click on Cabin/Lookout Rental Guide) and get far away from it all.

Fish and Shellfish

(*SEE ALSO* AQUACULTURE; CRABS; GEODUCK; RED TIDE; SALMON) Washington's aquatic resources include numerous species of marine and freshwater finfish and shellfish throughout its ocean and inland marine waters, thousands of miles of rivers and streams, and many lakes.

There are about 150 fish species that are considered important commercial and recreational species. Among the best known are salmon, steelhead, and trout. Saltwater species include bottom fish such as flounder and sole, rockfish, blennies, Irish lords, herring, and some fascinating creatures such as the fierce-looking but shy wolf eel.

Lakes and rivers support a number of freshwater species, including some, such as largemouth bass, that were introduced to the state as game fish. Shellfish species are also important both as recreational and commercial resources; they include Dungeness crab, clams, mussels, and oysters.

Commercial Fishing. The commercial fishing industry has undergone dramatic changes throughout the state's history. There was a time when rivers and streams were choked with salmon returning to spawn. While the fishing industry in Washington today comprises a smaller share of the gross state product than it did in its glory days, it is still significant.

Important commercial species landed in the state include chinook and coho salmon, halibut, groundfish, Pacific whiting, flounder, rockfish, and ocean perch. Shellfish species are also important commercial resources, including Dungeness crab and shrimp.

Washington Commercial Fish Landings (1997)

Finfish	Pounds Landed	Value
Salmon	22,359,769	$13,595,990
Sablefish	4,993,718	9,750,241
Halibut	3,893,709	9,739,443
Albacore Tuna	7,840,085	6,376,688
Rockfish	13,258,504	4,888,504
Sole	3,788,528	1,528,259
Hake	15,971,193	714,635
Pacific cod	1,465,682	567,376
Sturgeon	277,932	312,636
Herring	880,483	304,916
Flounder	2,715,602	282,963
Lingcod	653,465	272,892
Shark	1,387,896	201,061
Rainbow Trout	423,246	197,328
Smelts and Eulachon	153,446	100,616
Skates	630,225	57,174
Anchovy	130,292	41,615
Shad	14,441	2,111
Mackerel	1,567	78
Misc.	382,844	41,218

Shellfish	Pounds Landed	Value
Dungeness Crab	15,685,327	$31,671,300
Clam	2,077,873	25,771,974
Oyster	5,425,781	13,469,737
Shrimp	6,146,696	3,356,936
Mussel	272,782	2,493,578
Sea Urchin	1,039,638	1,188,735
Sea Cucumber	547,174	707,822
Scallop	1,410	22,159
Octopus	30,488	18,108
Cockle	1,312	782
Squid	1,426	333
Total	112,452,534	127,677,208

Source: National Marine Fisheries Service

Sport Fishing. More than 600,000 licensed anglers fish Washington's salt water, rivers, and lakes for sport. On the west side of the state, fishing is popular year-round. Nevertheless, there are traditional and established opening and closing dates. Opening day for freshwater lakes is traditionally the third Sunday in April. The rivers in the western portion of the state open traditionally on Memorial Day weekend. Anglers are encouraged to read carefully the fishing rules that are provided to them when they purchase a fishing license, as the seasons and size limit can vary by fish, by region, and even by year.

Saltwater fishing. Salmon is the big draw here. In 1995, anglers made an estimated 583,000 recreational salmon fishing trips. They caught about 327,000 salmon in salt water (another 190,000 were caught in fresh water). The state has more than 3,000 miles of saltwater coastline. Saltwater angling occurs in five reasonably well-defined regions: the Columbia River mouth, the Pacific coastline (including Willapa Bay and Grays Harbor), the Strait of Juan de Fuca, Puget Sound (including Hood Canal), and the San Juan Islands. The diversity of these regions is phenomenal. Anglers can brave the ocean on a large head boat, or fish protected coves from a canoe. In addition to Pacific salmon, ocean fishing also yields rockfish, cod and lingcod, halibut, sturgeon, smelt and herring, and ocean perch.

River fishing. The most popular river fish are steelhead. Steelhead are trout that spend a portion of their life feeding in the ocean. Like their cousins, the salmon, they return to fresh water to spawn. Steelhead average 5 to 10 pounds but can grow to more than 3 feet in length, and the largest steelhead weigh in at more than 40 pounds. Sturgeon, other varieties of trout, channel catfish, and many other fish also can be caught in Washington's rivers.

Lake fishing. Trout dominate freshwater fishing in Washington's many lakes. Rainbow trout are heavily stocked. Cutthroat are found east of the Cascades. Brook trout, brown trout, lake trout, golden trout, and grayling all can be caught in Washington's lakes. Outside of the mountain lakes, bass, blue gills, and catfish all keep the angler busy.

Shellfishing. State tidelands offer a cornucopia of shellfish. The intrepid recreationalist who goes after this quarry needs to make certain that the shellfish are taken from publicly owned tidelands that have been designated for the taking of

The coastal fishing fleet at port in Ilwaco. From *Washington II* by John Marshall.

shellfish, and that meet health standards (check for local conditions). Also check about licensing requirements. The sandy beaches of the ocean coast are known for abundant razor clam populations. Beaches on Puget Sound offer up littlenecks, butter clams, cockles, soft-shelled gapers, and horse clams. The largest and most exotic, the geoduck, is rare in the shallows but is abundant in muddy areas at diver depths. Clammers use either a shovel or a tube. A clam shovel has a long, slender, curved blade specially designed for digging rapidly down at a clam show. The tube looks just like it sounds. It is a length of pipe that you jam down over the clam show, then lift up to extract a core of sand, hopefully containing the clam. In addition to clams, recreationalists often go after red rock crabs and other crabs, which often can be found around piers and rocky areas.

Washington Department of Fish and Game, Natural Resources Bldg., 1111 Washington St. SE, Olympia, WA 98501; (360) 902-2200. http://www.wa.gov/ wdfw/fish/regs/fishregs.rtm (the complete rules for recreational shellfishing can be found on the Web).

Fish Hatcheries (See

ALSO MAP, PAGES 132–33) There are eight national fish hatcheries and 24 state hatchery complexes in Washington. The Washington Department of Fish and Wildlife (WDFW) operates the world's largest network of hatcheries—24 hatchery complexes with more than 90 rearing facilities (a hatchery complex may include production hatcheries, net pens, acclimation sites, and rearing ponds).

The original purpose of fish hatcheries was to restore the stocks of commercial and sport fish species that were decimated by a combination of factors, including overfishing and the building of dams across the state's major rivers. The first salmon hatcheries in Washington were owned and operated by commercial canneries, counties, and towns. The first salmon hatchery was built along the Kalama River in 1895, and the first trout hatchery was constructed in 1903 on Lake Chelan.

Today, hatcheries produce salmon, steelhead, trout, and warm-water fish species such as bass, perch, catfish, and walleye. A total of more than 300 million fish eggs are collected annually at the state hatcheries; altogether the state and national hatcheries release more than 250 million fish into rivers, streams, and lakes. The state hatcheries alone produce approximately 75 percent of all coho and chinook salmon, and 88 percent of all steelhead harvested statewide.

WDFW Hatchery Complexes.

Bingham Creek Willapa Bay Complex, Forks Creek, Nemah, Naselle

Cowlitz Complex, Cowlitz salmon, Cowlitz trout, Mossyrock

Dungeness Complex, Dungeness, Hurd Creek, Elwha

Eastbank Complex, Eastbank, Turtle Rock, Chelan, Lake Wenatchee

Elochoman Complex, Elochoman, Grays River, Beaver Creek

Grays Harbor Complex, Lake Aberdeen, Humptulips

Green River Complex, Issaquah, Soos Creek, Palmer Ponds, Cedar River

Hood Canal Complex, George Adams, Eells Springs, McKernan, Hoodsport

Kalama Complex, Kalama Falls, Fallert Creek, North Toutle

Klickitat Complex, Klickitat, Goldendale

Lakewood Complex, South Tacoma, Garrison, Chambers Creek

Lewis Complex, Lewis River, Merwin, Speelyai

Lyons Ferry Complex, Lyons Ferry, Tucannon

Minter Creek Complex, Minter Creek, Coulter Creek, Hupp Springs, Fox Island

Nooksack Complex, Kendall Creek, Samish, Lake Whatcom, Bellingham

Priest Rapids Complex, Priest Rapids, Columbia Basin, Ringold, Naches

Puyallup Complex, Puyallup, Voights Creek

Skagit Complex, Marblemount, Barnaby Slough, Baker Lake, Arlington, Whitehorse

Snohomish Complex, Wallace River, Reiter Pond, Tokul Creek

Sol Duc Complex, Sol Duc, Bogachiel, Shale Creek, Bear Springs

South Sound Complex, Tumwater Falls, McAllister, South Sound Net Pens, Skookumchuck

Spokane Complex, Ford, Sherman Creek, Spokane, Colville

Washougal Complex, Vancouver, Skamania, Washougal

Wells Complex, Wells, Methow, Omak, Similkameen

National Fish Hatcheries.

Carson National Fish Hatchery, Carson

Leavenworth National Fish Hatchery Complex (includes Entiat NFH, Winthrop NFH), Leavenworth

Little White Salmon Fish Hatchery Complex (includes Willard NFH), Cook

Makah National Fish Hatchery, Neah Bay

Quilcene National Fish Hatchery, Quilcene

Quinault National Fish Hatchery, Neilton

Spring Creek National Fish Hatchery, Underwood

National Fisheries Research and Technology Facilities.

In addition to the hatcheries, the U.S. Fish and Wildlife Service has several fisheries research and technology facilities in the state:

The **Abernathy Salmon Culture Technology** Center in Longview is researching the genetic aspects of fish restoration and recovery.

The **Olympia Fish Health Center** in Olympia provides fish health diagnostic, disease prevention, and therapeutic services to the national fisheries.

The **Lower Columbia River Fish Health Center** in Underwood is the Fish Health Center for the Lower Columbia River hatcheries (Spring Creek, Little White Salmon-Willard, Carson, Eagle Creek, Warm Springs, and Abernathy Salmon Culture Technology Center).

Forest (SEE ALSO NATIONAL FORESTS; OLD-GROWTH FORESTS)

Half of Washington State—21.4 million acres—is covered with forest. Of these lands, 64 percent are publicly owned or managed, and 34 percent are privately owned lands, about half of which are timber-producing forests. The U.S. Forest Service holds the largest share of public forest land—about 9 million acres—and the Washington Department of Natural Resources holds about 2.1 million acres.

The state's forestlands are classified by several types of ecosystems that are broadly defined by climate and elevation as coastal forest, lowland forest, subalpine and mountain forests, and intermountain region.

Coastal forests, which grow in low elevations along the coast, are by far the most lush. The Pacific Ocean climate greatly influences growing conditions, with mild temperatures, heavy rainfall (average rainfall reaches 130 inches per year), and summer fog. Sitka spruce, western red cedar, and western hemlock thrive in this wet, damp environment. Douglas fir is common on drier west- and south-facing slopes.

Lowland forests are those that stretch from the coastal region to the lower slopes of the Cascade Mountains. This region is the most heavily forested and harvested. Annual rainfall here averages about 70 inches, with moderate and mild temperatures. The dominant species are Douglas fir, western hemlock, and western red cedar. Big-leaf maple is also common, as is Pacific madrona, the region's only common broadleaved evergreen. Much of this region was logged early in the 20th century, so most of the forests consist of second- and third-growth Douglas fir.

Mountain forests are those at the 2,000- to 5,000-foot elevations on the flanks of the Olympics and the Cascades. The lower elevations have thick stands of close-growing evergreens, while at the higher elevations the trees thin out. At lower western elevations, Douglas fir, western hemlock, western red cedar, and Pacific silver fir thrive. In the mid-elevations of the drier eastern Cascades, lodgepole pine, ponderosa pine, grand fir, and western

larch join the Douglas fir.

Subalpine forests are those that exist at elevations of 5,000 to 7,000 feet along the high ridges and peaks of the Cascades, Olympics, and part of the Blue Mountains. Tree species have to be hardy to survive the harsher weather of the high country. Dominant species on the western slopes include alpine fir, lodgepole pine, Douglas fir, western white pine, and dwarf juniper. On the eastern slopes these species are joined by Engelmann spruce and alpine larch. There are also more meadows and glades breaking up the forest expanses in this region.

Intermountain forests are predominantly found through the Okanogan Highlands and Ferry, Stevens, and Pend Oreille Counties. This region also includes the lower east side of the Cascade Mountains and the Blue Mountains in southeastern Washington. Dry, arid conditions distinguish this region; annual rainfall ranges between 6 and 20 inches, and the temperature ranges from extreme heat in the summer to extreme cold in the winter. Ponderosa pine is well suited to this region because it is extremely drought-resistant.

Two unique forest ecosystems in this state are the temperate rain forest and old-growth forest. The Olympic Peninsula is home to one of the few temperate rain forests in the world, along the Hoh River.

A Natural Forest

In a natural forest, plants carpet its floor so densely that "nurselogs" offer seedlings a valuable perch. Logs also deliver ready-made nutrients when they fall, and accumulate still more as they decay... down-trees remain an important part of the forest community. What actually happens when a tree falls is this: The trunk is recruited to the forest floor ("recruitment" is a term used by forest ecologists). Beetles and nematodes and a great host of other organisms soon invade the log, bringing with them yeasts and the spores of fungi. These initiate a whole new cycle of nutrient build-up. —John Marshall, *Portrait of Washington*

Rain forest on the Olympic Peninsula. From *The Great Northwest Nature Factbook* by Ann Saling.

Rainfall can reach 240 inches per year there. Old-growth forest is generally considered to be areas that have not been significantly changed by fire, disease, or human intervention for a very long time, 200 years or longer. In Washington, there are still many places to see ancient stands of forest: on the Quinault Loop Trail on the Olympic Pensinsula, in the Grove of the Patriarchs in Mount Rainier National Park, and near Cougar on Mount St. Helens.

Forest Products Industry

Forests cover more than half of Washington, which ranks second only to Oregon in the production of lumber. More than 40 percent of the wood cut is used for lumber, about 40 percent is exported as roundwood, and the remainder is used for pulp and plywood. About two-thirds of the forestlands are owned by federal, state, or local governments and Indian tribes; the remaining third is privately owned by timber companies, family tree farmers, and private individuals.

There are two broad types of timberland in the state, with Douglas fir characteristic of the land west of the Cascades and ponderosa pine predominating in the drier lands east of the mountains. The most abundant single species is Douglas firs; about a fifth of all the Douglas fir in the country grow in Washington. Douglas fir makes up more than a third of the state's total lumber production. Western hemlock and ponderosa pine are other important commercial species. A typical 50-year-old Douglas fir, which has about 80 feet of "merchantable" height containing 380 board feet, is worth about $250.

The forest products industry is the second-largest manufacturing industry in the state. The industry accounts for about 58,000 full-time employees, and more than 200,000 related jobs, or about one in 13. This translates into a payroll of $2.2. billion a year, and $5.9 billion in purchases of goods and services from individuals and other businesses.

The forest products industry has undergone some difficult times in the past two decades. Increasing environmental restrictions to protect fish and wildlife habitat reduced the number of large, older trees that could be harvested. At the same time, reforestation of private forestlands intensified—private forestlands, which produce 75 percent of the state's timber supply, are planted with more than 200,000 new trees per day, or about 35 million tree seedlings per year. The forest products industry projects that commercial timber supplies will actually increase well into the 21st century as a result of these reforestation efforts.

Organizations and Events of Interest.

Camp 6 Logging Museum, 5400 Pearl St., Tacoma, WA 98407; (253) 752-0047. Camp 6 is filled with logging equipment from the era when "loggers were boss and steam was king!"

Mason County Forest Festival, first weekend after Memorial Day, Shelton, (800) 576-2021.

Deming Logging Show, second weekend in June, Deming, (360) 592-3051.

Sedro Woolley Loggerodeo, early July, Sedro Woolley, (360) 855-1841.

Presto!

Where there is logging, there is lots of leftover sawdust. In the 1920s, Robert T. Bowling, chief engineer of the Clearwater Timber Company, a division of Weyerhaeuser, was looking for practical uses for sawdust, splinters, and chips that were ordinarily burned as waste. He experimented with combinations of pressure, moisture, heat, and cooling to compress the wood waste, and in 1929, presto—the Pres-To Log was born. ⚹

Morton Loggers Jubilee, mid-August, Morton, (360) 498-5250.

Hoquiam Loggers Playday, first Saturday after Labor Day, Hoquiam, (360) 533-3447.

Lumberjack competitions feature events such as speed climbing, log chopping, ax throwing, tree topping, and truck driving.

Timber Harvests

Year	State Total	State Land	Private Land	Federal Land	Indian Land
	(in millions of board feet)				
1980	5,721	745	3,536	1,104	336
1981	4,890	468	3,275	888	259
1982	5,078	439	3,746	742	151
1983	6,087	548	4,027	1,274	238
1984	5,802	794	3,562	1,241	205
1985	5,964	1,014	3,588	1,149	213
1986	6,556	1,064	4,003	1,254	235
1987	7,035	970	4,387	1,441	237
1988	7,045	826	4,445	1,503	271
1989	6,852	842	4,596	1,152	262
1990	5,849	657	4,177	832	183
1991	5,104	535	3,683	714	172
1992	5,018	476	3,887	469	186
1993	4,329	461	3,338	338	192
1994	4,086	323	3,390	204	169
1995	4,392	496	3,510	156	230
1996	4,249	600	3,307	87	255

Source: Washington Office of Financial Management

Gambling

In 1997, there were about 5,100 licensed gambling facilities in Washington State, including casinos operated under compact by Indian tribes, card rooms, and licensed gambling activities of charitable/nonprofit organizations. Eleven of these were full-scale casinos operated by Indian tribes on Indian lands (*see* Indians). The gaming industry employed more than 4,000 people. Not counting the full-scale casinos (whose receipts are not publicly available), more than $740 million changed hands in the activities shown in the chart below.

Gambling Revenue (1997)

Punchboards/Pulltabs	$510,103,000
Bingo	183,444,000
Amusement games	27,292,000
Card rooms	16,045,000
Raffles	5,384,000
Fund-raising events	305,000
Source: Washington Gambling Commission	

Washington's state lottery was authorized in 1982. Revenues from the lottery have increased every year since its inception. In 1997, the state lottery produced $408 million in revenue, from the games shown in the chart below. About half the lottery revenues are deposited in the state general fund, and about half are allocated to higher education.

Lottery Revenue (1997)

Instant	$206,000,000
Lotto	121,900,000
Quinto	49,700,000
Daily Game	17,500,000
Daily Keno	12,800,000
Source: Washington Office of Financial Management	

Organizations of Interest.

Washington State Council on Problem Gambling, (800) 547-6133.

Washington State Gambling Commission, (800) 345-2529.

Washington State Lottery Commission, (800) 545-7510 (winning numbers), (360) 753-3337, www.wa.gov/lot/.

Geoduck

This giant denizen of the mud is not a myth; it's a humongous clam! The geoduck (pronounced "GOO-ee-duck) or, more formally, *Panopea generosa,* is the largest clam in North America. Their shells grow to about a foot long, and their siphons reach up another 2 or 3 feet. An average 3-pound geoduck may be a decade old. The largest geoducks have weighed in at about 35 pounds. Geoducks seem to stop growing at about 20 years, but some have lived to be more than 100, as measured by counting shell rings (similar to counting tree growth rings). Geoducks are found most commonly in muddy areas in Puget Sound. This is the only known location of a commercial geoduck harvest. In 1997, there were 12 designated geoduck harvest areas, all in waters more than 18 feet deep.

Geoducks

The adult geoduck stays put in its burrow for life and yet lives more than 140 years. (It stops growing after 20 years.) Greater Puget Sound bays and estuaries are the home of the densest population of geoducks in the Lower 48, especially in subtidal zones. An estimated 130 million of the ungainly animals live there.—Ann Saling, *The Great Northwest Nature Factbook*

Ghost Towns

The wind rustles the leaves, the boards creak. There is nothing left, not even hopes and dreams. Ghost towns are part of the legacy of the boom and bust cycles in mining and other resource-based industries. Washington has its share of ghost towns. Here are a few of our favorites, and how to find them.

Blewett. Located 21 miles north of Liberty on U.S. Highway 97. An old gold mining town, Blewett has a couple of dilapidated buildings. The most interesting site for mining buffs is an old stone arrastra, a water-powered ore crusher.

Bodie. The ghost town of Bodie, founded as a mill town in about 1900, is about 15 miles northeast of Wauconda; access from Highway 30, between

Wauconda and Republic. Bodie's residents worked for the Perkins Milling Company, a stamp mill that processed ore from mines in the area. When the mill shut down, so did Bodie. The mill burned in 1962; about six buildings remain, including the schoolhouse. Other ghost towns in the area are Old Toroda, Sheridan Mine Camp, and Sheridan.

Liberty. Fifteen miles northeast of Cle Elum is the ghost town of Liberty; access from U.S. Highway 97, northeast of Cle Elum. Gold was first discovered in the region in 1867. Liberty's fortunes waxed and waned with those of the gold miners. The boom of the 1860s and 1870s turned into the bust of the 1890s. The Klondike gold rush in the late 1890s lured the remaining miners away. Liberty's fortunes dwindled from then on, with brief interruptions. A dredge brought into the region in the 1920s rekindled some interest, for example. Today Liberty is a true ghost town. Log cabins, gold mining facilities, and the remains of business establishments can all be seen.

Molson. Three ghost towns are nestled east of Oroville, near the Canadian border; access from U.S. Highway 97, between Tonasket and Oroville. They began as mining towns, but the communities diversified into agriculture, before the towns died. Molson, founded in 1900, had a drugstore, a newspaper, and a hotel. Squabbles over title to the land beneath the town resulted in the establishments of two Molsons, Old Molson and new Molson. A brick schoolhouse, still standing, was constructed halfway between the two. The struggles between the old and new Molsons continued for many years and undoubtedly hand a hand in dooming the town. The last store in the area closed in 1955. Other ghost towns in the area are Bolster and Havillah.

Glaciers and Glaciation

Washington has the most extensive network of glaciers in the contiguous United States outside of Alaska, and evidence of its glacial past can be found in all parts of the state. During the last North American ice age, some 12,000 to 10,000 years ago, glaciers bulldozed their way across roughly the northern third of the state. The massive ice sheet picked up and moved soil, gravel, and even huge boulders as it progressed south, then dumped them as deposits of till, ridges called moraines, and outwashes of sand and gravel as the ice melted and receded back north. The large boulders seemingly plopped down in the middle of eastern Washington wheat fields—called erratics—were left there by glaciers (*see also* Erratics).

The high peaks of the Cascade and Olympic Mountains have just the right environmental conditions to maintain glaciers: elevations high enough to maintain permanent snowfields and plentiful snowfall in the winter. There are more than 500 glaciers in the state—the North Cascades alone have more than 300 and the Olympics have 60—covering a total area of 135 square miles.

Mount Rainier possesses the most extensive system of glaciers of any single U.S. peak outside Alaska. The largest glaciers hug the north and east slopes, protected from the sun. The Carbon River Glacier, more than 4 miles long, terminates at the lowest elevation (3,000 feet) of any glacier in the contiguous 48 states and contains the thickest ice—more than 700 feet at the 6,200-foot level. Nisqually Glacier is one of the world's most accessible glaciers. It is easily visible from the Nisqually River Bridge on the road between Longmire and Paradise, and from Paradise itself. It was the first U.S. glacier discovered, in 1857 during an ascent of

Looking Back

May 16, 1864

Asa Mercer arrived at a Seattle wharf accompanied by 11 marriageable women from New England to provide wives to the town's lonely, desperate bachelors.

Mount Rainier, and is the best documented glacier in the Western Hemisphere, with photographs dating back to 1884 and records of its size to 1857. Between that date and the present, it has retreated nearly a mile, perhaps an indicator of long-term climate change.

The Olympic Mountains, which are not as high or as cold as the Cascades, seem to prove to geologists that snowfall is more important than temperature in maintaining glaciers. Seven glaciers up to 900 feet deep wrap around two-thirds of Mount Olympus. Longest is the Hoh Glacier, which begins at about 5,500 feet elevation and extends down the mountain to the 4,000-foot level.

Golf

When the best golfers in the country converged on Redmond's Sahalee Golf Club for the 1998 PGA Championship, it put Washington on the map—golfwise. Sahalee regularly shows up on *Golf Digest*'s list of America's 100 Greatest Golf Courses, but there are some other notable courses as well.

The magazine also ranks the best "Most Affordable" and best "Upscale" courses— defined as being either above or below the dividing line of a $50 greens fee—based on such attributes as design, condition, and golfing experience. Desert Canyon (Orondo) and Semiahmoo (Blaine) made the best of the upscale list; Indian Canyon (Spokane), Kayak Point (Stanwood), Harbour Pointe (Mukilteo), and Meriwood (Lacey) made the best of the most afford- able list. Hangman Valley and Indian Canyon golf courses (Spokane) and Meadowood Golf Course (Liberty Lake) earned a spot on the list defined as a "Great Value," a balance of golf experience and affordabil- ity. In addition to the top 100 lists, other courses that were rated as among the best in the state are:

Apple Tree Golf Club, Yakima
Canterwood Golf and Country Club, Gig Harbor
Classic Country Club, Spanaway
Indian Summer Golf and Country Club, Olympia
Loomis Trail Golf Club, Blaine
McCormick Woods, Port Orchard
Port Ludlow Golf Club, Port Ludlow
Royal Oaks Country Club, Vancouver
Seattle Golf Club

As for quantity, golfers can choose among some 300 golf courses statewide, one-third spread over eastern and central Washington and the rest in western Wash- ington. The largest is Gold Mountain Golf Club near Bremerton, a 36-hole course that gets high marks from one local golf reviewer. There are also a handful of 27- hole courses for the truly zealous, but the majority (two-thirds) of the state's golf havens are 18 holes, with the rest being small 9-hole or dual-tee, 9-hole courses.

The state's oldest course, the Tacoma Country and Golf Club, founded in 1894, claims to be the oldest continuing golf club west of the Mississippi. The Spokane Coun- try Club can boast of being the site of the first Women's U.S. Open, held in 1946. Spokane was also site of the last time the PGA Championship was held in Washing- ton, in 1944 at Manito Golf and Country Club. This event is not just a big deal for the state's golfers, it is a money machine. Played every August, the PGA Championship pro- duces $45 million to about $80 million for host communities. Sahalee officials have already announced their wish to host the PGA Championship again. Don't buy a new visor just yet, however; the earliest it could return is 2007.

The Pacific Northwest Section of the Professional Golfers' Association of America hosts a full calendar of tournament play (national, regional, and local for professional and amateur, men and women, and senior and junior players) and holds seminars for area pro golfers. To get the latest tournament results and dates, click on the Pacific Northwest Section home page at PGA.com.

Events of Interest.
NFL Celebrity Golf Tournament, June, Ocean Shores, (800) 76-BEACH.
Surf & Turf Tournament, July, Chelan, (800) 4-CHELAN.

Government
Governance in the Evergreen State is a complex, multilayered, and multijurisdictional mixture of local, state, federal, and foreign governments. Because Washington shares a border with Canada, international entities are empowered to negotiate resource issues such as fisheries and energy. Nearly every agency of the federal government is represented in the state—from law enforcement to resource management to energy.

Many of the federal agencies with jurisdiction within the state are managers of public lands, such as the U.S. Forest Service, National Park Service, and Bureau of Land Management (*see* National Forests; National Parks). The Department of Defense maintains jurisdiction over military installations in the state (*see* Military). The extensive system of dams on the Columbia and Snake Rivers and their associated power grids are managed by the U.S. Army Corps of Engineers and the Bonneville Power Administration (*see* Bonneville Power Administration; Dams).

And the state's neighbors, Idaho and Oregon, share management of certain regional resources. Interstate entities include the Pacific Fishery Management Council, Pacific Northwest Electric Power and Conservation Planning Council (Northwest Power Planning Council), and Pacific States Marine Fisheries Commission.

Local governments include more than 277 municipalities (*see* Cities and Towns), 39 counties (*see* Counties), 65 different types of special use districts such as irrigation and public utility districts (*see* Special Districts), in-state regional planning councils, and Indian tribal governments (*see* American Indians). Among the regional agencies are 10 air pollution authorities, 33 economic development councils, 37 housing authorities, and 26 regional transit authorities.

The state government is composed of executive, legislative, and judicial branches (*see* Elected Officials; Judicial System; Legislature). In a 1998 evaluation of state governments, *Governing Magazine* and Syracuse University's Maxwell School graded all 50 states from A to F on five factors: financial management, capital management, personnel management, managing for results, and management of information technology. Washington was one of only four states that received the top grade of A minus. The state's annual budget is approximately $20.6 billion. The structure of Washington's state government is shown in the organization chart on pages 80–81.

Governor
(*SEE ALSO* ELECTED OFFICIALS) Over the past 150 years, 33 people have served as governor: 14 were appointed by U.S. presidents as territorial governors and 19 were elected as state governor. John R. Rogers, Samuel G. Cosgrove, and Ernest Lister died while in office; Dixy Lee Ray was the first—and only—woman to hold that office in this state; and Gary Locke was the first Chinese-American elected governor in the contiguous United States.

Votes Cast and Governor Elected (1990-96)

1992	
Mike Lowry	
Total vote	2,271,000
Percent/leading party	52.2/Dem.
1996	
Gary Locke	
Total vote	2,237,000
Percent/leading party	58.0/Dem.
Source: Congressional Quarterly	

Territorial Governors.
Isaac I. Stevens, 1853–1857
Fayette McMullen, 1857–1859
R. D. Gholson, 1859–1861
William H. Wallace, 1861
William Pickering, 1862–1866
(Continued on page 82)

Washington State Government Organization Chart (1998-99)

(State agencies based on gubernatorial appointment authority)

Legislative Branch

Senate/House of Representatives
Joint Legislative Audit and Review Committee
Office of the State Actuary
Legislative Transportation Committee
  Joint Legislative Systems Committee

Legislative Ethics Board Redistricting Commission
Legislative Evaluation and Accountability Program

Executive Branch, Statewide Elected Officers

Commissioner of Public Lands
  Department of Natural Resources
Insurance Commissioner

Lieutenant Governor

Treasurer
  Public Deposit Protection Commission

Attorney General
  Executive Ethics Board
Superintendent of Public Instruction
  Board of Education
Secretary of State
  Productivity Board

Governor

Puget Sound Water Quality Action Team
Governor's Office of Indian Affairs
Office of Family & Children's Ombudsman

Executive Branch, Office of the Governor

Agencies with Executive Appointed by the Governor

Environment & Natural Resources	General Government	Transportation	Health & Human Services	Education	Community Economics
Dept. Ecology	Off. of Finan. Management	State Patrol	Dept. Social & Health Services	School for the Blind	Dept. Community Trade & Economic Development Services
Dept. Agriculture • Commodity Commission	Dept. of Gen. Administration	Dept. Licensing • Occupational Regulatory Boards	Dept. of Labor & Industries	School for the Deaf	
Interagency Commission for Outdoor Recreation	Dept. Revenue	Traffic Safety Comm.	Dept. of Employment Security	Workforce Training & Education Coordinating Board	• Energy Services Council
Pollution Liability Insurance Program	Dept. Personnel Personnel Resources Board		Dept. of Health • Occupational Reg. boards		Office of Minority and Women's Business Enterprises
	Dept. Retirement Systems • Employee Retirement Benefits Board		Dept. of Corrections		
			Dept. of Veterans' Affairs		Commision on African-American Affairs
	Dept. Information Services		Council for Prevention of Child Abuse & Neglect		
	Lottery Commission				Commision on Asian-Pacific American Affairs
	Dept. Financial Institutions		Health Care Authority • Public Employees' Benefits Board		
	Military Dept.				Commision on Hispanic Affairs
	Public Printer		Dept. of Service for the Blind		
	Office of Admin. Hearings				Arts Commission
	Board of Accountancy				Economics, Revenue & Finance Council

80

Executive Branch, Office of the Governor *(continued)*

Agencies with Executive Appointed by a Board

Environment & Natural Resources	General Government	Transportation	Health & Human Services	Education	Community Economics
Fish & Wildlife Commission Dept. of Fish & Wildlife	Personnel Appeals Board	Transportation Commmission Dept. of Transp.	Human Rights Commission	Higher Education Coordinating Board	Convention and Trade Center
Parks & Recreation Commission	Liquor Control Board Public Employment Relations Commission	Board of Pilotage Commissioners	Indeterminate Sentence Review Board	Governing Boards of Four-Year	Housing Finance Commission
Environmental Hearings Office • Pollution Control Hearings Board • Shorelines Hearings Board • Forest Practices Appeals Board • Hydraulic Appeals Board	Board of Tax Appeals Public Disclosure Commission Board for Volunteer Firefighters & Reserve Officers	Marine Employees' Commission Transportation Improvement Board County Road Administration Board	Board of Industrial Insurance Appeals Criminal Justice Training Commission Sentencing Guidelines Commission	Institutions of Higher Education • U. of Washington • Wash. State University • Central Wash. U. • Eastern Wash. U. • Western Wash. U. • The Evergreen State College	
Conservation Commission	Utilities & Transportation Commission		Health Care Facilities Authority		
Columbia River Gorge Commission	Investment Board Gambling Commission		Board of Health & Technical	Board for Community and Technical Colleges Board of Trustees • Community Colleges • Technical Colleges	
Growth Management Hearings Boards • Eastern Washington • Central Puget Sound • Western Washington	Horse Racing Commission Statute Law Committee • Code Reviser Municipal Research Council				
Board of Natural Resources	Economic & Revenue Forecast Council			Joint Center for Higher Education	
	Caseload Forecast Council			Library Commission • State Library	
	Forensic Investigations Council			Higher Education Facilities Authority	
	Citizens' Commission on Salaries for Elected Officials			Wash. State Historical Society	
	State Capital Committee			Eastern Wash. State Historical Society	
	State Finance Committee				

Judicial Branch

Supreme Court Court of Appeals, Supreme Court Clerk, Law Library Superior Courts, Supreme Court Commissioner, Reporter of Decisions	District Courts, Administrator for the Courts, Commission on Judicial Conduct Municipal Courts, Office of Public Defense

Washington's first territorial governor, Isaac Stevens. Courtesy of University of Washington Libraries.

George E. Cole, 1866–1867
Marshall F. Moore, 1867–1869
Alvin Flanders, 1869–1870
Edward S. Salomon, 1870–1872
Elisha P. Ferry, 1872–1880
W.A. Newell, 1880–1884
Watson C. Squire, 1884–1887
Eugene Semple, 1887–1889
Miles C. Moore, 1889–statehood

State Governors.

Elisha P. Ferry (R-Seattle), 1889–1893
John H. McGraw (R-Seattle), 1893–1897
John R. Rogers (D-Puyallup), 1897–1901
Henry McBride (R-Seattle), 1901–1905
Albert E. Mead (R-Bellingham), 1905–1909
Samuel G. Cosgrove (R-Pomeroy), 1909
Marion E. Hay (R-Spokane), 1909–1913
Ernest Lister (D-Tacoma), 1913–1919
Louis F. Hart (R-Tacoma), 1919–1925
Roland H. Hartley (R-Everett), 1925–1933
Clarence D. Martin (D-Cheney), 1933–1941
Arthur B. Langlie (R-Seattle), 1941–1945
    and 1949–1957
Monrad Charles Wallgren (D-Everett),
    1945–1949
Albert D. Rosellini (D-Seattle), 1957–1965
Daniel J. Evans (R-Seattle), 1965–1977

Dixy Lee Ray (D-Fox Island), 1977–1981
John Spellman (R-Seattle), 1981–1985
Booth Gardner (D-Tacoma), 1985–1993
Mike Lowry (D-Seattle), 1993–1997
Gary Locke (D-Seattle), 1997-

Hanford

The Hanford Reservation occupies 560 square miles along the Columbia River, in an area known as the Hanford Reach, outside of Richland. Nuclear facilities at Hanford produced plutonium, the essential fuel of nuclear weapons. Hanford plutonium shortened the conquest of Japan in World War II, fueled the nuclear build-up in the 1950s, and won the Cold War in the 1980s. Yet the radioactive pollution from this effort contaminates the air, water, and soil in the region and over large reaches of the country, and will continue to do so for thousands of years. The facility that helped win the Second World War and the Cold War is today the world's largest environmental cleanup project.

Atomic scientists working feverishly to develop a super-weapon in World War II needed access to abundant electric power and cooling water. Facilities were built secretly at the Hanford Reach on the Columbia River in 1943. The first reactor, Hanford B, operated from 1944 to 1968. It made the fuel for the first atomic explosion, detonated in the desert near Alamogordo, New Mexico, on July 16, 1945. The Hanford B reactor was designated a National Mechanical Engineering Landmark in 1984.

Built in less than a year, as part of a crash program to shorten the Second World War, the Hanford B reactor had a minimum of environmental safeguards. In 1945, the first year of plutonium production, the Hanford B reactor released 500,000 curies of radioactive iodine (Iodine 131) into the environment. For purposes of comparison, the 1979 accident at the Three Mile Island nuclear power plant in Pennsylvania released about 20 curies of radiation. While environmental controls were added to the Hanford B reactor after the Second World War, and environmental controls were incorporated into later facilities built at the reservation, the production of plutonium along the Columbia River still produced huge amounts of radioactive pollution as a by-product.

In the 1960s, the peak years, nine plutonium production reactors produced fuel for the world's largest nuclear arsenal, the missiles housed in silos along the northern tier of the United States, the weapons carried in nuclear submarines that prowled the seas, and the long-range B-52 bombers poised to strike the enemy at a moment's notice. Today, just one reactor operates at Hanford, yet it remains a large, complex federal facility. Its workforce numbers about 11,000, and the annual budget is about $1.6 billion. Activities at the facility include waste management, storing spent nuclear fuel, cleaning up old contamination and restoring the environment, and applying and commercializing nuclear technologies.

Radioactive by-products, when concentrated in the human body, can alter the genetic makeup of cells. Excess radiation in the body is known to trigger certain forms of cancer. Once in the body, radioactive materials continue to affect cells until the radioactive materials decay. The amount of time necessary for radioactive materials to decay to a point where they no longer pose a health hazard varies, but for many radioactive materials it exceeds the lifetimes of humans.

Air pollution. The Hanford Dose Reconstruction Project estimated that 740,000 curies of Iodine 131 were released directly into the atmosphere from Hanford between 1944 and 1972. Radioactive iodine concentrates in the thyroid gland. Other common radiation by-products carried in the air are radioactive strontium and plutonium, which, after uptake into the human body, are concentrated in bone. Young children are especially at risk, because airborne radiation may land on vegetation, which is then taken up by grazing animals, notably cows, and passed on to humans via milk.

Water pollution. Cooling water from the Columbia River passed through the reactors at Hanford, where the water became irradiated. Additional radiation came from breaches of tanks and pipes, and purges of nuclear systems. One expert has estimated that, in the early 1950s, Hanford reactors discharged at least 8,000 curies of radioactive material per day into the Columbia River. People who ate fish and waterfowl at that time, who swam in or boated on the river, who irrigated their fields with river water, or who drank the river water below Hanford (for example, citizens of Pasco) would have been exposed to unhealthful levels of nuclear contamination from contact with the river

Hanford

Hanford is the site of Washington's only nuclear power plant, which began producing electricity in 1984. It is the sole product of the ill-fated public undertaking to build a statewide system of nuclear power plants that became known as WPPSS—pronounced "whoops"—which stands for Washington Public Power Supply System. The agency was formed in 1957 when 17 public and private utilities united to build larger plants and thus produce more power than they could separately. Its early projects—a small hydroelectric plant at Packwood Lake and a steam plant at Hanford—were completed successfully and on schedule, and WPPSS expanded its vision in the early 1970s to include construction of five nuclear power plants, three at Hanford and two near the town of Elma on the Satsop River. Within a decade the projects were stalled in a morass of cost overruns, politics, and bureaucratic bungling. In 1982 WPPSS, having decided to terminate construction on two plants and mothball two more, defaulted on its bond debt. It was the greatest such default in American history. In 1998 WPPSS decided it wanted to change its name to the more benign Energy Northwest. An energy conservation group by the same name declined to share the designation. ✺

(this in addition to the contamination from the fallout in the air).

Flora and fauna. Nuclear contamination becomes concentrated with each step up the food chain. One of the most critical pathways of contamination in humans is the consumption of plants and animals that themselves have become contaminated by having contact with or eating contaminated materials. Plants can have radiation concentrations that are thousands of times higher than the ambient level of contamination in air or water, for example.

The Hanford Nuclear Reservation represents the best and the worst of the nuclear age. The scientists and engineers at Hanford today devote themselves to safe storage of spent nuclear materials, to cleaning up the waste legacy of the past, and to applying nuclear technologies to improve humankind's lot in the future.

High Technology

Technology-based industries, which include such high-profile companies as Boeing and Microsoft, account for a huge share of Washington's economic base. According to a 1998 study by the Technology Alliance, these industries directly employ more than 266,451 people, and indirectly support one-third of the state's jobs (895,368 jobs). These industries pay more (their average labor income per job was $52,201), and sell a larger portion of their products and services out of state (76.5 percent, compared to an economy-wide average of 40 percent), making them important contributors to the gross state product.

The total sales of products and services amount to some $60.6 billion; total wages and income from direct employment are about $14 billion. Moreover, technology-

based industries have not only grown steadily over the last quarter decade, but some major sectors have developed that were minor or nonexistent 25 years ago. These include biotechnology and biomedical manufacturing, and software and computer services.

Types of Technology-Based Companies. Technology-based companies are loosely defined as those involved in research, development, and manufacturing of software and computer applications, chemicals and drugs, medical instruments and supplies, and electronics and electrical instruments and equipment. The major sectors are listed below.

Aerospace. (*See also* Aviation and Aerospace) Aerospace- and aviation-related employers generated almost 300,000 jobs in the Washington economy in 1997, 11.4 percent of total state employment.

Biotechnology. The research, testing, and manufacturing of drugs and medical instruments and supplies make up the biotechnology sector, which grew rapidly during the 1990s. Biotechnology and biomedical companies employ about 11,000 people directly. The sector includes noncommercial research organizations such as the Fred Hutchinson Cancer Rearch Center, the largest in the state and the largest recipient of research funds from the National Cancer Institute.

Software and computer services. Software and computer programming, data processing services, and computer-related service activity such as computer equipment leasing and maintenance and repair comprise this sector of technology-based industries. This sector has the highest labor income level of all technology-based industries, because of stock option benefits offered with employment. This sector is dominated by Microsoft, whose market is located largely outside the state. The software and computer services sector employs more than 40,000 people directly and supported a total of 193,000. It accounts for some 15 percent of the direct technology-based employment.

Computers and electronics. Composed

of computer and office equipment, electrical distribution equipment, electrical industrial apparatus, household audio and visual equipment, electronic components, and miscellaneous electrical equipment and supplies industries, this industry supported some 71,000 jobs in 1997, with 23,000 people directly employed in the industry.

Machinery and motor vehicles. This sector includes manufacturers of engines and turbines, construction and related machinery, industrial machinery, and motor vehicles and equipment. These companies employ some 13,800 people.

Chemicals and petroleum. Petroleum refining and production of industrial inorganic chemicals and agricultural chemicals employ some 4,000 people.

Specialized instruments and devices. These companies manufacture search and navigation equipment and measuring devices. They employ 8,100 workers.

Engineering, commercial research, and consulting services. This industry includes architectural and engineering services, commercial research services, and management consulting and public relations services segments. Each segment directly employees more than 20,000 people in Washington State.

Employment and Occupations. Washington State has a larger share of employment in technology-based industries than the nation as a whole. In 1997, this state had 46 percent more employment in these industries than the national average. This relatively high level of employment is associated with the aerospace sector, software and computer services (35 percent above the national average), and engineering, research, and management consulting services (17 percent above the national average).

Technology-based industries employ a wide range of occupations: engineering, mathematical and natural sciences managers, industrial production managers, engineers, architects, civil engineering technicians and technologists, design technicians and technologists, physical scientists, life scientists, physical and life science technicians and technologists, computer programmers, database administrators, mathematical scientists and related workers, social scientists, and medical and clinical laboratory technologists.

While employment in technology-based industries is concentrated strongly in the Seattle-Everett metropolitan area (due primarily to aerospace employment), there are firms located around the state in all counties but Garfield County. Twelve of 39 Washington counties have at least 1,000 persons employed in technology-based industries, while 25 counties have at least 100 persons employed in these sectors.

Research and Development. In 1995, Washington ranked 11th nationally in dollars spent on research and development, more than $5.2 billion, or 3.6 percent of the gross state product. Research and development activities at federal laboratories in the state, at the University of Washington and Washington State University, in industry, and in nonprofit research organizations are more important in Washington State than in the United States as a whole. The state has an especially strong concentration in funding of nonprofit research organizations. The University of Washington was the largest recipient of federal research funds of any public university in the United States in 1995.

Software. The remarkable growth that has occurred in software and computer services companies in the state is due in

Looking Back

June 17, 1897

Arrival in Puget Sound of the steamship *City of Portland*, loaded with a ton of gold, set off the Klondike gold rush. Washington's gold was earned mostly by outfitting the gold seekers.

part to changes in the industry as a whole over the past two decades. Formerly, software and computer services employment was primarily data processing for mainframe computers. With the advent of minicomputers and personal computers, employment in software and computer programming expanded while data processing jobs declined. Now a $3.5 billion industry, software is the fastest-growing industry in the state, according to the Washington Software Alliance. There are more than 1,600 computer software companies in the state, including such industry leaders as Microsoft, Adobe, and Attachmate. They produce PC business applications, minicomputer vertical applications, communications and utility software, games, operating systems, mainframe and supercomputer software, and engineering software. Washington is one of the top five states for employment in prepackaged software development, growing 137 percent in employment and nearly 500 percent in wages paid since 1988. Eastern King County has the highest concentration of software companies per capita in the country, and Spokane has a growing pool of 30-plus software companies employing some 1,800 people.

Hispanic Americans

The state's Hispanic population grew dramatically during World War II, due to the need for agricultural workers. As farmworkers went off to serve in the military, their departure created a desperate need for workers to plant and harvest Washington's crops. Farmers tried to fill the labor gap using students and other part-time workers, but they were not enough to do the job. So in 1942, the United States and Mexico agreed to allow Mexican laborers, called *braceros,* to enter the United States annually as temporary wartime workers, with the U.S. government providing transportation and housing for the workers. From 1943 to 1948, the *braceros* worked the fields throughout the state. The *bracero* program declined after the war, but the labor shortage did not, so farmers began recruiting migrant labor from other major agricultural regions of the United States. Eastern Washington eventually became a regular part of migrant workers' regular seasonal work route in the west. By the 1950s many migrants, primarily of Mexican descent, were regular seasonal residents, and some became year-round residents.

Today, the Hispanic population in Washington numbers 343,225, the largest single ethnic minority in the state and the fastest growing. Between 1990 and 1998, state population estimates indicate that, while the state's total population grew by more than 15 percent, the Hispanic origin population increased from 214,570 to approximately 343,000, a 60 percent growth in population.

Despite the increasing numbers of Hispanics who elect to live in the state's urban areas, the majority of the state's Hispanic community still live in the agricultural regions on the east side of the state. The Yakima County-Tri-Cities area has the largest Hispanic population—just more than 28 percent, or nearly one in three people, are Hispanic. Their cultural

---

Speaking the Language

The BASIC computer language was developed in 1964 for use on large mainframe computers. Software pioneers Paul Allen and Bill Gates adapted BASIC for use on one of the first commercially popular personal computers, the ALTAIR, in 1974-75. This success became the launchpad for the wildly successful and innovative Microsoft Corporation. The second stage of Microsoft's success centered on the development of a more sophisticated operating system for personal computers, known as DOS. While the DOS language to control computer operating systems had been developed initially by others, Gates and Allen secured a breakthrough when computer giant IBM chose the DOS operating system, to which Microsoft held licensing rights, for use in IBM's entry into the personal computer market in 1980. The rest, as they say, is history. ✳

contributions have added a decidedly vibrant Latin flavor to the region. There are Spanish-language radio stations, and Mexican films, restaurants, groceries, and festivals.

Organizations and Events of Interest.

Washington Commission on Hispanic Affairs, P.O. Box 40924, Olympia, WA 98504-0924; (360) 753-3159. The commission maintains a database of more than 1,000 Hispanic organizations, public service agencies, media, and contacts.

Cinco de Mayo, May, Pasco, (509) 545-0738.

Cinco de Mayo, May, Sunnyside, (800) 457-8089.

History

12,000-10,000 years before present. Clovis people, Marmes Man are among earliest known inhabitants.

9,600-9,300 years before present. Kennewick Man roams eastern Washington. The bones of this early state resident will be found in 1996.

1592 Juan de Fuca is rumored to have discovered the entrance to an inland sea in what is now Washington's northwest corner.

1774 Spaniard Juan Perez sails along the coast and names Santa Rosalia Mountain, later renamed Mount Olympus. Spaniards Bruno Heceta and Juan de la Bodega y Quadra send an expedition to near present-day Point Grenville and

claim the land for Spain. Mariners from Bodega's ship are killed by a band of Quinaults.

1778 British explorer Capt. James Cook charts the Washington coast en route to Vancouver Island.

1787 English explorer Charles Barkley explores and names the Strait of Juan de Fuca. English Capt. George Vancouver surveys the coast and inland waters. He names many Washington landmarks.

1792 American Capt. Robert Gray explores the mouth of the Columbia River and names it after his ship.

1805 Meriwether Lewis and William Clark reach the Pacific Ocean near Ilwaco.

1807 Trading post is built on the Columbia River.

1812 John Jacob Astor's Pacific Fur Company establishes forts at Okanogan and Spokane.

1818 The United States and England agree to jointly occupy the Oregon Territory (the agreement will last for nearly 30 years). The English North West Company establishes Fort Walla Walla.

1824 Hudson's Bay Company agent Dr. John McLoughlin moves the company from Astoria to Fort Vancouver to reinforce British control north of the Columbia River.

1829 Epidemics begin to ravage Indian tribes, which have no resistance to diseases brought by whites. The Chinook Indians along the Columbia River will be virtually wiped out within five years.

1836 Marcus and Narcissa Whitman establish a mission near Walla Walla. Migration of settlers over the Oregon Trail begins.

1841 Charles Wilkes brings his global scientific expedition to the region.

1843 Settlers of the Oregon Territory form a provisional government, which starts a border dispute between England and the United States. "Fifty-four forty or fight!" becomes a rallying cry.

1844 The first organized party of settlers reaches Puget Sound country. Led by Kentucky-born Michael T. Simmons, the party had intended to settle in Oregon but, learning that one of their party, a black man, George Washington Bush, would be prohibited from settling there, they continue north. Clark County, named after Capt. William Clark, is established.

1845 Lewis County is established and named after Capt. Meriwether Lewis.

1846 The United States and England agree to establish their international boundary at the 49th parallel. The Whitmans and 12 others are massacred by Cayuse Indians. The incident marks the beginning of the Northwest Indian wars. Peaceful coexistence will not be established for another 30 years.

1848 Oregon is officially designated a territory. Settlers begin heading north into present-day Washington to establish homes. The first Territorial Legislature convenes in Oregon City.

1850 Congress passes the Donation Land Law. It puts additional restriction on land claims: 320 acres were awarded to any white or half-white male who was an American citizen and had arrived prior to 1851; another 320 acres could be claimed by his wife.

1851 The Denny party lands on Alki Point, in what is now Seattle. Pacific County is established.

1852 Jefferson, Pierce, and King Counties are established.

1853 Washington is granted separate territorial status from Oregon. Isaac Stevens is appointed territorial governor and supervisor of Indian affairs. Sawmills are built on Puget Sound at Port Ludlow, Port Blakely, and Port Madison. Andrew J. Pope and William C. Talbot organize the Puget Mill Company. Island County is established.

1854 Governor Stevens begins negotiating treaties with Native American tribes. Chehalis, Wahkiakum, Whatcom, Skamania, Clallam, and Mason Counties are established.

1855 Conflicts break out between Indians and settlers at White River. The Northwest Indian wars will continue until 1859.

1857 Kitsap County is created from portions of King and Jefferson Counties. The discovery of gold in Idaho and British Columbia brings miners through Washington Territory.

1858 Spokane County is established.

1859 Congress ratifies treaties removing all tribes to reservations. Strained relations between England and the United States in the Northwest nearly result in war when an American shoots an Englishman's pig during a dispute on San Juan Island; the incident is called "The Pig War." Steamboat passenger service is extended along the Columbia River as far as The Dalles. Whitman Seminary is founded in Walla Walla. Klickitat County is established.

1861 Territorial University opens in Seattle; it will become the University of Washington. Snohomish County is established.

1862 City of Walla Walla is incorporated.

1863 Idaho Territory is formed, establishing Washington's eastern boundary. The first transcontinental telegraph links Washington Territory with the rest of the country. Stevens County is established.

1865 Yakima County is created.

1866 New hostilities erupt between Indians and settlers in Klickitat County.

1869 Settlers move across the Snake River into the Palouse.

1870 Washington's population approaches 24,000. Railroads have arrived, and the campaign for statehood begins.

1871 Whitman County is created. A sawmill is built near Spokane Falls.

1872 The Colville Indian Reservation is established.

1873 Three hundred railroad workers who haven't been paid go on strike. San Juan County is established.

1875 Columbia County is established

1877 The Army Corps of Engineers begins removing navigation obstacles from the middle and upper Columbia River.

1878 Timber and Stone Act authorizes sale to residents of up to 160 acres of timber or mineral land at $2.50 per acre. Intended to eliminate corruption, it instead will eventually allow mill companies to acquire sizeable holdings.

1880 Population is 75,116. The territory begins exporting wheat from the Palouse. Statehood campaign intensifies.

1881 Garfield County is created and named for President James A. Garfield.

1882 Congress passes anti-Chinese legislation, resulting in hardship and discrimination for Chinese living in Washington.

1883 Northern Pacific completes the rail link between the East Coast and Puget Sound, bringing an influx of new settlers. Adams, Douglas, Franklin,

Chief Seattle, one of Washington's most revered Indian leaders. Courtesy of University of Washington Libraries.

Asotin, Kittitas, and Lincoln Counties are established.

1885 Anti-Chinese riots break out in Seattle, Tacoma, and other towns. The Chinese are blamed for economic downturn.

1886 Longshoremen strike the Tacoma Mill Company for five days. They win a raise of 10 cents per hour and their own union.

1888 Congress passes an enabling act permitting Washington to prepare a state constitution, elect officials, and submit a petition for statehood. Pullman is incorporated; Okanogan County is established.

1889 Washington becomes the 42nd state on November 11. Its first governor is Elisha P. Ferry, formerly a territorial governor. The new state's population is 239,544. Fires sweep through Seattle, Spokane, and other cities.

1890 Population is 357,232. Washington State University is founded at Pullman. Henry Hewitt Jr., a partner in the St. Paul & Tacoma Lumber Company, organizes a syndicate to found Everett at the mouth of the Snohomish River.

1891 Coal miners go on strike. Conflict erupts when mine owners recruit

African-Americans, who have been shut out of the unions, as strikebreakers.

1893 Great Northern Railway reaches Seattle.

1896 Gold is discovered in Alaska in 1896, and Seattle becomes the gateway to the Klondike. From 1897 to 1908, Seattle merchants sell gear and food to prospectors. Along Columbia River, fights break out between fishermen from Oregon and fish trap operators in Washington.

1899 Mount Rainier National Park is established. Chelan and Ferry Counties are formed.

1900 Frederick Weyerhaeuser buys 900,000 acres of forest, and founds the enormous company that bears his name. Mammoth sawmills are built around Puget Sound and in the lower Columbia region.

1902 More than 110 forest fires from Eugene to Bellingham burn an estimated 700,000 acres and turn the sky black for hundreds of miles.

1903 Child labor laws are adopted. Fire burns 20 acres of the Aberdeen business district and surrounding homes.

1905 Washington leads the states in lumber production, a position it will retain until the late 1930s. The U.S.

Department of the Interior approves irrigation for the Yakima Valley. Benton County is created.

1907 In Seattle, 19-year-old Jim Casey founds American Messenger Company. It will become United Parcel Service of America, Inc. (UPS), the largest package-delivery company in the world.

1909 The Alaska-Yukon-Pacific Exposition is held in Seattle. Grant County is established. In Spokane, the Industrial Workers of the World (IWW)—nicknamed the "Wobblies"—begin a national labor protest that will become known as the Spokane Free Speech Fight.

1910 Washington grants women the right to vote. It is the fifth state to do so.

1911 The Legislature approves one of the first workmen's compensation systems in the nation, a triumph for progressivism. Pend Oreille County is established.

1912 Lumber workers—members of the IWW—strike in Grays Harbor County.

1913 The State Board of Park Commissioners is created.

1916 Washingtonians vote to go dry, predating national Prohibition by three years. The Boeing Company flies its first

A group of Wobblies—Industrial Workers of the World—poses in front of their local headquarters.
Courtesy of University of Washington Libraries.

aircraft (a seaplane) in Seattle. Long-shoremen strike all along the West Coast, including Washington. A campaign to revive the flagging IWW in the lumber camps results in violence as Wobblies are attacked by vigilantes while at a meeting in Everett. Five Wobblies and two vigilantes are killed, and 51 people are wounded in what will become known as the Everett Massacre.

1917 The nation enters World War I, and Camp Lewis opens south of Tacoma. Strikes by lumber workers halt 75 percent of the lumber output of Washington, Oregon, and Idaho.

1918 Tacoma and Seattle build shipyards for war ship construction.

1919 An encounter between Wobblies and the American Legion in Centralia ends in violence. Several men are killed, one is lynched, and across the state almost 1,000 Wobblies are jailed. The Seattle General Strike lasts five days. It is peaceful, despite propaganda from employers' associations saying that the strike is affiliated with the Russian Revolution and encouraging violence against dissenters and radicals. Miners at Wilkeson shut down mines, demanding a 14 percent wage raise and better working conditions.

1921 One of the region's largest banks fails. There are so many automobiles on the roads, the state establishes a motorcycle highway patrol.

1922 Labor strikes spread to typographical and railroad workers.

1928 Permanent capitol building is completed in Olympia. There are two dozen pulp and paper plants operating in the state.

1930 Public Utility Districts are authorized to buy and sell water power. During the next decade, voters all over the state will approve local PUDs.

1933 The New Deal Civilian Conservation Corps (CCC) begins clearing trails, fighting forest fires, and planting trees throughout the state. The Legislature appropriates state park funds for an emergency relief program similar to the CCC. Construction of Grand Coulee Dam begins.

1934 Strikes in the next several years will affect shipping industry, lumber, and newspaper publishing.

1938 Bonneville Dam is completed.

1940 An aluminum plant is built at Vancouver, taking advantage of Washington's new cheap water power.

1941 Japanese nationals and Japanese Americans are interned in eastern Washington and Idaho. Grand Coulee Dam is finished, beginning the reclamation of thousands of acres of arid land. Henry Jackson is elected to the House of Representatives.

1943 Hanford begins converting uranium to plutonium. Warren Magnuson wins his first term to the U.S. Senate.

1948 Aerospace workers go on strike against Boeing. The state's Joint Legislative Fact-Finding Committee on un-American Activities holds hearings on Communist activity among University of Washington faculty.

1950 A disastrous flood kills three people in Garfield County.

1958 Boeing's 707 jet airliner begins commercial flights.

1962 Seattle hosts the Century 21 world's fair, which brings the Space Needle to Seattle—along with millions of visitors.

1968 Two national wilderness areas are established in the North Cascades—Glacier Peak Wilderness and Pasayten Wilderness. A 10-year effort is begun to clean up Lake Washington, and the state passes air and water pollution measures.

Looking Back

November 5, 1916

Seven people were killed and 50 wounded in a clash between vigilantes and Wobblies in what became known in labor history as the "Everett Massacre."

1970-71 The first 747 wide-body "jumbo jet" enters service. Its development pushes Boeing to the edge of bankruptcy. The company lays off 60 percent of its workforce. A major economic downturn prompts the famous billboard "Will the last person leaving Seattle please turn out the lights?" The trans-Alaska pipeline project is launched—and, as in the Klondike gold rush, people, equipment, and supplies pass through the Puget Sound area. Trade with Pacific Rim countries increases dramatically.

1974 Spokane holds a world's fair— "Progress without Pollution." Native Americans file a lawsuit in federal court, claiming violation of their 1855 treaty fishing rights. In Tacoma, Judge George Boldt rules in favor of the Indians and guarantees them half of the fish caught off reservations. The ruling will be upheld by the Supreme Court.

1975 William H. Gates III and Paul Allen found Microsoft Corporation.

1976 Dixy Lee Ray, a Democrat and former chairwoman of the U.S. Atomic Energy Commission, becomes the first woman governor of the state.

1979 Seattle Sonics win the NBA championship.

1980 Mount St. Helens erupts in a cataclysmic display that kills 57 people and causes billions of dollars of damage.

After nearly four decades in the Senate, senior Senator Warren G. Magnuson, a Democrat, is voted out of office in the Reagan Republican landslide.

1983 Senator Henry M. Jackson dies while still in office.

1990 The northern spotted owl is listed as a threatened species. Efforts to protect this and other species lead to logging restrictions and set off economic and political controversy between environmentalists and the timber industry.

1995 Thomas S. Foley, powerful Democratic Congressman from Spokane who has been Speaker of the House of Representatives since 1989, loses his Congressional seat to the Republican Revolution.

1997 Gary Locke becomes the first Asian-American governor in the continental United States.

Horse Racing

Horse racing runs from June through November at Emerald Downs in Auburn, from August through November at Playfair Race Course in Spokane, and in April and September-October at Sun Downs in Kennewick. Horse races are also held for a few days in association with regional fairs, including the following:

Columbia County Fairgrounds (May)
Southeast Washington Fairgrounds (May, August, September)

Grays Harbor Fairgrounds (July)
Benton-Franklin County Fairgrounds
Waitsburg Fairgrounds

In 1996, there were 2,826 registered race horse owners in the state, 464 registered trainers, and 136 jockeys. A total of $93,374,000 was wagered on races at Emerald Downs and $49,645,000 was wagered at Yakima Meadows. These figures include both on-site wagers ($80,234,000) and off-site wagers from parimutuel satellite locations ($62,784,000). **Daily Racing Form**, 12559 26th Ave. NE, Seattle, WA 98125; (206) 365-9300.

Hospitals

Most Washingtonians, according to a 1996 report by the Washington Department of Health (*The Health of Washington State*), consider themselves to be in pretty good health. While that same report found room for improvement, overall health-care accessibility and availability is high in most parts of the state. Not surprisingly, there are more health-care providers per capita, more facilities, and quicker response times for emergencies in urban areas than in rural ones.

There are 103 hospitals in the state, according to the Washington State Hospital Association; 52 are private and 51 are public. Of the private facilities, 6 are for-profit businesses and 46 are nonprofit institutions. Of the public facilities, 6 are federal and 45 are state or local. They include 94 general hospitals, 3 children's hospitals, 4 psychiatric hospitals, and 2 rehabilitation and chemical dependency centers. Slightly more than half of all hospitals are urban (51 percent), but the urban hospitals are much, much larger (250 beds on average for urban hospitals versus about 60 beds on average per rural hospital).

Hospitals and Healthcare Facilities.

Adams County. Othello Community Hospital, Othello; East Adams Rural Hospital, Ritzville.

Asotin County. Tri-State Memorial Hospital, Clarkston.

Benton County. Kennewick General Hospital, Kennewick; Prosser Memorial Hospital, Prosser; Carondelet Behavioral Health Center and Kadlec Medical Center, Richland.

Chelan County. Lake Chelan Community Hospital, Chelan; Cascade Medical Center, Leavenworth; Central Washington Hospital, Wenatchee.

Clallam County. Forks Community Hospital, Forks; Olympic Memorial Hospital, Port Angeles.

Clark County. Southwest Washington Medical Center, Vancouver.

Columbia County. Dayton General Hospital, Dayton.

Cowlitz County. PeaceHealth, St. John Medical Center, Longview.

Ferry County. Ferry County Memorial Hospital, Republic.

Franklin County. Lourdes Health Center, Pasco.

Garfield County. Garfield County Memorial Hospital, Pomeroy.

Grant County. Columbia Basin Hospital, Ephrata; Coulee Community Hospital, Grand Coulee; Samaritan Healthcare, Moses Lake; Quincy Valley Hospital, Quincy.

Grays Harbor County. Grays Harbor Community Hospital, Aberdeen; Mark Reed Hospital, McCleary.

Island County. Whidbey General Hospital, Coupeville.

Jefferson County. Jefferson General Hospital, Port Townsend.

King County. Auburn Regional Medical Center, Auburn; Overlake Hospital Medical Center, Bellevue; Highline Community Hospital, Burien; St. Francis Hospital, Federal Way; BHC Fairfax Hospital, Evergreen Community Health Care, Kirkland; Group Health Eastside Hospital, Redmond; Valley Medical Center, Renton; Children's Hospital and Regional Medical Center, (Seattle) Group Health Central Hospital, Harborview Medical Center Regional Hospital, Northwest Hospital,

Providence Seattle Medical Center, Swedish Health Services/Ballard and First Hill, University of Washington Medical Center, Vencor Seattle Hospital, Virginia Mason Medical Center, Seattle.

Kitsap County. Harrison Memorial Hospital, Bremerton.

Kittitas County. Kittitas Valley Community Hospital, Ellensburg; Enumclaw Community Hospital, Enumclaw.

Klickitat County. Klickitat Valley Hospital, Goldendale; Skyline Hospital, White Salmon.

Lewis County. Providence Centralia Hospital, Centralia; Morton General Hospital, Morton.

Lincoln County. Lincoln Hospital, Davenport; Odessa Memorial Hospital, Odessa.

Mason County. Mason General Hospital, Shelton.

Okanogan County. Okanogan-Douglas County Hospital, Brewster; Mid-Valley Hospital, Omak; North Valley Hospital, Tonasket.

Pacific County. Ocean Beach Hospital, Ilwaco; Willapa Harbor Hospital, South Bend.

Pend Oreille County. Newport Community Hospital, Newport.

Pierce County. Good Samaritan Hospital, Puyallup; Allenmore Hospital, Madigan Army Medical Center, Mary Bridge Children's Hospital, Puget Sound Hospital, St. Clare Hospital, St. Joseph Medical Center, Tacoma General Hospital, Tacoma.

Skagit County. Island Hospital, Anacortes; Affiliated Health Services, Mount Vernon.

Snohomish County. North Snohomish County Health System, Cascade Valley Hospital, Arlington; Stevens Healthcare, Edmonds; Providence General Medical Center, Everett; Providence Pacific Clinic, Valley General Hospital, Monroe.

Spokane County. Deer Park Health Center and Hospital, Deer Park; Deaconess Medical Center, Empire Health Services, Holy Family Hospital, 92nd Medical Group (Fairchild AFB), Sacred Heart Medical Center, Shriners Hospitals for Children,

---

Innovation

The scene is common today, at least on TV. The heart attack victim is revived by applying electric shock paddles to the chest. Dr. Karl William Edmark, a cardiovascular surgeon from Seattle, developed this invention from 1959 to 1962. Edmark's company subsequently developed a lightweight, portable defibrillator, which is now even being used on commercial airplanes. ✷

Valley Hospital and Medical Center, Spokane.

Stevens County. St. Joseph's Hospital, Chewelah; Mount Carmel Hospital, Colville.

Thurston County. Capital Medical Center, Providence St. Peter Hospital, Olympia.

Walla Walla County. St. Mary Medical Center, Walla Walla General Hospital, Walla Walla.

Whatcom County. St. Joseph Hospital, Bellingham.

Whitman County. Whitman Hospital and Medical Center, Colfax; Pullman Memorial Hospital, Pullman.

Yakima County. Sunnyside Community Hospital, Sunnyside; Providence Toppenish Hospital, Toppenish; Providence Yakima Medical Center, Yakima Valley Memorial Hospital, Yakima.

Hot Springs
Natural hot springs are often associated with active volcanic regions. The Cascades, the Olympics, and the entire western portion of the state are particularly well endowed. The United States Geological Survey documents 18 hot springs or pools in Washington. A few of these may be trivial or hard to enjoy—located in volcanic craters, for example—but others are inviting and easily accessible. Some are within easy reach of the large urban areas that ring Puget Sound. Several have been developed as resorts.

Below is a selection of the most accessible or worthwhile hot spring or pool destinations. Seek them out. Wash away the stress of civilization. Remember to use these resources responsibly, so that they remain open for all to use.

Baker Hot Springs. Natural sandy pool, water temperature 109° F, 7 gallons per minute. Clothing optional. Located in Mount Baker-Snoqualmie National Forest, north of Concrete. On Highway 20, 5 miles east of Hamilton, turn north on Grandy Creek Rd. toward Baker Lake. Beyond FS Rd. 1144 and after 3.2 miles, reach the parking area. Trail begins on the left, at the north end of the parking area; it's a 600-yard walk. Access to the trail may require a trail permit. Check with the local ranger station before proceeding, or the forest headquarters, (800) 627-0062.

Kennedy Hot Springs. Soaking pool fed by 96° F spring, 30 gallons per minute. Clothing optional. Located in Mount Baker-Snoqualmie National Forest, in the Glacier Peak Wilderness, near the Pacific Crest Trail. From Darrington, take FS Rd. 20 southeast about 8 miles to its intersection with FS Rd. 23. Drive to the end of FS Rd. 23, which is the trailhead for Trail 643 up White Chuck Canyon. Hike in 5 miles to the spring. Access to the trail may require a trail permit. Check with the local ranger station before proceeding, or the forest headquarters, (800) 627-0062.

Olympic Hot Springs. Crude but lovely rock pools on a forested hillside, 100° F–120° F water, up to 135 gallons per minute, depending on the pool and the time of year. Clothing somewhat optional. Located in Olympic National Park. From Port Angeles, go 10 miles west on U.S. Highway 101, turn south, and follow signs to Elwha Valley. Continue south to the end of the road and park. Walk the well-defined trail up Boulder Creek about 2 miles into the hot springs area. This destination is only for the truly determined, since part of the road washed out, extending the hike to the hot springs to 5 or 6 miles.

Scenic Hot Springs. Wooden soaking box, 122° F water from several springs, 30 gallons per minute; water flows through a hose into the 4-by-6-foot soaking box. Located on a steep hillside above the Tye River. From Skykomish, go 10 miles on U.S. Highway 2 east to the town of Scenic. Cross the bridge over the railroad, turn right (south), and follow the powerline road. Park and walk east under the powerline. Between the fourth and fifth tower, an unmarked path diverges on the right up the hill to the springs.

St. Martins on the Wind Hot Springs. Three sandy pools, 107° F water. Clothing optional. Located on the property of Carson Hot Springs Resort (see below), which requests a small donation for access, within sight of a waterfall on the bank of a small river. From the Highway 14 bridge over the Wind River, go 0.75 mile east, then turn north on Berge Rd. Drive 0.75 mile to a hard left turn onto Indian Cabin Rd. Go 0.5 mile to a flat parking area under a powerline. Take a 20-minute rock-hop up the river. Follow signs and instructions.

Developed Hot Spring Resorts (fees charged).

Carson Hot Mineral Springs Resort, P.O. Box 370, Carson, WA 98610; (509) 427-8292. Men's and women's bathhouses with 126° F water piped in. The bathhouses are attended, and sweat wraps and other services are available. From intersection of Highway 14 and Bridge of the Gods over the Columbia River, go east on Highway 14 and watch for signs.

Doe Bay Village Resort, P.O. Box 437, Olga, WA 98279; (360) 376-2291. Located in an idyllic spot at the mouth of a cove on

Orcas Island with a laid-back, casual atmosphere. Mineral water is pumped at 105° F into two outdoor pools. From the Orcas Island ferry in the San Juan Islands, go north on Horseshoe Highway through Eastsound to the resort at the eastern end of the island.

Goldmyer Hotsprings, c/o 202 N. 85th St., Suite 106, Seattle, WA 98103; (206) 789-5631. Located in an old mineshaft with 120° F water. Facilities are maintained by a nonprofit volunteer organization that requests prior reservations and a daily donation. The springs are a 0.5-mile hike from the road. Directions provided after reservation is made.

Notaras Lodge, 242 Main St. E., Soap Lake, WA 98851; (509) 246-0462. Motel with in-room hot tubs, also a public bathhouse; 95° F–100° F water is from Soap Lake. Massage available. Located north of Ephrata on Highway 17 in the town of Soap Lake.

Sol Duc Hot Springs Resort, P.O. Box 2169, Port Angeles, WA 98362; (206) 327-3583. Modern, full-service family resort located in Olympic National Park. Swimming pool is 128°, cooled to 101°F–105° F, 50 gallons per minute. From U.S. Highway 101, 2 miles west of Fairholm, take Soleduc River Rd. 12 miles south to the resort.

Hunting
Washington offers exceptional hunting for big game, small game, and birds, including waterfowl. As in other states, hunters need to be trained in safe hunting practices, obtain a state license, and obey season and bag limits. **Washington Department of Fish and Wildlife,** 1111 Washington St. SE, Olympia, WA 98501; (360) 902-2200. Complete information can be found on-line at http://www.wa.gov/wdfw/huntcorn.htm.

Big game. Elk and deer are the main targets, but Washington hunters also go after bear, mountain goat, and mountain sheep. Elk and deer are hunted throughout the state. In 1996, 84,000 licensed elk hunters bagged nearly 7,000 elk out of an estimated population of 54,000. About 181,000 deer hunters took home nearly 40,000 deer out of a total population of about 390,000. Bear, goat, and sheep are hunted in the rugged high country. Fewer than 2,500 bear are killed each year. Fewer than 1,000 mountain goats are taken each year. Because there are fewer than 600 mountain sheep in the state, competition for the few licenses that are awarded is very keen.

Small game. Small game includes upland birds, waterfowl, rabbits, and a few other species (squirrels are protected in Washington State because of their important role in spreading seeds from cones). In 1996, hunters took about 134,000 grouse, 134,000 pheasants, 84,000 quail, 54,000 partridge, and at least 18,000 rabbits.

Waterfowl. Washington straddles the Pacific Flyway. Waterfowl migrants and residents, all of which are hunted, include at least 17 species of ducks. Some of the best table fare are canvasback, pintail, mallard, teal, wood duck, redhead, ringneck, ruddy, and black duck. The poorest eating ducks are generally thought to be goldeneye, coot, and bufflehead.

Hydroplanes
Anyone who has spent a summer in Seattle or the Tri-Cities can distinguish the distinctive rumble of the thunderboats from miles away. Hydroplanes, those massive muscle boats that leave giant roostertails in their nearly 200-miles-per-hour wakes and are known to sometimes go airborne—but not on purpose—have been a sporting fixture in the state since the early 1950s. The first race of these motorboat giants in Washington was held on Lake Washington in 1951, and Seattle sportswriters loved them enough to establish the Hydroplane Hall of Fame in 1960 (in 1982 it became part of the Hydroplane and Raceboat Museum).

The thunderboats race every year in Seattle in August. While the city has hosted at least one world championship and several major national events, the big summer races have consistently been part of the city's big summer do, Seafair, even though the name of the prize has changed over time. In eastern Washington, the Tri-Cities holds the other summer hydro blowout, on the Columbia River. It started as the Atomic Cup and is now the Budweiser Columbia Cup. Both the Seattle and

A hydroplane racing on the Columbia River near the Tri-Cities. Courtesy of Tri-City Water Follies.

Tri-Cities events are Unlimited Hydroplane Racing Association (UHRA) sanctioned events, which means the results are included in the point scoring for the World Championships. www.hydrdos.org.

Motorboat race fans can also satisfy their need to watch speed at several regattas featuring smaller, but no less exciting, race boats sponsored by the American Power Boat Association (APBA). These races,

Lap Records: Seattle, Lake Washington (2 miles)

Year: Boat, Driver	Qualfii-cation Lap	Compe-tition Lap	6-mile Heat	10-mile Heat	28-mile Race
1993: *Miss Budweiser*, Chip Hanauer	162.451				
1995: *Miss Budweiser*, Chip Hanauer	162.543				
1993: *Kellogg's Frosted Flakes*, Mike Hanson		155.207			
1993: *Winston Eagle*, Mark Tate			150.890		
1991: *Winston Eagle*, Mark Tate				141.776	
1993: *Kellogg's Frosted Flakes*, Mike Hanson					140.011

Lap Records: Tri-Cities, Columbia River (2.5 miles)

Year: Boat, Driver	Qualifi-cation Lap	Compe-tition Lap	7.5-mile Heat	12.5-mile Heat	35-mile Race
1994: *Miss Budweiser*, Chip Hanauer	168.486				
1995: *Smokin' Joe's*, Mark Tate	169.055				
1994: *Miss Budweiser*, Chip Hanauer	158.590				
1996: *Smokin' Joe's*, Mark Tate		160.910			
1994: *Miss Budweiser*, Chip Hanauer			156.957		
1994: *Miss Budweiser*, Chip Hanauer				148.130	
1995: *Smokin' Joe's*, Mark Tate				149.980	
1994: *Miss Budweiser*, Chip Hanauer					152.157
Source: Unlimited Hydroplane Racing Association					

which feature several classes of motorboats, are held throughout the state, including Lake Chelan in Chelan, Lawrence Lake in Yelm, and Puget Sound at Poulsbo. Check the APBA racing schedule on-line at http://www.apba-boatracing.com/schedule.htm.

Straightaway Records: Lake Washington

Year: Boat, Driver		Mph
1950: *Slo-Mo-Shun IV*, Stanley Sayres		160.323
1952: *Slo-Mo-Shun IV*, Stanley Sayres		178.497
1957: *Hawaii Kai III*, Jack Regas		187.627
1960: *Miss Thriftway*, Bill Muncey		192.001

Hydro Winners Over the Years

APBA Gold Cup.
1958: Seattle, *Hawaii Kai III*, Jack Regas
1959: Seattle, *Maverick*, Bill Stead
1962: Seattle, *Miss Century 21*, Bill Muncey
1965: Seattle, *Miss Bardahl*, Ron Musson
1967: Seattle, *Miss Bardahl*, Billy Schumacher
1973: Tri-Cities, *Miss Budweiser*, Dean Chenoweth
1974: Seattle/Sand Point, *Pay 'n Pak*, George Henley
1975: Tri-Cities, *Pay 'n Pak*, George Henley
1981: Seattle, *Miss Budweiser*, Dean Chenoweth
1984: Tri-Cities, *Atlas Van Lines*, Chip Hanauer
1985: Seattle, *Miller American*, Chip Hanauer

Apple Cup, Lake Chelan.
1958: *Miss Bardahl*, Norm Evans
1959: *Miss Pay 'n Save*, Chuck Hickling
1960: *Miss Thriftway*, Bill Muncey

Atomic Cup, Tri-Cities.
1966: *Miss Budweiser*, Bill Brow
1967: *Miss Bardahl*, Billy Schumacher
1968: *Miss Eagle Electric*, Warner Gardner
1969: *Myr's Special*, Dean Chenoweth
1970: *Pay 'n Pak's Lil' Buzzard*, Tommy Fults
1971: *Miss Madison*, Jim McCormick

1972: *Atlas Van Lines*, Bill Muncey
1977: *Atlas Van Lines*, Bill Muncey

Budweiser Columbia Cup, Tri-Cities.
1997: *PICO American Dream*, N. Mark

Budweiser Cup, Seattle.
1987: *Miss Budweiser*, Jim Kropfeld

Columbia Cup, Tri-Cities
1976: *Atlas Van Lines*, Bill Muncey
1978: *Miss Budweiser*, Ron Snyder
1979: *Atlas Van Lines*, Bill Muncey
1980: *Atlas Van Lines*, Bill Muncey
1981: *The Squire Shop*, Chip Hanauer
1982: *The Squire Shop*, Tom D'Eath
1983: *American Speedy Printing*, Jack Schafer Jr.
1985: *Miller American*, Chip Hanauer
1986: *Miller American*, Chip Hanauer
1987: *Miss Budweiser*, Jim Kropfeld
1988: *Miss Budweiser*, Tom D'Eath
1989: *Cooper's Express*, Mitch Evans
1990: *Miss Budweiser*, Tom D'Eath
1991: *Winston Eagle*, Mark Tate
1992: *Miss Budweiser*, Chip Hanauer
1993: *Miss Budweiser*, Chip Hanauer
1994: *Miss Budweiser*, Chip Hanauer
1995: *Smokin' Joe's*, Mark Tate
1996: *PICO American Dream*, Dave Villwock

Emerald Cup, Seattle.
1982: *Atlas Van Lines*, Chip Hanauer
1983: *Miss Budweiser*, Jim Kropfeld
1986: *Miller American*, Chip Hanauer

Freedom Cup, Seattle.
1984: *Miss Budweiser*, Jim Kropfeld

Lake Washington, Seattle.
1951: *Slo-mo-shun V*, Lou Fageol
1952: *Slo-mo-shun IV*, Stan Dollar
1953: *Slo-mo-shun IV*, Joe Taggart and Lou Fageol
1954: *Slo-mo-shun V*, Lou Fageol
1955: *Gale V*, Lee Schoenith
1957: *Miss Thriftway*, Bill Muncey

Rainier Cup, Seattle.
1988: *Miss Budweiser*, Tom D'Eath
1989: *Miss Circus Circus*, Chip Hanauer

1990: *Miss Circus Circus*, Chip Hanauer
1991: *Miss Budweiser*, Scott Pierce
1992: *The Tide*, George Woods Jr.

Seafair Trophy, Seattle.
1956: *Shanty I*, Russ Schleeh
1960: *Miss Thriftway*, Bill Muncey
1963: *Tahoe Miss*, Chuck Thompson
1964: *Miss Bardahl*, Ron Musson
1966: *My Gypsy*, Jim Ranger
1969: *Miss Budweiser*, Bill Sterett
1970: *Miss Budweiser*, Dean Chenoweth
1971: *Pride of Pay 'n Pak*, Billy Schumacher
1972: *Atlas Van Lines*, Bill Muncey
1975: *Pay 'n Pak*, George Henley
1976: *Miss Budweiser*, Dean Chenoweth
1977: *Atlas Van Lines*, Bill Muncey
1978: *Atlas Van Lines*, Bill Muncey
1979: *Atlas Van Lines*, Bill Muncey

Texaco Cup, Seattle.
1993: *Miss Budweiser*, Chip Hanauer
1994: *American Dream*, Dave Villwock
1995: *Miss Budweiser*, Chip Hanauer
1996: *PICO American Dream*, Dave Villwock
1997: *PICO American Dream*, N. Mark Evans

UIM Worlds Championship.
1968: Seattle, *Miss U.S.*, Bill Muncey
1973: Seattle, *Pay'n Pak*, Mickey Remund
1974: Tri-Cities, *Pay'n Pak*, George Henley
1980: Seattle, *Atlas Van Lines*, Bill Muncey

World Championship, Seafair, Seattle.
1961: *Miss Bardahl*, Ron Musson

Organizations and Events of Interest.
Hydroplane and Raceboat Museum, 1605 S. 93rd St., Bldg. E-D, Seattle, WA 98108; (206) 764-9453. The only public museum dedicated to powerboat racing, with vintage hydroplanes and an extensive collection of memorabilia.

Budweiser Columbia Cup for Unlimited Hydroplanes, July, Columbia River, Columbia Park, Kennewick, off Highway 240. 3-5 laps of a 2.5-mile course.

General Motors Cup at Seafair, August, Lake Washington, Seattle, 3–5 laps of a 2-mile course.

International Border
The state shares an international border with Canada, at the 49th parallel from Idaho to the Strait of Georgia on land, and in the channels that skirt west around the San Juan Islands, around the east end of Vancouver Island, and through the middle of the Strait of Juan de Fuca. The official ports of entry along the U.S.-Canada border in Washington are Port Angeles, Friday Harbor, Point Roberts, Blaine, Lynden, Sumas, Nighthawk, Oroville, Ferry, Danville, Laurier, Frontier, Boundary, and Metaline Falls.

When the 49th parallel was established as the international border, it created an interesting geographic anomaly—it disconnected the 5-mile tip of the Point Roberts peninsula from the rest of Washington. Point Roberts, which dips south from British Columbia below the 49th parallel, is accessible only by water or by driving through Canada.

Islands
Washington's large marine coastal region and the Columbia River are settings for hundreds of islands. Some are heavily developed; some are rural and bucolic. Some have regular access by ferry;

San Juan Islands. Photo by John Marshall.

some are accessible only by boat, and some are the protected province of seabirds and wildlife. The major island groupings are found in the state's northwestern corner, where the San Juan Archipelago and the inland waters of Puget Sound and its approaches harbor concentrations of large and small islands and island groups. Below is only a sampling of some of the best known.

San Juan Islands. The San Juan Islands are Washington's largest and best-known island group. In 1979, the Washington State Board on Geographic Names distinguished the San Juan Islands as a distinctive group within the larger San Juan Archipelago, designating the San Juan Islands as those "west of Rosario Strait." The largest and most populated islands of the San Juan group are Orcas, San Juan, Lopez, and Shaw. These islands have regular ferry service from the mainland, and San Juan Island has air service as well. Other smaller islands include Stuart, Spieden, Waldron, Henry, Patos, Sucia, Matia, Clark, Blakeley, Decatur, and Center Islands, and numerous other tiny islands and rocks. The San Juan Islands comprise San Juan County.

The group was visited and named in 1792 by Spanish navigators, and settled by English and American fur trappers and traders. Both Great Britain and the United States laid claim to the islands, but they became part of the United States in 1872 following the settlement of a boundary dispute with Great Britain. The scenic San Juans are a popular vacation destination, and getting there during the summer months can mean lengthy waits in the ferry line. The car queue can be avoided if you happen to be a healthy outdoor type who is willing to tour the islands by bicycle, or if you own or rent a boat.

Strait of Juan de Fuca and North of Puget Sound. The Strait of Juan de Fuca and the waters between Rosario Strait and the mainland have a number of unique islands. Protection Island, a rocky island in the Strait of Juan de Fuca 2 miles north of the entrance to Port Discovery Bay, was named by Capt. George Vancouver because it sheltered Port Discovery Bay and could be fortified for military protection. Today, its name is more indicative of its environmental status as a haven for seabirds. East of Rosario Strait and north of Whidbey Island are several good-sized islands that are inhabited year-round. Lummi and Guemes Islands are populated and have regular ferry service. Fidalgo Island, connected to the mainland by bridge, is home to one of northwestern Washington's larger towns, Anacortes, which is the terminus of the ferry that runs through the San Juan Islands. Fir Island, formed by the Skagit River delta, is a rural agricultural area. Cypress and Sinclair Islands in Rosario Strait are largely unpopulated and accessible only by private boat.

Island County. Whidbey and Camano Islands together comprise Island County. Whidbey Island was determined to be the longest offshore island in the continental United States in 1992, when Congress declared Long Island, New York, to be a peninsula, not an island. Whidbey is also the largest island in Puget Sound; it is 45 miles long, 10 miles across at its widest part, and 235 square miles in area, and has 200 miles of shorelines, eight lakes, and four state parks. Deception Pass, at the island's north end, is notorious for its 8-knot tidal current. Directly east of Whidbey Island across Saratoga Passage is smaller Camano Island, which is separated from the mainland by Davis Slough. Camano and Whidbey are both largely rural and residential. Whidbey is home to the Whidbey Island Naval Air Station.

Puget Sound. The northernmost islands of Puget Sound are

Looking Back

April 29, 1965

The Puget Sound region was shaken by a 6.5-magnitude earthquake, the strongest one since the 7.1-magnitude earthquake of April 13, 1949.

Marrowstone and Indian Islands, just south of the entrance to Puget Sound and just west of the mainland of the Olympic Peninsula. Farther south are the exurban islands of Bainbridge, Vashon, and Maury, all situated west of Seattle and north of Tacoma, and accessible by regular and frequent ferry service. Bainbridge was once home to small farms, but is now an upscale community, many of whose inhabitants commute to work in Seattle. The island is 11 miles long and about 4 miles wide. Another urban and heavily populated island is Mercer Island, located in Lake Washington east of Seattle. In the southernmost reaches of Puget Sound lies another cluster of islands, most of which are inhabited. They include Hartstene, Fox, Squaxin, Anderson, and McNeil. The latter is best known as the site of a state penitentiary (formerly a federal penitentiary). Finally, a favorite island for visitors is Blake Island, site of a state marine park and a popular local Indian salmon bake.

Coastal Islands. The Pacific coast is dotted with many barren rocks, but only a couple islands of notable size. Destruction Island, some 4 to 5 miles off the northwest coast, is 49 acres of rocky ground that is home to a large population of horn-billed auklets. Spanish explorer Bruno Heceta named the island Isla de Dolores, or Island of Sorrows, after he lost six crewmembers to an Indian attack at Point Grenville. Tatoosh Island, just north of Cape Flattery, is home to a lighthouse built in 1857 to guide ships entering the Strait of Juan de Fuca. Long Island, a wildlife refuge in Willapa Bay, while not an offshore island, is one of the larger islands along the Pacific coast.

Columbia River. Numerous small islands can be found in the Columbia River, especially its middle and lower reaches. Largest is Puget Island, in the lower Columbia, which is accessible by ferry. Bachelor, Reed, Lady, Skamania, and Miller Islands are some of the other larger islands.

Judicial System

The multilevel judicial system in Washington State includes local courts, state courts, federal courts, and tribal courts.

Local Courts

Local courts, or courts of limited jurisdiction, are located in counties and municipalities. They include district courts, municipal courts, and justice of the peace courts. District court judges are elected to four-year terms on nonpartisan ballots. District and municipal courts hear civil cases (with limited liability, less than $35,000), criminal cases within certain liability limits, and violations of municipal ordinances. The majority of cases heard by these courts are traffic violations.

Filings for District Courts, Municipal Courts, and Justice of the Peace Courts (1996)

	State/County Matters	Municipal Matters
Traffic infractions	401,356	377,439
Non-traffic infractions	7,611	21,250
DWI and related	23,252	14,205
Other traffic misdemeanors	72,166	88,538
Non-traffic misdemeanors	68,394	95,770
Felony preliminary	8,297	NA
Civil	108,183	0
Domestic violence protection	12,896	574
Small claims	28,494	NA
Total	730,649	597,776

Source: Washington State Judiciary

State Courts

Superior Courts. The state is divided into 30 judicial districts, each district having one or more superior court judge assigned to it, a total of 164 superior court judges in all. Superior court judges are elected to four-year terms. These are the courts of general jurisdiction. They hear civil matters, property and tax cases, probate, and domestic matters. Their jurisdictions also extend over all criminal cases beyond those tried by the courts of limited jurisdiction, and they also hear appeals from those courts. A total of 3,983 trials (2,212 criminal and 1,771 juvenile) were conducted in the Superior Court in 1996.

Filings for Superior Court (1996)

	Criminal Cases
Homicide	330
Sex crimes	1,753
Assault	3,220
Robbery/burglary, etc.	10,076
Controlled substances	10,215
Other felonies	5,441
Lower court appeals	1,032
Total criminal cases	32,067
Total criminal trials	2,212
	Civil cases
Torts	12,776
Commercial/contract	15,124
Property rights	18,296
Domestic relations/paternity	52,630
Other civil cases	25,290
Appeals	768
Total civil cases	124,884
	Other cases
Probate	14,548
Guardianship	2,543
Mental illness	7,453
Juvenile cases	47,114
Juvenile trials	1,771
Total other cases	71,658

Appeals Court. The Appeals Court reviews lower court decisions. It is organized into three divisions, and each division is divided into three districts: Division 1 has nine judges, Division 2 has six judges, and Division 3 has five judges. The division headquarters are located in Seattle, Tacoma, and Spokane, respectively. Appeals Court judges are elected to six-year terms.

Filings for Appeals Court (1996)

Criminal appeals	1,753
Civil appeals	1,375
Personal restraint petitions	548
Other petitions	507
Total filings	4,183

Supreme Court. The Supreme Court is the head of the judicial branch of state government and the court of last resort for the state. Nine judges serve on the Supreme Court. They are elected to six-year terms on nonpartisan ballots.

Filings for State Supreme Court (1996)

Criminal appeals	13
Civil appeals	97
Criminal petitions	396
Civil petitions	297
Personal restraint petitions	38
Other petitions	391
Disciplinary proceedings	13
Total cases filed	1,245

Source: Washington State Judiciary

Federal Courts

The federal court system in Washington State includes the U.S. District Court, the U.S. Court of Appeals, and U.S. Bankruptcy Court. The U.S. District Court and U.S. Bankruptcy Court each operate in two regions, the Western Washington District and the Eastern Washington District. The U.S. Court of Appeals represents the Ninth Circuit. The federal courts have varying numbers of judges.

U.S. District Courts. Most federal cases are initially tried and decided in the U.S. district courts, the federal courts of general trial jurisdiction. A district may itself be divided into divisions and may

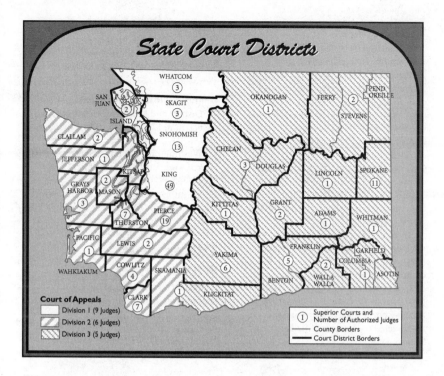

State Court Districts

Court of Appeals
- Division 1 (9 Judges)
- Division 2 (6 Judges)
- Division 3 (5 Judges)

① Superior Courts and Number of Authorized Judges
— County Borders
— Court District Borders

have several places where the court hears cases. District court judges are appointed for life by the President of the United States, with the advice and consent of the Senate. Congress authorizes judgeships for each district based in large part on the caseload. Magistrate judges also handle a variety of matters including civil consent cases, misdemeanor trials, preliminary hearings, and pretrial motions.

U.S. District Court, Western Washington District, six district judges, three senior judges, six magistrate judges.

U.S. District Court, Eastern Washington District, five district judges, two magistrate judges.

Each district court has a bankruptcy unit that hears and decides petitions of individuals and businesses seeking relief from bankruptcy under the federal bankruptcy code; there are four categories of such cases. Bankruptcy judges are appointed by the U.S. Court of Appeals for a term of 14 years.

U.S. Bankruptcy Court, Western Washington District, five bankruptcy judges.

U.S. Bankruptcy Court, Eastern Washington District, two bankruptcy judges.

U.S. Court of Appeals, Ninth Circuit.
The intermediate appellate courts in the federal judicial system are the courts of appeals. They are often referred to as circuit courts. They review matters from the district courts, the U.S. Tax Court, and certain federal administrative agencies. Judges who sit on the courts of appeals are appointed for life by the President of the United States, with the advice and consent of the Senate. Each court of appeals consists of six or more judges, depending on the caseload.

Washington is part of the Ninth Circuit, headquartered in San Francisco, California; it includes Alaska, Arizona, California, Hawaii, Idaho, Montana, Nevada, Oregon, Washington, Guam, and the Northern Mariana Islands. The U.S. Court of Appeals in Washington has one circuit judge and three senior judges.

Tribal Courts

Tribal courts have jurisdiction on Indian reservations. Each tribe has its own particular set of laws, and the tribal courts handle a full array of civil and criminal cases. Non-Indians are often parties to cases, either as plaintiffs or as defendants. Criminal jurisdiction, however, is limited to prosecution of Indians officially enrolled in federally recognized tribes or Canadian bands only. There are tribal courts on the Colville, Kalispel, Lummi, Makah, Puyallup, Quileute, Quinault, Spokane, Squaxin Island, and Yakama Reservations.

In addition to individual tribal courts, the Northwest Intertribal Court System (NICS) provides three full-time and various contract circuit-riding judges, two prosecutors, code-writers, and appellate court personnel to 10 western Washington tribes—the Chehalis, Hoh, Muckleshoot, Nooksack, Port Gamble S'Klallam, Sauk-Suiattle, Shoalwater Bay, Skokomish, Swinomish, and Tulalip—and two affilliate tribes, the Jamestown S'Klallam and the Stillaquamish tribes. **Northwest Intertribal Court System (NICS)**, 144 Railroad Ave., Suite 302, Edmonds, WA 98020; (425) 774-5808.

Organizations of Interest.

District and Municipal Court Judges Association, 1206 S. Quince St., Olympia, WA 98504; (360) 753-3365.

Washington State Bar Association, 2101 Fourth Ave., fourth floor, Seattle, WA 98121-2330; (206) 727-8200.

Washington State Trial Lawyers Association, 1511 State Ave., Olympia, WA 98506; (360) 786-9100.

Lakes and Reservoirs

There are more than 8,000 lakes and ponds across Washington, many of them man-made reservoirs created by dams. The larger share of lakes and reservoirs are found in eastern Washington. The region has 4,051 lakes that cover a total area of 432,662 acres—

William O. Douglas

Washington's most distinguished jurist was Supreme Court Justice William Orville Douglas. Douglas joined Franklin Roosevelt's administration in 1937 as chairman of the Securities and Exchange Commission, which was established to police the stock markets following the crash of 1929 and the onset of the Great Depression. A great favorite and poker-playing pal of the President, Douglas was nominated by Roosevelt to the U.S. Supreme Court in 1939, where he served until his retirement in 1975. First as a scholar at Yale University and later in government, Douglas was a leading legal proponent of the government's power to regulate the economy and business. On the court, he became a champion for human rights and freedom of expression. In public and private life he was an ardent conservationist, and crusaded tirelessly for conservation causes, including efforts to set public land aside as parks and wilderness. Conservative critics disliked his open views on obscenity and civil disobedience, his concern for the protection of criminals, and his penchant for marrying younger women.

Born in 1898 in Minnesota, Douglas grew up in Yakima. As a teenager, he would tramp through the nearby Cascade Mountains; these experiences inculcated a love of wilderness in him, which influenced him greatly. Even late in life, when on the Supreme Court, Justice Douglas would return each summer to his country house on Goose Prairie, a roadless tract in the Cascades, near Yakima. During those many summers, court officials from the 9th (Northwest) would have to traipse on foot into Goose Prairie whenever an urgent court action required the Justice's attention.

Douglas graduated from Whitman College in Walla Walla (1920), and worked his way through Columbia Law School. He died in 1980. ✳

more than double the area of lakes in western Washington, which has some 3,887 lakes and reservoirs with a total surface area of 176,920 acres.

The state's lakes range from vast reservoirs to the tiny, jewel-like alpine lakes that fill the tarns and cirques of the high Cascades and Olympics.

Many of the state's largest lakes are reservoirs; only 10 of the 30 largest lakes are natural. Lake Chelan is the largest natural lake in the state; it is 55 miles long, varies in width from 1 to 2 miles, and is the third-deepest lake in the United States, at 1,486 feet. The largest reservoir is Lake Franklin D. Roosevelt, which stretches for 151 miles behind Grand Coulee Dam. Perhaps the most unusual lake is Soap Lake, northeast of Ephrata. When the wind blows, it whips up a foam on this alkaline lake that washes against the shore. Its waters, which are purported to contain more than 20 chemicals, are believed by some people to have useful medicinal properties. Sun Lakes State Park in northwest Grant County includes a chain of seven lakes—Blue, Park, Falls, Deep, Perch, Rainbow, and Reflection Lakes—that are remnants of an ancient riverbed of the Columbia.

Largest Lakes

Lake Franklin D. Roosevelt, behind Grand Coulee Dam	79,000 acres
Umatilla Lake, behind John Day Dam	52,000 acres in Washington
Lake Wallula, behind McNary Dam	38,800 acres in Washington
Lake Chelan	33,104 acres
Potholes Reservoir	28,200 acres
Banks Lake	24,900 acres
Lake Washington	22,138 acres
Ross Lake, behind Ross Dam	11,678 acres
Moses Lake	6,815 acres
Osoyoos Lake	5,729 acres in Washington
Lake Whatcom	5,127 acres
Swift Reservoir	4,588 acres
Merwin Lake	4,089 acres
Lake Cushman	4,003 acres
Yale Reservoir	3,801 acres

Laws The state constitution, amended or new laws enacted by the Legislature, and laws passed by the citizens as initiatives and referendums form the basis of state law. Washington's first state constitution was written at a constitutional convention held in Walla Walla in 1878. However, while the voters approved it, the territory's attempts to join the union failed to pass every Congress for the next 10 years as Republicans and Democrats fought to deny statehood to any territory that they thought would tip the balance of power in the other camp's favor. Finally, in 1888 an omnibus statehood bill was approved that allowed Washington, along with North Dakota, South Dakota, and Montana, to proceed through the steps leading to statehood. In 1889, Washington convened its second constitutional convention and adopted a constitution. Two controversial amendments failed to make it into the 1889 document—women's suffrage and prohibition. Since then, a number of important amendments have been added 1to the constitution.

Amendments to the constitution must be approved by two-thirds of both the State House of Representatives and the State Senate, and by a majority of the electorate. Proposed amendments may also be drawn up by a constitutional convention and ratified by voters. The constitution does not provide for direct popular amendment. Indirect popular amendment can occur through an arduous process resulting in a constitutional convention. This process begins with the Legislature. Both houses must approve a call for a convention, which must then be approved by the voters. If approved, delegates must be elected, the convention must meet, and its product must be submitted to the voters. Twice, attempts to convene a constitutional convention were rebuffed by the voters, in 1918 and in the late 1960s.

Bills submitted to the Legislature must receive a simple majority vote of both the State House of Representatives and State

Senate to become law. If the governor vetoes a bill submitted for his or her signature, the Legislature may override the veto.

In 1912, provisions were added that authorized initiatives, referendums, and recalls as a means of direct citizen decision making. The initiative is the direct power of the voters to enact new laws or to change existing laws. The referendum gives the voters an opportunity to approve or reject proposed legislation or laws enacted by the Legislature. To propose an initiative or referendum, voters must follow procedures outlined by the Public Disclosure Commission and the Secretary of State. They must circulate and file petitions containing a number of signatures of registered voters equal to or in excess of 8 percent of the votes cast for the office of governor in the last gubernatorial election.

Washington laws are codified in the Revised Code of Washington (RCW). Directives on how laws are to be administered are found in the Washington Administrative Code (WAC). The RCW, the WAC, and the complete text of the state constitution can be found on the Internet at http://access.wa.gov/government/awconst.a sp.; the text of the RCW can be found at http://wsl.leg.wa.gov/wsladm/ rcw.htm; the text of the WAC can be found at http://www.mrsc.org/wac.htm. The text of the state constitution's Bill of Rights can be found in the appendix.

Law Enforcement

(*SEE ALSO* PRISONS) Law enforcement agencies in Washington cover a range of jurisdictions, which include federal, state, county, city, tribal, special district (such as ports and parks), and institutional (such as universities). There are 9,292 full-time, sworn-in local, county, and state police officers in the state (or 17 police officers per 10,000 population): 5,430 are local officers, 906 are state police, and 2,553 are county or district sheriff's officers. All commissioned law enforcement officers in the state (except the State Patrol) are trained at the Washington State Criminal Justice Training Commission's Basic Law Enforcement Training Academy near Seattle. Advanced training and regional courses are conducted throughout the state.

The federal government enforces federal law through a number of agencies in the state: the Federal Bureau of Investigation (Bellingham, Everett, Olympia, Seattle, Silverdale, Spokane, and Tacoma), the Border Patrol (Bellingham, Colville, Lynden, and Oroville), the Bureau of Alcohol, Tobacco and Firearms (Seattle, Spokane, and Yakima), the Drug Enforcement Administration (Blaine, Richland, Seattle, Spokane, Vancouver, and Yakima), the Secret Service (Seattle and Spokane), the U.S. Marshal's Office (Seattle, Spokane, Tacoma, and Yakima), and U.S. Customs Service (Aberdeen-Hoquim, Anacortes, Bellingham, Blaine, Everett, Friday Harbor, Longview-Kelso, Lynden, Metaline Falls, Moses Lake, Northport, Olympia, Oroville, Port Angeles, Port Townsend, Seattle, Spokane, Sumas, Tacoma, and Yakima).

Organizations of Interest.
Criminal Justice Training Center, 19010 First Ave. S., Seattle, WA 98148; (206) 439-3740.

Washington Association of Sheriffs and Police Chiefs, 2629 12th Court SW, Olympia 98502; (360) 586-3221.

Washington State Law Enforcement Association, 509 E. 12th, P.O. Box 7369, Olympia, WA 98507; (360) 943-7566.

Washington State Patrol, General Administration Bldg., P.O. Box 42600, Olympia, WA 98504-2600; (360) 753-6540.

Legislature

The Washington State Legislature consists of the Senate (49 members) and House of Representatives (98 members). The Legislature convenes every year; sessions begin the second Monday in January and last up to 60 consecutive days in even-numbered years, and up to 105 consecutive days in odd-numbered years. Special legislative sessions are convened as needed for a specific purpose and for not more than 30 consecutive days. The Legislature must approve special sessions by a two-thirds vote. The session that convenes in January 2000 will be the 58th Washington Legislature.

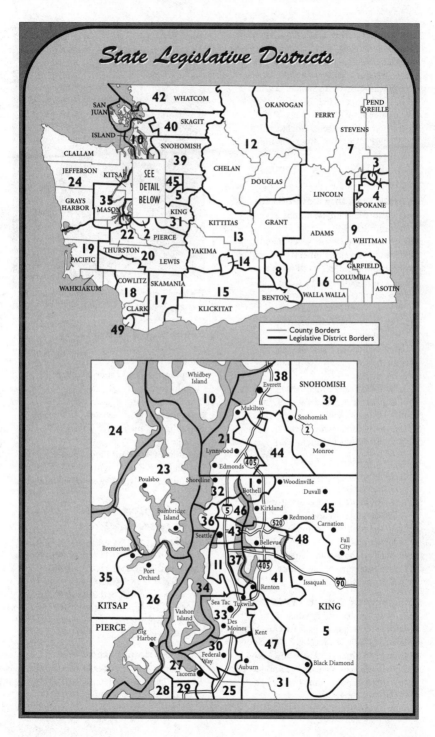

State Legislative Districts

County Borders
Legislative District Borders

Washington State Senate

Senators are elected to four-year terms; half are elected at the general election held in November of each even-numbered year.

Washington State Senate, Legislative Bldg., P.O. Box 40482, Olympia, WA 98504-0482; (360) 786-7550. http://www.leg.wa.senate/default.htm.

Senate Office Buildings, Olympia: Legislative Building (LEG), Irving R. Newhouse Building (IRN), John A. Cherberg Building (JAC).

Senate Standing Committees.

Agriculture and Environment (seven members)
Commerce and Labor (seven members)
Education (seven members)
Energy and Utilities (seven members)
Financial Institutions, Insurance, and Housing (seven members)
Government Operations (seven members)
Health and Long-Term Care (seven members)
Higher Education (nine members)
Human Services and Corrections (seven members)
Law and Justice (11 members)
Natural Resources and Parks (11 members)
Rules (11 members)
Transportation (15 members)
Ways and Means (21 members)

Senate Officers (1999).

President of the Senate, Lieutenant Governor Brad Owen
President Pro Tempore, Senator R. Lorraine Wojahn
Vice President Pro Tempore, Senator Albert Bauer
Secretary of the Senate, Tony Cook
Deputy Secretary of the Senate, Brad Hendrickson

Democratic Caucus (1999).

Majority Leader, Sid Snyder
Majority Caucus Chair, Harriet A. Spanel
Majority Floor Leader, Betti L. Sheldon
Majority Whip, Rosa Franklin
Majority Caucus Vice Chair, Ken Jacobsen
Majority Assistant Floor Leader, Calvin Goings
Majority Assistant Whip, Tracey Eide

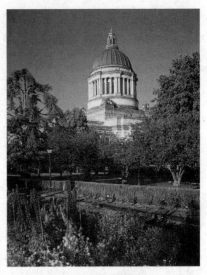

The State Capitol building in Olympia. From *Portrait of Washington* by John Marshall.

Republican Caucus (1999).

Republican Leader, Dan McDonald
Caucus Chair, Patricia S. Hale
Republican Floor Leader, Stephen L. Johnson
Republican Whip, Alex A. Deccio
Republican Deputy Leader, Dino Rossi
Republican Caucus Vice Chair, Joseph Zarelli
Republican Assistant Floor Leader, Bill Finkbeiner
Republican Assistant Whip, Jim Honeyford

Washington State House of Representatives

Representatives serve for two-years.

Washington State House of Representatives, Legislative Bldg., P.O. Box 40600, Olympia, WA 98504-0600; (360) 786-7750. http://www.leg.wa.gov/house/default.htm

House of Representatives Office Buildings, Olympia: John L. O'Brien Bldg. (JLOB), Legislative Bldg. (LEG).

Standing Committees.

Agriculture and Ecology (11 members)
Appropriations (31 members)
Capital Budget (11 members)

(Continued on page 112)

Washington State Senate Roster (1999-2000)

District	Senator (Political Party)	Address*	Phone
1	Rosemary McAuliffe (D)	402-A JAC	(360) 786-7600
2	Marilyn Rasmussen (D)	409 LEG	(360) 786-7602
3	Lisa Brown (D)	338 JAC	(360) 786-7604
4	Bob McCaslin (R)	112 IRN	(360) 786-7606
5	Dino Rossi (R)	109-A IRN	(360) 786-7608
6	James West (R)	204 IRN	(360) 786-7610
7	Bob Morton (R)	115-D IRN	(360) 786-7612
8	Patricia Hale (R)	303 LEG	(360) 786-7614
9	Larry Sheahan (R)	109-B IRN	(360) 786-7620
10	Mary Margaret Haugen (D)	435 JAC	(360) 786-7618
11	Margarita Prentice (D)	419 JAC	(360) 786-7616
12	George Sellar (R)	401-C LEG	(360) 786-7622
13	Harold Hochstatter (R)	115-B IRN	(360) 786-7624
14	Alex Deccio (R)	407 LEG	(360) 786-7626
15	Jim Honeyford (R)	106-A IRN	(360) 786-7684
16	Valoria Loveland (D)	316 JAC	(360) 786-7630
17	Don Benton (R)	109-B IRN	(360) 786-7632
18	Joseph Zarelli (R)	203 IRN	(360) 786-7634
19	Sid Snyder (D)	311 LEG	(360) 786-7636
20	Dan Swecker (R)	103 IRN	(360) 786-7638
21	Paul Shin (D)	412-B LEG	(360) 786-7640
22	Karen Fraser (D)	417 JAC	(360) 786-7642
23	Betti Sheldon (D)	410-A LEG	(360) 786-7644
24	Jim Hargrove (D)	412-A LEG	(360) 786-7646
25	Calvin Goings (D)	410 JAC	(360) 786-7648
26	Bob Oke (R)	110 IRN	(360) 786-7650
27	R. Lorraine Wojahn (D)	309 LEG	(360) 786-7652
28	Shirley Winsley (R)	205 IRN	(360) 786-7654
29	Rosa Franklin (D)	410 LEG	(360) 786-7656
30	Tracey Eide (D)	406 JAC	(360) 786-7658
31	Pam Roach (R)	202 IRN	(360) 786-7660
32	Darlene Fairley (D)	425 JAC	(360) 786-7662
33	Julia Patterson (D)	422 JAC	(360) 786-7664
34	Michael Heavey (D)	403 LEG	(360) 786-7667
35	Tim Sheldon (D)	408 LEG	(360) 786-7668
36	Jeanne Kohl-Welles (D)	432 JAC	(360) 786-7670
37	Adam Kline (D)	431 JAC	(360) 786-7688
38	Jerilita (Jeri) Costa (D)	405 JAC	(360) 786-7674
39	Val Stevens (R)	105 IRN	(360) 786-7676
40	Harriet Spanel (D)	312 LEG	(360) 786-7678
41	Jim Horn (R)	107 IRN	(360) 786-7680
42	Georgia Gardner (D)	424 JAC	(360) 786-7682
43	Pat Thibaudeau (D)	414 JAC	(360) 786-7628
44	Jeanine Long (R)	102 IRN	(360) 786-7686
45	Bill Finkbeiner (R)	201 IRN	(360) 786-7672
46	Ken Jacobsen (D)	427 JAC	(360) 786-7690
47	Stephen Johnson (R)	401-B LEG	(360) 786-7692
48	Dan McDonald (R)	303 LEG	(360) 786-7694
49	Al Bauer (D)	406 LEG	(360) 786-7696

*LEG = Legislative Building, IRN = Irving R. Newhouse Building, JAC = John A. Cherberg Building

Source: Washington State Senate

Washington State House Roster (1999)

District	Representative (Political Party)	Address*	Phone
1	Rosemary McAuliffe (D)	402-A JAC	(360) 786-7600
2	Marilyn Rasmussen (D)	409 LEG	(360) 786-7602
1	Al O'Brien (D)	JLOB 324	(360) 786-7928
1	Mike Sherstad (R)	JLOB 424	(360) 786-7900
2	Roger Bush (R)	JLOB 415	(360) 786-7824
2	Scott Smith (R)	JLOB 413	(360) 786-7912
3	Jeff Gombosky (D)	JLOB 319	(360) 786-7946
3	Alex Wood (D)	JLOB 318	(360) 786-7888
4	Larry Crouse (R)	JLOB 331	(360) 786-7820
4	Mark Sterk (R)	JLOB 419	(360) 786-7984
5	Philip Dyer (R)	JLOB 337	(360) 786-7852
5	Brian Thomas (R)	JLOB 203	(360) 786-7876
6	Brad Benson (R)	JLOB 437	(360) 786-7922
6	Duane Sommers (R)	JLOB 332	(360) 786-7962
7	Cathy McMorris (R)	JLOB 435	(360) 786-7988
7	Bob Sump (R)	JLOB 405	(360) 786-7908
8	Jerome Delvin (R)	JLOB 416	(360) 786-7986
8	Shirley Hankins (R)	LEG 401	(360) 786-7882
9	Mark Schoesler (R)	LEG 402	(360) 786-7844
9	Larry Sheahan (R)	JLOB 333	(360) 786-7942
10	Barry Sehlin (R)	JLOB 205	(360) 786-7914
10	David Anderson (D)	JLOB 338	(360) 786-7884
11	Eileen Cody (D)	JLOB 304	(360) 786-7978
11	Velma Veloria (D)	JLOB 303	(360) 786-7862
12	Clyde Ballard (R)	LEG 3FL	(360) 786-7999
12	Linda Evans Parlette (R)	JLOB 440	(360) 786-7832
13	Gary Chandler (R)	JLOB 407	(360) 786-7932
13	Joyce Mulliken (R)	JLOB 436	(360) 786-7808
14	Jim Clements (R)	JLOB 433	(360) 786-7856
14	Mary Skinner (R)	JLOB 434	(360) 786-7810
15	Jim Honeyford (R)	JLOB 404	(360) 786-7960
15	Barbara Lisk (R)	LEG 3FL	(360) 786-7874
16	Bill Grant (D)	LEG 412	(360) 786-7828
16	Dave Mastin (R)	LEG 404	(360) 786-7836
17	Marc Boldt (R)	JLOB 403	(360) 786-7994
17	Jim Dunn (R)	JLOB 402	(360) 786-7976
18	Thomas Mielke (R)	JLOB 418	(360) 786-7850
18	John Pennington (R)	LEG 409	(360) 786-7812
19	Mark Doumit (D)	JLOB 309	(360) 786-7870
19	Brian Hatfield (D)	JLOB 317	(360) 786-7806
20	Gary Alexander (R)	JLOB 427	(360) 786-7990
20	Richard DeBolt (R)	JLOB 330	(360) 786-7896
21	Mike Cooper (D)	JLOB 241	(360) 786-7950
21	Renee Radcliff (R)	JLOB 439	(360) 786-7972
22	Sandra Singery Romero (D)	LEG 415	(360) 786-7940
22	Cathy Wolfe (D)	JLOB 320	(360) 786-7992
23	Paul Zellinsky Sr. (R)	JLOB 423	(360) 786-7934
24	Jim Buck (R)	JLOB 406	(360) 786-7916
24	Lynn Kessler (D)	LEG 412	(360) 786-7904
25	Jim Kastama (D)	JLOB 315	(360) 786-7968

*JLOB = John L. O'Brien Building, LEG = Legislative Building. Source: Washington State House

Washington State House Roster (1999) *(continued)*

District	Representative (Political Party)	Address*	Phone
25	Joyce McDonald (R)	JLOB 417	(360) 786-7948
26	Tom Huff (R)	JLOB 204	(360) 786-7802
26	Patricia Lantz (D)	JLOB 340	(360) 786-7964
27	Ruth Fisher (D)	JLOB 314	(360) 786-7930
27	Debbie Regala (D)	JLOB 302	(360) 786-7974
28	Michael Carrell (R)	JLOB 422	(360) 786-7958
28	Gigi Talcott (R)	JLOB 426	(360) 786-7890
29	Steven Conway (D)	JLOB 306	(360) 786-7906
29	Brian Sullivan (D)	JLOB 341	(360) 786-7996
30	Tim Hickel (R)	JLOB 420	(360) 786-7898
30	Maryann Mitchell (R)	JLOB 421	(360) 786-7830
31	Eric Robertson (R)	LEG 407	(360) 786-7846
31	Les Thomas (R)	JLOB 401	(360) 786-7866
32	Patty Butler (D)	JLOB 308	(360) 786-7880
32	Grace Cole (D)	JLOB 307	(360) 786-7910
33	Karen Keiser (D)	JLOB 321	(360) 786-7868
33	Jim McCune (R)	JLOB 335	(360) 786-7834
34	Dow Constantine (D)	JLOB 240	(360) 786-7952
34	Erik Poulsen (D)	JLOB 243	(360) 786-7938
35	Bill Eickmeyer (D)	JLOB 322	(360) 786-7902
35	Peggy Johnson (R)	JLOB 334	(360) 786-7966
36	Mary Lou Dickerson (D)	JLOB 305	(360) 786-7860
36	Helen Sommers (D)	JLOB 301	(360) 786-7814
37	Dawn Mason (D)	JLOB 339	(360) 786-7944
37	Kip Tokuda (D)	JLOB 323	(360) 786-7838
38	Jeri Costa (D)	JLOB 242	(360) 786-7864
38	Pat Scott (D)	LEG 414	(360) 786-7840
39	Hans Dunshee (D)	JLOB 336	(360) 786-7804
39	John Koster (R)	JLOB 414	(360) 786-7816
40	Jeff Morris (D)	JLOB 326	(360) 786-7970
40	David Quall (D)	JLOB 239	(360) 786-7800
41	Ida Ballasiotes (R)	JLOB 431	(360) 786-7926
41	Mike Wensman (R)	JLOB 412	(360) 786-7894
42	Georgia Gardner (D)	JLOB 325	(360) 786-7980
42	Kelli Linville (D)	JLOB 327	(360) 786-7854
43	Frank Chopp (D)	LEG 415	(360) 786-7920
43	Edward Murray (D)	LEG 414	(360) 786-7826
43	Karen Schmidt (R)	JLOB 328	(360) 786-7842
44	Dave Schmidt (R)	LEG 404	(360) 786-7982
44	Bill Thompson (R)	JLOB 438	(360) 786-7892
45	Bill Backlund (R)	JLOB 425	(360) 786-7822
45	Kathy Lambert (R)	JLOB 428	(360) 786-7878
46	Marlin Appelwick (D)	LEG 3FL	(360) 786-7886
46	Phyllis Kenney (D)	JLOB 316	(360) 786-7818
47	Jack Cairnes (R)	JLOB 430	(360) 786-7858
47	Suzette Cooke (R)	JLOB 429	(360) 786-7918
48	Bill Reams (R)	LEG 402	(360) 786-7936
48	Steve Van Luven (R)	LEG 401	(360) 786-7848
49	Don Carlson (R)	JLOB 432	(360) 786-7924
49	Val Ogden (D)	JLOB 342	(360) 786-7872

*JLOB = John L. O'Brien Building, LEG = Legislative Building. Source: Washington State House

Commerce and Labor (nine members)
Criminal Justice and Corrections
　(12 members)
Education (11 members)
Energy and Utilities (13 members)
Finance (15 members)
Financial Institutions and Insurance
　(11 members)
Government Administration (13 members)
Government Reform and Land Use
　(11 members)
Health Care (11 members)
Higher Education (nine members)
Law and Justice (13 members)
Natural Resources (11 members)
Rules (19 members)
Trade and Economic Development
　(nine members)
Transportation Policy and Budget
　(27 members)

Composition of State Legislature, by Political Party Affiliation (Election Years 1990-98)

	House	Senate
1990	58 D, 40 R	24 D, 25 R
1992	65 D, 33 R	28 D, 21 R
1994	38 D, 60 R	25 D, 24 R
1996	45 D, 53 R	23 D, 26 R
1998	49 D, 49 R	27 D, 22 R

Source: The Council of State Governments

Libraries
Public libraries were opened at Tacoma, Seattle, and Spokane in the 1890s, and almost every community in the state is now provided with library service. There are almost 2,500 libraries in Washington State library districts, counties and municipalities, school districts, colleges and universities, government agencies, and private organizations. Each year, these libraries circulate an average of 10.2 books for every Washington resident, a circulation rate second only to Ohio.

The Washington State Library in Olympia is the oldest library in Washington. It was founded as the territorial library in 1853. Other major libraries in Washington include the University of Washington library, which has the largest collection of materials on the history of the Pacific Northwest in the country; the Washington State University Library, at Pullman; and the State Law Library, at Olympia.

Summary of Libraries in Washington State.
69 public libraries, with 310 outlets
42 state academic libraries, with 78 outlets
More than 1,800 K-12 public school
　libraries in 296 school districts
74 publicly funded special libraries, such as
　law libraries, military libraries, and the
　State Library
More than 203 private libraries

Selected Washington Libraries

County Libraries.
Asotin County Library, 417 Sycamore St., Clarkston, WA 99403.

Fort Vancouver Regional Library, 1007 E. Mill Plain Blvd., Vancouver, WA 98663.

Jefferson County Rural Library District, P.O. Box 990, Port Hadlock, WA 98339.

King County Library System, 300 Eighth Ave. N., Seattle, WA 98109.

Kitsap Regional Library, 1301 Sylvan Way, Bremerton, WA 98310.

Mid-Columbia Library District, 4101 E. Lattin Rd., West Richland, WA 99353.

North Central Regional Library, 238 Olds Station Rd., Wenatchee, WA 98801.

North Olympic Library System, 2210 S. Peabody, Port Angeles, WA 98362.

Orcas Island Library District, 87 Rose St., Eastsound, WA 98245.

Pend Oreille County Library District, 116 S. Washington, Newport, WA 99156.

Pierce County Library System, 3005 112th St. E., Tacoma, WA 98446.

Sno-Isle Regional Library, 7312 35th Ave. NE, Marysville, WA 98271.

Spokane County Library District, 4322 N. Argonne Rd., Spokane, WA 99212.

Timberland Regional Library, 415 Airdustrial Way SW, Olympia WA 98501.

Yakima Valley Regional Library, 102 N. Third St., Yakima, WA 98901.

Public Libraries.

Bellingham Public Library, P.O. Box 1197, Bellingham, WA 98227.

Camas Public Library, 421 NE Franklin St., Camas, WA 98607.

Carpenter Memorial Library, 302 Penn Ave., Cle Elum WA 98922.

Ellensburg Public Library 209 N. Ruby St., Ellensburg, WA 98926.

Longview Public Library, 1600 Louisiana, Longview, WA 98632.

Milton Memorial Library, 1000 Laurel St., Milton, WA 98354.

Neill Public Library, 210 N. Grand Ave., Pullman, WA 99163.

Ocean Shores Library, P.O. Box 669, Ocean Shores, WA 98569.

Puyallup Public Library, 324 S. Meridian, Puyallup, WA 98371.

Renton Public Library, 100 Mill Ave. S., Renton, WA 98055.

Seattle Public Library, 1000 Fourth Ave., Seattle, WA 98104.

Spokane Public Library, 906 W. Main Ave., Spokane, WA 99201.

Tacoma Public Library, 1102 Tacoma Ave. S., Tacoma, WA 98403.

Walla Walla Public Library, 238 E. Alder, Walla Walla, WA 99362.

University and College Libraries.

Central Washington University Library, 400 E. Eighth Ave., Ellensburg, WA 98926.

Centralia College Library, 600 W. Locust, Centralia, WA 98531.

Clover Park Technical College, Miner LRC 4500, Steilacoom Blvd. SW, Lakewood, WA 98499.

Columbia Basin College Library, 2600 N. 20th Ave., Pasco, WA 99301.

Eastern Washington University Libraries, 816 F St., MS 84, Cheney, WA 99004.

Edmonds Community College Library, 20000 68th Ave. W., Lynnwood, WA 98036.

The Evergreen State College Library, 2700 Evergreen Pkwy. NW, Olympia, WA 98505.

Highline Community College Library, P.O. Box 98000, MS 25-4, Des Moines, WA 98198.

Peninsula College Glann Library, 1502 E. Lauridsen Blvd., Port Angeles, WA 98362.

Pierce College, LRC 9401, Farwest Dr. SW, Tacoma, WA 98335.

Seattle Central Community College, IRS 1701 Broadway (2BE 2101), Seattle, WA 98122.

Spokane Community College Library, 1810 N. Greene St., MS 2160, Spokane, WA 99217.

Tacoma Community College, Wanamaker Library, 6501 S. 19th St., Tacoma, WA 98466.

University of Washington Libraries, FM-25, Seattle, WA 98195.

Walla Walla Community College Library, 500 Tausick Way, Walla Walla, WA 99362.

Washington State University Libraries, Pullman, WA 99164.

Whitman College Penrose Library, 345 Boyer Ave., Walla Walla, WA 99362.

Yakima Valley Community College Library, P.O. Box 1647, Yakima, WA 98907.

Organizations of Interest.

Washington Library Association, 4016 First Ave. NE, Seattle, WA 98105-6502; (206) 545-1529. http://www.wla.org/fslibs.html.

Lighthouses Lighthouses

have been a picturesque part of Washington's maritime history since the first one was built to aid mariners approaching the mouth of the Columbia River in 1856. Lights, fog signals, and lightships were important guides to

North Head Lighthouse just north of the mouth of the Columbia River. Courtesy of Washington State Parks & Recreation Commission.

mariners along the Pacific coast and the inland waters. Lighthouses were originally operated by the U.S. Lighthouse Service, then they were transferred to the U.S. Coast Guard in the 1930s. Most lighthouses and fog signals are now automated, and automated buoys have replaced the old lightships.

Many of the original lighthouses still stand, and a number of them are easily accessible by automobile and are open to the public: 11 are on the National Register of Historic Places. One, the North Head Lighthouse at Cape Disappointment, is part of the state parks system, which maintains the lightkeepers residence as a vacation rental. Some of the original towers have been replaced by not-so-picturesque steel towers; however, there are still plenty of beautiful old lighthouses that are worth a visit, and many are right in the middle of cities and towns. In addition to lighthouses, anchored lightships marked dangerous shoals and reefs. One of the two surviving lightships open to visitors is moored at Lake Union in Seattle. For more information about lighthouses and lightships, visit the **Coast Guard Museum Northwest,** Pier 36, Seattle.

Inland Waters.

Kitsap Peninsula: Point No Point Lighthouse (1879), Hansville.

Marrowstone Island: Marrowstone Point Lighthouse (1888), Fort Flagler State Park.

Maury Island: Point Robinson Lighthouse (1885). Open weekends, noon to 4:00 P.M.

Mukilteo: Mukilteo Lighthouse (1906).

Olympia: Dofflemyer Point Lighthouse (1887).

Patos Island: Patos Island Lighthouse (1893), access from Lime Kiln Point State Park.

Port Townsend: Point Wilson Lighthouse (1879), at Fort Worden State Park. Still has the classical Fresnel lens.

Rosario Strait: Burrows Island Lighthouse (1906).

San Juan Island: Cattle Point Lighthouse (1888) and Lime Kiln Lighthouse (1919), San Juan Island National Historical Park.

Seattle: Alki Point Lighthouse (1913), West Seattle. West Point Lighthouse (1881), Discovery Park, Magnolia. This was the last lighthouse in Washington to be automated.

Strait of Juan de Fuca: Ediz Hook Lighthouse (1861). New Dungeness Lighthouse (1857), Dungeness Spit. Slip Point Lighthouse (1905), Clallam Bay. Smith Island Lighthouse (1858).

Stuart Island: Turn Point Lighthouse (1893).

Tacoma: Browns Point Lighthouse (1903).

Whidbey Island: Admiralty Head Lighthouse (1861), Keystone.

Pacific Coast.

Columbia River: Cape Disappointment Lighthouse (1856), next to Fort Canby State Park. North Head Lighthouse (1898), 2 miles north of Cape Disappointment Lighthouse.

Destruction Island: Destruction Island Lighthouse (1891).

Tatoosh Island: Cape Flattery Lighthouse (1857).

Westport: Grays Harbor Lighthouse (1898), also called Westport Lighthouse.

Willapa Bay: Willapa Bay Light (1858).

Mammals

(*SEE ALSO* COUGAR; ELK; ENDANGERED SPECIES; WHALES) Wildlife that roams throughout this geographically diverse state include the smallest fur-bearers, herds of hoofed animals, large carnivores, and sleek marine mammals. Mammals in Washington live in habitats ranging from marine waters and islets to arid prairies to alpine forests and meadows.

Among the hoofed animals are deer, elk, and mountain goats. The Olympic Peninsula is home to the rare Roosevelt elk, and the lower Columbia has herds of endangered Columbia white-tailed deer. Rocky Mountain and California bighorned sheep are both native to this state's mountains. Rocky Mountain sheep—more commonly known as the mountain goat—are thriving especially in the Olympic Mountains, much to the detriment of the delicate alpine flora, according to biologists.

Black bear in the North Cascades. From *Washington II* by John Marshall.

At the top of the food chain are the large carnivores, including the black bear, cougar, and bobcat. Black bears are found primarily in the high country of the various mountain ranges. Cougars are found throughout the state, and the elusive bobcat is rarely seen at all. The bobcat, or lynx, is primarily found in northeastern Washington in the high country of the Pasayten Wilderness. Both bears and cougars are finding themselves increasingly at odds with encroaching civilization. Sightings of cougars or even a bear in a backyard at the outer edge of a suburban neighborhood is not unusual, even throughout the heavily populated Pugetopolis.

Among the smaller mammals are numerous squirrels and chipmunks, as well as marmots and mountain beavers. Hoary marmots (the largest North American species) live in the lower elevations of the Cascades, and the Olympic marmot is found only high in the Olympics. The mountain beaver is not actually a beaver; it is more closely related to voles than beavers. It lives only in the Northwest.

Along the marine coast, marine mammals feed on the abundant marine life.

Washington Natives

Bighorn sheep are native to Washington and lived in the region for an uninterrupted period from the last ice age to the early 20th century. Rocky Mountain bighorns were native to the Selkirk and Blue Mountains in the far eastern part of the state, and California bighorns lived in the Okanogan highlands and on the eastern slopes of the Cascades. The introduction of domestic livestock is thought to have been largely responsible for the disappearance of bighorns from Washington by the early 1930s.

In 1967, the Washington Department of Game (now the Department of [Fish and] Wildlife) released some California bighorns from a British Columbia herd onto Clemans Mountain. Subsequent releases have been made, and although the population fluctuates, the Clemans Mountain herd now numbers about 38 animals. Washington's total bighorn population is estimated at about 750, of which 210 are the Rocky Mountain subspecies. Each year the Department of Fish and Wildlife holds a drawing to determine which hunters will receive one of a small number of permits to hunt Washington's bighorns.—Susan Ewing, *Going Wild in Washington and Oregon* ✻

In addition to whales, harbor seals, California sea lions, and sea otters occur in the state's waters. The sea lions have been especially easy to spot. In Seattle, they have been annual visitors to the locks that separate Union Bay and Puget Sound, where they've made the fish funneling through the fish ladders their own personal smorgasbord.

The state's extensive wilderness areas and many wildlife refuges provide ample opportunities for viewing wildlife. In addition to the many wildlife guides available in bookstores, you can find out more about where to view some of these spectacular creatures on the **Washington Department of Fish and Wildlife**'s Web site at http://www.wa.gov/wdfw/lands/wildarea.htm.

Marine Pilots and Vessel Traffic Services

A pilot is a master mariner with expert local knowledge and superior ship-handling skills. Foreign ships entering Washington waters are required to take on a state-licensed pilot. The pilot remains with the vessel until the termination of the voyage. Upon embarkation, the process is repeated in reverse. For ships in domestic trades, including tugs and barges (except inland towing industry vessels), the person piloting the vessel must hold a federal first-class pilot's license. State-licensed pilots are overseen by the state Pilotage Commission, whose members are appointed by the governor.

State-licensed pilots for Puget Sound are picked up at Port Angeles. The Dungeness Spit is an excellent location to watch oceangoing vessels pick up and drop off state-licensed pilots (bring a pair of binoculars). The organizations listed below provide state-licensed pilots to foreign vessels and others.

Foreign vessels transiting Puget Sound and entering Canada take on Canadian pilots. Foreign vessels entering the Columbia River take on Oregon-licensed pilots.

Marine traffic in Puget Sound is monitored continuously by a vessel traffic monitoring service (VTS) operated by the U.S. Coast Guard. Bona fide groups can tour the VTS, located on the Seattle waterfront; arrangements may be made by calling (206) 217-6050.

Organizations of Interest.
Grays Harbor Pilots, P.O. Box 123, Aberdeen, WA 98520; (360) 532-2761.

Puget Sound Pilots, 101 Stewart St., Suite 900, Seattle, WA 98101; (206) 728-6400.

Microsoft Corporation

Microsoft was founded in 1975 by William H. Gates III and Paul Allen, who were friends from high school. At that time they were living in Albuquerque, New Mexico, and collaborating on a programming language for the first personal computer. They formed Microsoft and moved the company to Redmond a few years later. After contracting with then computer giant IBM to provide an operating system for IBM's new personal computers, Microsoft grew quickly. It is the largest computer software company in the world. Today, in addition to its software operating platforms, the company produces widely used software and multimedia applications, such as Word, Excel, Encarta, and many others. The company has also expanded into the Internet and entertainment fields. It is a partner in DreamWorks Interactive, an interactive multimedia entertainment venture, and a joint television and Internet venture with the NBC network, called MSNBC. The company has offices worldwide and employs more than 20,000 people.

Microsoft's home campus in Redmond. Courtesy of Microsoft Corporation.

Mileage

Driving distances between cities. *Indicates the shortest route by ferry.

Aberdeen																						
163	Anacortes
172	39	Bellingham
82	78	89	Bremerton
426	316	324	338	Colville
198	179	189	110	232	Ellensburg
258	220	231	170	168	63	Ephrata
108	143	93	131	449	241	299	Forks
240	281	292	212	315	106	162	348	Goldendale
288	284	295	216	208	109	96	347	114	Kennewick-Pasco
72	226	234	145	488	260	320	180	223	317	Long Beach
96	203	214	122	425	200	257	204	146	240	78	Longview
143	18	28	61	303	161	202	150	263	267	205	186	Mount Vernon
50	137	148	59	377	149	209	158	212	246	112	67	120	Olympia
144	87	116	71	392	187	245	56	289	293	206	184	94	121	Port Angeles
122	*41	*70	49	346	154	207	102	257	260	185	162	*48	99	46	Port Townsend
376	357	368	288	147	182	153	419	246	137	437	359	339	328	365	333	Pullman
83	78	89	*1	338	110	170	132	212	216	146	126	60	60	77*	50*	288	Seattle
45	118	126	37	375	147	120	408	249	142	431	362	311	320	354	316	76	280	Spokane
79	110	121	36	350	122	272	243	110	204	118	40	224	106	222	201	339	164	343	Vancouver
335	331	342	262	229	156	134	393	163	53	368	290	313	293	339	307	114	262	158	254	Walla Walla
237	173	184	139	212	75	47	252	178	132	299	254	155	188	198	160	199	138	164	288	178	Wenatchee
203	211	222	143	262	36	93	274	70	86	244	167	193	161	219	187	193	142	196	180	132	108	Yakima

Military

Military All of the uniformed services are represented in Washington. The Department of Defense spends more than $2 billion in contract awards and more than $3 billion in military payroll in the state. Total active-duty personnel number more than 60,000, their dependents add more than 91,000 people to the state's population, and civilian personnel number nearly 23,000. In addition to active military, there are more than 600,000 veterans of the armed services in the state, the largest segment being Vietnam veterans. The major bases are the McChord and Fairchild Air Force Bases, Fort Lewis (U.S. Army), and Navy installations in Bremerton, Everett, and Seattle and on Whidbey Island and Hood Canal.

U.S. Air Force Installations.

McChord Air Force Base, south of Tacoma, was established in 1940 and operated as a bomber base during World War II. Soon after the war, the base became home to the 62nd Trooper Carrier Wing, which is now named the 62nd. In addition to its role in support of combat operations, the 62nd has flown numerous humanitarian rescue and supply missions. Its cargo aircraft evacuated military personnel and dependents from the Philippines after the eruption of Mount Pinatubo, flew supplies and medical personnel to areas devastated by hurricanes and blizzards, air-dropped supplies in support of scientific ventures to remote areas such as Antarctica, and even flew a whale—the film-star orca from *Free Willy*, named Keiko—from Oregon to Iceland. There are more than 40 C-141 B Starlifters based at McChord, which each carry a crew of five. Beginning in mid-1999, McChord's C-141s will be replaced over about five years by C-17s. During the 1998 biannual Air Force Air Mobility Rodeo, a week of ground and air competition, the 62nd Airlift Wing team won top honors as the best C-141 Starlifter wing in the world.

Fairchild Air Force Base, outside of Spokane, was built in 1942 as the Spokane Army Air Depot, serving as a repair depot for damaged aircraft returning from the Pacific Theater during World War II. The base was renamed in 1950, in memory of the late Air Force Vice Chief of Staff General Muir S. Fairchild, a native of Bellingham. In 1971, it became a wing and assumed control over all Air Force survival schools, and in the latest military reorganization, the 92nd Bomb Wing was redesignated the 92nd Air Refueling Wing, and Fairchild AFB was transferred from Air Combat Command (ACC) to Air Mobility Command (AMC), in a ceremony marking the creation of the largest air refueling wing in the Air Force. Dubbed as the new "tanker hub of the Northwest," the wing is capable of maintaining an air bridge across the nation and the world in support of U.S. and allied forces. Fairchild currently has more than 60 active-duty and Air National Guard KC-135 aircraft assigned.

U.S. Army Installations. Fort Lewis, south of Tacoma, was born out of World War I, when in 1917 Pierce County voted to purchase 70,000 acres for donation to the federal government for use as a military base, becoming the first military installation to be created as the result of an outright gift of land by the citizens themselves. It was named Camp Lewis in honor of explorer Meriwether Lewis. Fort Lewis is the home of I Corps; 1st Brigade, 25th Infantry Division; 3rd Brigade, 2nd Infantry Division; 1st Special Forces Group (Airborne); Fifth Army West, Fourth ROTC Region Headquarters, 2nd Battalion 75th Ranger Regiment; and other nondivisional support units and tenant organizations. I Corps is involved in the operation and training of active, reserve, and National Guard units from Alaska to Alabama, and from Pennsylvania to Puerto Rico.

Madigan Army Medical Center, also south of Tacoma, is home to the Northwest Regional Medical Command, which includes U.S. Army medical facilities in six states: Washington, Alaska, Oregon, Idaho, Nevada, and California. It supports U.S. Army National Guard and U.S. Army Reserve units in all six states.

In addition to Fort Lewis and Madigan, the U.S. Army maintains a training and firing center outside of Yakima, and the U.S. Army Corps of Engineers maintains and manages federal dams and locks, and navigable waterways.

U.S. Navy Installations. The U.S. Navy's installations in Washington include the Whidbey Island Naval Station, Everett Carrier Homeport, Naval Submarine Base at Bangor and Silverdale, the Naval Shipyard and Naval Hospital at Bremerton, and Seattle Naval Air Station. The Commander, Naval Base Seattle (COMNAVBASE), is the regional coordinator for the Navy in Washington, Oregon, and Alaska. Additionally, Seattle is the reporting senior in the CINCPACFLT Chain of Command for NAS Whidbey Island, NAVSTA Everett, and SUBBASE Bangor. Naval ships stationed at these facilities include aircraft carriers, destroyers, and Trident nuclear submarines.

Ships based at Naval Station Everett: USS *Abraham Lincoln,* USS *Chandler,* USS *David R. Ray,* USS *Fife,* USS *Ford,* USS *Ingraham,* USS *Paul F. Foster.*

Ships based at Puget Sound Naval Shipyard, Bremerton: USS *Bridge,* USS *Camden,* USS *Carl Vinson,* USS *Mount Hood.*

Armed Services

	Total	Army	Navy	Marines	Air Force
Active-duty personnel	60,884	20,000	31,837	5,339	9,047
Family members	91,517	22,100	56,704	14,679	12,713
Civilian personnel	23,892	5,400	15,325	541	3,167
Source: U.S. Census Bureau					

A lifeboat from the Coast Guard's National Motor Lifeboat School near Ilwaco. Courtesy of the U.S. Coast Guard.

Submarines based at Bangor: USS *Ohio,* USS *Michigan,* USS *Florida,* USS *Georgia,* USS *Henry M. Jackson,* USS *Alabama,* USS *Alaska.*

The Whidbey Island Naval Air Station was commissioned in 1942 as a seaplane and training base. Whidbey's 19 active-duty squadrons fly EA-6B Prowler electronic countermeasure (radar jamming) aircraft, P-3C Orion patrol craft, and EP-3E Aries II fleet air reconnaissance aircraft. The air station also maintains a Search and Rescue Unit, flying the UH-3H helicopter, as well as UC-12B aircraft for fleet logistic support. Whidbey is also the center of Naval Air Reserve activity in the area.

U.S. Coast Guard Installations.

Washington is part of the 13th District of the U.S. Coast Guard, which is made up of many different operational and administrative (support) units. Most Coast Guard operations in the Pacific Northwest include dramatic cliff and offshore rescues, marine inspections, fisheries law enforcement patrols, and myriad other Coast Guard missions. Coast Guard Vessel Traffic Service Puget Sound works jointly with its Canadian counterparts to ensure

that more than 250,000 ships and ferries bound for Vancouver, B.C., Seattle, and Tacoma transit safely through Puget Sound and the Strait of Juan de Fuca. **13th Coast Guard District Office,** (206) 220-7000.

Pacific Northwest and Pacific Ocean Coast Guard resources: HH 65-A Dolphin helicopter; Island Class patrol boats; Point Class patrol boats; 44- and 52-foot motor lifeboats; 41-foot utility boat (range, 280 nautical miles; maximum speed, 26 knots); 30-foot surf rescue boat (range, 150 miles; maximum speed, 31 knots); Polar Class icebreakers (399 feet, crew 139), *Polar Sea* and *Polar Star,* Seattle; high-endurance cutters (378 feet, crew 178), *Mellon* and *Midgett,* Seattle; endurance cutter (210 feet, crew 82), *Active,* Port Angeles.

Aids to Navigation Team Puget Sound, (206) 217-6918.

Bellingham Station, (360) 734-1692.

Cape Disappointment Station, (360) 642-2382.

Grays Harbor Station, (360) 268-0121.

Group/Air Station, Port Angeles, (360) 457-2226.

Loran Station, George, (509) 785-2752.

Marine Safety Office Puget Sound, (206) 217-6200.

National Motor Lifeboat School, (360) 642-2384.

Neah Bay Station, (360) 645-2236.
Quillayute River Station, (360) 374-6469.
Seattle Station, (206) 217-6750.
Vessel Traffic Service Puget Sound, (206) 217-6040.

Washington Army National Guard.

Headquartered at Fort Lewis, the 66th Aviation Brigade is one of the four major subordinate commands of the Washington Army National Guard. Its commander is responsible for units not only in Washington, but in 14 other states as well—these include Arizona, California, Idaho, Kansas, Mississippi, Montana, North Dakota, South Carolina, Utah, and Vermont. **Washington National Guard,** Bldg. 1, Camp Murray, Tacoma, WA 98430-5000; (253) 512-8000.

Organizations of Interest.

Coast Guard Museum/Northwest, Pier 46, 1519 Alaskan Way S., Seattle, WA 98134; (206) 217-6993. Features ship and boat models and uniforms, and tours of two high-endurance cutters and two ice-breakers docked at the pier.

Fairchild Heritage Museum, 2nd

Combat Support Group/CCEM, Fairchild AFB, WA 99011; (509) 247-2100.

Fort Lewis Military Museum, P.O. Box 331001, Fort Lewis, WA 98433-1001; (253) 967-7206.

McChord Air Museum, 100 Main St., McChord AFB, WA 98438-1109; (206) 984-2485.

Mothball Fleet and Museum Ship: USS Turner Joy, destroyer. Located one block from the Navy yard in Bremerton, the USS *Turner Joy* is (in)famous for the Tonkin Gulf incident during the Vietnam War. Visitors can also tour carriers, submarines both nuclear and conventional, cruisers, and other ships. The USS *Missouri,* or "Mighty Mo," a major attraction in Bremerton since 1955, was moved to Honolulu in 1998.

Naval Underseas Warfare Museum, 1 Garnet Way, Keyport, WA 98345; (360) 396-4148. The museum, located adjacent to the Navy torpedo test facility, has models of support ships and boats, and actual research and rescue submarines.

Mima Mounds
A geological puzzle, thousands of small (up to 7 feet tall and 40 feet in diameter), circular mounds cover large grassy regions outside of

Mima mounds near Olympia. From *The Great Northwest Nature Factbook* by Ann Saling.

Olympia. Their origin is unknown; explanations include frost heave effects, odd remnants of receding glaciers, buffalo wallows, anthills, shell middens, even gravel fish nests from prehistoric lakes! The 445-acre Mima Mounds Natural Area is the best place to see more than 4,000 of these geological oddities. The Mima Mounds are listed as a National Natural Landmark.

Minerals and Gems

A few interesting gemstones found in the state are of interest to rockhounds. Amethysts can be found southeast of Mount Vernon, fire opals are occasionally found near Pullman—they were mined there around 1891—and rare blue agates are found near Ellensburg. Jasper, garnets, jadeite, tourmaline, and beryl can also be found in the state.

Despite a gold rush in 1854 at Fort Colville on the upper Columbia, the state's mineral reserves proved to be less flashy than those of other western states. Gold is still mined in the state, primarily in Ferry and Okanogan Counties, and the state was the nation's ninth-largest producer of gold in 1997. The highest-value mining products are much less glamorous than gold or silver, however. Gold and magnesium metal represented close to 30 percent of the state's nonfuel mineral value, but about 65 percent of the state's nonfuel mineral production is construction sand and gravel, crushed stone, and portland cement. In 1997, the state ranked 26th in the nation in total non-fuel mineral production, with a total value of $522 million.

Washington Division of Geology and Earth Resources, Washington Department of Natural Resources, P.O. Box 47007, Olympia, WA 98504-7007; (360) 902-1450.

Mount Rainier (SEE ALSO CASCADE MOUNTAINS; GLACIERS AND GLACIATION; NATIONAL PARKS; VOLCANOES AND VOLCANISM)

Mount Rainier (14,410 feet), the fifth-highest peak and highest volcano in the United States, and Washington's highest peak, dominates the horizon on both sides of the Cascade Range. Named by British explorers after a

Coals to Newcastle

Newcastle Beach Park in Bellevue is named for one of three coal-mining towns that sprang up in 1868 after coal was discovered nearby. More than 150 million tons of coal and waste rock were mined from 1868 to 1963 and, in the days before rail, transported to steam barges on Lake Washington just south of the park. At one time, the town of Newcastle boasted the second-largest population in Washington, after Seattle.—Barbara Sullivan, *Seattle Picnics* ✻

British naval admiral, it was called Tahoma, the "Mountain that was God," by the local Native Americans, but many western Washingtonians simply call it "The Mountain." Three peaks—Liberty Cap, Point Success, and Columbia Crest, the highest—radiate from the summit, blanketed by glaciers. Its 34 square miles of glaciers comprise the largest glacial system on a single peak in the United States outside of Alaska.

Mount Rainier is a dormant volcano, not an extinct one. Rainier has sputtered and rumbled over four major periods in the last 10,000 years, and there have been minor eruptions as recently as the early 1800s. The greater danger, however, is from mud slides that occur when volcanic heating warms glacial ice and starts an unstable mass of mud and debris tumbling down the mountainside.

Mount Rainier was once nearly 16,000 feet high, before material sloughed off its highest reaches and crashed down its flanks. The world's largest such event, the Osceola mudflow, plowed its way along the White and Nisqually Rivers all the way to Puget Sound (*see also* Osceola Mudflow). Geologists have recently warned that a future mudflow down the Nisqually and Puyallup Rivers could lay waste to a large area between Tacoma and Seattle.

The mountain is the centerpiece of a magnificent national park. Timber flourishes at elevations of up to 5,000 feet. Above that

The summit of Mt. Rainier. From *The Great Northwest Nature Factbook* by Ann Saling.

Measuring Mount Rainier's Height

Mount Rainier is the tallest of Washington's many peaks. To check its height, surveyors in 1988 carried equipment to the summit for a remeasurement. They recorded signals from satellites, the first use of modern celestial technology for assessing a terrestrial peak. Their results—14,411 feet, accurate within inches—were released during the state's Centennial celebration, 80 years after the first measurement. That first measurement, in 1909, placed the height at 14,150 feet. Four years later, this was changed to 14,408 feet. Then in 1956, the mountain "grew" an additional 2 feet to 14,410 feet. More telling, however, than the changing figures is that, although Mount Rainier ranks fifth in height among the peaks of the Lower 48 states, it is the highest above its immediate base. Longmire's elevation is only 2,760 feet, whereas the champion peak, Mount Whitney, California (14,495 feet above sea level), and the soaring peaks of the Colorado Rockies start from land already a mile high.—John Marshall, *Portrait of Washington* ❋

altitude, alpine meadows gradually take over. Timberline begins at about 6,500 feet. Mount Rainier National Park was established by Congress in 1899. It contains 62 major lakes, 30 large waterfalls, and more than 700 species of flowering plants. A dramatic scenic highway encircles the mountain. Most tourist activities are centered at Paradise, located on a south-facing shoulder of the mountain just below timberline. Another way to see the mountain is to walk the Wonderland Trail, which also encircles the mountain.

The mountain has been climbed many times since the first ascent in 1852, and was the site of the country's worst climbing accident in 1981, when 11 climbers were swept into a crevasse to their deaths. The most popular routes are the Disappointment Cleaver route, from Paradise, and the Emmons route. A guide service provides both training and equipment for the multi-day climb, from May through September.

Mount St. Helens (SEE ALSO CASCADE MOUNTAINS, NATIONAL PARKS, VOLCANOES AND VOLCANISM)

Mount St. Helens was Washington's fifth-highest peak before it blew 1,300 feet off its top in 1980. The 8,364-foot mountain is now just the 30th-tallest peak in the state. That blast, which occurred at 8:31 A.M. on May 18, 1980, was one of the worst volcanic eruptions in recent U.S. history. It spewed huge clouds of ash that turned day into night in Yakima and rained down ash as far away as Montana;, devastated about 150 square miles around the mountain, including 57,000 acres of timber; and killed 57 people. Mudflows roared down the mountain and filled the shipping channel in the Columbia River.

After nearly 20 years, Washington's famous volcano has become a national volcanic monument, and a major attraction and recreational area. Thousands of ghost trees flattened by the blast still litter the slopes. But the area has also demonstrated the rejuvenating power of nature, as plants and animals have returned. The Mount St. Helens National Volcanic Monument can be reached from U.S. Highway 12 by automobile, or let your fingers do the walking to the Volcanocam on the World Wide Web at www.fs.fed.us/gpnf/mshnvm/volcanocam.

Mt. St. Helens erupting on May 18, 1980. Courtesy of U.S. Geological Survey.

Mountains (SEE ALSO CASCADE

MOUNTAINS; GLACIERS AND GLACIATION; MOUNT RAINIER; MOUNT ST. HELENS; OLYMPIC MOUNTAINS; VOLCANOES AND VOLCANISM) There are more than 500 named mountains in Washington State. The largest mountains, great, glaciated volcanic peaks of the Cascade Range,

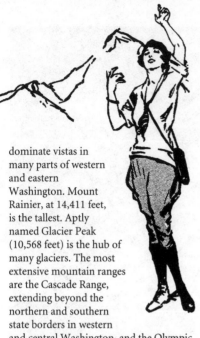

dominate vistas in many parts of western and eastern Washington. Mount Rainier, at 14,411 feet, is the tallest. Aptly named Glacier Peak (10,568 feet) is the hub of many glaciers. The most extensive mountain ranges are the Cascade Range, extending beyond the northern and southern state borders in western and central Washington, and the Olympic Range, on the Olympic Peninsula. Two smaller ranges are the northern end of the Blue Mountains extending from Oregon into Washington's southeastern corner, and the southern end of Canada's Selkirk Range, extending into Washington's northeastern corner.

Blue Mountains. This mountain range is located in Columbia, Garfield, and Asotin Counties in the southeastern corner of the state. Named for their lovely blue color when seen from a distance, up close these mountains were considered an obstacle to early pioneers and ranchers. Two of their peaks thought to be especially hard to travel during winter were named by local cattlemen as Mount Horrible and Mount Misery.

Coast Range. The Coast Range is a mountain system that runs from southern Alaska to Baja California. Washington's Olympic Mountains are considered part of the Coast Range. The system's lowest elevations are found in southern Washington, in the Willapa Hills, and in Oregon; its highest peaks are found in the Olympic Mountains.

Selkirk Mountains. The southern tail of the Selkirk Range, most of which lies north of the Canadian border, dips down into Washington in Pend Oreille County east of the Pend Oreille River.

Museums
Washington has a wide range of museum collections, both specialized and general. The Seattle metropolitan area has several large art museums, including the main Seattle Art Museum, the Seattle Asian Art Museum, the Charles and Emma Frye Art Museum, and the Henry Gallery of the University of Washington. Historical museums can be found in nearly every county in the state. There are also numerous private historical foundations in pioneer homes and specialized exhibits such as maritime facilities and old military forts. Science and technology and natural history museums associated with universities and nonprofit organizations include the Museum of Flight at Boeing Field and the Pacific Science Center in Seattle. Information about some specialized museums is listed with other entries in this book; for example, military museums and agricultural history collections. The following is a sampling of the state's museums.

Art Museums.
Bellevue Art Museum, 301 Bellevue Square, Bellevue, WA 98004; (425) 454-3322.

Cheney Cowles Museum, 2316 W. First Ave., Spokane, WA 99204; (509) 456-3931.

Frye Art Museum, 704 Terry, Seattle, WA 98104; (206) 622-9250.

Henry Art Gallery, University of Washington, Seattle, WA 98195; (206) 543-2280.

Maryhill Museum of Art, 35 Maryhill Museum Dr., Goldendale, WA 98620; (509) 773-3733.

Seattle Art Museum, 100 University St., Seattle, WA 98101; (206) 654-3100.

Seattle Asian Art Museum, 1400 E. Prospect, Volunteer Park, Seattle, WA 98112; (206) 654-8900.

Tacoma Art Museum, 1123 Pacific Ave., Tacoma, WA 98402; (253) 272-4258.

History and Cultural Collections.
Clallam County Historical Society and Museum, 223 E. Fourth St., Port Angeles,

WA 98362; (360) 417-2364.

Clark County Historical Museum (includes former Grant House Museum), 1511 Main, Vancouver, WA 98660; (360) 695-4681.

East Benton County Historical Society and Museum, 205 Keeaydin Dr., Kennewick, WA 99336-5683; (509) 582-7704.

Edmonds Historical Museum, P.O. Box 52, Edmonds, WA 98020; (425) 774-0900.

Foothills Historical Society Museum, 175 Cottage, P.O. Box 530, Buckley, WA 98321; (360) 829-1291.

Fort Walla Walla Museum, 755 Myra Rd., Walla Walla, WA 99362-9460; (509) 525-7703.

Franklin County Historical Society and Museum, 305 N. Fourth Ave., Pasco, WA 99301; (509) 547-3714.

Gig Harbor Peninsula Historical Society and Museum, P.O. Box 744, Gig Harbor, WA 98335-0744; (253) 858-6722.

Grays Harbor Historical Seaport, 813 E. Heron St., Grays Harbor, WA 98520; (360) 532- 8611.

Kitsap County Historical Society Museum, 280 Fourth St., P.O. Box 903, Bremerton, WA 98337-0206; (360) 479-6226. http://www.waynes.net/kchsm/.

Lewis County Historical Museum, 599 NW Front Way, Chehalis, WA 98532; (360) 748-0831.

Mukilteo Historical Museum, 304 Lincoln Ave., Mukilteo, WA 98275; (425) 355-2144.

Museum of History and Industry, 2700 24th Ave. E., Seattle, WA 98112; (206) 324-1125.

Nordic Heritage Museum, 3014 NW 67th St., Seattle, WA 98117; (206) 789-5707.

North Central Washington Museum, 127 S. Mission St., Wenatchee, WA 98801; (509) 664-3340.

Okanogan County Historical Society and Museum, 1410 Second N., P.O. Box 1129, Okanogan, WA 98840-1129; (509) 422-4272.

Spanaway Historical Society Museum, 812 E. 176th St., P.O. Box 741, Spanaway, WA 98387-0741; (253) 536-6655.

Washington State History Museum, 1911 Pacific Ave., Tacoma, WA 98402; (888) BE-THERE, (253) 272-WSHS.

Westport Maritime Museum, 2201 Westhaven Dr., P.O. Box 1074, Westport, WA 98595-1074; (360) 268-0078. http://www.westportwa.com/museum/.

Maryhill Museum sits on a bluff overlooking the Columbia River south of Goldendale. Photo by Steve Terrill, courtesy of Maryhill Museum of Art.

Whatcom Museum of History and Art, 121 Prospect St., Bellingham, WA 98225; (360) 676-6981.

Whitman County Historical Society, Perkins House, P.O. Box 67, Colfax, WA 99111-0067; (509) 332-1029.

Yakima Valley Museum, 2105 Tieton Dr., Yakima, WA 98902; (509) 248-0747.

Science and Natural History Museums.

Burke Museum of Natural History and Culture, NE 45th and 17th Ave. NE, University of Washington, Seattle, WA 98195; (206) 543-5590.

Charles R. Conner Natural History Museum, Washington State University, Pullman, WA 99164-4236; (509) 335-3515.

Pacific Science Center, 200 Second Ave. N., Seattle Center, Seattle, WA 98109; (206) 443-2001.

Specialty Museums.

Children's Activity Museum, 400 N. Main, Ellensburg, WA 98926; (509) 925-6789.

The Children's Museum, 305 Harrison, Seattle, WA 98109; (206) 441-1768.

Hands On Children's Museum, 106 11th Ave. SW, Olympia, WA 98501; (360) 956-0818.

Mindport Exhibits, 111 Grand Ave., Bellingham, WA 98225; (360) 647-5614.

Odyssey Maritime Discovery Center, 2201 Alaskan Way, Pier 66, Seattle, WA 98121; (206) 374-4000.

Rosalie Whyel Museum of Doll Art, 1116 108th NE, Bellevue, WA 98004; (425) 455-1116.

Mushrooms With the

western side of this state's reputation for moisture, dampness, fog, drizzle, rain, and just downright precipitation, it is not surprising that it is a great place to find fungi.

There are more than 2,000 species of mushrooms in the region, and literally dozens of edible mushroom species, including the delectable and desirable chanterelles and morels. The edible species include the following:

King bolete (*Boletus edulis*)

Golden chanterelle and white chanterelle (*Cantharellus cibarius* and *C. subalbidus*)

Horn of plenty (*Craterellus cornucopioides*)

Coral tooth mushroom (*Hericium abietis*), also called coral hydnum

Spreading-hedgehog mushroom (*Hydnum repandum*)

Shaggy parasol (*Lepiota rachodes*)

Edible morel (*Morchella esculenta*)

Black picoa (*Picoa carthusiana*), also called Oregon black truffle

Cauliflower mushroom (*Sparassis crispa*)

Matsutake, pine mushroom, or white matsutake (*Tricholoma magnivelare* and *T. ponderosum*)

Oregon white truffle (*Tuber gibbosum Gilkey*)

Commercial harvesting of wild mushrooms grew dramatically during the 1990s, primarily of *Boletus edulis, Cantharellus cibarius, Morchella esculenta,* and *Tricholoma magnivelare.* A good day of picking can earn a wild harvester hundreds of dollars, which has also resulted in poaching and even in altercations over harvest areas. In 1989, Washington State passed the first law in the country requiring licensing of mushroom buyers and dealers and annual harvest reporting for commercial wild mushrooms. Fall is the biggest season for wild mushrooms. The rains and mild temperatures are perfect for their growth.

Few mushroom species are seriously poisonous, but in Washington there have been cases of mushroom poisoning, especially among recent Asian immigrants who have gathered and eaten deadly Amanita species that resemble a species widely consumed in Asia. Another deadly

mushroom resembles some Psilocybe— "magic mushroom"—species. If you gather wild mushrooms, be sure you correctly identify your mushrooms before you eat them; even cooking does not eliminate the toxins, which can be dangerous. Members of the Puget Sound Mycological Society will help identify mushrooms; call them at (206) 522-6031. If you fear you may have eaten poisonous mushrooms, call Poison Control at (206) 526-2121 or (800) 732-6985, or call 911.

White button (*Agaricus*) mushrooms are also grown as an agricultural product. The value of production in 1997-98 was estimated at $14.4 million.

National Forests (SEE ALSO WILDERNESS)

There are eight national forests in Washington State, six located entirely within the state and two that share area with bordering states. Altogether, national forestland comprises more than 10 million acres in Washington. These national forests contain 10,000 miles of rivers and stream, 7,000 miles of trails, 23 formally designated wilderness areas, 500 developed campgrounds, 13 downhill ski areas, and thousands of miles of forest roads open to the public.

Maps of the national forests can be obtained (for $3 each) at Forest Service offices, and at outdoor equipment and information stores and centers. Information about the national forests can be obtained over the Worldwide Web at www.fs.fed.us/r6/. You can also make reservations for campsites for national forest campgrounds in Washington on the Web at http://nrrc.com/. Cabins and fire lookouts are also available for rent. The Washington and Oregon national forests comprise the Forest Service's Region 6, headquartered in Portland, Oregon. **Pacific Northwest Region,** 333 SW First Ave., Portland, OR 97208.

Colville National Forest. The 1.03-million-acre Colville National Forest is located in the northeastern corner of the state between Roosevelt Lake and the Idaho border. **Colville National Forest,** 765 S.

Main St., Colville, WA 99114; (509) 684-7000. www.fs.fed.us/cvnf.

Highlights: **Noisy Creek Mountain Sheep Feeding Station** at the base of Hall Mountain near Sullivan Lake provides close views of bighorn sheep. The best viewing is in December or January. Hike and ride along **400 miles of trails.** Access to the **Kettle Crest, Abercrombie-Hooknose, Thirteen-mile,** and **Selkirk Mountains.** The 10-mile **State Trail,** an old wagon trail between Albian Hill and Lambert Creek, connects to the **Kettle Crest National Recreation Trail.** The **Sherman Pass Scenic Byway,** between Republic and Kettle Falls on Highway 20, offers breathtaking views and provides access to numerous recreation trails and sites. The byway showcases the history and culture of Native Americans, wildfires, early settlers, and mining and forest management.

Gifford Pinchot National Forest.

The Gifford Pinchot National Forest comprises 1.3 million acres of land in southwestern Washington. It includes the 110,000-acre Mount St. Helens National Volcanic Monument. **Gifford Pinchot National Forest,** P.O. Box 8944, Vancouver, WA 98669-8944; (360) 750-5000. www.fs.fed.us/gpnf.

Highlights: **Mount St. Helens National Volcanic Monument.** Hike and ride on more than **1,000 miles of trails,** including the **Pacific Crest National Scenic Trail.**

Kaniksu National Forest. The Kaniksu National Forest is part of 2.5 million acres of public lands that lie within the panhandle of northern Idaho and extend into eastern Washington and western Montana. Of the total area, 298,311 acres lie within Washington State. The forest is situated in the east-central part of the Columbia Plateau, between the Cascade Mountains to the west and the Bitterroots to the east. **Kaniksu National Forest,** 3815 Schreiber Way, Coeur d'Alene, ID 83814-8363; (208) 765-7307.

Highlights: **Priest Lake Museum and Visitor Center** opened in 1900 with information and displays about the area. Located at Luby Bay, just north of Hills Resort, Idaho, adjacent to Priest Lake. In the **Roosevelt Grove** of ancient cedars, located 11 miles north of Nordman, Idaho, some trees are more than 1,000 years old. **Granite Falls,** adjacent to the Roosevelt Grove of ancient cedars, is a spectacular sloping falls that gushes over solid granite. An overlook trail goes above the falls for a dramatic view from a sheer cliff face. A **scenic drive** connects Nordman, Idaho, with Metaline Falls, Washington, via Pass Creek Pass.

Mount Baker-Snoqualmie National Forest. The 1.7-million-acre Mount Baker-Snoqualmie National Forest extends over 140 miles along the western slopes of the Cascade Mountains from the Canadian border to the northern boundary of Mount Rainier National Park. Nearly 3 million people in or near the Puget Sound metropolitan area are 40 to 70 miles west of the forest. This, coupled with the fact that

Douglas-fir cones

four major mountain passes cross the Cascades through the national forest, makes this one of the most visible national forests in the country. **Mount Baker-Snoqualmie National Forest,** 21905 64th Ave. W., Mountlake Terrace, WA 98043; (800) 627-0062. www.fs.fed.us/r6/mbs/.

Highlights: Picturesque beauty ranges from glacier-cut valleys to the rugged ice-capped mountains of the North Cascades. Glaciers dominate the northern portion, where some mountains rise far above 7,000 feet. The most prominent is 10,778-foot **Mount Baker,** located in the Mount Baker Wilderness, one of eight wilderness areas in the forests. **Wilderness areas** cover 42 percent of the total forest acreage. Subalpine meadows between Mount Baker and Mount Shuksan can be viewed at the end of the **Mount Baker Scenic Byway.** Mount Baker, Stevens Pass, Snoqualmie, and Crystal Mountain **ski areas** are located here.

Okanogan National Forest. The 1.7-million-acre Okanogan National Forest, located in northern Washington, includes the Pasayten and Lake Chelan-Sawtooth Wildernesses. Vegetation in the forest varies from grass and shrubs in the lowest elevations near the Columbia River, to the beautiful ponderosa pine at mid-elevations, to the Douglas fir in the Cascade Mountains and the subalpine and alpine zones at elevations above 6,000 feet The area is famous for its mule deer herds, sports fisheries in the various lakes and streams, and acres and acres of backcountry to traverse. **Okanogan National Forest,** 1240 S. Second Ave., Okanogan, WA 98840; (509) 826-3275. www.fs.fed.us/r6/oka/okafacts.html.

Highlights: Washington Pass Scenic Overlook, along the **North Cascades National Scenic Highway** (Highway 20), provides spectacular views of Liberty Bell Mountain (7,790 feet). Highway 20 is usually open from late April through November. Hart's Pass provides an unexcelled view of the North Cascades from 7,500-foot Slate Peak. The pass is a major trailhead for the **Pacific Crest National Scenic Trail.** North Cascades Smokejumper

Base, 4 miles south of Winthrop on County Rd. 9129, is the birthplace of the Forest Service smokejumper program. Visitors are welcome to tour the base during the summer.

Olympic National Forest. Most of the Olympic National Forest's 632,324 acres lie on timbered ridges and in valleys from 500 to 3,500 feet above sea level. The peaks and meadows of Olympic National Park rise above the national forest. This area provides habitat for about 60 species of mammals, over 200 bird species, seven reptile species, and 15 amphibian species. More than 3,000 Roosevelt elk roam the national forest on the western side of the mountains. **Olympic National Forest,** 1835 Black Lake Blvd. SW, Olympia, WA 98512-5623; (360) 956-2400. www.fs.fed.us/r6/olympic.

Highlights: **Olympic rain forest,** on the west side of the Olympic Peninsula, provides a chance to visit one of the few temperate rain forests. Nature trails wind through lush, moist stands of trees that receive more than 200 inches of rainfall each year. **Hurricane Ridge,** accessible via a paved road, gives motorists a look into the high mountain country of Olympic National Park. The **Pacific coast** is accessible from U.S. Highway 101 at Kalaloch and by spur roads to the mouth of the Hoh River, to La Push, and to Rialto Beach.

Umatilla National Forest. The Umatilla National Forest, located in the Blue Mountains of southeastern Washington and northeastern Oregon, covers 1.4 million acres (319,349 acres of it in Washington) of diverse landscapes and plant communities. The forest has some mountainous terrain, but most of the forest consists of V-shaped valleys separated by narrow ridges or plateaus. The landscape also includes heavily timbered slopes, grassland ridges and benches, and bold basalt outcroppings. Elevations range from 1,600 to 8,000 feet above sea level.

Umatilla is an Indian word meaning "water rippling over sand." Explorers Lewis and Clark passed this way in 1805, and Marcus and Narcissa Whitman crossed the area in 1836 to establish a mission near

Walla Walla. Thousands of emigrants followed the Oregon Trail through this area on their way west. **Umatilla National Forest** has two Washington Ranger Districts: 71 W. Main, Pomeroy, WA 99347; (509) 843-1891. 1415 W. Rose St., Walla Walla, WA 99362; (509) 522-6290. www.fs.fed.us/r6/uma/.

Highlights: Clearwater Lookout/Heliport, built in 1935, is a 99-foot tower offering a bird's-eye view of the **Wenaha-Tucannon Wilderness. Kendall Skyline Road** offers spectacular views of the area. It started as a private road prior to World War I, and was completed in the 1930s by the Civilian Conservation Corps. FR 40 travels along ridgetops with panoramic views of the Blue Mountains, the Wenaha-Tucannon Wilderness, the Eagle Cap Wilderness, and Wallowa Mountains.

Wenatchee National Forest. The 2.2-million-acre Wenatchee National Forest extends about 140 miles along the east side of the crest of the Cascade Mountains. The Lake Chelan-Sawtooth, Glacier Peak, Henry M. Jackson, Alpine Lakes, William O. Douglas, Norse Peaks, and Goat Rocks Wilderness Areas comprise approximately 40 percent of the forest area. **Wenatchee National Forest,** 215 Melody Lane, Wenatchee, WA 98801; (509) 662-4335. www.fs.fed.us/r6/wenatchee/forest/contact.htm.

Highlights: **Lake Chelan** lies within an 80-mile glacial valley, near the center of the state. Rolling hills at the southern end contrast with the spectacular fjordlike quality at the northern end. The **Pacific Crest National Scenic Trail** traverses the length of the national forest (a total of 153 miles of the 2,500-mile Mexico-Canada trail). It passes through spectacular alpine scenery within six wilderness areas.

National Marine Sanctuaries

The Olympic Coast Marine Sanctuary, created in 1994, covers 3,310 square miles of marine waters off the rugged Olympic Peninsula coastline from Cape Flattery to the mouth of the Copalis River. The sanctuary averages approximately 38 miles seaward, including covering much of the continental shelf, and protects diverse marine habitats, including rocky and sandy shores, kelp forests, seastacks and islands, and open ocean. Among its varied marine life are tufted puffins, bald eagles, northern sea otters, gray whales, Pacific salmon, and dolphins. Cultural programs are operated with the Makah, Quileute, Hoh, and Quinault Indian Nations. Ecotourism programs are coordinated with state agencies and regional tourism organizations. **Olympic Coast Marine Sanctuary,** 138 W. First St., Port Angeles, WA 98362; (360) 457-6622. E-mail: ocnms@ocean.nos.noaa.gov.

The National Oceanic and Atmospheric Administration (NOAA) and Washington State have been working since 1988 to designate a second marine sanctuary in the state, which would be known as the Northwest Straits National Marine Sanctuary. It would include the waters encompassing the San Juan Islands, northern Puget Sound, and the Strait of Juan de Fuca. A variety of important marine habitats can be found throughout the Northwest Straits, including kelp forests, eelgrass beds, submerged marine banks, rocky shores and islands, and sand- and mudflats. More than 20 species of visiting and resident marine mammals depend on these habitats and the marine resources they support, including the only resident population of orcas, or killer whales, in the continental United States. The area's 200-plus fish species include salmon, halibut, herring, rockfish, and lingcod; its more than 100 species of marine birds include auklets, loons, grebes, gulls, terns, shorebirds, and the single largest concentration of breeding bald eagles in the continental United States. Well over 2,000 species of marine invertebrates live in these fertile waters, along with hundreds of species of marine algae and plants.

National Natural Landmarks

The National Natural Landmarks Program, established in 1962 by the U.S. Secretary of the Interior, identifies and encourages the protection of sites in the United States that contain the best examples of geological and ecological components of the nation's landscape. Sites can be recommended by private citizens or from inventories by outside groups, such as the State Natural Heritage Programs. Scientists then evaluate recommended areas, using the national significance criteria. If a site fulfills the requirements for landmark status, and if a majority of the private property owners do not object to the designation, the area's nomination is considered by a final advisory board. Once designated, the area is listed on the National Registry of Natural Landmarks. To date, 587 sites have been designated as National Natural Landmarks; 17 of them are in

Washington State. The majority of the state's national natural landmarks are geological features related to the glacial processes that shaped eastern Washington.

Eastern Washington.

Boulder Park and **McNeil Canyon Haystack Rocks.** These two adjacent sites contain the greatest concentration and best examples of erratics, large boulders deposited by glaciers, on the Columbia Plateau, possibly in the country.

Davis Canyon. This area contains examples of antelope bitterbrush/Idaho fescue shrub steppe.

Drumheller Channels. This butte-and-basin scabland is a place where isolated hills are interspersed with shallow depressions scoured out by massive ancient floods.

Gingko Petrified Forest. Two features make this petrified forest distinctive: the large number of genera and species represented, and the unusual preservation of fossils in lava flows. This area is also a state park.

Grand Coulee. This coulee, which is a steep gulch or water channel, is the largest in the Columbia Plateau.

Grande Ronde Feeder Dikes. These "feeder dikes" were channels that fed the voluminous Miocene lava flows of the Columbia Plateau.

Grande Ronde Goosenecks. "Goosenecks" are those loopy bends formed by a meandering river or stream.

The Great Gravel Bar of Moses Coulee. This example of gravel bars deposited by ancient floods on the Channeled Scablands is the largest.

Rose Creek Preserve. The preserve constitutes the best remaining example of the aspen (*Populus tremuloides*) phase of the hawthorn (*Crataegus douglasii*)/cow parsnip (*Heracleum lanatum*) habitat type.

Sims Corner Eskers and **Kames.** These examples are the best of Pleistocene ice stagnation landforms in the Columbia Plateau and western United States.

Steptoe and **Kamiak Buttes.** Steptoe Butte is the type example of a steptoe, an isolated hill or mountain surrounded by lava flows (named after General Steptoe,

who served during Washington's Indian wars in the 19th century). Kamiak Butte is an excellent place to observe the Palouse loess substrate.

Umtanum Ridge Water Gap. Water gaps have been cut through several anticlinal ridges between Ellensburg and Yakima by the antecedent Yakima River. State Route 821 passes through the gap, where folded rocks illustrate results of tectonic stress and stream cutting.

Wallula Gap. Glacial-outburst waters that crossed the Channeled Scablands during the Spokane floods were channeled through Wallula Gap. For several weeks, up to 200 cubic miles of water per day was delivered to a gap that could discharge less than 40 cubic miles per day. Water filled the Pasco Basin and the Yakima and Touchet Valleys to form temporary Lake Lewis.

Withrow Moraine and **Jameson Lake Drumlin Field.** This ice-age terminal moraine, material deposited at the receding edge of a glacier, is the only one in the Columbia Plateau. Drumlins are elongated hills created by glaciers. Together, these features are excellent examples of how the continental glaciers eroded materials in some places and deposited them in others.

Western Washington.

Mima Mounds. These mounds are a superb example of this mysterious topography.

Nisqually Delta. The delta supports one of the five best-known examples of the Washington-Oregon Salt Marsh Subtheme of the Temperate Coastal Salt Marsh Theme in the North Pacific Border Region. The delta is a major resting area for migratory waterfowl.

Point of Arches. These arches are spectacular examples of the results of shoreline erosion.

National Parks The
National Park Service administers national parks; national historical parks, sites, and reserves; and national recreation areas. All units of the park system have equal legal standing. In Washington State, the system (Continued on page 134)

National Forests, Parks, Wilderness Areas, & Wildlife Refuges

National Forests

1. Colville National Forest
2. Gifford Pinchot National Forest
3. Mount Baker–Snoqualmie National Forest
4. Okanogan National Forest
5. Olympic National Forest
6. Wenatchee National Forest

National Parks, Monuments, Historic Sites/Preserves/Parks, and Recreation Areas

7. Ebey's Landing National Historic Reserve
8. Fort Vancouver National Historic Reserve
9. Klondike Gold Rush National Historical Park
10. Lake Chelan National Recreation Area
11. Lake Roosevelt National Recreation Area
12. Mount Rainier National Park
13. Mount St. Helens National Volcanic Monument
14. North Cascades National Park
15. Olympic National Park
16. San Juan Island National Historical Park
17. Whitman Mission National Historic Site

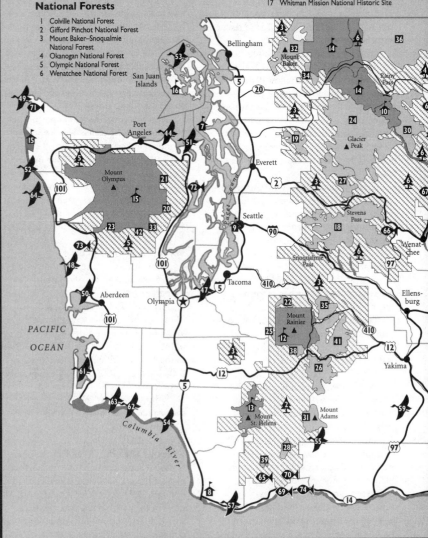

Wilderness Areas

18 Alpine Lakes	31 Mount Adams
19 Boulder River	32 Mount Baker
20 The Brothers	33 Mount Skokomish
21 Buckhorn	34 Noisy-Diobsud
22 Clearwater	35 Norse Peak
23 Colonel Bob	36 Pasayten
24 Glacier Peak	37 Salmo-Priest
25 Glacier View	38 Tatoosh
26 Goat Rocks	39 Trapper Creek
27 Henry M. Jackson	40 Wenaha-Tucannon
28 Indian Heaven	41 William O. Douglas
29 Juniper Dunes	42 Wonder Mountain
30 Lake Chelan–Sawtooth	

National Wildlife Refuges

43 Columbia National Wildlife Refuge Complex
44 Dungeness National Wildlife Reserve
45 Little Pend Oreille National Wildlife Refuge
46 McNary National Wildlife Refuge
47 Nisqually National Wildlife Refuge Complex
48 Copalis National Wildlife Refuge
49 Flattery Rocks National Wildlife Refuge
50 Grays Harbor National Wildlife Refuge
51 Protection Island National Wildlife Refuge
52 Quillayute Needles National Wildlife Refuge
53 San Juan Islands National Wildlife Refuge
54 Ridgefield National Wildlife Refuge Complex
55 Conboy Lake National Wildlife Refuge
56 Pierce National Wildlife Refuge
57 Steigerwald Lake National Wildlife Refuge
58 Saddle Mountain National Wildlife Refuge
59 Toppenish National Wildlife Refuge
60 Turnbull National Wildlife Refuge
61 Willapa National Wildlife Complex
62 Julia Butler Hansen National Wildlife Refuge of Columbian White-Tailed Deer
63 Lewis and Clark National Wildlife Refuge
64 Washington Islands Refuges

National Fish Hatcheries

65 Carson National Fish Hatchery
66 Leavenworth National Fish Hatchery Complex
67 Entiat National Fish Hatchery
68 Winthrop National Fish Hatchery
69 Little White Salmon National Fish Hatchery Complex
70 Willard National Fish Hatchery
71 Makah National Fish Hatchery
72 Quilcene National Fish Hatchery
73 Quinault National Fish Hatchery
74 Spring Creek National Fish Hatchery

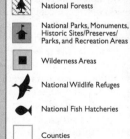

National Forests

National Parks, Monuments, Historic Sites/Preserves/ Parks, and Recreation Areas

Wilderness Areas

National Wildlife Refuges

National Fish Hatcheries

Counties

includes three national parks; six national historic parks, sites, or reserves; and four national recreation areas. National recreation areas and national monuments are not necessarily administered by the park service, but by the agency on whose land they are located; for instance, Mount St. Helens National Volcanic Monument is administered by the U.S. Forest Service, as it is in Gifford Pinchot National Forest.

Olympic National Park. Olympic National Park was originally established as Mount Olympus National Monument in 1909, and later established as a national park in 1938. It was also designated a Biosphere Reserve in 1976 and a World Heritage Site in 1981. One of the top 20 most visited parks in the National Park Service system, it encompasses most of the Olympic Mountains, including one of the finest remaining areas of virgin rain forest in the Pacific Northwest, and a strip of rugged Pacific coast. Mount Olympus (7,965 feet), the highest peak of the Olympic Mountains, has six glaciers on its slopes; a total of more than 60 active glaciers are found in the park. The park contains more than 1,200 species of higher plants, over 200 species of birds, and about 60 species of mammals—many found only on the Olympic Peninsula. Wildlife in the park includes the rare Roosevelt elk, black-tailed deer, cougar, black bear, and otter. Seals, sea lions, and numerous marine birds inhabit the coastal portion.

U.S. Highway 101 provides the main access to the park, with a few spur roads leading to the outer edge of the park, but there are no roads through the rugged heart of the Olympics. The park is a true wilderness park, with 95 percent of its area designated as wilderness—no roads, no accommodations, no services.

Park rangers offer free campfire programs, nature walks, and talks during the summer months. For an in-depth look at the natural and human resources of the park, visitors are invited to participate in one of the many programs offered at the **Olympic Park Institute,** 111 Barnes Point Rd., Port Angeles, WA 98362; (360) 928-3720. E-mail: opi@olympus.net. Olympic

Park Institute is a private, nonprofit educational organization whose mission is to inspire environmental stewardship through education. It conducts programs that emphasize direct, hands-on learning experiences for adults and children.

The park has 16 established campgrounds, many of which are open year-round, and accommodations at Kalaloch Lodge and Lake Crescent Lodge. Boats can be rented at Fairholm Visitor Service Area, Log Cabin Resort, and **Lake Crescent Lodge,** (360) 452-0330. During the winter months, there is skiing at Hurricane Ridge, and guided snowshoe walks are offered each weekend.

Hoh Visitor Center, Hoh Rain Forest, (360) 374-6925.

Hoodsport Ranger Station, on the east side of the Olympic Peninsula, (360) 374-5254.

Olympic National Park Superintendent, 600 E. Park Ave., Port Angeles, WA 98362; (360) 452-0330, TDD (360) 452-0306.

Olympic Park Visitor Center, 3002 Mount Angeles Rd., Port Angeles, WA 98362; (360) 452-0330.

Mount Rainier National Park. Mount Rainier National Park contains vast expanses of pristine old-growth forests, sub-alpine flower meadows, spectacular alpine scenery, and great opportunities for stimu-lating outdoor recreation. The park, established on March 2, 1899, is the fifth-oldest national park in the United States. It encompasses 378 square miles (235,612.5 acres).

More than 2 million visitors enjoy Mount Rainier National Park every year. Entrance fees are collected year-round. They range from a $5 seven-day, single-person fee for anyone entering the park by foot, bicycle, or motorcycle to $20 for a park pass good for one year, and lifetime pass programs for seniors and the disabled. The park features two rustic inns, The National Park Inn at Longmire and the Paradise Inn at Paradise, and six automobile campgrounds with approximately 600 individual and five group sites. There is a 14-day limit during July and August for the campgrounds. Fees range from $10 to $14

View of the Olympic Mountains. From *Garden Touring in the Pacific Northwest* by Jan Whitner.

per night. Reservations can be made on-line up to three months in advance through the National Park Reservation Service, and some campgrounds allow visitors to reserve a site upon arrival on a space-available basis. Wilderness permits are required for overnight stays in the backcountry and wilderness throughout the year.

Each year more than 4,500 people successfully climb to the 14,411-foot summit of Mount Rainier. However, this climb is not for the faint of heart, short of breath, or out of shape. Climbers must register with a ranger before climbing, and check out upon returning. Solo climbing requires advance written approval by the park superintendent. Climbers must pay $15 for each person attempting a summit climb, or purchase a $25 annual pass, designed for individuals making multiple climbs during one year. One-day climbing instruction, two-day summit climbs, and five-day climbing seminars are conducted by **Rainier Mountaineering, Inc.,** 535 Dock St., Suite 209, Tacoma, WA 98402; (253) 627-1105.

Henry M. Jackson Memorial Visitor Center, Paradise, (360) 569-2211, ext. 2328.

Longmire Museum, (360) 569-2211, ext. 3314.

Mount Rainier Guest Services, Inc. (reservations for Longmire and Paradise Inns), P.O. Box 108, Ashford, WA 98304; (360) 569-2275.

Mount Rainier National Park, Park Superintendent, Tahoma Woods, Star Route, Ashford, WA 98304-9751; (360) 569-2211.

Ohanapecosh Visitor Center, open late May into October, (360) 569-2211, ext. 2352.

Sunrise Visitor Center, open late June into September, (360) 569-2211, ext. 2357.

North Cascades National Park.

North Cascades National Park contains the most rugged section of the northern Cascade Mountains. High, jagged peaks intercept moisture-laden winds, producing glaciers, icefalls, waterfalls, and other water phenomena in this wild alpine region where lush forests and meadows, plant and animal communities thrive in the valleys.

About 400,000 people visit the park each

year. The park and recreation areas are always open, but access is limited by snow in winter. Note that State Route 20 (North Cascades Scenic Highway), the major access to Ross Lake National Recreation Area (see below), is partially closed from approximately mid-November to mid-April. Exact opening and closing dates depend on weather, snow depths, and avalanche hazards. Visitation is highest in August, lowest in January.

Only two gravel roads enter the North Cascades National Park: the Cascade River Road from Marblemount and the Stehekin Valley Road. The second road does not connect to any roads outside the Stehekin Valley, which is accessible only by floatplane (Chelan Airways) or by boat (Lake Chelan Boat Company) from Chelan. There is no road access into Stehekin, or any other part of Lake Chelan National Recreation Area. In the Stehekin Valley, the National Park Service and Stehekin Adventure Company provide bus service along the road from late May through mid-October. The buses provide access to many trailheads along the Stehekin Valley Road. The park maintains 386 miles of trails throughout the North Cascades Complex, which includes the Ross Lake and Lake Chelan National Recreation Areas. A free permit, issued on a first-come, first-served basis, is required for overnight stays in the backcountry. The most up-to-date and complete information on trail and climbing conditions is available at information centers. The park complex has many wayside exhibits, museum exhibits at both visitor centers, and five self-guiding interpretive trails. A number of outfitters have permits to outfit and guide horseback trips, hiking trips, technical climbs, and float trips.

Golden West Visitor Center, Stehekin Landing, (360) 856-5700, ext. 340.

North Cascades National Park, Headquarters, 2105 State Route 20, Sedro-Woolley, WA 98284; (360) 856-5700, TDD (360) 856-5700 ext. 310.

North Cascades Visitor Center, Newhalem, (206) 386-4495.

Wilderness Information Center, Marblemount, (360) 873-2250.

Other Park Service Sites.

Ebey's Landing National Historical Reserve. Authorized in 1978, this reserve was the first national reserve established in the United States. It protects 19,000 acres on Whidbey Island that were important to Washington's exploration and settlement. P.O. Box 774, Coupeville, WA 98239; (360) 678-6084.

Fort Vancouver National Historic Site. Fort Vancouver, in present-day Vancouver, Washington, was the original western headquarters of the British Hudson's Bay Company, a fur-trading company that operated throughout northern North America from the 1600s into the 19th century. Designated a national historic site in 1961 (it was originally a national monument), it features restored buildings and a museum that displays artifacts from the area. 612 E. Reserve St., Vancouver, WA 98661; (360) 696-7655.

Klondike Gold Rush National Historical Park, Seattle Unit. Located in Pioneer Square in downtown Seattle, this tiny unit of the National Park Service is the southern portion of the Alaska park. Seattle was the

Blockhouse at Ebey's Landing National Historical Reserve, Coupeville, Whidbey Island. From *Washington II* by John Marshall.

jumping-off point to the Klondike; here, gold seekers bought supplies and boarded ships heading north. The park building contains exhibits about the 1890s gold rush and its impact on the region. 117 S. Main St., Seattle, WA 98104; (206) 553-7220.

Lake Chelan National Recreation Area. Located in northern Washington just south of North Cascades National Park, the 62,887-acre recreation area includes the northern section of Lake Chelan. Surrounded by mountains and the Okanogan National Forest and the Wenatchee National Forest, the recreation area is accessible only via boat, plane, or foot. 2105 State Route 20, Sedro Woolley, WA 98284; (360) 856-5700.

Lake Roosevelt National Recreation Area. Originally established as Coulee Dam National Recreation Area in 1946, it was renamed in 1997. Located in northeastern Washington, it features Franklin D. Roosevelt Lake, formed by the Grand Coulee Dam on the Columbia River. Nearly all of the 150-mile-long lake is under the jurisdiction of the recreation area. Portions of the lake are located within both the Colville Indian Reservation and the Spokane Indian Reservation. The area includes two historic sites: St. Paul's Mission, built by Native Americans in 1845 and operated until the 1870s, and Fort Spokane, established in the early 1880s. Four buildings associated with the fort have been restored. 1008 Crest Dr., Coulee Dam, WA 99116; (509) 633-9441.

Mount Baker National Recreation Area. This recreation area was created in 1984 to accommodate the use of snowmobiles when snow levels are sufficient (greater than 2 feet at Schriebers Meadow Trailhead). During the summer months, the area is used for hiking and camping. 21905 64th Ave. W., Mountlake Terrace, WA 98043; (425) 775-9702.

Nez Perce National Historical Park. Authorized in 1965, this 2,110-acre historical park includes 38 individual sites located in four states—Idaho, Montana, Oregon, and Washington. The sites commemorate the Nez Perce culture and history, including their famous struggle against the U.S. government in 1877. Other sites are associated with settlers, trappers, traders, missionaries, and explorers of the Pacific Northwest, including the Lewis and Clark expedition. The two sites in Washington State are located on the Colville Indian Reservation northeast of Spokane. Rte. 1, Box 100, Spalding, ID 83540; (208) 843-2261.

Ross Lake National Recreation Area. This 118,000-acre recreation area is part of the North Cascades National Park Complex. It includes three reservoirs: 12,000-acre Ross Lake, 910-acre Diablo Lake, and 210-acre Gorge Lake—water gateways to more remote areas. The three lakes are surrounded by forests, mountains, and glaciers. 2105 State Route 20, Sedro Woolley, WA 98284; (360) 856-5700.

San Juan Island National Historical Park. This site on San Juan Island commemorates the end of a boundary dispute between the United States and Great Britain, known as the "Pig War." The hostilities began when, in 1859, an American farmer killed a pig owned by a British settler on ground whose ownership was in question. The site features restored 19th-century buildings associated with the dispute. P.O. Box 429, Friday Harbor, WA 98250; (360) 378-2240.

Whitman Mission National Historic Site. The site of the Waiilatpu mission, built by Marcus and Narcissa Whitman in 1836, features a museum and the graves of the Whitmans and other settlers killed by Cayuse Indians, who blamed the white settlers for the deaths of many Cayuse who died from an outbreak of measles. The national historic site was named in 1963, but originally authorized in 1936. The site is located west of Walla Walla. Rte. 2, Box 247, Walla Walla, WA 99362; (509) 529-2761.

National Register of Historic Places

The National Register of Historic Places is the nation's official list of buildings, structures, objects, sites, and districts worthy of preservation for their significance in American history, architecture, archaeology, and culture. National Register listings should not be confused with local historic property and historic district designations. Properties and districts listed in the National Register sometimes also receive local designation, but there is no direct correlation between the two.

There are about 1,200 such places located throughout Washington State. They include farms, mansions, and cabins; public buildings such as courthouses, libraries, schools, and post offices; Forest Service ranger stations and lookouts; industrial sites such as hydroelectric power stations, mines, and mills; bridges and railroad stations; and even a garage, a jail, and an aircraft tower. The entire list can be perused on the Internet, at http://www.nr.nps.gov/nrishome.htm. Below is a sampling from around the state.

Alderton School, Alderton
American Firebrick Company, Mica
Anderson Island School, Anderson Island
Arndt Prune Dryer, Ridgefield
Arthur Foss (tugboat), Moss Bay, Kirkland
Asotin Clarkston Public Library, Clarkston
Auburn Public Library, Auburn
Bainbridge Island Filipino Community Hall, Bainbridge Island
Bank of Starbuck, Starbuck
Beaver School, Beaver
Benewah Milk Bottle, Spokane
Birdsey D. Minkler House, Lyman
Black Warrior Mine, North Cascades National Park, Stehekin
Blewett Arrastra, Cashmere
Boistfort High School, Curtis
Boundary Marker No. 1, U.S.-Canada border, Point Roberts
Burlington Carnegie Library, Burlington
Burr Cave, Walker
Cape Disappointment Historic District, Ilwaco
Capitol Theatre, Yakima
Chamber's Prairie—Ruddell Pioneer Cemetery, Lacey
Chicago Milwaukee St. Paul & Pacific Railroad Depot, Kittitas
Chief Joseph Memorial, Nespelem
Chimacum Post Office, Chimacum
Clallam Aircraft Warning Service Observation Tower, Agnew

Claquato Church, Claquato
Cloverland Garage, Cloverland
Columbia River Gillnet Boat Altoona Cannery, Altoona
Columbia River Quarantine Station, Knappton
Curlew School, Curlew
Denver and Rio Grande Western Railroad Business Car No. 101, Othello
Dungeness School, Dungeness
Elbe Evangelical Lutheran Church, Elbe
Everett Carnegie Library, Everett
First Day Advent Christian Church, Goldendale
Fort Flagler, Marrowstone Island
Fort Nisqually Site, Du Pont
Fort Okanogan, Bridgeport
Fort Spokane Military Reserve Route, Miles
Fort Steilacoom, Steilacoom
Frederick W. Winters House, Bellevue
Gallaher House, Mansfield
Galster House, Lower Hadlock
Garfield County Courthouse, Pomeroy
Glines Canyon Hydroelectric Power Plant, Port Angeles
Grandview State Bank, Grandview
Grays River Covered Bridge, Grays River
Hanford B Reactor, Hanford
Hiram F. Smith Orchard, Oroville
Holy Cross Polish National Catholic Church, Pe Ell
Hoquiam's Castle, Hoquiam
Hudsons Bay Gristmill Site, Kettle Falls
Hulda Klager Lilac Gardens, Woodland
Indian Shaker Church, Marysville
International Boundary, along U.S.-Canada border, Hozomeen
Irondale Jail, Irondale
Italian Rock Ovens, Cheney
J. C. Barron Flour Mill, Oakesdale
Jaaska House and Warehouse, Rochester
John R. Jackson House, Chehalis
Klipsan Beach Life Saving Station, Klipsan Beach
Lake Chelan Hydroelectric Power Plant, Chelan
Laughlin Round Barn, Castle Rock
Lime Kiln Light Station, San Juan Island
Longview Community Store, Longview
Lower Baker River Hydroelectric Power Plant, Concrete
Lucerne Guard Station, Lucerne

Looking Back

July 2, 1979

The U.S. Supreme Court voted six to three to uphold most aspects of the Boldt Decision, granting Washington Indian tribes half of the commercial fish catch.

Nature and Wildlife Preserves (SEE ALSO MAP, PAGES 132–33)

State Natural Area Preserves.

Natural Area Preserves (NAPs), managed by the Department of Natural Resources (DNR), are established to protect high-quality examples of typical or unique natural features, particularly rare plants and animals. The preserve system includes 25,000 acres in 47 sites, with an average size of 536 acres. In eastern Washington, habitats protected on preserves include outstanding examples of arid-land shrub-steppe, grasslands, vernal ponds, oak woodlands, subalpine meadows and forest, ponderosa pine forests, and rare plant habitats. Western Washington preserves include five large coastal preserves supporting high-quality wetlands, salt marsh, and forested buffers. Other habitats include mounded prairies, sphagnum bogs, natural forest remnants, raptor habitat, and grassland balds. NAPs are managed to allow natural processes to occur as much as possible with minimal human intervention. Preserves are open for research and educational uses by written permission. Certain uses, including recreation, may be restricted on Natural Area Preserves.

Badger Gulch, Klickitat County, 180 acres. High-quality examples of three native plant associations of forest-steppe boundary in south-central Washington.

Bald Hill, Thurston County, 298 acres. Stream sides, mossy rocks, cliff crevices, vernally wet grassland, and exposed rock outcrops with plant communities of the Puget Trough region.

Barker Mountain, Okanogan County, 120 acres. Mid- to upper-elevation ridgetops, with ledges and steep, rocky slopes with examples of shrub-steppe and conifer forest of the Okanogan Highlands.

Bone River, Pacific County, 2,453 acres. Highest-quality salt marsh vegetation remaining in Willapa Bay; includes tideflats, sloughs, freshwater streams, freshwater wetlands, and conifer forests. Critically important waterfowl habitat.

Camas Meadows, Chelan County, 310 acres. Pristine example of sphagnum bog ecosystem.

Carlisle Bog, Grays Harbor County, 310 acres. Wetland and aquatic ecosystems of the Olympic Peninsula.

Castle Rock, Grant County, 81 acres. Five shrub-steppe communities, three vernal alkaline ponds, and a segment of a permanent stream.

Chehalis River Surge Plain, Grays Harbor County, 2,330 acres. The largest and highest-quality, spruce-dominated, surge plain wetland in the state.

Chopaka Mountain, Okanogan County, 2,764 acres. Examples of alpine turf communities, subalpine forests, and a subalpine pond with an associated riparian system.

Clearwater Bogs, Jefferson County, 504 acres. Three bog ecosystems and associated forested drainages.

Cleveland Shrub Steppe, Klickitat County, 640 acres. Two shrub-steppe plant associations.

Columbia Falls, Skamania County, 514 acres. High-quality forest plant communities, including nine vascular plants endemic to the Columbia River Gorge.

Columbia Hills, Klickitat County, 3,593 acres. Washington's largest populations of three rare plants.

Cypress Highlands Skagit County, 1,072 acres. Rare low-elevation freshwater wetlands and native fescue grasslands interspersed between forests of Douglas fir and lodgepole pine, western red cedar, or Rocky Mountain juniper.

Dabob Bay, Jefferson County, 356 acres. Coastal spits with good quality native vegetation, non-vegetated tideflats, and forested upland buffer.

Davis Canyon, Okanogan County, 293 acres. One of few remaining examples of the meadow-steppes once found in eastern Washington. Designated a National Natural Landmark.

Entiat Slopes, Chelan County, 640 acres. Steep slopes and a large population of a state threatened plant species.

Goose Island, Grays Harbor County, 12 acres. A large colony of nesting seabirds.

Gunpowder Island, Pacific County, 152 acres. Nesting seabird colonies.

Kahlotus Ridgetop, Franklin County, 239 acres. Remnant example of grass-dominated steppe in the Columbia Basin.

Kennedy Creek, Mason County, 66 acres. Marsh area, with a remnant of a larger tidal river marsh that includes tideflats, portions of two stream channels, and an area of upland buffer. Important shorebird habitat.

Kings Lake Bog, King County, 309 acres. Two types of Puget Trough wetland ecosystems.

Little Pend Oreille River, Stevens County, 253 acres. An example of Okanogan Highlands mid-elevation stream and riparian ecosystem.

Marcellus Shrub Steppe, Adams County, 122 acres. Examples of shrub-steppe grasslands dominated by two sagebrush species, and examples of alkali vernal ponds.

Methow Rapids, Okanogan County, 66 acres. Large granitic boulders and remnants of two Columbia Basin native plant associations.

Roosting bald eagles. From Going Wild in Washington and Oregon by Susan Ewing.

Mima Mounds, Thurston County, 445 acres. A National Natural Landmark that is a representative example of "mima mound" topography, a native grassland ecosystem, and a rare Puget Trough plant species.

Niawiakum River, Pacific County, 797 acres. Intact tidal river system with best salt marsh vegetation remaining in Willapa Bay and some of the best along the entire Washington-Oregon coast.

North Bay, Grays Harbor County, 1,043 acres. One of the highest-quality coastal freshwater and sphagnum bog systems remaining in Washington.

Oak Patch, Mason County, 17 acres. Example of Oregon white oak woodland and an Oregon white oak-conifer mosaic.

Olivine Bridge, Skagit County, 148 acres. An example of native vegetation on serpentine soils at low elevations in the western Cascades and mixed conifer forest.

Pinecroft, Spokane County, 100 acres. High-quality examples of native ponderosa pine/grassland communities.

Point Doughty, San Juan County, 56 acres. Orcas Island native plant association representative of the "rain shadow" vegetation of the San Juan Islands.

Riverside Breaks, Okanogan County, 35 acres. High-quality remnants of two native plant associations and a population of sensitive vascular plants.

Rocky Prairie, Thurston County, 36 acres. Examples of "mima mound" topography and native grassland.

Sand Island, Grays Harbor County, 8 acres. Nesting seabird colonies.

Selah Cliffs, Yakima County, 64 acres. Cliffs and talus slopes containing the largest known population of a threatened plant species.

Skagit Bald Eagle, Skagit County, 1,546 acres. Critical bald eagle roosting site that complements nearby Skagit River Bald Eagle Natural Area.

Skookum Inlet, Mason County, 105 acres. Salt marsh communities, tideflats, and second-growth forest.

Snoqualmie Bog, King County, 79 acres. Two types of Puget Trough wetland ecosystems.

Spring Creek Canyon, Lincoln County, 235 acres. Basalt canyons with forest and shrub-steppe ecosystems.

Trout Lake, Klickitat County, 670 acres. March and cotton wood forests. Home to one of only three populations of the (threatened species candidate) Oregon spotted frog.

The Two-Steppe, Douglas County, 355 acres. Largest remaining shrub-grassland ecosystem in the northwest Columbia Basin.

Upper Dry Gulch, Chelan County, 320 acres. Canyon with shrub-steppe habitat and largest known population of an endangered plant species.

Whitcomb Flats, Grays Harbor County, 5 acres. Nesting seabird colonies.

Willapa Divide, Pacific County, 272 acres. Three coniferous forest ecosystem types and associated mid-elevation stream and riparian systems.

State Natural Resources Conservation Areas. Natural Resources Conservation Areas (NRCAs), managed by the Department of Natural Resources (DNR), were established to protect outstanding examples of native ecosystems; habitat for endangered, threatened, and sensitive plants and animals; and scenic landscapes. The program, established in 1987, includes 24 sites on more than 47, 000 acres; the sites vary in size from fewer than 10 to nearly 10,000 acres. Habitats protected include island and marine ecosystems, alpine lakes and glaciers, relatively undisturbed examples of upland and wetland forests, and old-growth forests. Conservation areas also protect geologic, cultural, historic, and archaeological sites. Certain recreational uses may alter sensitive natural features on NRCAs, so management plans identify low-impact uses that do not adversely affect the resource values NRCAs were established to protect.

Cattle Point, San Juan County, 93 acres on San Juan Island. Wildlife and important plant species with freshwater wetland, grasslands, waterfront, and mature conifer forest.

Clearwater Corridor, Jefferson County, 2,323 acres. The Commission on Old Growth Alternatives for Washington's Forest Trust Lands (1989) recommended this area's preservation. A coastal forest of Sitka spruce, western hemlock, red alder, and bigleaf maple.

Cypress Island, Skagit County, more than 3,700 acres. Miles of waterfront and excellent examples of coniferous forests and wetland ecosystems, and rare bird species.

Dishman Hills, Spokane County, 518 acres. Potholes, ponds, ridges, and gullies, with seven different plant communities and one of the last remaining populations of an endangered plant.

Elk River, Grays Harbor County, more than 3,500 acres. The largest, highest-quality estuarine system remaining in Washington or Oregon. It includes tideflats, sloughs, salt marshes, freshwater wetlands, and forested uplands. Critically important waterfowl and shorebird habitat.

Granite Lakes, Skagit County, 603 acres. Abutting the Glacier Peak Wilderness Area; contains 160-year-old stands of silver fir, mountain hemlock, and associated plant communities.

Greider Ridge, Snohomish County, 6,700 acres. Spectacular mid- to high-elevation subalpine areas with exposed rocks and cliffs.

Hat Island, Skagit County, 91 acres. In Padilla Bay between Anacortes and Bayview; provides important bird habitat.

Klickitat Scenic River, Yakima County, 470 acres. Spectacular views of the undammed and free-flowing river contribute to this area.

Lake Louise, Whatcom County, 137 acres. Bogs, wetlands, hardwood thickets, and mixed conifer forests.

Lummi Island, Whatcom County, 661 acres. Forested shoreline with steep, rocky headlands.

Merrill Lake, Cowlitz County, 114 acres. Forest cover of mixed conifers and hardwoods along a shoreline of statewide significance. Prime habitat for birds of prey.

Morning Star, Snohomish County, 10,000 acres. Extremely steep and rugged terrain, old-growth timber, and numerous small alpine lakes and glaciers.

Mount Pilchuck, Snohomish County, 9,600 acres. Low-elevation to alpine forests and meadows.

Mount Si, King County, 8,000 acres. Popular hiking area; encompasses the entire Mount Si/Little Si/Mount Teneriffe/Green Mountain ridge crest.

Rattlesnake Mountain Scenic Area, King County, 1,771 acres. Facing Mount Si to the north, this area is managed with King County to protect additional ridge views in the I-90 corridor.

Shipwreck Point, Clallam County, 471 acres. One of the last open stretches of beach on the Strait of Juan de Fuca.

South Nemah, Pacific County, 1,452 acres. One of the last small uncut drainages in the Willapa Hills with 300-year-old western red cedars and habitat for many sensitive wildlife species.

South Nolan, Jefferson County, 213 acres. Old-growth temperate forest with scattered wetlands; many trees more than 500 years old.

Table Mountain/Greenleaf Peak, Skamania County, 2,800 acres. Within the Columbia River Gorge National Scenic Area and part of a large forest ecosystem that supports a wide variety of wildlife. Wetland basin, vertical rock faces, and spectacular views.

Teal Slough, Pacific County, 8.5 acres. Supports a remnant coastal old-growth forest.

West Tiger Mountain Tradition Plateau, King County, 4,500 acres. Dense forests, wetlands, talus slopes, and scenic vistas. Adjacent to the Tiger Mountain State Forest.

White Salmon Oak, Klickitat County, 319 acres. Contains representatives of all the Oregon white oak communities now found in the White Salmon River drainage. These communities, which are quickly disappearing from Washington, provide an important glimpse of the region's pre-settlement landscape.

Woodard Bay, Thurston County, more than 600 acres. Shoreline, wetlands, and old-growth forest just minutes from downtown Olympia.

State Wildlife Areas. The Washington Department of Fish and Wildlife (WDFW) is directed to manage 25 wildlife areas to maintain or enhance habitats for fish and wildlife and provide compatible wildlife-oriented recreation. More than 840,000 acres are managed in parcels of a few hundred to tens of thousands of acres. There are also more than 600 one- to five-acre sites that provide access to lands and waters for fishing, hunting, and other recreational uses. Call (360) 902-2200 for a copy of the complete management plan for a given wildlife area.

Chesaw Wildlife Area
Chief Joseph Wildlife Area
Colockum Wildlife Area
Columbia Basin Wildlife Area
Cowlitz Wildlife Area
Johns River Wildlife Area
Klickitat Wildlife Area
L. T. Murray Wildlife Area
Lake Terrell Wildlife Area
Methow Wildlife Area
Oak Creek Wildlife Area
Olympic Wildlife Area
Scatter Creek Wildlife Area
Scotch Creek Wildlife Area
Sherman Creek/Le Cleur Creek
   Wildlife Area
Sinlahekin Wildlife Area
Skagit Wildlife Area
Snoqualmie Wildlife Area
South Puget Sound Wildlife Area
Sunnyside Wildlife Area
Swanson Lakes Wildlife Area
Tunk Habitat Area
Vancouver and Shillapoo Lakes
   Wildlife Area
Wells Wildlife Area
William T. Wooten Wildlife Area

National Wildlife Refuges. The federal government operates a number of national wildlife refuges in Washington State, under the jurisdiction of the U.S. Fish and Wildlife Service. They include:

Arid Lands National Wildlife Refuge Complex (Hanford ALE and Saddle Mountain NWR), 3250 Port of Benton Blvd., Richland, WA 99352; (509) 371-1801.

Columbia National Wildlife Refuge Complex, 735 E. Main St., Othello, WA 99344; (509) 488-2668.

Dungeness National Wildlife Reserve,

33 S. Barr Rd., Port Angeles, WA 98362; (360) 457-8451.

Little Pend Oreille National Wildlife Refuge, 1310 Bear Creek Rd., Colville, WA 99114; (509) 684-8384.

McNary National Wildlife Refuge (managed by Umatilla, Oregon, NWR), 64 Maple Rd., Burbank, WA 99323; (509) 547-4942.

Nisqually National Wildlife Refuge Complex, 100 Brown Farm Rd., Olympia, WA 98516; (360) 753-9467. The Nisqually NWR complex includes the San Juan Islands NWR, Protection Island NWR, Copalis NWR, Flattery Rocks NWR, Quillayute Needles NWR, amd Grays Harbor NWR.

Ridgefield National Wildlife Refuge Complex, 301 N. Third St., Ridgefield, WA 98642; (360) 887-4106. The complex includes Conboy Lake NWR, Franz NWR, Pierce NWR, Ridgefield, and Steigerwald Lake NWR.

Toppenish National Wildlife Refuge (under Mid-Columbia River NWRC in Oregon), 21 Pumphouse Rd., Toppenish, WA 98948; (509) 865-2405.

Turnbull National Wildlife Refuge, 26010 S. Smith Rd., Cheney, WA 99004; (509) 235-4723.

Washington Maritime National Wildlife Refuge Complex (includes Protection Island NWR and San Juan Islands NWR), Islands Refuges, 33 S. Barr Rd., Port Angeles, WA 98362; (360) 457-8451.

Willapa National Wildlife Complex, HC 01, Box 910, Ilwaco, WA 98624; (360) 484-3482. It includes the Julia Butler Hansen Refuge for the Columbian White-tailed Deer NWR, Lewis and Clark NWR, and Willapa.

Newspapers

Washington has a long tradition of a healthy and vociferous press. In addition to more than a couple dozen daily newspapers and some 160 weekly newspapers, the state is served by a number of ethnic newspapers (these include newspapers that cover news for the Cambodian, Hispanic, Filipino, Jewish, Korean, Chinese, Vietnamese, and American Indian communities), special-interest papers such as *Fishing & Hunting News* and *Seattle Gay News,* and periodicals covering business and industry, the arts, law, the environment, and local history.

National papers and news bureaus that maintain a Northwest Bureau include the *New York Times, Wall Street Journal,* the Associated Press, and Reuters.

Washington newspapers and correspondents have garnered national awards for journalism. The prestigious Pulitzer Prize has been awarded to the following:

1950, National Reporting, Edwin O. Guthman, *The Seattle Times,* for his series on the clearing of Communist charges against University of Washington Professor Melvin Rader.

1975, Spot News Photography, Gerald H. Gay, *The Seattle Times,* for his photograph of four exhausted firefighters titled "Lull in the Battle."

1981, Local General Spot News Reporting, The Longview Daily News Staff, *The Longview Daily News,* for coverage of the eruption of Mount St. Helens.

1982, Local Investigative Specialized Reporting, Paul Henderson, *The Seattle Times,* for reporting that cleared an innocent man who had been convicted of rape.

1984, Feature Writing, Peter Mark Rinearson, *The Seattle Times,* for his story titled "Making It Fly," about the building of the Boeing 757.

1990, National Reporting, Ross Anderson, Bill Dietrich, Mary Ann Gwinn, and Eric Nalder, *The Seattle Times,* for coverage of the *Exxon Valdez* oil spill disaster.

1997, Investigative Reporting, Eric Nalder, Deborah Nelson, and Alex Tizon, *The Seattle Times,* for their investigation of

corruption in a federally sponsored housing program for Native Americans.
1997, Beat Reporting, Byron Acohido, *The Seattle Times,* for coverage of the aerospace industry, notably an investigation of rudder control problems on Boeing's popular 737 jetliner.
1999, Editorial Cartooning, David Horsey, *The Seattle Times.*

Daily Newspapers in Washington State.

Aberdeen Daily World
Bellingham Herald
Bremerton Sun
The Chronicle (Centralia)
Columbia Basin Herald (Moses Lake)
The Columbian (Vancouver)
The Daily (UW, Seattle)
Daily Evergreen (WSU, Pullman)
Daily Journal of Commerce (Seattle)
The Daily News (Pullman)
Daily Record (Ellensburg)
Eastside Journal (Bellevue)
The Everett Herald
Herald-Republic (Yakima)
The Longview Daily News
The Olympian
The Oregonian (Vancouver, Clark County News Bureau)
Peninsula Daily News (Port Angeles)
Seattle Post-Intelligencer
The Seattle Times
South County Journal (Kent)
The Spokesman-Review (Spokane)
Sunnyside Sun Daily News
Tacoma Daily Index
Tacoma Morning Tribune
Tri-City Herald
Union-Bulletin (Walla Walla)
Wenatchee Daily World

Organizations of Interest.

Newspaper Publishers Association, Washington, 3838 Stone Way N., Seattle, WA 98103; (206) 634-3838. http://www.wnpa.com. The Web site contains links to nearly all local weekly newspapers.

Pacific Northwest Newspaper Guild, 2900 Eastlake Ave. E., Suite 220, Seattle, WA 98102; (206) 328-1190.

Old-Growth Forests

Old growth refers to forests that grow undisturbed by fire, disease, or human interference until the trees reach full maturity. This may take as long as 200 years. Old-growth forests have an abundance of very large trees with complex layers of branches and crown foliage, and dead and decaying wood on the forest floor. Stands of old-growth forests can be admired at these locations:

Federation Forest State Park, Enumclaw. You'll see some very large Douglas firs and some of the largest western red cedars in the "Land of the Giants." Head east on Highway 410, and turn right at the Interpretive Center sign about 17 miles east of Enumclaw.

Grove of the Patriarchs, Stevens Canyon, Mount Rainier National Park. Some trees here are more than 700 years old. From Highway 123, the Stevens Canyon entrance to Mount Rainier National Park, continue to the parking lot beyond the Ohanapecosh River bridge.

Quinault Loop Trail, Olympic Peninsula. Here are 500-year-old Douglas firs up to 8 feet in diameter. Turn east off Highway 101 onto the South Shore Road.

Olympia
Olympia (pop. 39,070), located on Budd Inlet in the southernmost reaches of Puget Sound, is Washington's capital and one of its oldest cities. The site of the first customs house on Puget Sound, Olympia was designated the capital when the Washington Territory was formed in 1853. State government is the town's biggest employer—some 21,000 people working in state government live here.

The town's dominant landmark is the domed capitol building, designed after the U.S. capitol. Besides the capitol building, which houses the state Legislature and governor's office, the capitol campus includes the state's Supreme Court building, the State Library, the Governor's Mansion, and numerous state agency offices. More than 30 landscaped acres with seasonal floral displays surround the capitol campus, and the city also features three colleges, a downtown waterfront boardwalk, a farmers' market, and a Japanese garden.

The State Capital Museum, located in historic Lord Mansion, is the best place to begin learning about the state's capital and its political and cultural history. The capitol building and governor's mansion are open to visitors. Daily tours are conducted for the capitol; tours of the Governor's Mansion require a reservation. Other interesting sites include:

Capitol Conservatory. This greenhouse was constructed by the Work Projects Administration in 1939.

Korean War Veterans Memorial. Built in 1993 on the East Campus across the footbridge from the State Capitol Visitor Center.

Old Capitol Building. This downtown Olympia building served as the Capitol (1901-1928) before the present capitol building was constructed.

Vietnam Veterans Memorial. Built in 1987 on the hillside east of the Insurance Building.

Organizations of Interest.

State Capitol Visitor Center, 14th St. and Capitol Way, Olympia, WA 98504; (360) 586-3460.

Washington State Capital Museum, 211 W. 21st Ave., Olympia, WA 98501; (360) 753-2580.

Washington State Capitol Tours, (360) 586-TOUR.

Olympic Mountains

(*SEE ALSO* NATIONAL PARKS) The Olympic Mountains dominate the Olympic Peninsula. They are part of the Coast Range mountain system that runs the length of the west coast of North America. Heavily glaciated Mount Olympus (7,965 feet)—named for the home of the Greek gods—is the highest peak.

The Olympics are among the youngest mountains in North America, with rocks dating from as recent as 3 million years ago. Glaciers sculpted the peaks and streams, and rivers fed by snow- and glacier-melt cut deep valleys. Large glacial erratic boulders lie scattered on the mountain slopes. The

Mountain goats in Olympic National Park. From *The Great Northwest Nature Factbook* by Ann Saling.

Olympics contains some 50 permanent snowfields. Lush, northern rain forest vegetation dominates at lower elevations. The dramatic terrain and setting of the Olympic Mountains can be appreciated from Hurricane Ridge, which can be reached by car from Port Angeles.

Most of the Olympic Range lies within Olympic National Park (908,720 acres). Paved roads only skirt the park. Most of the park, which was designated a World Heritage Site by the United Nations in 1981, is undisturbed coniferous forest and glaciated mountain terrain. These lands provide an undisturbed home to over 200 species of birds and about 60 species of mammals, including the rare Roosevelt elk. Mountain goats were introduced into the Olympics in the 1920s and now thrive in the interior.

Osceola Mudflow

Washington's volcanoes have been known to erupt violently in large mudflows that take down an entire face of the volcano. The Osceola mudflow was one such volcanic event. More than 5,700 years ago, this violent mudflow raced down the White River Valley on the north flank of Mount Rainier all the way to today's Commencement Bay, at Tacoma. More than a half cubic mile of debris washed down the mountain, and the summit of the mountain was lowered by 1,500 feet. Mount Rainier has suffered more than 50 such catastrophic mudflows in the last 10,000 years. Geologists predict that more will occur in the future.

Outdoor Recreation (See also Skiing and Snowboarding; Trails; Water Sports)

Washington's diverse landscape of mountains, waterways, seacoast, and extensive forests provides abundant opportunities for outdoor recreation. Hiking and camping are extremely popular activities. Whether you are car camping or backpacking—for those with strong backs and legs—state and national parks contain thousands of campsites that range from rugged undeveloped sites with no facilities to developed campgrounds complete with hot showers.

The state's craggy mountains provide many challenges for mountain climbing, mountain biking, and rock climbing. Among the truly intrepid are some 10,000 people who every year scale Mount Rainier, about half of whom make it to the summit. There are a number of guides and outfitters who lead groups to the summit. Perhaps the best known is Lou Whittaker, a world-renowned mountain climber, and co-owner

of **Rainier Mountaineering, Inc.,** 35 Dock St., Suite 209, Tacoma, WA 98402; (253) 627-6242. Mount Rainier is a popular destination for many world-class climbers, who like to train here. While not the world's tallest mountain, it is nonetheless a daunting challenge, even for experienced climbers.

Mountain biking is another activity that has grown in popularity among those who like to head for the hills. The Washington State Department of Transportation has a huge list of links to bicycling resources in Washington State and across the country. http://www.wsdot.wa.gov/ppsc/bike/.9

Interagency Committee for Outdoor Recreation, 1111 Washington St. SE, P.O. Box 40917, Olympia, WA 98504-0917; (360) 902-3000.

Pacific Coast (See also Puget Sound and Inland Waters)

Along the Pacific Ocean boundary of Washington runs the longest roadless seacoast in the contiguous states, the most undeveloped and primitive Pacific Ocean shore, and its last undisturbed coastal ecosystem. The coastal water over which the state has jurisdiction comprises 2,511 square miles; the coast extends for 157 miles from north to south. The principal indentation is Puget Sound, which is connected with the Pacific Ocean by the Strait of Juan de Fuca. Other

Outdoor Inventions

Two contributions to the comfort of outdoor enthusiasts everywhere were developed by innovative Washingtonians. Sno-Seal, in the familiar blue and white can, was the brainchild of Ome Daiber, a Seattle sporting goods manufacturer. He developed the product in the 1930s. The secret, we are told, is beeswax, which is more water-repellent than other waxy or oily substances. Sno-Seal also employs emulsifying ingredients to help it sink into the leather and not rub off or be greasy to the touch.

Eddie Bauer, another local sporting goods businessman, developed and popularized the down jacket. Bauer had a brush with hypothermia in 1934, when he neglected to bring a heavy wool jacket on a trip to the Olympic Peninsula. He recalled a Russian uncle who swore by goose-down clothing, which kept him warm during the Russo-Japanese War, in 1904. Bauer was already working with goose down—for manufacturing fishing flies and badminton shuttlecocks. He began to experiment with clothing. Early attempts at light, down-filled jackets were distributed to friends, who waxed enthusiastic about the new product. The first commercial down entered the clothing trade in 1936. ✤

major coastal indentations are Willapa Bay and Grays Harbor. Long, sandy beaches border the southwestern coast between the bays and the Pacific Ocean. Rugged cliffs and headlands border the ocean side of the Olympic Peninsula. From Cape Flattery at the Strait of Juan de Fuca south to Kalaloch, the narrow, 60-mile-long roadless shore is the last wild stretch of seacoast in the United States.

Beaches. Beaches along Washington's northern coast tend to be rocky headlands interspersed by coves with sand and cobble. One of the most beautiful of all of Washington's northern beaches is Point of Arches, which is accessible only by a challenging trail. Point of Arches displays the full spectrum of sea rock sculpted by waves in great and picturesque abundance: windows and arches cut into rock, towering sea stacks, islets and offshore rocks hundreds of feet high. Farther south lies Ruby Beach on the Olympic Peninsula, with its swaths of colorful sand formed by wave action that has ground garnet crystals into pinkish sand.

Long stretches of sandy beach line the southern half of the coast. The longest uninterrupted stretch of beach is the 28-mile Long Beach Peninsula. Long Beach juts north along the coast from the mouth of the Columbia River, forming the western edge of Willapa Bay.

Headlands. Among the more dramatic coastal features are the dramatic high cliffs and bluffs that overlook the Pacific Ocean. On the north end, Cape Flattery, at the tip of the Olympic Peninsula, marks the most northwesterly land in the Lower 48 states, and Cape Alava extends farther west than any other land in the Lower 48 states. On the south end, Cape Disappointment is the most distinctive promontory. The headland is the site of the state's first lighthouse, and marks the north entrance to the Columbia River. It was named by Capt. John Meares, who in 1788 failed to locate what became known as the Columbia River.

Bays and Harbors. Willapa Bay and Grays Harbor, the two major bays on the

> *Ocean's Fury*
>
> One awesome manifestation of the frequent fury of waters off the outer coast is the lengthy graveyard of ships. Stretching from Southeast Alaska to Oregon, the havoc represents almost every maritime country and most decades over several centuries.... Off Cape Flattery, Washington, lie more than 150 oceangoing ships and cargo once worth billions of dollars.—Diane Swanson, *The Emerald Sea* ✱

Washington coast, are both important wildlife estuaries. Willapa Bay has many flats exposed at low tide, and the bay is renowned for oyster growing. Grays Harbor is accessible by oceangoing ships. Both of these large estuaries, critical elements of the Pacific Flyway, support huge populations of migrating birds.

PAC-10
PAC-10 is short for the Pacific-10 Atlantic Conference, an athletics league of 10 western universities, including Washington's two largest state institutions. The schools that comprise the PAC-10 are:

Arizona State University, Sun Devils
California State, Golden Bears
Oregon State University, Beavers
Stanford University, Cardinal
University of Arizona, Wildcats
University of California Los Angeles, Bruins
University of Oregon, Ducks
University of Southern California, Trojans
University of Washington, Huskies
Washington State University, Cougars

The PAC-10 is host to the Rose Bowl. The league sponsors 10 men's sports and 11 women's sports. In addition to football, the conference schools field teams in baseball, basketball, cross-country running, golf, gymnastics, rowing, soccer, softball, swimming, tennis, track and field, volleyball, and wrestling. The PAC-10 also belongs to the Mountain Pacific Sports Federation (MPSF) in five other men's sports and two other women's sports.

Apple Cup*—The First 100 Years

Year	Final Score	Location	Year	Final Score	Location
1900	UW 5, WSU 5	at UW	1954	WSU 26, UW 7	at WSU
1901	WSU 10, UW 0	at WSU	1955	UW 27, WSU 7	at UW
1902	UW 16, WSU 0	at UW	1956	UW 40, WSU 26	in Spokane
1903	UW 10, WSU 0	at WSU	1957	WSU 27, UW 7	at UW
1904	UW 12, WSU 6	at UW	1958	WSU 18, UW 14	in Spokane
1907	WSU 11, UW 5	at UW	1959	UW 20, WSU 0	at UW
1908	UW 6, WSU 6	at UW	1960	UW 8, WSU 7	in Spokane
1910	UW 16, WSU 0	at WSU	1961	UW 21, WSU 17	at UW
1911	UW 30, WSU 6	at UW	1962	UW 28, WSU 21	in Spokane
1912	UW 19, WSU 0	at UW	1963	UW 16, WSU 0	at UW
1913	UW 20, WSU 0	at UW	1964	UW 14, WSU 0	in Spokane
1914	UW 45, WSU 0	at UW	1965	UW 27, WSU 9	at UW
1917	WSU 14, UW 0	at UW	1966	UW 19, WSU 7	in Spokane
1919	UW 13, WSU 7	at WSU	1967	WSU 9, UW 7	at UW
1921	WSU 14, WSU	at UW	1968	WSU 24, UW 0	in Spokane
1922	UW 16, WSU 13	at WSU	1969	UW 30, WSU 21	at UW
1923	UW 24, WSU 7	at UW	1970	UW 43, WSU 25	in Spokane
1924	UW 14, WSU 0	at UW	1971	UW 28, WSU 20	at UW
1925	UW 23, WSU 0	at WSU	1972	WSU 27, UW 10	in Spokane
1926	WSU 9, UW 6	at UW	1973	WSU 52, UW 28	at UW
1927	UW 14, WSU 9	at UW	1974	UW 24, WSU 17	in Spokane
1928	UW 6, WSU 0	at UW	1975	UW 28, WSU 27	at UW
1929	WSU 20, UW 13	at WSU	1976	UW 51, WSU 32	in Spokane
1930	WSU 3, UW 0	at UW	1977	UW 35, WSU 15	at UW
1931	UW 12, WSU 9	at UW	1978	UW 38, WSU 8	in Spokane
1932	UW 0, WSU 0	at UW	1979	UW 17, WSU 7	at UW
1933	WSU 17, UW 6	at WSU	1980	UW 30, WSU 23	in Spokane
1934	UW 0, WSU 0	at UW	1981	UW 23, WSU 10	at UW
1935	UW 21, WSU 0	at WSU	1982	WSU 24, UW 20	at WSU
1936	UW 40, WSU 0	at UW	1983	WSU 17, UW 8	at UW
1937	UW 7, WSU 7	at WSU	1984	UW 38, WSU 29	at WSU
1938	UW 28, WSU 0	at UW	1985	WSU 21, UW 20	at UW
1939	WSU 6, UW 0	at WSU	1986	UW 44, WSU 23	at WSU
1940	UW 33, WSU 9	at UW	1987	UW 34, WSU 19	at UW
1941	UW 23, WSU 13	at WSU	1988	WSU 32, UW 31	at WSU
1942	UW 0, WSU 0	at UW	1989	UW 20, WSU 9	at UW
1943	WSU 9, UW 6	at UW	1990	UW 55, WSU 10	at WSU
1945	WSU 7, UW 0	at UW	1991	UW 56, WSU 21	at UW
1946	UW 21, WSU 7	at WSU	1992	WSU 42, UW 23	at WSU
1947	UW 20, WSU 0	at UW	1993	UW 26, WSU 3	at UW
1948	WSU 10, UW 0	at WSU	1994	WSU 23, UW 8	at WSU
1949	UW 34, WSU 21	at UW	1995	UW 33, WSU 30	at UW
1950	UW 52, WSU 21	in Spokane	1996	UW 31, WSU 24	at WSU
1951	WSU 27, UW 25	at UW	1997	WSU 42, UW 35	at UW
1952	UW 33, WSU 27	in Spokane	1998	UW 16, WSU 9	at WSU
1953	WSU 25, UW 20	at UW			

*University of Washington Huskies vs. Washington State University Cougars
Source: University of Washington Athletics Department

Palouse

Washington's southeastern corner is known as the Palouse. It is a region about 85 miles by 100 miles characterized by rolling hills thick with wheat, picturesque small towns, and eastern Washington's largest university, Washington State University—known affectionately as "Wazzu." The rich soil here defined the region's shape and settlement. The Palouse Hills are made of fertile volcanic soil carried to the area by steady winds and piled in thick layers. This soil, called loess, is considered some of the most fertile soil in the West. Settlers began moving into the Palouse in 1869, and within a few years the best lands were already snatched up and producing wheat. Despite early fears about how to get crops to market, by the mid-1880s the Palouse and Walla Walla Valley together were producing more than 7 million bushels of wheat every year. In one year alone, from 1881 to 1882, the value of Palouse wheat shipped down the Columbia River leapt from a little over $0.5 million to $3 million. Lentils are another major crop in the Palouse, which hosts the National Lentil Festival, one of only two lentil festivals in the world (the other is in France).

Petroglyphs and Pictographs

The Columbia Plateau is rich in Native American rock carvings (petroglyphs) and paintings (pictographs). In all, there are more than 750 known sites from The Dalles to the Rocky Mountains, and from the Fraser River to the Hells Canyon of the Snake. The drawings and carvings, which date from more than 3,000 years ago until the late 1800s, record the goings-on of daily life as well as religious ritual. Images depict humans or animals, or geometric symbols. The representations are naturalistic, stylized, or highly abstract. Hunters recorded their success; shamans made images to ward off evil spirits. The coming of the horse in the 1600s is recorded in the images.

Petroglyphs were made either by pecking at the base rock with a harder stone, or by incising the surface. Petroglyphs are

Losing It

Palouse Falls has a drop of 198 feet, and the water is chocolate brown with soil from Palouse fields. Measurements in the winter of 1962-63 showed 22 million tons of sediment going over the falls, equivalent to 160 acres of soil 80 feet deep. That was the worst erosion year on record. Average erosion is about half of that.—John Marshall, *Portrait of Washington* ✳

Palouse Falls. Photo by John Marshall

most often found on basalt, a hard, dense volcanic stone with a usually uniformly colored, relatively smooth surface.

The pigments used for making pictographs were made from minerals in the region; for example, crushed iron oxides for red and yellow colors. Certain clays in the region yielded white pigments, and copper oxides provided blue-green. Charcoal and manganese oxide provided black pigments. The pigments were often applied as fingerpaints. Sometimes a brush, a feather, or a twig was employed. The mineral pigments have great staying power, because they have actually stained the rock surface. Many pictographs are as old as petroglyphs.

Fortunately, a number of Columbia Plateau rock art sites have been protected and are open to the public.

Cowiche Creek. Excellent examples of pictographs are located just northeast of Yakima. From I-82, take the Naches exit north of town. Go west on U.S. Highway 12 for 4 miles to Ackley Rd. Turn south on Ackley, then immediately turn west on Powerhouse Rd. for about 0.5 mile to a large interpretive sign. A pathway runs from the sign to the pictographs on the columnar basalt cliff south of the road.

Gingko Petrified Forest State Park. Petroglyphs salvaged from the area flooded by Wanapum Dam were moved to this state park. They include fine renderings of hunting scenes. Exit I-90 at Vantage (30 miles east of Ellensburg). Proceed less than 1 mile north.

Horsethief Lake State Park. Located on the north bank of the Columbia just above The Dalles, this park contains a large concentration of rock art in a natural setting. Across the Columbia from The Dalles. At the junction of U.S. Highway 197 and Highway 14, proceed east on Highway 14 approximately 2 miles, to the park entrance. Within the park, proceed past the administrative offices to a parking area near the railroad tracks that parallel the river. The trail to the rock art leads west from this parking lot, below a rimrock of low basalt cliffs. Rock art is scattered over 0.5 mile along this trail.

Long Lake and Little Spokane Pictographs. The Long Lake pictographs are reached by following Highway 291 from Spokane to milepost 28, about 6 miles past the town of Tumtum. A path leads from the parking area to two separate areas. The pictographs on the Little Spokane River can be reached from Rutter Pkwy., a few miles north of Spokane. There is a small park devoted to the pictographs.

Petroglyphs and pictographs have been salvaged many times from dam and road construction. Some of these fine examples of early art can be seen at other locations, including:

Fort Okanogan State Park Visitor Center, 5 miles east of Brewster.

Ice Harbor Dam Overlook, on the Snake River 12 miles east of Pasco.

Maryhill Museum, on Highway 14, 4 miles west of Maryhill, along the Columbia River.

Petroglyphs at Horsethief Lake State Park. Courtesy of Washington State Parks & Recreation Commission.

North Central Washington Museum, Wenatchee.

Priest Rapids Dam, on display in the picnic area, about 20 miles south of the I-90 bridge at Vantage.

Prosser City Park, 30 miles west of Richland.

Rocky Reach Dam Museum, north of Wenatchee.

Roosevelt Park, on Highway 14, 1 mile east of Roosevelt, along the Columbia River.

Wells Dam Overlook, 10 miles north of Chelan.

Physical Geography

Washington is the 19th largest state in the United States. Its total area is 70,637 square miles; the total land area is 66,581 square miles and total water area is 4,055 square miles. The state's inland waters cover 1,545 square miles, and the coastal waters over which the state has jurisdiction comprise 2,511 square miles. From east to west, the state is roughly 350 miles and 240 miles from north to south. The approximate mean elevation is 1,700 feet. The highest point is Mount Rainier, elevation 14,411 feet; the lowest elevation is sea level. The geographic center of the state is located in Devils Gulch, just west of the north end of Mission Ridge (due south of Cashmere and southwest of Wenatchee).

The state extends from the 45th to the 49th parallel of north latitude, and from 116 degrees west to 124 degrees, 40 minutes west longitude. The state is bordered on the north by Canada, on the east by Idaho, on the south by Oregon, and on the west by the Pacific Ocean. The Columbia River forms the border between Oregon and Washington from the Pacific Ocean to just east of McNary Dam.

The state is divided into up to eight major natural regions or physiographic provinces (depending on which definitions one uses): the Olympic Peninsula and Willapa Hills (the Olympic Mountains, while often lumped together with the Coast Range, are considered a distinct physiographic region from Willapa Hills, which are part of the Coast Range); the Puget

Trough, also called the Puget Lowland, the region of glacially scoured lowland that lies between the coastal and Cascade Mountains from Puget Sound; the Cascade Mountains, also considered as two distinct provinces, the Northern and Southern Cascades; the Okanogan Highlands in the northeastern part of the state; the Columbia Basin; and a small portion of the Blue Mountains in the southeastern corner of the state.

Place Names
Place names in Washington State reflect successive waves of occupation and settlement. Place names are formally approved by the Washington State Board on Geographic Names. The Tacoma Public Library maintains a complete database of Washington place names on its Web site at tpl.lib.wa.us. **Washington State Board on Geographic Names,** Department of Natural Resources, P.O. Box 47032, Olympia, WA 98504-7032; (360) 902-1230.

Native American names appear throughout the state, from Seattle to Spokane. The name Seattle was bestowed by the original territorial pioneers in 1852, in honor of the chief of the Duwamish and Suquamish tribes, who occupied the land on which the settlers settled. Spokane is named for an Indian tribe that inhabits the region where that city was established.

The earliest European explorers who left names behind were the Spanish, who ventured north from their holdings in California in the late 1700s. Remnants of Spanish exploration can be found in the names of San Juan, Orcas, and Camano Islands, as well as the Strait of Juan de Fuca.

English explorers followed. Mount Rainier, Hood Canal, and Dungeness were all named by English explorers. Peter Rainier and Samuel Hood were British admirals who were much renowned for defeating American colonists during the American revolutionary war. Dungeness was named after a reach of the English Channel.

American explorers followed the British, and preceded the territorial government and permanent settlers. Bainbridge Island is named for an early American naval hero,

Commodore William Bainbridge, who defeated the British in the War of 1812; he also captained the famed *Constitution,* which is the oldest U.S. naval vessel (on view in Boston Harbor, Massachusetts). Mount Constitution on Orcas Island was named by Lieutenant Wilkes after the famous naval vessel. Wilkes also named Elliott Bay during his exploring expedition; he had three crew members named Elliott along with him.

Early trappers and settlers retained and misspelled Indian names, such as Okanogan and Snohomish. Others repeated names from the old country (Kent, Geneva), and still others named their new homesteads out of eternal optimism (Acme, Paradise).

Foresters, not surprisingly, were the first to name many places in the wild reaches of the state. Bald Eagle Mountain, Eel Glacier, Fire Mountain, Fall Creek, Forest Mountain, Forlorn Lakes, Graves Creek, Jasper Mountain, Lake Edna, and Little Pete Lake are among many places that U.S. Forest Service personnel named for sweethearts, horses, and notable natural features.

After the region became a territory, place names often honored early settlers and civic and business leaders (La Conner, Ellensburg, Bush Prairie).

Postmasters played an especially important role in naming their communities, as did railroad and government officials. Railroad men had a particularly important role, as every station required a name. Deming, Fletcher, Lyman, and Raymond were all named by postmasters. Arlington, Benton City, and Cle Elum were given their names by railroad men.

Plants (*SEE* FOREST; MUSHROOMS; OLD GROWTH FORESTS)

The Pacific Northwest, with its diversity of terrain and climate, supports a wide variety of plant ecosystems and communities. These variations include the moist cool regions west of the Cascade mountains, the cool rugged subalpine and alpine terrain of the various mountain ranges, miles of marine-influenced coastline and estuaries, interior valleys and river basins, and semiarid high desert plateau. Some native plants are wide-ranging; others are confined to specific, well-defined areas. All are affected by such environmental factors as temperature, precipitation, and wind; soil chemistry, porosity, and drainage; and elevation, slope, and substrate. Another factor—wildfires—also affects the region's vegetation.

In general, in western Washington and along the eastern slopes of the Cascades and the mountains of northeastern and southeastern Washington, forests dominate, although the character of those forests

Skunk cabbage

varies (*see also* Forest). Along the western slope of the Cascades and the Olympic Mountains, the trees grow closer together, there is less light reaching the forest floor, and the vegetation on the forest floor is thick and lush. Here, ferns, mosses, fungi, and lichens are abundant. The state flower, the coast rhododendron, can grow quite tall here, unlike in more open areas, where it tends to be more compact. Other shrubs and woody plants found in the understory are Oregon grape, mock orange, salal, and devil's club. The conifer species found here below timberline are predominantly western hemlock, western red cedar, and Douglas and other firs. Also found here are madrona trees and Garry oak. While there is not a great variety of wildflowers in the coastal forest understory, beargrass thrives in a wide range of altitudes, from 3,000 feet on Oregon's Mount Hood down to sea level

Sword ferns

in Washington's Olympic Mountains.

Similar elevations on the east side of the Cascades and other eastern Washington mountains tend to be characterized by ponderosa and lodgepole pine with sparse undergrowth. As the terrain levels out along the high desert plateau, the vegetation is characterized as shrub-steppe, the driest of Washington's vegetation zones. Sagebrush, greasewood, and perennial grasses, particularly bluebunch wheatgrass, are typical of this region, along with low-lying bluegrass and cheatgrass.

In the high mountain regions, subalpine and alpine plant communities take over. Timberline tends to be at about 5,000 to 6,000 feet. Above these elevations, the mountain meadow zone features a wide variety of wildflowers, such as avalanche lily, glacier lily, columbine, paintbrush, penstemon, and pasqueflower (also known as western anemone). A favorite viewing area for alpine wildflowers is the meadows at Paradise on Mount Rainier.

The coastal region, with its sand dunes, estuaries, and headlands, is another distinctive area for plants. Trees and shrubs that grow along the edge of sand beaches and dunes include salt-resistant plants, such as various beach grasses. Rushes and sedges are found along estuaries, and in some places in the shallow waters, large eelgrass beds support a rich marine biota. Two of the largest eelgrass beds on the West Coast are found in Washington: in Willapa Bay on the Pacific coast and Padilla Bay south of Bellingham. Off the rocky northern coast, large offshore kelp forests thrive.

Finally, among the state's native plants are some delicious edible berries—wild Pacific blackberry, salmonberries, and wild huckleberries are found in many areas— and some not-so-desirable plants, some of which are classified as "exotic pest plants." The Pacific Northwest Exotic Pest Plant Council, (206) 616-5020, maintains a list of those plants that they consider have "the potential to disrupt or alter the natural ecosystem function, composition, and diversity of the site it occupies."

The Washington Natural Heritage Program keeps track of all rare and sensitive species, including those considered threatened or endangered in the state. **Washington Natural Heritage Program,** Department of Natural Resources, P.O. Box 47016, Olympia, WA 98504-7016; (360) 902-1688.

Endangered Species.

Artemisia campestris ssp. *borealis,* northern wormwood

Aster jessicae, Jessica's aster

Astragalus pulsiferae var suksdorfii, Ames' milk-vetch

Astragalus sinuatus, Whited's milk-vetch

Cypripedium parviflorum, yellow lady's-slipper

Delphinium leucophaeum, Pale larkspur

Eriogonum codium, Umtanum desert buckwheat

Hackelia venusta, showy stickseed

Lesquerella tuplashensis, Whitebluffs bladderpod

Liparis loeselii, twayblade

Lobelia kalmii, Kalm's lobelia

Lupinus sabinii, Sabin's lupine

Lupinus sulphureus var kincaidii, Kincaid's sulfur lupine

Sidalcea hirtipes, hairy-stemmed checkermallow

Rubus nigerrimus, Northwest raspberry

Oxytropis campestris var wanapum, Wanapum crazyweed

Threatened Species.

Allium dictuon, blue mountain onion

Aster borealis, rush aster

Astragalus australis var. *olympicus,* Cotton's milk-vetch
Astragalus columbianus, Columbia milk-vetch
Calochortus nitidus, broad-fruit mariposa
Camissonia pygmaea, dwarf evening-primrose
Cimicifuga elata, tall bugbane
Corydalis aquae-gelidae, Clackamas corydalis
Cusickiella douglasii, Douglas' draba
Cypripedium fasciculatum, clustered lady's-slipper
Delphinium viridescens, Wenatchee larkspur
Dodecatheon austrofrigidum, frigid shootingstar
Eatonella nivea, white eatonella
Erigeron howellii, Howell's daisy
Erigeron oreganus, gorge daisy
Eryngium petiolatum, Oregon coyote-thistle
Filipendula occidentalis, queen-of-the-forest
Haplopappus liatriformis, Palouse golden-weed
Juncus kelloggii, Kellogg's rush
Lathyrus holochlorus, thin-leaved peavine
Lathyrus torreyi, Torrey's peavine
Lobelia dortmanna, water lobelia
Loeflingia squarrosa var. *squarrosa,* Loeflingia
Lomatium rollinsii, Rollins' desert-parsley
Lomatium tuberosum, Hoover's desert-parsley
Meconella oregana, white meconella
Navarretia tagetina, marigold navarretia
Ophioglossum pusillum, adder's-tongue
Orthocarpus bracteosus, rosy owl-clover
Oxytropis campestris var. *columbiana,* Columbia crazyweed
Penstemon barrettiae, Barrett's beardtongue
Petrophyton cinerascens, Chelan rockmat
Phacelia lenta, sticky phacelia
Platanthera chorisiana, Choris' bog-orchid
Poa laxiflora, loose-flowered bluegrass
Poa unilateralis, ocean-bluff bluegrass
Polemonium carneum, great polemonium
Polemonium

pectinatum, Washington polemonium
Ranunculus reconditus, obscure buttercup
Rorippa columbiae, persistent sepal yellowcress
Salix sessilifolia, soft-leaved willow
Silene seelyi, Seely's silene
Silene spaldingii, Spalding's silene
Sisyrinchium sarmentosum, pale blue-eyed grass
Sullivantia oregana, Oregon sullivantia
Tauschia hooveri, Hoover's tauschia
Trifolium thompsonii, Thompson's clover

Organizations of Interest.
Washington Native Plant Society, P.O. Box 28690, Seattle, WA 98118-9890; (206) 323-3336, (888) 288-8022.

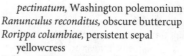

Cedars

Cedars require 60 to 120 inches of rain a year. In moist, rich bottomland, the massive trees dominate undisturbed groves indefinitely, reaching 200 feet tall with a diameter of up to 15 or 20 feet. More tolerant of shade than most conifers, cedars once dominated old-growth forests along the Washington coast....Northwest Coast Indian tribes used western red cedar wood and bark more extensively than any other native plant, for cooking utensils, burial boxes, enormous war canoes, and many other uses. Some planks they split for their longhouses measured 40 feet long, 4 inches thick, and 3 feet wide. The straight-grained wood splits easily, and is light yet firm and almost knot free.—Ann Saling, *The Great Northwest Nature Factbook* ❊

Politics
Washington politics is a healthy mix of the liberal tradition of the densely settled cities around Puget Sound, the innate conservatism of the rural areas, and the strong progressivism tradition brought to the region by Scandinavian settlers a century ago. The political process in Washington is also very open: Voters can participate directly in law-making, and are not restricted by political party when voting for candidates in primary and general elections.

Initiatives and Referendums.
Washington was one of the first states to adopt the initiative and referendum process, as an amendment to the state constitution in 1912. The process gives citizens the power to enact new laws or change existing ones.

There are two types of initiatives: initiatives to the people, which are submitted to the voters at a general election, and initiatives to the Legislature. The Legislature can adopt the initiative as proposed, reject or refuse to act, in which case it is submitted to the voters, or approve an amended version, in which case both the amended and original versions are submitted to the voters. Any registered voter, acting individually or on behalf of an organization, may propose an initiative, but the sponsor must obtain a certain number of signatures of legal voters (8 percent of the number of votes previously cast for governor) to get the initiative placed on the ballot. Initiatives appearing on the ballot require a simple majority to become law, except for gambling or lottery measures, which require 60 percent approval.

The referendum process allows voters the final say regarding laws proposed or approved by the Legislature, except for emergency laws (those necessary to preserve the public peace, health, or safety, and for the support of state government and its existing institutions). There are two types of referendums: Referendum bills are proposed laws referred to the electorate by the Legislature, and referendum measures are laws recently passed by the Legislature that are placed on the ballot because of petitions signed by voters. A referendum is passed by a simple majority, except gambling and lottery measures, which require 60 percent of the vote.

Office of the Secretary of State, Attention: Initiative and Referendum Coordinator, P.O. Box 40237, Olympia, WA 98504-0237; (360) 586-0400. http://www.wa.gov/sec/elections.htm.

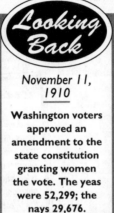

Looking Back

November 11, 1910

Washington voters approved an amendment to the state constitution granting women the vote. The yeas were 52,299; the nays 29,676.

Running For Office
Candidates must file their intent to run for elective office with the Secretary of State's office or county elections office between the fourth Monday in July through the next succeeding Friday. Candidates for most offices must also submit a filing fee, which varies from zero to 1 percent of the elective office's annual salary. Candidates can run by entering the primary as a major party candidate, as a minor party candidate, or as an independent candidate by qualifying through a nominating convention, or by filing a declaration to stand-in as a write-in candidate.

Political Parties
Washington distinguishes between major and minor political parties. Major political parties are those that have had at least one nominee for President, U.S. Senator, or a statewide office who received at least 5 percent of the total election vote cast at the last preceding general election held in an even-numbered year.

Major Political Parties.
Washington State Democratic Central Committee, 616 First Ave., Suite 300, Seattle, WA 98104; (206) 583-0664, fax (206) 583-0301. E-mail: waparty@democrats.org. http://www.wa-democrats.org.

Washington State Republican Party, 16400 Southcenter Pkwy., Suite 200, Seattle, WA 98188; (206) 575-2900, fax (206) 575-1730. E-mail: wsrp@seanet.com. http://www.wsrp.org.

Minor Political Parties.
American Heritage Party, P.O. Box 1534, Mead, WA 99021; (888) 396-6247, fax (509) 738-4663. E-mail: ahp@americanheritageparty.org. http://wwwamericanheritageparty.org.

Freedom Socialist Party, 5018 Rainier Ave. S., Seattle, WA 98118-6110; (206) 722-2453, fax (206) 723-7691. E-mail: freedomsoc@igc.apc.org. http://www.socialism.com.

Libertarian Party, P.O. Box 20732, Seattle, WA 98102; (800) 353-1776. E-mail: director@lpws.org. http://www.lpws.org.

Populist Party, 1916 Pike Pl., Suite 695, Seattle, WA 98101; (206) 781-5617.

Reform Party of Washington State, 1122 E. Pike St., Suite 539, Seattle, WA 98122; (206) 625-3303 or (360) 866-8619, fax (360) 866-8619 or (206) 329-0396. http://washington.reformparty.org. E-mail: telfordp@olywa.net.

Socialist Workers Party, 1405 E. Madison St., Seattle, WA 98122; (206) 323-3429. E-mail: 74461.2544@compuserve.com.

Campaign Financing

Washington State established a Public Disclosure Commission in 1973 to provide the public with information about who provides financial support to candidates and political committees, and where and how much lobbyists spend in the political process. Candidate or political committee treasurers must report the source and amount of campaign contributions over $25 and list campaign expenditures. The occupation and employer of individuals giving $100 or more to a campaign must also be identified. Campaign finance reports are available at the Public Disclosure Commission's Office in Olympia and at county elections offices.

Contributions to U.S. Senate and House of Representatives candidates are regulated by federal law. The limits on contributions to candidates and political committees from individuals are:

To candidates for state Legislature: $550, primary election; $550, general election.

To candidates for governor, lieutenant governor, and other statewide elected officials: $1,100, primary; $1,100 general election.

No limit to political parties, ballot issue committees, or political action committees, but during the 21 days before the general election, a person may contribute no more than $5,000 to a local or judicial office candidate, political party, or other political committee. Contributions from corporations, unions, businesses, associations, and similar organizations are permitted, subject to limits and other restrictions. Among the biggest spenders in running for office or pushing an issue, the Public Disclosure Commission lists the following from its "Most Money" journal.

Initiatives. Most money spent FOR an initiative: $6,259,692, Initiative 48, Sports Stadium/Exhibition Center, 1997.

Most money spent OPPOSING a single initiative: $3,406,425, Initiative 676, Handgun device, 1997.

Most money spent in an initiative campaign by BOTH sides: $6,986,439, Initiative 48, Sports Stadium/Exhibition Center, 1997.

LEAST amount spent in a winning initiative campaign: $14,006, Initiative 316, Mandatory Death Penalty, 1975.

Statewide Elected Offices. Most money raised and spent by a single candidate for governor: $2,946,810 raised, $2,925,898 spent, by Booth Gardner, 1984.

Most money spent by all candidates: $8,883,283 in 1996 by Locke, Craswell, Inslee, Rice, Foreman, Maleng, Waldo, Tharp, Roach, Hanson, Brazier, Zetlen, Said, and Englerius, combined.

Most money spent by a single candidate for statewide elected office (other than governor): $804,941 by Ann Anderson, Commissioner of Public Lands, 1992.

Most money spent by all candidates for a single statewide elected position (other than governor): $1,488,960 for attorney general, 1992, position won by Christine Gregoire.

State Senate. Most money spent by a single candidate: $301,807 by Ray Schow, 1998, 30th District.

Most money spent by all candidates in a single race: $504,887 for 36th District, 1990, seat won by Ray Moore.

State House of Representatives. Most money spent by a single candidate: $193,862 by Joe King, 1990, 49th District.

Most money spent by all candidates in a

single race: $323,528 for 23rd District, 1998, seat won by Paul Zellinsky Sr.

PACS. Ten most active political action committees (PACS), by reported expenditures (1996):

Washington Federation of State Employees
    Legislative Fund
United for Washington
Washington Education Association
Washington State Taxpayers Committee
Washington Conservation Voters
Candidates Political Action Fund
Retail Action Council
Washington Chiropractic Trust
Washington State Machinists Council
Washington State Labor Council, AFL-CIO

Organizations of Interest.

Elections Division, Office of the Secretary of State, Legislative Bldg., P.O. Box 40220, Olympia, WA 98504-0220; (360) 902-4151, fax (360) 586-5629, TDD (800) 422-8683. E-mail: elections@secstate.wa.gov.

Washington State Public Disclosure Commission, 7111 Capitol Way, Room 403, P.O. Box 40908, Olympia, WA 98504-0908; (360) 753-1111, fax (360) 753-1112. http://www. washington.edu/pdc.

Population

The U.S. Census Bureau numbers Washington's residents at 5,610,000. It is the 15th most populous state, and among the 10 fastest-growing states, with a 15.3 percent net change in population—that means an additional 744,000 residents—from 1990 to 1997; most of the growth occurred from 1990 to 1995 (11.7 percent). Population per square mile of land area in the state is 84.3 persons. The state's population change for this time period includes 570,000 births, 289,000 deaths, 98,000 immigrants from

foreign countries, and 352,000 residents who moved from elsewhere in the United States. In addition, there are an estimated 52,000 undocumented immigrants in the state. The racial makeup of the state includes 196,000 African Americans; 100,000 American Indians, Eskimos, and Aleuts; and 311,000 Asians and Pacific Islanders. Persons who claim Hispanic origin number 340,000.

Looking Back

June 16, 1936

The bill creating Olympic National Park was signed into law. It was considered a victory of conservation over lumber interests that had attempted to exclude vast stands of commercially valuable hemlock from the park.

Ports
Washington has 76 public port districts scattered along Puget Sound, the Pacific coast, and the Columbia River. In 1996, of the $87 billion of trade moving through the state, waterborne cargo flowing through Washington's ports accounted for $54 billion. Approximately one in five jobs throughout the state are connected to trade, and many of those jobs are in port areas.

According to the Washington Public Ports Association and the Washington Council on International Trade, Washington is the fifth-largest exporting state in the United States; one-third of all U.S. grain exports move through the Columbia/Snake River system. While Washington State represents about 2 percent of the nation's population, its ports handle 6.6 percent of all U.S. exports and receive a 5.8 percent share of the nation's imports. The ports of Seattle and Tacoma together comprise the second-largest container load center in North America.

The port districts are public agencies run by elected commissioners, and they comprise the largest locally controlled port system in the world. In addition to waterborne trade, port districts operate marinas, airports, railroads, and industrial sites.

Washington Public Ports Association, P.O. Box 1518, Olympia, WA 98507-1518; (360) 943-0760.

Top Ports (1996)

	Value of Waterborne Trade
Port of Seattle	$31.1 billion
Port of Tacoma	17.7 billion
Port of Vancouver	1.4 billion
Port of Longview	1.2 billion
Port of Kalama	1.2 billion
Port of Bellingham	508 million
Port of Aberdeen/Hoquiam	469 million
Port of Everett	214 million
Port of Anacortes	207 million

Source: Washington Public Ports

Distance from Port of Seattle to Other Ports

City	Miles	Nautical Miles
Los Angeles	954	829
Anchorage	1,414	1,229
Honolulu	2,677	2,326
Panama	3,651	3,173
Tokyo	4,791	4,164
Seoul	5,180	4,501
Hong Kong	6,483	5,634
Buenos Aires	6,885	5,983
Sydney	7,737	6,723
Singapore	8,070	7,013
Jakarta	8,373	7,276

Prisons
The Washington State Department of Corrections employs 6,000 men and women to administer and supervise more than 12,000 offenders housed in 12 institutions and 19 work training and pre-release facilities. In addition, there are more than 81,000 supervised offenders in the community.

Prison Population (December 1998)

Institution	Capacity	Total Population	% of Capacity
Ahtanum Facility	120	102	85
Airway Heights	1,936	2,040	105
Cedar Creek	400	386	97
Center for Women	680	690	101
Clallam Bay	858	899	105
Coyote Ridge	400	397	99
Larch Center	400	380	95
McNeil Annex	235	232	99
McNeil Island	1,124	1,174	104
Monroe Reformatory	776	1,118	144
Olympic Center	340	347	102
Pre-release	499	531	106
Shelton Center	1,205	1,735	144
Special Offender Center	144	141	98
Twin Rivers	834	843	101
Walla Walla Penitentiary	1,875	2,431	130
Work Ethic Camp	200	185	93
Work Release	682	610	89
Totals	12,708	14,241	112

Source: Washington State Department of Corrections

Prison Demographics

Age and Gender		Percentages
Average age	34.4	
Male	12,302	92.8
Female	924	7.2

Race	
White	71.1
Black	22.5
Hispanic	13.4
American Indian	3.3
Asian	2.4
Other	0.7

Length of Sentence	
Less than 2 years	16.3
2-5 years	26.9
5-10 years	27.7
More than 10 years	26.8
Life without release	2.3

Type of Offense	
Murder	12.4
Manslaughter	1.5

Prison Demographics (continued)

Type of Offense (continued)	Percentages
Sex crimes	22.5%
Robbery	10.0%
Assault	15.4%
Property	15.0%
Drug crimes	22.0%
Other/unknown	1.2%

Recidivism

Nearly one-third of first-time prisoners return to prison within five years of release.

The return rates by offense categories are:

Property crimes	43%
Person crimes	31%
Drug crimes	26%
Sex crimes	20%

Source: Washington State Department of Corrections

Changing Prison Population.

The prison population is increasing as a result of legislative and judicial changes. The offender population has been growing faster than the state population since 1988, as sentencing changes have increased the offender population.

In 1987, drug offenders accounted for 4 percent of the population, property offen-ders 21 percent, and violent offenders 75 percent. By 1997, the drug offender population reached nearly 24 percent, while property offenders decreased to 14 percent and violent offenders decreased to 62 percent.

Recent laws have increased sentence lengths. This has contributed to an increased aging offender population. The number of offenders age 50 and over more than doubled over the past 10 years. Older offenders require more care, incur more health problems, and generally have higher costs associated with them.

Legislation has also increased the incarceration of youthful offenders. From 1997 to 2000, there is projected to be a 360 percent increase in the number of youthful offenders. The number of female offenders is also projected to increase. Female offenders have a higher rate of drug abuse as well as higher rates of HIV infection.

Corrections Costs.

The Department of Corrections accounts for about 8 percent of the state general funds budget. One prison bed costs taxpayers nearly $1 million over 30 years. Operating costs account for more than 76 percent of these costs. The annual cost per offender reached a high of $18,707 in 1988. In fiscal year (FY) 1997, the cost per offender, adjusted for inflation, was $15,207. The average cost per bed is approximately $23,500 per year. The average cost per offender on supervision in the community is $780 per year. Corrections costs will be more than $900 million in the 1997-1999 biennium. These costs are projected to grow by as much as 46 percent within the next five years.

Death Penalty.

From 1904 through October 1998, there have been 76 executions in Washington State. As of December 1998, 14 people were on death row. Death sentences are carried out at the Washington State Penitentiary. Death is inflicted by intravenous injection or, at the election of the prisoner, by hanging.

State Institutions.

Ahtanum View Corrections Complex, 2009 S. 64th Ave., Yakima, WA 98903; (509) 573-6300. This minimum-security facility is designed for elderly and medically disabled offenders who need assistance with activities of daily living.

Airway Heights Corrections Center, 11919 W. Sprague Ave., P.O. Box 1899, Airway Heights, WA 99001-1899; (509) 244-6700. At this medium- and minimum-security facility, work opportunities include janitorial, bindery, food services, refurbishing personal computers, optical laboratory, maintenance, laundry, motor pool, recreation, clerical, library, natural resources programs, community work crews, and groundskeeping. Educational programs are provided by Spokane Community College.

Cedar Creek Corrections Center, 1 Bordeaux Rd., P.O. Box 37, Littlerock, WA 98556; (360) 753-7278. Offenders housed at this facility work in Department of Natural Resources programs, and also in asbestos abatement, removal of underground storage tanks, panel assembly, and general labor.

Clallam Bay Corrections Center, 1830 Eagle Crest Way, Clallam Bay, WA; (360) 963-2000. Composed of four close-custody units, four medium-security units, and one intensive-management unit, this facility's work experiences include office chair manufacturing, data entry, and telemarketing projects for state agencies. Educational programs are provided by Peninsula College.

Coyote Ridge Corrections Center, 1301 N. Ephrata, P.O. Box 769, Connell, WA 99326-0769; (509) 545-2328. About half the offenders from this minimum-security facility work off-site for nonprofit organizations and public agencies.

Larch Corrections Center, 15314 NE Dole Valley Rd., Yacolt, WA 98675-6300; (360) 260-6300. At this facility accessed by unpaved forest roads, most offenders work in general forest management under the supervision of the Department of Natural Resources.

McNeil Island Corrections Center, 1403 Commercial St., P.O. Box 88900, Steilacoom, WA 98388-0900; (253) 588-5281. This island facility is reached by a 20-minute ferry ride. It includes the main institution and a minimum-custody annex. Work assignments include food service, maintenance, fire crew, barbers, recreational aides, teachers' aides, library assistants, laundry workers, clerks, janitors, carpenters, painters, welders, plumbers, electricians, and steamfitters.

Olympic Corrections Center, 11235 Hoh Mainline, Forks, WA 98331; (360) 374-6181. Most offenders work with the Department of Natural Resources.

Twin Rivers Corrections Center, 16920 16th SE, P.O. Box 888, Monroe, WA 98272-0888; (360) 794-2400. This medium-security facility includes facilities for sex offenders and mentally ill and seriously disturbed offenders. Limited work opportunities focus primarily on mental health treatment. Edmonds Community College provides training and educational programs.

Washington Corrections Center for Women, 960 Bujacich Rd. NW, P.O. Box 17, Gig Harbor, WA 98335-0017; (253) 858-4200. Two unique programs are offered: the Prison Pet Partnership Program, which trains dogs to assist handicapped individuals, and the "Children's Center," a program offering offenders the opportunity to practice learned positive parenting skills with their children in a safe, structured environment.

Washington Corrections Center, W. 2321 Dayton Airport Rd., P.O. Box 900, Shelton, WA 98584; (360) 436-4433. This is the reception, testing, and classification center for all male offenders, with the exception of inmates sentenced to death, seriously fragile offenders under age 18, and mental cases, who are sent to Twin Rivers. The reception center is a close-security facility.

Washington State Penitentiary, 1313 N. 13th St., Walla Walla, WA 99362-1065; (509) 525-3610. At this facility for long-term, older, violent, and more serious offenders, work experience includes institutional support positions in food service, license plate manufacture, sheet and welded metal fabrication, wood and upholstery restoration, sign production and refurbishing, mattress production, hog and dairy farms, and duffel bag manufacture.

Washington State Reformatory and Farm, 16700 177th Ave. SE, P.O. Box 777, Monre, WA 98272-0777; (360) 794-2600. The farm is located 5 miles from the main institution of Twin Rivers.

County Jails. County jails in the state have an average daily population in excess of 9,000.

Professional Sports

Washington State's cities and towns field a number of professional and semi-pro sports teams, although the best known are the three Seattle major league ball clubs: the Mariners baseball team, the Seahawks football team, and the SuperSonics basketball team. The Mariners and Seahawks, which played in the Kingdome from the time it was built in the 1970s, both have new stadiums. The new Mariners ballpark, named Safeco Field, saw its first game July

15, 1999; the Seahawks' new stadium is scheduled to be completed in 2002. The SuperSonics began playing in the renovated KeyArena in the Seattle Center in 1995.

Major and Minor League Baseball

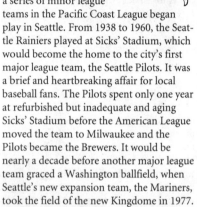

Minor league baseball has been a fixture in Washington since the late 1800s, when what would become a series of minor league teams in the Pacific Coast League began play in Seattle. From 1938 to 1960, the Seattle Rainiers played at Sicks' Stadium, which would become the home to the city's first major league team, the Seattle Pilots. It was a brief and heartbreaking affair for local baseball fans. The Pilots spent only one year at refurbished but inadequate and aging Sicks' Stadium before the American League moved the team to Milwaukee and the Pilots became the Brewers. It would be nearly a decade before another major league team graced a Washington ballfield, when Seattle's new expansion team, the Mariners, took the field of the new Kingdome in 1977.

Nearly 20 years later, Seattleites were reminded that what the American League giveth, the American League can taketh away. So when the specter of their beloved Mariners moving to another city arose in 1995, the Legislature cobbled together a public/private finance package to build a shiny new stadium so that baseball could be enjoyed outdoors—the way it always has been by Washington's minor league teams. Mariners ticket holders are protected from the rain by a retractable roof. The new Safeco Field seats 46,621 and its field is 3.13 acres. The roof has three panels and takes 20 minutes to open or close.

The Mariners' farm system teams include the Everett AquaSox and Tacoma Rainiers in state, and the Orlando Rays, Lancaster (California) JetHawks, Wisconsin Timber Rattlers (fifth year), and Peoria (Arizona) Mariners out of state. Peoria, Arizona, is also the home of the Mariners' spring training facility.

Seattle Mariners, Administrative Offices, P.O. Box 4100, 83 King St., third floor, Seattle, WA 98104; (206) 628-3555. Email: mariners@ mariners.org. http://www. mariners.org.

Minor League Baseball. One does not have to live in or travel to Seattle to catch the excitement of professional baseball. While it is not the bigs, minor league baseball is just as exciting to many hometown fans. You can catch the minors in Tacoma, Everett, Spokane, Yakima, and the Tri-Cities. The games are played outdoors, just like in the big leagues, but bring your own umbrella if it looks like rain.

Everett AquaSox, Northwest League. Affiliation: Seattle Mariners. Memorial Stadium, 3802 Broadway, Everett, WA 98201; (425) 258-3673.

Spokane Indians Baseball, Class A. Affiliation: Kansas City Royals. 602 N. Havana, Spokane, WA; (509) 535-2922.

Tacoma Rainiers, Pacific Coast League. Affiliation: Seattle Mariners. Cheney Stadium, 2502 S. Tyler, Tacoma, WA 98405; (253) 752-7707.

Tri-City Posse, Western Baseball League. Affiliation: Locally owned. Tri-Cities Stadium, 6200 Burden Rd., Pasco, WA; (509) 547-6773.

Yakima Bears, Class A. Affiliation: Los Angeles Dodgers. Yakima County Stadium at Central Washington Fairgrounds. 810 W. Nob Hill Blvd., Yakima, WA 98902; (509) 457-5151.

Basketball

The Seattle SuperSonics of the National Basketball Association are Washington's big-ticket basketball show. The Sonics first took the court in Seattle for the 1967-68 season. By the the late 1970s, they were one of the league's elite teams, reaching the NBA Finals in two straight seasons and winning the crown in 1978-79 under Coach Lenny Wilkens. After an up-and-down decade in the 1980s, Seattle became one of the league's best teams again in the 1990s under Coach George Karl, reaching the playoffs seven times and the finals in 1995–96 against the powerhouse Chicago

Bulls. The series was predicted to be a rout for Chicago, but the Sonics won games 4 and 5 before losing the championship to the Bulls in game 6. In 1998, the Sonics replaced Coach Karl with former Phoenix coach Paul Westphal.

Professional and semi-pro basketball in Washington has also included professional women's basketball and semi-pro basketball in Yakima. In 1997 and 1998, Seattle was home, too briefly, to the Seattle Reign of the American Basketball League, which went out of business after just two years. In Yakima, basketball fans can catch the action of the Yakima Suns at the Sundome. The team is part of the developmental league for the NBA Sonics, Blazers, and Kings affiliations. Spokane takes basketball to the streets in June each year during Hoopfest, the largest 3-on-3 basketball tournament in the United States.

Seattle SuperSonics, 190 Queen Anne Ave. N., Box 900911, Seattle, WA 98109-9711; (206) 283-DUNK. Home court: KeyArena, First Ave. N. between Thomas and Republican, Seattle.

Seattle SuperSonics Team History

Season	Wins	Losses	% of wins
1967-68	23	59	.280
1968-69	30	52	.366
1969-70	36	46	.439
1970-71	38	44	.463
1971-72	47	35	.573
1972-73	26	56	.317
1973-74	36	46	.439
1974-75	43	39	.524
1975-76	43	39	.524
1976-77	40	42	.488
1977-78	47	35	.573
1978-79	52	30	.634
1979-80	56	26	.683
1980-81	34	48	.415
1981-82	52	30	.634
1982-83	48	34	.585
1983-84	42	40	.512
1984-85	31	51	.378
1985-86	31	51	.378
1986-87	39	43	.476
1987-88	44	38	.537
1988-89	47	35	.573

(continued)

The Seattle Mariners at their old home stadium, the Kingdome. Courtesy of Kingdome Media Relations Office.

Seattle SuperSonics Team History
(continued)

Season	Wins	Losses	% of wins
1989-90	41	41	.500
1990-91	41	41	.500
1991-92	47	35	.573
1992-93	55	27	.671
1993-94	63	19	.768
1994-95	57	25	.695
1995-96	64	18	.780
1996-97	57	25	.695
1997-98	61	21	.744

Football

Professional football arrived in the Northwest in 1974 when Seattle was granted an expansion team. In their first year of play, 1976, the Seahawks were sixth in the league in attendance, despite a 2-12 record. The team changed hands several times and in 1997 was purchased by local multibillionaire Paul Allen, who made construction of a new stadium part of the package. Voters approved a statewide referendum to build the $400 million facility as a public-private endeavor. The new stadium will replace the 20-year-old Kingdome, the team's home stadium, on the existing site just south of downtown Seattle. It will have 72,000 seats, including 7,000 club seats and 82 suites, and roof protection for 70 percent of the fans with an open-air, natural-grass field.

Seattle Seahawks, 11220 NE 53rd St., Kirkland, WA 98033; (888) NFL-HAWK.

Hockey

The Western and West Coast Hockey Leagues are represented in Washington in Seattle, Spokane, the Tri-Cities, and Tacoma.

Western Hockey League.

Seattle Thunderbirds. Home: KeyArena, Seattle. 1813 130th Ave. NE, Suite 210, Bellevue, WA 98005; (206) 448-7825, (425) 869-7825. www.seattle-thunderbirds.com.

Spokane Chiefs. Home: Spokane Arena. 700 W. Mallon, Spokane, WA 99201; (509) 328-0450. www.spokanechiefs.com.

Tri-City Americans. Home: Tri-Cities Coliseum. 7100 W. Quinault, Arena Level, Kennewick, WA 99336; (509) 736-0606. www.amshockey.com.

West Coast Hockey League.

Tacoma Sabercats. Home: Tacoma Dome. 1111 Fawcett Ave. S., Suite 204, Tacoma, WA 98402; (253) 627-2673.

Soccer

While world league soccer has not made the inroads in the United States that it has in other countries, it is still a sport with widespread appeal and there are several professional and semi-professional teams in the state. The Seattle Sounders are the state's only A-League soccer team, the highest level of competition in the United System of Independent Soccer Leagues (USISL), which is composed of different levels in indoor, outdoor, amateur, and women's leagues in the United States and Canada. The A-League is a Division II professional league by the United States Soccer Federation. Other teams in Washington play in the USISL Premier Development Soccer League (PDSL); they are the Yakima Reds, the Spokane Shadow, the Seattle Bigfoot, and the Hibernians of Bellevue.

A-League.

Seattle Sounders. Home: Renton Memorial Stadium. 10838 Main St., Bellevue, WA 98004; (800) 796-KICK, (206) 622-3415, fax (425) 643-3515. www.seattle-sounders.com.

Premier Development Soccer League.

Hibernians. Stadium: Various sites. P.O. Box 1557, Bellevue, WA 98009-1557; (206) 781-5877.

Spokane Shadow Soccer. Home: Joe Albi Stadium. 4918 W. Everett Ave., Spokane, WA 99205; (509) 326-4625.

Yakima Reds. Home: Marquette Stadium. P.O. Box 9187, Yakima, WA 98909; (509) 453-2086.

Public Transportation

The state's 26 public transit authorities serve more than 4.5 million people. This means that about 83 percent of Washingtonians are within the service area of a public transit provider. These transit services, listed below, carried about 138 million passengers over 94 million revenue service miles in 1994. The largest public transit system in the state is Metro Transit of King County, which has a fleet of about 1,300 vehicles serving an annual ridership of more than 75 million within a 2,128-square-mile area. In 1996, voters approved a transportation system that will add light rail to the Puget Sound region. Over the next 10 years, the Puget Sound Regional Transit Authority (called both Sound Transit and RTA), the agency implementing the system, will add electric light rail, commuter rail, and regional express bus routes to the region's transit system.

Public Transit Authorities.
Ben Franklin Transit (Kennewick, Pasco, and Richland)
Clallam Transit
Community Transit (Snohomish County)
Community Urban Bus Service (Kelso and Longview)
Cowlitz Transit Authority
C-Tran (Clark County, Vancouver)
Everett Transit
Grant Transit Authority
Grays Harbor Transit Authority
Intercity Transit (Thurston County)
Island Transit (Whidbey Island)
Jefferson Transit Authority (Port Townsend)
King County Transit (Metro)
Kitsap Transit (Bremerton)
Link (Chelan and Douglas Counties)
Mason County Transportation Authority
Pacific Transit System
Pierce Transit
Prosser Rural Transit (Benton County)
Pullman Transit (Whitman County)
Regional Transit Authority
Skagit Transit Authority
Spokane Transit Authority
Twin Transit (Lewis County)
Valley Transit (Walla Walla County)
Whatcom Transportation Authority (Bellingham)
Yakima Transit

Intercity Bus Service.
Borderline Stage, (509) 684-3950. Colville, Spokane, and Trail, BC.
Columbia Bus Systems, (800) 342-0210. Seattle, Yakima, Richland, Pasco, Pullman, and Walla Walla.
Greyhound Bus Lines, (800) 231-2222. Statewide.
Northwestern Trailways, (800) 366-3830. Everett, Seattle, Tacoma, Wenatchee, Moses Lake, Spokane, Pullman, and Moscow and Lewiston, Idaho.
Olympic Bus Lines, (800) 550-3858. Port Angeles-Sea-Tac Airport.

Puget Sound and Inland Waters

(SEE ALSO ISLANDS) East from the Pacific Ocean are 1,545 square miles of protected inland waters that make up Washington's northwestern corner. The passageway to the inland sea is the Strait of Juan de Fuca, which early explorers mistakenly thought might be part of the much-sought Northwest Passage through North America. The major components of the inland waters are the Strait of Juan de Fuca, the San Juan Archipelago, Puget Sound, and Hood Canal. While the entire watery region is sometimes referred to as Puget Sound, the sound itself is actually just that portion that extends south from Admiralty Inlet. The waters and shores of this region contain deep, sheltered harbors, bays, and inlets; long sandy spits and peninsulas; narrow water passes and channels; and hundreds of islands. Some of the region's most outstanding features are listed below.

Puget Sound. Puget Sound, an arm of the Pacific Ocean and a defining feature of western Washington, extends about 80 miles from Admiralty Inlet to Olympia. Puget Sound covers nearly 1,000 square miles, is the nation's second-largest estuary, and is divided into several branches navigable by large vessels. The principal ports of the sound are Seattle, Tacoma, Everett, and Olympia on the eastern shore, Bremerton on the western shore, and Port Townsend at the entrance. Puget Sound is a large, glacier-carved basin. Its deepest point lies at 920 feet, just south of the Kingston-Edmonds ferry route. Puget Sound is named for Peter Puget, a British naval officer who accompanied the British explorer George Vancouver to the Pacific Northwest.

Strait of Juan de Fuca. This 90-mile-long international waterway between British Columbia and Washington, with an average width of 13 miles, extends from the Pacific Ocean at Cape Flattery to the vicinity of Port Townsend in the United States and to Victoria, British Columbia, in Canada. The waterway was named for a Greek sailing master, Apostolos Valerianos, who called himself Juan de Fuca and claimed that he discovered the Strait in 1592 while employed by the Spanish government. Other major straits include Haro and Rosario. Haro Strait is an irregular channel between the San Juan Archipelago and Vancouver Island and other smaller Canadian islands. It marks the international boundary between British Columbia and the United States. Rosario Strait extends north and south between the San Juan Islands, and connects the Strait of Juan de Fuca with Georgia Strait to the north.

Hood Canal. Hood Canal is a long (about 80 miles), hook-shaped tidal channel that separates the Kitsap Peninsula from the Olympic Peninsula. The channel is crossed by one of the state's famed floating bridges (it sank in a violent storm in 1979 and had to be replaced), and Trident nuclear submarines ply its waters as they leave and return to the navy base at Bangor. Its more natural highlights include numerous seals and shellfish.

Dungeness Spit and Ediz Hook. Extending 5.5 miles into the Strait of Juan de Fuca near Port Angeles, Dungeness Spit is the longest natural sand spit in the United States. The western outer shore of the 100-yard-wide spit is exposed to the strait and the prevailing winds; the protected inner eastern shore curves around calm, shallow, 556-acre Dungeness Bay with an enclosed harbor, tideflats, and saltwater marsh. The spit and the adjacent tide line form the Dungeness National Wildlife Refuge. Lying within the rain shadow of the Olympic Mountains, the spit receives only about 15 inches of rain a year. To the east, another spit, 1-mile-long Ediz Hook, forms Port Angeles Harbor.

Bays and Harbors. The shoreline of the inland sea is convoluted by hundreds of bays, inlets, and harbors. The deepwater

Dungeness Spit. Photo by Susan Dupere.

Harbor seals. From *Going Wild in Washington and Oregon* by Susan Ewing,

bays provided perfect locations for ports, so it is not surprising that most early settlements were located near bays and harbors. On Puget Sound, the largest cities are located along protected bays: Tacoma on Commencement Bay, Seattle on Elliott Bay, Bremerton on Sinclair and Dyes Inlets, Olympia on Budd Inlet, Bellingham on Bellingham Bay. On the Strait of Juan de Fuca, Neah Bay, Port Angeles Harbor, and Sequim Bay are major indentations.

Radio and Television Stations

Washington has a full range of radio and television stations—all types of music, talk, news, and specialized audiences are represented. The state's largest ranked radio markets, according to Arbitron, a radio marketing research company, are Seattle-Tacoma (ranked 14th nationally), Spokane (87th), Yakima (193rd), and the Tri-Cities (207th). Television stations include local access and cable stations (not listed here).

The National Academy of Television Arts and Sciences hands out its Northwest regional awards each year in June. In 1998, the 34th such annual awards, the following people were dubbed the best in the Northwest in television.

Outstanding Daily Newscast: KIRO News at 10, KIRO-TV News Staff, Seattle.
Outstanding Reporting, Spot News: "Marina Collapse," April Zepada, John Knorr, Frances Turean, KOMO, Seattle.
Outstanding Reporting, Hard News: "China White," Lisa Hughes, Brian Miller, KIRO, Seattle.
Outstanding Reporting, Soft Feature, "The Enchantments," John Yeager, Jeannine Daigle-Moore, Mark Morache, KIRO, Seattle.
Outstanding Reporting, Same Day Feature: "Reggie's Big Find," Julie Blacklow, Mark Morache, KIRO, Seattle.
Outstanding Reporting, Humorous Feature: "It's a Wonderful Sports Town," Erick Johnson, Bryan O'Donnell, Darrin Tegman, KOMO, Seattle.
Outstanding Reporting, Investigative News: "Junkies Take Cabs," Brad Stone, Linda Byron, Randy Eng, KING, Seattle.
Outstanding Reporting, Sports: "Fan Catch," Eric Johnson, Darrin Tegman, KOMO, Seattle.
Outstanding Reporting, News Series: "Gadget Week: Garage Door, Code Grabber, Baby Monitor," Ross McLaughlin, Alison Grande, KIRO, Seattle.
Outstanding Reporting, Specialty Reporting: "Environmental Reporting," Scott Miller, KING, Seattle.
Documentary, Historical/Biographical: "The Beatles in Seattle," Ken Morrison, KOMO, Seattle.
Public Affairs Special, Studio: "Ice Storm '96," KXLY, Spokane.
Public Affairs Special, Location: "Hot Highs," Elaine Purchase, Christian Raaum, Dan Ibabao, KOMO, Seattle.
Public Affairs Series, Location: "In Color," Deborah Horne, Theresa Bujnoch, Eric Alexander, KIRO, Seattle.
Information Special: "Over Beautiful British Columbia," Jeff Gentes, Marc Pingry, KCTS, Seattle.
Informational Series, Studio: "Computerized Babies—Northwest Afternoon," Steve Boyd, Doug Irvine, James Owen, KOMO, Seattle.
Informational Segment, Magazine or Short Format: "Earth Agenda: Return of the Eagle," Sharon Howard, KOMO, Seattle.
Entertainment, Special: "Almost Live's Dinner and a Movie," Bill Stainton, KING, Seattle.

Entertainment, Series: "Almost Live," Bill Stainton, KING, Seattle.

Entertainment, Segment—Magazine or Short Format: "Last Horizons," Nancy Guppy, KING, Seattle.

Instructional, Segment—Magazine or Short Format: "Bosnia: Lessons in Democracy," Elaine Purchase, Charles O'Farrell, Tri Ngo, KOMO, Seattle.

Children and Youth Programming, Special: "Safety Central," Terry Severson, Christine Hughes, Doug Wetz, Kevin Williams, KCPQ, Tacoma.

Children and Youth Programming, Series: "Watch This: Air Force One," George Butts, Blake Hurley, Anita Woo, KING, Seattle.

Children and Youth Programming, Segment—Magazine or Short Format: "Candles in the Snow," Elaine Purchase, Charles O'Farrell, Dan Ibabao, KOMO, Seattle.

Fine Arts, Segment—Magazine or Short Format: "Time of Your Life—The Fabulous Follies," Terry Murphy, Chris Raaum, Tri Ngo, KOMO, Seattle.

Sports, Segment—Magazine or Short Format: "The Air Chair," Blake Hurley, Tom Bishop, John Stofflet, KING, Seattle.

Community Service Award: "For Kid's Sake," KOMO-TV Staff, KOMO, Seattle.

Individual Achievement, Anchor: Dan Lewis, KOMO, Seattle.

Individual Achievement, Host/Talent: Jim Dever, KING, Seattle.

Individual Achievement, Reporter: Christine Chen, KSTW, Tacoma.

Radio Stations

City	Call Letters	Channel	Affiliation/Format
Tacoma	KVTI	90.9 FM	Clover Park Technical College
Aberdeen	KBKW	1450 AM	Talk
	KDUX	104.7 FM	Classic rock
	KXRO	1320 AM	News/weather/sports
Anacortes	KLKI	1340 AM	Talk radio
Auburn	KBSG AM	1210 AM	Oldies
	KGRG	89.9 FM	Green River Community College
Bellevue	KASB	89.3 FM	Bellevue High School
	KBCS	91.3 FM	Bellevue Community College
Bellingham	KAFE	104.3 FM	Soft rock
	KBFW	930 AM	New country
	KGMI	790 AM	News
	KPUG	1170 AM	News and sports
	KUGS	89.3 FM	Western Washington University
	KZAZ	91.7 FM	Northwest Public Radio
Burien	KGNW	820 AM	Christian talk
Centralia	KCED FM	91.3 FM	Centralia College
	KITI	95.1 FM	*Live 95*
Chehalis	KACS	90.5 FM	Contemporary Christian
Chelan	KOZI FM	1230 AM & 93.5 FM	
Cheney	KEWU	89.5 FM	Eastern Washington State University
	KEYF FM	101.1 FM	Oldies
	KOOP	550 AM	Eastern Washington State University
Clarkston	KNWV	90.5 FM	Northwest Public Radio
Colfax	KCLX	1450 AM	
	KRAO	102.5 FM	
Cottonwood	KNWO	90.1 FM	Northwest Public Radio
Dayton	KZHR	92.5 FM	
Eatonville	KKBY	104.9 FM	
Edmonds	KCMS	105.3 FM	Christian music
Ellensburg	KCAT	91.1 FM	Central Washington State University
	KCWU	88.3 FM	
	KNWR	90.7 FM	Northwest Public Radio
Ephrata	KTAC	93.9 FM	

City	Call Letters	Channel	Affiliation/Format
	KTBI	810 AM	
	KULE AM	730 AM	
	KULE FM	92.3 FM	
Everett	KSER	90.7 FM	
	KWYZ	1230 AM	Korean broadcasting
Kennewick	KFLD	870 AM	Sports
	KONA	610 AM	
	KONA	105.3 FM	
	KTCR	1340 AM	
Longview	KLYK	105.5 FM	
	KUKN	94.5 FM	
	KLOG	1490 AM	
Mercer Island	KMIH	104.5 FM	Independent
Moses Lake	KLWS	91.5 FM	Northwest Public Radio
	KMLW	88.3 FM	
Mount Vernon	KAPS	660 AM	Country
	KBRC	1430 AM	
	KSVR	90.1 FM	Independent
Newport	KMJY AM	700 AM	
	KMJY FM	104.9 FM	
Olympia	KAOS	89.3FM	The Evergreen State College
	KGY AM	1240 AM	Full service/adult contemporary
	KGY FM	96.9 FM	
	KRXY	94.5 FM	
Pasco	KEYW	98.3 FM	*The Key*
	KGDN	101.3 FM	
	KGSG	93.7 FM	
Port Angeles	KIKN	1290 AM	Country
	KNWP	90.1 FM	Northwest Public Radio
	KONP	1450 AM	
Pullman	KRFA	91.7 FM	Northwest Public Radio
	KUGR	95.1 FM	
	KWSU	1250 AM	Northwest Public Radio
	KZUU	90.7 FM	Washington State University
	KZZL	99.5 FM	
Richland	KALE	960 AM	
	KEGX	106.5 FM	*The Eagle*
	KFAE	89.1 FM	Northwest Public Radio
	KIOK	94.9 FM	*Thunder Country*
Seattle	KBKS	106.1 FM	*Kiss 106.1*
	KBLE	1050 AM	Inspirational
	KCMU	90.3 FM	National Public Radio, University of Washington
	KING	98.1 FM	
	KIRO	710 AM & 100.7 FM	News, talk, and sports
	KISW	99.9 FM	
	KIXI	880 AM	Music
	KJR	950 AM & 95.7 FM	Sports (AM)
	KKDZ	1250 AM	*Radio Disney*, music and talk for children
	KKOL	1300 AM	CNN news, conservative talk shows
	KLFE	1590 AM	Christian
	KLSY	92.5 FM	
	KMPS	94.1 FM	
	KNHC	89.5 FM	Nathan Hale High School
	KNWX	770 AM	Business
	KNDD	107.7 FM	
	KOMO	1000 AM	News, talk

City	Call Letters	Channel	Affiliation/Format
	KPLZ	101.5 FM	*Star 101.5*
	KRPM	1090 AM	Classic country
	KSRB	1150 AM	Soul
	KUBE	93.3 FM	
	KUOW	94.9 FM	National Public Radio, University of Washington
	KVI	570 AM	Talk
	KWJZ	98.9 FM	
	KYCW	96.5 FM	*Young Country 96.5*
	KZOK	102.5 FM	
Spokane	KAGU	88.7 FM	Gonzaga University
	KAEP	105.7 FM	*The Peak*
	KAQQ	590 AM	*Q59*
	KDRK	93.7 FM	*Cat Country 94*
	KEEH	104.7 FM	*Positive Life Radio*
	KEYF	101.1 FM	Oldies
	KGA	1510 AM	
	KHTQ	94.5 FM	
	KISC	98.1 FM	*98 Kiss FM*
	KKZX	98.9 FM	
	KMBI AM	1330 AM	
	KMBI FM	107.9 FM	
	KNFR	96.1 FM	
	KPBX	91.1 FM	Spokane Public Radio
	KSFC	91.9 FM	Spokane Falls Community College
	KSPO	106.5 FM	
	KTRW	970 AM	
	KWRS	90.3 FM	Whitworth College
	KXLY AM	920 AM	*NewsRadio 920*
	KXLY FM	99.9 FM	*Classy 99.9*
	KZZU	92.9 FM	
Sunnyside	KAYB	88.1 FM	
Tacoma	KCCR	94.5 FM	Pacific Lutheran University
	KBSG FM	97.3 FM	
	KBTC	91.7 FM	
	KMTT	103.7 FM	*The Mountain*
	KPLU	88.5 FM	Jazz; Pacific Lutheran University Public Radio
	KUPS	90.1 FM	University of Puget Sound
	KVTI	90.9 FM	*I-91*
Walla Walla	KGTS	91.3 FM	
	KNLT	95.7 FM	
	KTWY	93.3 FM	*Way-FM*
	KUJ FM	99.1 FM	
	KWCW	90.5 FM	Whitman College
	KWWS	89.7 FM	Northwest Public Radio
Wenatchee	KKRT	900 AM	
	KKRV	104.9 FM	
	KPLW	89.9 FM	*Positive Life Radio*
	KPQ AM	560 AM	
	KPQ FM	102.1 FM	*Soft Rock 102*
Yakima	KATS	94.5 FM	
	KFFM	107.3 FM	
	KMWX	1460 AM	
	KNWY	90.3 FM	Northwest Public Radio
	KYAK	930 AM	

Television Stations

City	Call Letters	Channel	Affiliation
Bellingham	KVOS	12	Independent
Pullman	KWSU	10	PBS
Seattle	KCTS	9	PBS
	KING	5	NBC
	KIRO	7	CBS
	KOMO	4	ABC
	KONG	16	Independent
	KTZZ	22	Independent
Spokane	KAYU	28	FOX
	KHQ	6	NBC
	KREM	2	CBS
	KSPS	7	PBS
	KXLY	4	ABC
Tacoma	KBTC	28	PBS
	KCPQ	13	FOX
	KSTW	11	UPN
	KTBW	20	Trinity
Tri-Cities	KEPR	19	CBS
	KNDU	25	NBC
	KTNW	31	PBS
	KVEW	42	ABC
Wenatchee	KCWT	27	ABC
Yakima	KAPP	35	ABC
	KIMA	29	CBS
	KNDO	23	NBC
	KYVE	47	PBS

Organizations of Interest.

National Academy of Television Arts and Sciences, 217 Ninth N., Seattle, WA 98109; (206) 575-3444.

Washington Association of Broadcasters, 924 Capitol Way S., Olympia, WA 98501; (360) 705-0774.

Broadcasting Pioneer

Edward R. Murrow, one of the most prominent journalists from Washington State, was a pioneer of television news. He rose to international acclaim as a war correspondent. Broadcasting from London during the blitz in World War II, his standard opening line, "This... is London," was one of the most famous handles of the era. Murrow attended Washington State College (now Washington State University), where he was elected student body president. Murrow left radio for television in 1948, at the dawn of commercial television, to host the "See It Now" series, a program regarded as the first modern television news program. ✳

Railroads (SEE ALSO

TRANSPORTATION) Washington's freight rail system consists of the operations of 13 common carriers, including 10 line-haul carriers, one nonoperating rail line owner, and two switching/terminal companies. There are about 3,102 miles of track in the system. Sixty-eight percent of the track is owned by the Burlington Northern Santa Fe (BNSF), and 12 percent is owned by the Union Pacific (UP). In addition to common carrier rail lines, there are several non-common carrier lines that move freight within the state that would otherwise move over public roads. The system has declined with the closure of many branch lines (a loss of about 2,000 miles of lines since 1970), but main lines carry increasing amounts of freight.

Freight carried in Washington includes farm products, lumber and wood products, food and related products, metallic ores, and containers/trailers on flat cars. Common carrier railroads currently operate freight terminals in the vicinity of Seattle, Spokane, and Tacoma. A number of other rail yards are used for car classifications, switching, storage, and maintenance.

The BNSF and UP share one north-south alignment between Oregon and Tacoma. From Tacoma to Seattle, each railroad operates over its own track. BNSF is the only line that runs north of Seattle to Canada. BNSF, the only east-west railroad in the state, has three Cascade Mountain crossings: the Cascade Tunnel (Stevens Pass), the Columbia River Gorge, and Stampede Pass. The UP connects from Portland up the Oregon side of the Columbia River to Pasco. Both UP and BNSF maintain track between Pasco and Idaho through Spokane.

Main-line railroad in Washington costs about $25,000 per track-mile per year to maintain (double that for double tracks). Annual expenditures to maintain the system are about $100 million. The state has estimated that the railroads save the taxpayers nearly $800 million in avoided highway congestion costs and road damages.

Amtrak operates intercity rail passenger service on trackage owned by the BNSF. Passenger service is maintained between Seattle and Vancouver, BC; Seattle and Portland, Oregon; Seattle and Spokane; and Spokane and Portland. The north-south corridor from Eugene, Oregon, to Vancouver, BC, through Portland and Seattle has been designated the Pacific Northwest Rail Corridor. It is one of five national rail corridors to be developed for high-speed rail passenger service. Annual ridership as of 1997 was just under a half million passengers. The Washington State Department of Transportation anticipates a 75 percent increase in intercity rail passenger service over the next 20 years.

Organizations of Interest.

Mount Rainier Scenic Railroad, P.O. Box 921, Elbe, WA 98330; (888) STEAMII, (360) 569-2588.

The Northwest Railway Museum, Snoqualmie Depot, P.O. Box 459, Snoqualmie, WA 98065; (425) 888-3030.

The Great Northern Railroad

Railroads built the West, and James Jerome Hill built the Great Northern, one of the greatest of them all. The Great Northern, initially running from St. Paul, Minnesota, to Seattle, Washington, was built entirely without government subsidy, a rarity for the time. It enabled wheat and other crops to be shipped expeditiously to the Orient—the first global trade corridor—and also opened up eastern U.S. markets for western U.S. timber. Jim Hill was born in Ontario, Canada, in 1838. While his railroad empire originated out of St. Paul, Minnesota, Seattle was its terminus, and Hill spent much time in the Northwest. In fact, his many efforts to attract settlers to the vicinity of his railroad line helped spur immigration to the Northwest. His railroad had agents in Europe who encouraged immigration. He offered free land, free cows, anything to attract settlement to the regions crossed by the Great Northern. He truly was an empire builder. James Hill died in 1916.✳

Washington State Railroads Historical Society Museum, 122 N. Tacoma Ave., Pasco, WA 99301; (509) 543-4159.

Yakima Valley Rail and Steam Museum, P.O. Box 889, Toppenish, WA 98948; (509) 865-1911. Open to the public seven days a week during the summer. Train rides on the Toppenish, Simcoe & Western Railroad are offered to the public during the summer and early fall.

Red Tide

Red tide is the common name for a phenomenon caused by a small marine organism that turns the water a color similar to tomato soup. The technical name for red tide is paralytic shellfish poisoning, or PSP. The PSP toxin is produced by a species of dinoflagellate, a microscopic photosynthesizing organism that lives in marine waters. The species that causes PSP in Washington waters is *Alexandrium catenella* (formerly known as *Gonyaulax catenella*). Under the right combination of sunlight, water temperature, salinity, and nutrients, *Alexandrium* reproduces very rapidly. During such a "bloom," shellfish such as oysters, mussels, clams, and scallops can accumulate PSP toxins, and while it does not hurt the shellfish, it is dangerous to humans who eat them. PSP can cause symptoms that range from numbness and tingling of the lips and tongue to death in extreme cases. Symptoms usually develop within one to two hours of consumption and disappear within 12 to 24 hours. There is no known antidote for the PSP toxin. In life-threatening cases, artificial respiration is necessary.

The water does not always turn red during a bloom of *Alexandrium*. The absence of color does not ensure that shellfish from affected waters are safe to eat; nor does a reddish tinge in the water mean that shellfish are unsafe. Several similar, non-toxic organisms also can color the water red, orange, or purple. The only way to be certain that the water is safe is by laboratory testing, and the Washington Department of Health routinely tests shellfish-growing areas for PSP.

The Department of Health Shellfish Office maintains a toll-free 24-hour PSP hotline (800-562-5632) and a Web page (www.doh.wa.gov/ehp/sf) to identify recreational beaches closed to shellfishing.

Rivers

(SEE ALSO COLUMBIA RIVER; WATERFALLS; WATER SPORTS) Washington has a wealth of rivers—from the mighty but mild and dammed Columbia, to wild and scenic rivers, to the untamed rivers with white-water rapids. All of Washington's rivers drain toward the Pacific Ocean, in three major hydrologic regions: the Columbia River system, the Coast system, and the Puget Sound region. The Columbia River system totals some 67,750 square miles in the state, and all of the major rivers in eastern Washington flow into it. The principal tributaries are (from upstream to downstream) the Pend Oreille, Spokane, Okanogan, Methow, Wenatchee, Yakima, and Snake Rivers.

The Coast system of rivers stretches from the Strait of Juan de Fuca to the estuary of the Columbia River. The rivers in this region that flow directly into the Pacific Ocean include the Quinault, Chehalis, Grays, and Willapa Rivers.

A number of smaller rivers in northwestern Washington drain into Puget Sound and its northern approaches. They include (from north to south) the Skagit, Stillaguamish, Snoqualmie, Skykomish, Cedar, Puyallup, and Nisqually Rivers.

Wild and Scenic Rivers. The National Wild and Scenic River System seeks to preserve the character and landscape of specially designated rivers. There are three designated Wild and Scenic Rivers in Washington:

Klickitat River. The Klickitat rises on the eastern slope of the Cascades near Cispus Pass, and winds through deep, rocky canyons for about 60 miles to join the Columbia near Lyle, in Klickitat County. Its designated reach is 10 miles from the confluence with Wheeler Creek, near the town of Pitt, to the confluence with the Columbia River. The river flows into the Columbia inside the Columbia Gorge National Scenic Area. Fishing, recreation, and scenic views are excellent.

Skagit River. The Skagit is the largest river that drains into Puget Sound. The segment of the river designated as scenic is 99 miles; another 58.5 miles are classified as recreational. It includes the segment from the pipeline crossing at Sedro Woolley upstream to and including the mouth of Bacon Creek. The Skagit features one of the largest concentrations of bald eagles in the Lower 48 states in a region characterized by rugged canyons, glacier-clad mountains, and densely forested slopes.

White Salmon River. The White Salmon rises on the west slope of Mount Adams and flows into the Columbia Gorge. The designated reach is 9 miles from its confluence with Gilmer Creek, near the town of B Z Corner, to its confluence with Buck Creek. This river flows through a deep, narrow, rocky gorge. The angling for spawning salmon is notable, and the many springs and stable summer flows provide outstanding white-water boating.

White-water Rivers. Washington is home to some of the best white-water rafting and kayaking in the world. White-water rivers are classified from Class I (very tame) to Class VI (nearly impossible). A few of the many great white-water rivers are listed below; for more complete information, there are a number of published guidebooks to white water, and many river outfitters have sites on the World Wide Web.

The **Green River** has continuous Class III to IV rapids, along with waterfalls and beautiful hanging gardens in the Green River Gorge.

The **Klickitat** offers Class II and III rapids, fun but not difficult, and a spectacular, 700-foot canyon.

The **Methow** is a great river for beginners, with big water, tall waves, and Class III and IV rapids that are not technically difficult.

The **Nooksack**'s narrow canyon section requires precise maneuvering.

The **Sauk River** has nearly continuous Class III to IV rapids.

The **Skykomish,** only one hour from Seattle, is a challenging Class IV to V run, depending on water flow.

The **Tieton River** is a roller coaster of

Class III rapids in the fall when the Rimrock Dam is opened. The river flows between towering columnar basalt cliffs.

The **Wenatchee River** is very popular among rafters. It has huge roller-coaster rapids rated Class III and IV, but is not considered technically difficult.

White Salmon has a steep gradient creating Class III and IV rapids.

Organizations of Interest.

Adopt-A-Stream Foundation, P.O. Box 5558, Everett, WA 98206; (425) 316-8592.

American Rivers—Northwest Regional Office, 150 Nickerson St., Suite 311, Seattle, WA 98109; (206) 213-0330.

American Whitewater Affiliation—Washington, 4930 Geiger Rd. SE, Port Orchard, WA 98366-9351; (360) 876-6780.

Columbia River Conservation League, 2407 S. Irving St., Kennewick, WA 99337; (509) 735-0102.

Rivers Council of Washington, 509 10th Ave. E., Suite 200, Seattle, WA 98102; (206) 568-1380.

Washington Scenic Rivers Program, State Parks and Recreation Commission, 7150 Clearwater Lane, KY-11, Olympia, WA 98504-5711; (360) 902-8533.

Wild and Scenic Rivers Program, http://www.nps.gv/rivers/.

Roads and Highways (SEE ALSO

TRANSPORTATION; VEHICLE AND DRIVER'S LICENSES) Washington's highway system represents an investment of tens of billions of dollars. The state system includes 714 miles of interstate highways, 214 miles of other freeways and expressways, and 7,178 miles of principal and minor arterials. Together with major and minor collectors and local roadways, the system totals more than 96,000 miles of roads.

The annual total of vehicles on the roadways continues to rise. The first state-constructed highway, in 1896, connected Bellingham to Republic by way of Marblemount and Twisp. There were 763 automobiles on Washington's roads in 1906, 70,000 in 1916, and 5.3 million in

Washington Road and Highway Facts (1996)

Miles of roads: 79,555 (764 miles of interstate highways)
Vehicle miles traveled: 49.2 billion (13.3 billion on interstates)
Number of highway accidents: 252,792
Accidents per 100 million miles: 285
Number of highway fatalities: 977
Fatalities per 100 million miles: 1.4
Leading causes of accidents: excessive speed; failure to yield right of way; inattention; alcohol
Pedestrian/car accidents (total of 613 fatalities): 1,887 (annual average)
Bicycle/car accidents (total of 71 fatalities); 1,449 (annual average)
Source: Washington Department of Transportation

1996. These numbers have contributed to Seattle's distinction of sharing a three-way tie with Los Angeles and San Francisco-Oakland as having the worst rush-hour traffic in the United States (ranking based on 1996 statistics).

Mountain Passes. The Cascade Mountains are crossed by road through a number of mountain passes. Weather conditions, especially during the winter, can be treacherous and it is a good idea for drivers to be aware of road and weather conditions. Mountain pass road conditions are monitored and reported daily on the Washington State Department of Transportation Web site at http://traffic.wsdot.wa.gov/sno-info/, and on radio and television weather and driving reports. Under severe snow conditions, snow tires and chains may be required to travel across the mountain passes. Some passes are closed for the better part of the winter; others may close for brief periods of time during especially heavy snowfall. The passes are listed below from highest to lowest elevation.

Sherman Pass, State Route 20, elevation 5,575 feet.

Washington Pass (North Cascades Highway), State Route 20, elevation 5,477 feet.

Chinook Pass, State Route 410, elevation 5,430 feet (to Crystal Mountain Boulevard, elevation 4,400 feet).

Rainy Pass (North Cascades Highway), State Route 20, elevation 4,855 feet.

Cayuse Pass, State Route 123, elevation 4,675 feet.

White Pass, U.S. Highway 12, elevation 4,500 feet.

Mount Baker Highway, State Route 542, elevation 4,250 feet.

Blewett Pass, U.S. Highway 97, elevation 4,102 feet.

Stevens Pass, U.S. Highway 2, elevation 4,061 feet.

Satus Pass, U.S. Highway 97, elevation 3,107 feet.

Snoqualmie Pass, Interstate 90, elevation 3,022 feet.

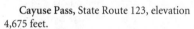

The Mullan Road

One of the earliest and most important roads built in Washington was called the "Mullan Road" (after its chief architect, Army Captain John Mullan)—624 miles of wagon ruts that ran from Fort Benton, Montana, on the Missouri River to Fort Walla Walla. Construction began in 1859 and was completed in 1862, costing $230,000, paid for by the federal government. The Mullan Road was an important route west and was heavily traveled. In 1992, a section of the old Mullan Road was made part of the Washington and Idaho Centennial Trail. Today it accommodates bicyclists, hikers, and horseback riders along the Spokane River from Spokane to Coeur d'Alene, Idaho. ✷

Scenic Highways. While Washington may have a nasty rush-hour problem in one part of the state, there are some beautiful drives to take elsewhere. Among the federally designated National Scenic Byways are Mount Baker Scenic Highway (State Route 542), Spirit Lake Memorial Highway at Mount St. Helens (State Route 504), North Cascades Scenic Highway (State Route 20) with its spectacular viewpoint at Washington Pass, Columbia River Gorge (State Route 14), Pacific Coast Scenic Byway (U.S. Highway 101), Stevens Pass Greenway (U.S. Highway 2), White Pass Scenic Byway (U.S. Highway 12), Cascade Loop (I-5, State Route 20, U.S. Highway 97, and U.S. Highway 2), Cascade Valleys Heritage Corridor (Highway 202), Lewis and Clark Trail Highway (U.S. Highway 12 and State Route 14), North Pend Oreille Scenic Byway (State Route 31), and Sherman Pass Scenic Byway (State Route 20).

Rodeos
Nothing says The West like cowboys, and there is no better way to experience cowboys than to see them ridin' a bronc or ropin' a steer at a local rodeo.

Rodeos can be found throughout Washington, although the majority are held in eastern Washington. The two best known are the Ellensburg Rodeo, held each Labor Day weekend, and the Omak Stampede, with its famous and controversial—animal rights activists charge the course is too dangerous for the horses—suicide race. The race consists of 20 riders going hell-bent for leather down a steep embankment, fording the river, climbing back up the other side, and racing to the rodeo grounds.

Some rodeos include events sanctioned by the Professional Rodeo Cowboys Association (PRCA), which means that competitors are accumulating points for national standings in specific rodeo events and for the overall champion cowboy competition.

Events of Interest.
Elma-Grays Harbor Indoor Pro Rodeo, March, Elma, (360) 482-4500. NPRA sanctioned.

U.S. Team Roping Championship, March, Pasco, (509) 543-2997.

Grand Coulee Mule Gymkhana, April, Grand Coulee, (509) 633-1083. Rodeo events on mules.

Pasco-Columbia Basin College Rodeo Challenge, April, Pasco, (509) 543-2997.

Coulee City PRCA Last Stand Rodeo, May, Coulee City, (509) 632-5497.

Grand Coulee Colorama Festival and PWRA Rodeo, May, Grand Coulee Dam (509) 633-3074.

Winthrop Memorial Day Rodeo, May, Winthrop, (509) 996-2125.

Colville PRCA Rodeo, June, Colville, (509) 684-5973, (509) 684-4849.

Glenwood Rodeo, June, Glenwood, (509) 364-3355.

Newport PWRA Rodeo, June, Newport, (509) 447-5812.

Rosalia Battle Days/Rodeo, June, Rosalia, (509) 523-3311.

Timber Bowl Rodeo Darrington, June, Darrington, (888) 338-0976.

Tonasket Founders Day Rodeo, June, Tonasket, (509) 486-4297. PRCA rodeo.

Tonasket Pony Express Friendship Ride, June, between Tonasket and Princeton, BC, (509) 486-4297.

Washington State High School Rodeo, June, Pasco, (509) 543-2997, (509) 543-1914.

Cheney Rodeo Days, July, Cheney, (509) 235-8480. PRCA rodeo.

Dream Riders Junior Rodeo, July, Newport, (509) 447-5812, (509) 447-2095.

Lewis County Roundup Rodeo, July, Chehalis, (360) 330-2088.

Toppenish Rodeo and Pow Wow, July, Toppenish, (800) 569-3982.

Toppenish Eagles Junior Rodeo, July, Toppenish, (800) 569-3982.

Evergreen State Fair and Rodeo, August, Monroe, (360) 794-7832.

Goldendale-Klickitat County Fair and Rodeo, August, Goldendale, (509) 364-3325.

Kennewick Horse Heaven Roundup (PRCA), August, Kennewick (509) 269-4472.

Long Beach Annual Rodeo, August, Long Beach, (800) 451-2542. NPRA.

Moses Lake Roundup, August, Moses Lake, (509) 765-7765. PRCA rodeo.

Omak Stampede and World Famous

Steer wrestling at the Ellensburg Rodeo. From *Washington II* by John Marshall.

Suicide Race, August, Omak, (800) 933-6625. PRCA rodeo.

Roy Pioneer Rodeo, August, Roy, (206) 843-1113.

Sumas Junior Rodeo, August, Sumas, (360) 988-2104.

Columbia River Pro Rodeo Association, September, Pasco, (509) 547-2476. PRCA rodeo.

Ellensburg Rodeo, September, Ellensburg, (800) 637-2444.

Othello Rodeo, September, Othello, (800) 684-2556.

Puyallup Fair Rodeo, September, Puyallup, (253) 841-5047. PRCA rodeo.

Walla Walla Fair and Frontier Days, September, Walla Walla, (509) 527-3247. PRCA rodeo.

Winthrop Labor Day Rodeo, September, Winthrop, (509) 996-2125. PWRA rodeo.

Pasco Wrangler's Last Chance, October, Pasco, (509) 543-2297. PRCA rodeo.

Salmon (*SEE ALSO* FISH AND SHELLFISH; FISH HATCHERIES) Pacific salmon are born in fresh water, migrate to the ocean, and return as adults to the streams where they were born to spawn and die.

Prior to European settlement, the waters of Washington State teemed with salmon, which provided the dietary mainstay for the coastal native populations. More than a century of heavy fishing, dams on the rivers, timbering, and other habitat alterations have taken their toll. Today's salmon populations are much reduced, and some individual runs of salmon on specific streams are acknowledged to be threatened with extinction. Five distinct species of salmon are found in Washington waters.

King or chinook salmon (*Oncorynchus tshawytscha*): Least abundant, but largest, often running 30 to 40 pounds and sometimes up to 100 pounds. Spawns May to January.

Coho or silver salmon (*Oncorynchus kisutch*): Widespread, but less abundant than sockeye, pink, and chum salmon. Runs 6 to 12 pounds. Spawns November to January, but begins entering rivers in August.

Sockeye or red salmon (*Oncorynchus nerka*): Less abundant than pink and chum. Length to 33 inches, can weigh up to 15 pounds but most are 3½ to 8 pounds.

Pink or humpback salmon (*Oncorynchus gorbuscha*): Most abundant of all

Top Trophy Salmon, Freshwater

Species	Weight (lbs.)	Caught by	From	Date
Atlantic	8.96	Gregory Karl Lepping	Goat Lake	September 13, 1992
Atlantic, sea-run	9.59	John L. Dahll	Puyallup River	September 6, 1995
Chinook	68.26	Mark Salmon	Elochoman River	October 5, 1992
Chum	27.97	Johnny Wilson	Satsop River	October 19, 1997
Coho	23.5	David Bailey	Satsop River	January 12, 1986
Sockeye	10.6	Gary Krasselt	Lake Washington	July 20, 1982

Top Trophy Salmon, Saltwater

Species	Weight (lbs.)	Caught by	From	Date
Chinook	70.5	Chet Gausta	Sekiu	September 6, 1964
Chum	19.9	Arnold Hansen	Point No Point	October 8, 1988
Coho	20.6	Joseph A. Christian	Westport	August 27, 1996
Pink	6.38	Rodney M. Hansen	Mukilteo	August 25, 1997

Source: Washington State Department of Fish and Wildlife

species, weighs 3 to 5 pounds. This species has a two-year life cycle. Returns to rivers to spawn July to September.

Chum or dog salmon (*Oncorynchus keta*): Second in abundance to pink salmon, average weight 9 pounds, but can weigh more than 30 pounds. Returns to rivers to spawn between July and December, sometimes as late as March.

Seattle
Washington's largest city, Seattle is consistently ranked as one of the best cities in the country in which to live or work. Home to major corporate successes such as Boeing, Microsoft, Nintendo, and Starbucks, the region has undergone dramatic growth that causes those who

came before to shudder at the transformation of the skyline and the region. The burgeoning population (539,670) also strains the local highways and other urban infrastructure, and has earned the city top honors in a national "worst traffic" survey.

Despite its growth pains, Seattle retains its charm. It still maintains a large fishing fleet and is a world-class shipping center. The city's flavor derives in part from its waterfront and its mix of modern skyscrapers and historic districts such as the Pike Place Market, a working farmers market, and Pioneer Square. There is also the much-maligned weather. While rainy periods set in for weeks during the winter, the sun is likely to shine at least part of each day in the other three seasons.

Though there were already settlements in the territory by 1850, the first white settlers set foot in what is now Seattle in 1851. The city's founders included entrepreneurs looking to establish a sawmill and supply timber by ship to San Francisco and other fast-growing Pacific coast cities, and in its early days the city's economy was based on the surrounding forests. With the completion of transcontinental railroads in the 1870s, Seattle eventually became a major transshipment and trading center for Alaska and Asia.

Like a number of western cities that were built primarily with wood-frame buildings, downtown Seattle was consumed by a tragic fire, in 1889. The modern city dates from the rebuilding that followed, boosted by the Klondike gold rush that began in 1896. Modern Seattle was shaped as well by industrial expansion that took off with the airplane industry during World War II.

Seattle's popular Pike Place Market. Photo by Susan Dupere.

Gas Works Park

You can easily identify Gas Works Park at the north end of Lake Union by the hulking skeleton of the old gas manufacturing plant at the water's edge. Built in 1906, the gasworks operated until 1956, when it was abandoned. The city bought the site in 1962 and trucked in tons of dirt and sawdust to produce topsoil for growing grass over sludge and tar left by the gasworks. Now there is little hint of what was once an industrial wasteland.—Barbara Sullivan, Seattle Picnics ❀

In 1962, Seattle celebrated its urban success by hosting a world's fair called "Century 21." The fairgrounds, the monorail, and the skyline signature Space Needle are legacies of this event.

In the 1980s, Seattle entrepreneurs founded entire new industries, including the coffee culture typified by Starbucks and the software industry dominated by Microsoft, founded by Seattle natives Paul Allen and Bill Gates. Major developments and campuses have sprouted east of Lake Washington to accommodate growth spurred by the software industry.

Skiing and Snowboarding

Skiing is big business in Washington and getting bigger, with cross-country skiing becoming even more popular than downhill skiing. In the Cascades, in the Kettle Range, the Selkirks, and the Blue Mountains, you will see cross-country skiers, alone or in groups, on the thousands of miles of groomed trails. The Methow Valley has some of the best cross-country skiing areas, with 150 kilometers of marked and groomed trails. There are also thousands of acres of public land to ski on, especially in the national forests. Logging roads are a good place to cross-country ski because they are usually closed to vehicles during the winter.

The downhill ski areas are stretched along the Cascades from Mount Baker to

Mount Rainier, and smaller ones are located farther east. Snow on the western slopes of the Cascades is usually wetter and heavier than that east of the mountains.

Snowboarding is the only part of the downhill ski industry that has shown growth in recent years. The wide boards work well on all kinds of snow. Mount Baker is a popular area for boarders.

Badger Mountain, Waterville, WA 98858; (509) 745-8760, (509) 745-8479, (509) 745-8470. Located 35 miles north of Wenatchee. Area: 3,000 acres with 4,500 to 3,000 feet elevation. Three tow lifts. Downhill and cross-country skiing, and ice skating.

Bear Mountain Ranch, Chelan, WA 98816; (509) 682-5444. Area: 55 kilometers of groomed trails. Cross-country skiing.

Crystal Mountain, Crystal Mountain, WA 98022; (360) 663-2300, (206) 825-5044. Located on Mount Rainier. Area: 7,000 to 4,000 feet elevation and 32 major runs; 1,000 acres of backcountry. Ten chair lifts. Downhill and cross-country skiing.

Echo Valley, Monson, WA 98831; (509) 682-4002, (509) 687-3167, (509) 687-3162. Area: 3,500 to 3,000 feet elevation. One poma lift, three rope tows. Downhill and cross-country skiing.

49 Degrees North, Chewelah, WA 99109; (509) 935-6649, snow phone (509) 935-6649. Area: 5,773 to 3,928 feet elevation. Four double-chair lifts. Downhill and cross-country trails.

Hurricane Ridge, Olympic Peninsula, WA 98392; (360) 452-0329. Located 17 miles from Port Angeles. Two rope tows and a poma lift. Downhill and cross-country skiing.

Leavenworth Ski Hill and Leavenworth Winter Sports Club, Leavenworth, WA 98826; (509) 548-5115, (509) 548-5807. Area: 1,850 to 1,300 feet elevation. Two rope tows. Downhill skiing and cross-country trails with double-set tracks and a skating lane.

Loup Loup Ski Bowl, Omak, WA 98841; (509) 826-2720, (800) 225-6625, (509) 826-4371. Area: 5,240 to 4,040 feet elevation. Two tow bars. Downhill skiing.

Methow Valley Ski Touring, Winthrop, WA 98862; (800) 422-3048, ski conditions

(800) 682-5787, Methow Valley Ski Touring Association (509) 996-3287. Area: About 200 kilometers of groomed trails, with hut-to-hut skiing, the longest ski-trail system in the state, and one of the longest in the country. Cross-country skiing.

Mission Ridge, Wenatchee, WA 98807; (800) 245-3922, (509) 663-7631, snow phone (800) 374-1693. Area: 6,740 to 4,600 feet elevation; 2,080 acres with 33 runs, the longest is 5 miles. Four double-chair lifts, two rope tows. Downhill, cross-country, and telemark skiing.

Mount Baker, Bellingham, WA 98226; (360) 734-6771, snow phone (360) 671-0211. Area: 5,050 to 3,500 feet. Two quad lifts, six double-chair lifts, one rope tow. Downhill skiing and snowboarding. This mountain leads the nation in snowfall (600-inch annual average) and is a mecca for snowboarders.

Mount Spokane Ski Area, Spokane, WA 99021; (509) 238-6281. Area: 5,883 to 4,367 feet elevation, 25 runs, longest run is 1.5 miles. Five chairs. Downhill skiing.

Mount Spokane State Park, Spokane, WA; (509) 238-4258, snow conditions

A New Ski

The K2 Corporation of Vashon Island, Washington, developed the first commercially practical fiberglass snow ski, in 1965. The fiberglass ski initially was a mid-market alternative to inexpensive wooden skis and high-end metal skis, which were manufactured by the Head Corporation. K2 stands for Bill and Don Kirschner, brothers who founded the company. K2 was an outgrowth of the brothers' fiberglass mold and construction business. The original fiberglass ski included a slim core of spruce, which was wrapped with fiberglass, with the fibers all running in the same direction. This "wet wrap" method kept costs down and produced a strong, highly flexible ski. While K2 skis are still manufactured on Vashon Island, the Kirschner Brothers sold their interests many years ago. ✤

(509) 238-4025. Located 25 miles north of Spokane. Area: 30 kilometers of groomed trails. Cross-country skiing.

Mount Tahoma Scenic Trails, Ashford, WA 98304; (253) 472-4402, snow conditions (360) 569-2451. Area: More than 103 miles, groomed and ungroomed. Cross-country, hut-to-hut skiing with three huts, one yurt (three-night maximum).

North Cascade Heli-Skiing, Mazama, WA 98833; (509) 996-3272. Area: Elevations up to 8,000 feet.

Scottish Lakes, Leavenworth, WA 98826; (888) 944-2267, (206) 844-2000. Located 17 miles west of Leavenworth off U.S. Highway 2. Area: 5,000 feet elevation, 17 miles of backcountry trails. Backcountry ski touring, lodging, snowshoeing, sledding, snowboarding.

Sitzmark, Tonasket, WA 98855; (509) 485-3323, (509) 486-2700. Area: 4,950 to 4,300 feet elevation, 2 to 7 kilometers of groomed trails. One double-chair lift, one tow. Downhill and cross-country skiing and snowboarding.

Ski Bluewood, Dayton, WA 99328; (509) 382-4725, snow conditions (509) 382-2877. Area: 5,400 to 4,300 feet elevation, 430 skiable acres, 24 trails, 5 kilometers of snowmobile trails, 5 kilometers of cross-country trails. Two triple-chair lifts, one platter lift. Downhill and cross-country skiing, snowmobiling.

Squilchuck Ski Bowl, Wenatchee, WA 98807; (509) 662-1651, (509) 663-6543. Located on the road to Mission Ridge. Two rope tows.

Stevens Pass, (206) 634-0200, (206) 634-1645. A popular commuter area 80 miles northeast of Seattle on U.S. Highway 2, Stevens is known for its steady, healthy snowfall and, increasingly, its diverse terrain. The front side is a beginner/intermediate paradise now graced by a new high-speed lift, and the recent addition of new back-side runs and lifts has elevated the mountain to standout status. Area: 5,800 to 4,000 feet elevation, 26 runs, 1,125 acres. Four triple-chair lifts, six double-chair lifts, three rope tows. Downhill skiing.

Summit at Snoqualmie (formerly Alpental/Snoqualmie/Ski Acres/Hyak),

A skier at Stevens Pass Ski Area in the Cascade Mountains. From *Washington II* by John Marshall.

Snoqualmie Pass; (206) 232-8182, snow conditions (206) 236-1600. Area: 5,400 to 2,602 feet elevation. Nineteen double-chair lifts, eight triple-chair lifts, one quad-chair lift, nine rope tows. Downhill skiing and snowboarding.

The Summit at Snoqualmie Nordic Center, Snoqualmie Pass; (425) 434-6646, (206) 236-1600. Area: 55 kilometers of groomed trails, 4 kilometers of lighted trails. Cross-country skiing.

White Pass Village, White Pass, WA 98937; (509) 672-3100, (509) 248-6966, (206) 634-0200, (206) 572-4300. Area: 6,000 to 4,500 feet elevation, 635 acres of open slopes, several miles of trails. One high-speed quad chair; three double-chair lifts; one rope tow. Downhill and cross-country skiing.

Sno-Park. The Washington State Parks and Recreation Department maintains a series of plowed lots on state, federal, and private lands. Recreationists pay for the plowing, signing, and maintenance of the facilities through a permit program. To be legally parked in a designated Sno-Park, a vehicle must have a permit; the price is $7 for a day, $10 for three days, and $20 for a full season (the permit is is also good for lots in Oregon and Idaho). More than 50 Sno-Park lots are kept plowed and open specifically for nonmotorized users, and 60 more can be used by snowmobiles. The Parks Department publishes a booklet with descriptions and maps for all groomed cross-country trails ($4), and maps showing multi-use Sno-Park lots ($5). Permits and maps can be purchased at U.S. Forest Service district offices, at most outdoor retail shops, from Washington State Parks at (800) 233-0321, or on the Internet at www.parks.wa.gov/xsnopark.htm.

Organizations of Interest.

Cross-country ski reports, (206) 632-2021, (206) 632-7787.

Downhill ski reports, (206) 634-0200, (206) 634-0071.

Mountain pass information, (206) 976-7623, (206) 455-7900.

Office of Winter Recreation, Washington State Parks and Recreation Office, 7150 Clearwater Lane, Olympia, WA 98504-2662; (206) 586-0185. *Washington State Groomed Cross Country Ski Trails* is a guide available from the office (also available at most outdoor recreation stores and ranger stations).

Washington ski report, (206) 634-2754.

Slug
One of the state's best-known molluscs is a slug—a very big slug, to be exact. The honorable banana slug (*Ariolimax columbianus*) is commonly 4 to 6 inches long, and sometimes reaches more than 10 inches when crawling. Slugs are most active at night and in dim, humid conditions, because they need the humidity to replenish liquid that is consumed in their prodigious production of slime. Slime is very important to the slug. It provides both traction and lubrication, and also protects the slug's sole. Banana slugs can be eaten. Fry them after removing the slime by soaking the slugs in vinegar. They taste just like the more expensive French "escargots"—though whether one should announce such a substitution to one's dinner guests is at best questionable.

Nuisance slugs in the garden can sometimes be controlled by providing them with pie tins of beer. They find the beer irresistible and do not survive the debauch.

Snake River
Rising in Yellowstone National Park in Wyoming, the Snake River cuts across southeastern Washington to empty into the Columbia River in Franklin County. The river runs a total of 1,038 miles. On the border between Washington and Idaho, the Snake River has cut Hells Canyon. The deepest gorge on the North American continent, Hells Canyon is 7,000 feet deep and more than 40 miles long. The Snake River is navigable by barge clear through the state of Washington to Lewiston, Idaho.

Special Districts

Special districts are independent governmental entities operated by elected officials. Special districts provide specific services in areas that lie beyond municipal boundaries or to areas that cross different boundaries. Washington has more types of special districts than most states—more than 65 different types. The major types are school, fire, port, utility, and transit districts.

Cemetery Districts
Community Councils (county, city)
Conservation Districts
Cultural Arts, Stadium, and Convention Districts
Diking, Drainage, and Flood Control Districts
Education Districts
Emergency Medical and Emergency Service Communication Districts
Fire Protection Districts
Health Districts
Housing Authorities
Irrigation Districts
Joint Operating Agencies
Legal Authorities (hydroelectric projects)
Library Districts
Metropolitan Municipal Corporations
Park and Recreation Districts
Pest Control Districts (mosquito, pest, and weed)
Public Facilities Districts

Public Hospital Districts
Public Utility Districts
Reclamation Districts
Sewer and Sewerage Improvement Districts
Solid Waste Districts
Transportation Districts (includes ports, airports, public transit, and others)
TV Reception Improvement Districts
Water Districts

Speed Limits

The basic rule of speed on Washington's highways is codified in the Revised Code of Washington, which states: "(1) No person shall drive a vehicle on a highway at a speed greater than is reasonable and prudent under the conditions and having regard to the actual and potential hazards then existing. In every event speed shall be so controlled as may be necessary to avoid colliding with any person, vehicle, or other conveyance on or entering the highway in compliance with legal requirements and the duty of all persons to use due care. (2) Except when a special hazard exists that requires lower speed for compliance with subsection (1) of this section, the limits specified in this section or established as hereinafter authorized shall be maximum lawful speeds, and no person shall drive a vehicle on a highway at a speed in excess of such maximum limits." The limits are:

25 miles per hour on city and town streets
50 miles per hour on county roads
60 miles per hour on state highways

Drivers must also drive at appropriate reduced speed "when approaching and crossing an intersection or railway grade crossing, when approaching and going around a curve, when approaching a hill crest, when traveling upon any narrow or winding roadway, and when special hazard exists with respect to pedestrians or other

Looking Back

1875

George Washington Bush, born a black slave in Virginia, founded the city of Centralia, which was to become an important logging and railroad center.

traffic or by reason of weather or highway conditions."

Spokane

Spokane (population 188,300) is the state's second-largest city, eastern Washington's largest, and the largest city between Seattle and Minneapolis. By stretching a historical point, Spokane can claim to be the first Western settlement in the Pacific Northwest; England's North West Company opened a trading post here in 1810, and the site has been continuously occupied ever since. Spokane's growth took off, however, in the 1870s with the coming of the railroads. Astute, or possibly wily, city fathers succeeded in attracting two railroads through town, the Northern Pacific—the first railroad to complete a northern crossing of the continent—and the Great Northern Railway. Seated at the junction of the two lines, Spokane was able to obtain favorable freight rates that spurred agriculture and ranching in the region.

In 1974, Spokane hosted Expo '74, a world's fair that not only brought international attention to the city, but left it transformed. The fairgrounds were created out of a rundown industrial area, which is now Riverfront Park, 100 acres along the Spokane River in the middle of the city.

Skywalking

By the 1890s, Spokane was beyond the boomtown stage. Building styles and techniques were contemporary with the rest of the nation. Today, skywalks link these structures—"largest and oldest skywalk network in the United States except for Minneapolis-St. Paul." The enclosed corridors convert most of Spokane's downtown section into a kind of mall.
—John Marshall, *Portrait of Washington* ✳

Spotted Owl

Most Washingtonians won't ever see a spotted owl (*Strix occidentalis caurina*), but it remains important as an indicator species, because it nests in old-growth timber. Spotted owls grow up to 19 inches tall and may have a wingspan of a foot or more. They lack the ear tufts of many other owls and have round heads. Owl vision is much more sensitive to light than human vision; this feature is critical to their success as nocturnal hunters.

State Parks

Washington's state parks run the gamut from magnificent natural areas such as old-growth forest to natural geological and other wonders, to historical and cultural sites, to spectacular vistas and viewpoints.

Spotted owl. From The Great Northwest Nature Factbook by Ann Saling.

The state park system, like those in most far western states, came late, attendant upon large-scale automobile travel and rising public interest in preserving wild lands for recreation and cultural heritage for posterity. Neither budget nor parks existed until 1915. The early parks came from private donations; for example, Moran State Park on Orcas Island.

During the Depression years, the state park system benefited from government efforts directed at reducing unemployment through public works projects. From 1933 to 1938, Civilian Conservation Corps (CCC) workers developed park sites, trails, and facilities. Today the state park system encompasses 260,000 acres. Funds for park acquisition and maintenance are drawn from driver's license and other fees, revenue from the enforcement of highway laws, from park concessions and leases, and from legislative appropriations.

The accompanying map identifies all of Washington's state parks; the listing below highlights selected parks. To find out more about the parks and park activities—for example, where and when to fish, or where to find the best and most isolated beach—call the state parks information center at (800) 233-0321. For a map of the state park system, send $3 to **Washington State Parks and Recreation Commission**, P.O. Box 42650, Olympia, WA; or visit the Parks Department on the Internet at www.parks.wa.gov/.

Washington State parks campsites and lodgings are served by a central reservation system. Call Reservations Northwest, (800) 452-5687, to make a reservation in more than 60 of the parks, or E-mail the Parks Department at res.nw@state.or.us or from the Internet at http://www.parks.wa.gov/mapinfo.htm.

State Park Highlights.

Beacon Rock State Park. Located 35 miles east of Vancouver on Highway 14, in Skamania County. Beacon Rock is a landmark for Columbia River travelers. Lewis and Clark camped by it in November 1805 and gave it its name. A hiking trail to the top leads to a spectacular view of the Columbia River and countryside.

Blake Island State Park. Located 3 miles directly west of Seattle, in central Puget Sound, between Vashon and Bainbridge Islands, in Kitsap County. Access is by tour boat in connection with the Tillicum Indian Village, or by private boat. The park has 5 miles of beaches with magnificent views of the Olympic Mountains, Mount Rainier and Mount Baker, and the Seattle skyline. Blake Island is believed to be the birthplace of Chief Seattle.

Crawford State Park. Located in Pend

Oreille County. Take Highway 31 out of Metaline, then proceed to Boundary Dam, and then via a Forest Service road to Crawford. Gardner Cave is the featured attraction. It is the second-largest limestone cavern in Washington. Guided cave tours are given.

Crystal Falls State Park. Located 15 miles east of Colville on Highway 20, in Stevens County. There is a view of the falls and Little Pend Oreille River.

Dash Point State Park. Located off Highway 509 in Federal Way, in Pierce and King Counties. It has popular, accessible beach walking with outstanding views of Puget Sound.

Deception Pass State Park. Located 9 miles north of Oak Harbor and 9 miles south of Anacortes on Fidalgo and Whidbey Islands, in Island and Skagit Counties. Its spectacular promontory is a fine vantage point of Puget Sound and the Straits of Georgia and Juan de Fuca.

Dry Falls Interpretive Center. Located 7 miles southwest of Coulee City on Highway 17, in Grant County. Open May-September. Exhibits tell the story of the creation of this geological phenomenon. The building overlooks the giant precipice and affords a magnificent view of the Grand Coulee, of which Dry Falls is a central feature.

Federation Forest State Park. Located 18 miles southeast of Enumclaw on Highway 410, in King County. The park contains old-growth forest, remnants of the original wagon road in the region, and remains of old cabins and signs of early logging.

Flaming Geyser State Park. Located between Black Diamond and Enumclaw on Highway 169, in King County. The park, located at the downstream end of the Green River Gorge, is a popular take-out point for rafters and kayakers enjoying white-water adventures in the gorge. The namesake, the flaming geyser, is caused by methane gas seeping from an underlying coal seam; when ignited, it creates a small torch flame in a rock pit. The flaming geyser was once featured in *Ripley's Believe It or Not*. Flaming Geyser Lodge sleeps 15; call (360) 902-8600.

Fort Canby State Park. Located 2.5 miles southwest of Ilwaco at the confluence of the Columbia River and the Pacific Ocean, in Pacific County. Lewis and Clark arrived at Cape Disappointment in November 1805. The mouth of the Columbia River, with its lava headlands, shifting sand dunes, and submarine sands, is known as the graveyard of the Pacific. Lighthouses have occupied this location since the late 1800s. Fort Canby was initially constructed during the Civil War (1863). Gun batteries presently in the park were constructed in the late 1890s, and reconstructed in the early years of World War II. Cabins and yurts are available to rent (for reservations, call 800-452-5687), as well as the North Head lighthouse keeper's house, which sleeps eight.

Fort Columbia State Park. Located 2 miles southeast of Chinook, in Pacific County. This fort, along with Fort Canby and Fort Stevens on the Oregon side, constituted the harbor defense of the Columbia River from 1896 until 1947, through the Spanish-American War and World Wars I and II. The area was the home of the Chinook Indians and their famed Chief Comcomly. Capt. Robert Gray dropped anchor near here after his discovery of the Columbia River. The quaint steward's house sleeps four; reservations, (800) 452-5687.

Fort Flagler State Park. Located on the north end of Marrowstone Island, across the bay from Port Townsend, in Jefferson County. Fort Flagler, along with the heavy batteries of Fort Worden and Fort Casey,

Looking Back

September 26, 1944

With famous nuclear physicist Enrico Fermi looking on, the first reactor at Hanford began operation. Plutonium production commenced by the end of the year.

Deception Pass State Park from Whidbey Island side of the pass. Photo by John Marshall.

once guarded the entrance to Puget Sound. These posts, established in the late 1890s, became the first line of a fortification system designed to prevent a hostile fleet from reaching such targets as the Bremerton Naval Yard and the cities of Seattle, Tacoma, Olympia, and Everett. Fort Flagler has two vacation houses, once part of the fort's staffing quarters; reservations, (360) 902-8600.

Fort Worden State Park. Located within the city limits of Port Townsend, in Jefferson County. At the time they were built, these forts that guarded the entrance to Puget Sound had the most modern weapons and fortifications. Their giant cannons became obsolete with the advent of more sophisticated weapons. Fort Worden's grounds and building were refurbished in the 1970s for vacation housing and also for a conference and educational center. Performing arts events are frequently held there today, and 32 refurbished quarters are available for rent; reservations, (360) 385-4730.

Gingko Petrified Forest State Park. Located where I-90 crosses the Columbia River at Vantage, in Kittitas County. The park is an area of exposed petrified wood

and logs, which grew as long ago as the Miocene epoch. The existence of the petrified wood was discovered during highway construction in the early 1930s.

Goldendale Observatory State Park. Located 1 mile north of Goldendale, in Klickitat County. The observatory houses a 24.5-inch reflecting telescope, one of the largest in the United States, which is available for public use. For permission to use the observatory, contact the staff by E-mail at Goldobs@gorge.net.

Kanaskat-Palmer State Park. Located 11 miles east of Enumclaw and Highway 410 via Farman Rd., in King County. A natural forest setting at the upstream end of the Green River Gorge makes this a popular put-in for kayakers, rafters, and others seeking white-water thrills and adventure.

Lake Lenore Caves State Park. Located 8 miles south of Sun Lakes State Park and 8 miles north of Soap Lake, on Highway 17, in Grant County. Caves formed by meltwaters plucking basalt from the walls of the coulees were later used as shelters by prehistoric humans. A trail from near the north end of Lake Lenore leads to some of these caves.

Lewis and Clark State Park. Located 12 miles south of Chehalis on Jackson Highway (old U.S. Highway 99), in Lewis County. The park contains one of the last stands of lowland old-growth forest. The John R. Jackson House was the first American pioneer home built north of the Columbia River. There's a great view of Mount St. Helens (the crater is visible). The dominant historical feature of the park is the old north spur of the Oregon Trail.

Lincoln Rock State Park. Located 7 miles north of East Wenatchee on U.S. Highway 2, on the east bank of the Columbia River, in Chelan County. A prominent geological feature resembles the profile of Abraham Lincoln, hence the name for this park.

Maryhill State Park. Located 12 miles south of Goldendale on Highway 14, in Klickitat County. Tycoon Sam Hill built a concrete castle for his wife, Mary, on a hill near the park, thus the name Maryhill. Sam made an unsuccessful attempt at establishing a colony of Belgian Quakers preceding World War II. Sam's home (3 miles from the park), now a museum, as well as a full-scale concrete replica of Stonehenge (1 mile from the park), which he had built as a memorial to those who died in World War I, are open to the public.

Moran State Park. Located on Orcas Island, in San Juan County. There are astounding views of the San Juans, the Cascades, the Olympics, and Puget Sound from the top of Mount Constitution (accessible by road). The park was the former estate of Robert Moran, onetime shipbuilder and mayor of Seattle. Camp Moran vacation house on the shore of Cascade Lake sleeps up to 10 people; call (360) 902-8600.

Old Fort Townsend. Located 4 miles south of Port Townsend, in Jefferson County. This park atop a 150-foot cliff commands a scenic view of Admiralty Inlet, Port Townsend Bay, and the Cascade Mountains. The fort was established in 1856, built with hewn-log timbers and clamshells, which were burned and ground for plaster. Troops were sent from the fort in July 1859 to help in a boundary dispute with England over San Juan Island, which came to be known as the "Pig War."

Palouse Falls State Park. Located 6 miles north of Lyons Ferry and 17 miles south of Washtucna, in Franklin County. Glacial floods formed a series of waterfalls along the Palouse River before it entered the Snake River. Palouse Falls, 198 feet high, is the only one remaining today. It is most spectacular in the spring and early summer.

Peace Arch State Park. Located on the U.S.-Canadian border at Blaine, in Whatcom County. The arch commemorates the signing of the Treaty of Ghent in 1814 and the Rush-Bagot Agreement of 1817, ending the War of 1812. The treaties provided for an unguarded U.S.-Canadian border from the Bay of Fundy to the Strait of Juan de Fuca. The Peace Arch, a 67-foot, jointly maintained structure straddling the border, is surrounded by extensive flowerbeds.

Peshastin Pinnacles State Park. Located 2 miles east of Cashmere, in Chelan County. Unique sandstone spires and formations are a popular rock-climbing area.

Rainbow Falls State Park. Located 18 miles west of Chehalis and 8 miles east of Pe Ell on Highway 6, in Lewis County. A falls above the bridge creates the namesake rainbow.

Ranald MacDonald's Grave State Park. Located 18 miles northwest of Curlew Lake State Park on Mid Way Rd., in Ferry County. Ranald MacDonald—no relation to the 20th-century fast-food clown—was a 19th-century adventurer and son of a Scotsman and a Chinook princess. He learned Japanese as a youth from sailors at Fort Vancouver. Years later, he purposefully had himself shipwrecked in Japan and worked his way across the country to the capital, where he taught English to the Japanese and promoted friendlier relations between Japan and the United States.

Steamboat Rock State Park. Located 12 miles south of Grand Coulee on Highway 155, in Grant County. The signature columnar basalt butte, which dominates the area, was once an island in the ancient Columbia River bed.

Sun Lakes State Park. Located 7 miles
(Continued on page 190)

Washington State Parks

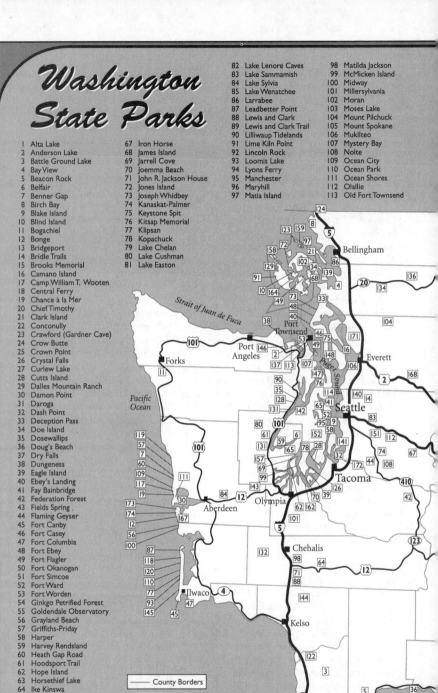

1 Alta Lake	67 Iron Horse
2 Anderson Lake	68 James Island
3 Battle Ground Lake	69 Jarrell Cove
4 Bay View	70 Joemma Beach
5 Beacon Rock	71 John R. Jackson House
6 Belfair	72 Jones Island
7 Benner Gap	73 Joseph Whidbey
8 Birch Bay	74 Kanaskat-Palmer
9 Blake Island	75 Keystone Spit
10 Blind Island	76 Kitsap Memorial
11 Bogachiel	77 Klipsan
12 Bonge	78 Kopachuck
13 Bridgeport	79 Lake Chelan
14 Bridle Trails	80 Lake Cushman
15 Brooks Memorial	81 Lake Easton
16 Camano Island	
17 Camp William T. Wooten	
18 Central Ferry	
19 Chance à la Mer	
20 Chief Timothy	
21 Clark Island	
22 Conconully	
23 Crawford (Gardner Cave)	
24 Crow Butte	
25 Crown Point	
26 Crystal Falls	
27 Curlew Lake	
28 Cutts Island	
29 Dalles Mountain Ranch	
30 Damon Point	
31 Daroga	
32 Dash Point	
33 Deception Pass	
34 Doe Island	
35 Dosewallips	
36 Doug's Beach	
37 Dry Falls	
38 Dungeness	
39 Eagle Island	
40 Ebey's Landing	
41 Fay Bainbridge	
42 Federation Forest	
43 Fields Spring	
44 Flaming Geyser	
45 Fort Canby	
46 Fort Casey	
47 Fort Columbia	
48 Fort Ebey	
49 Fort Flagler	
50 Fort Okanogan	
51 Fort Simcoe	
52 Fort Ward	
53 Fort Worden	
54 Ginkgo Petrified Forest	
55 Goldendale Observatory	
56 Grayland Beach	
57 Griffiths-Priday	
58 Harper	
59 Harvey Rendsland	
60 Heath Gap Road	
61 Hoodsport Trail	
62 Hope Island	
63 Horsethief Lake	
64 Ike Kinswa	
65 Illahee	
66 Indian Painted Rocks	

82 Lake Lenore Caves	98 Matilda Jackson
83 Lake Sammamish	99 McMicken Island
84 Lake Sylvia	100 Midway
85 Lake Wenatchee	101 Millersylvania
86 Larrabee	102 Moran
87 Leadbetter Point	103 Moses Lake
88 Lewis and Clark	104 Mount Pilchuck
89 Lewis and Clark Trail	105 Mount Spokane
90 Lilliwaup Tidelands	106 Mukilteo
91 Lime Kiln Point	107 Mystery Bay
92 Lincoln Rock	108 Nolte
93 Loomis Lake	109 Ocean City
94 Lyons Ferry	110 Ocean Park
95 Manchester	111 Ocean Shores
96 Maryhill	112 Olallie
97 Matia Island	113 Old Fort Townsend

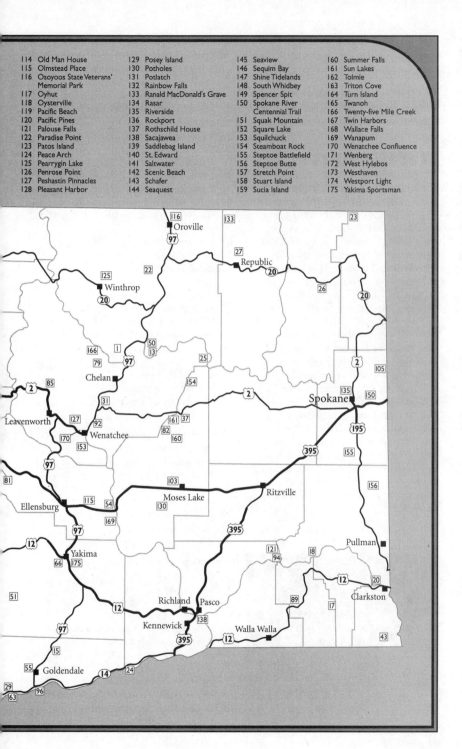

southwest of Coulee City on Highway 17, in Grant County. The park is situated in the lower Grand Coulee below and including Dry Falls. Plunge pools from the falls formed four of the seven lakes in the park. The park is on the north side of more than 10,000 acres of the best example of the Channeled Scablands.

State Symbols

State motto: *Alki. Alki* is an Indian word that means "by and by." This motto first appeared on the territorial seal designed by Lt. J. K. Duncan of Gov. Stevens's surveying expedition. On one side it pictures a log cabin and an immigrant wagon with a fir forest in the background. On the other side, a sheet of water is traversed by a steamer and sailing vessel, with a city in perspective. The goddess of Hope and an anchor are in the center. The figure is pointing at the significant word, *Alki*. As the story goes, the first settlement on Alki Point was named New York. The new settlement was slow to grow, therefore, with tongue in cheek the settlers renamed the settlement New York-Alki, meaning "New York by and by."

State seal: Designed in 1889 by jeweler Charles Talcott, using an ink bottle, a silver dollar, and a postage stamp.

State flower: Coast rhododendron. In 1892, Washington women selected the coast rhododendron as the state flower because they wanted an official flower to enter in a floral exhibit at the 1893 World's Fair in Chicago.

Coast rhododendron. Photo by John Marshall.

State flag: Similar to the state seal. Adopted by law in 1923, the flag has a dark green bunting with the state seal in the center.

State Capitol Building: The present capitol in Olympia was first occupied by the Legislature in March 1927. The design greatly resembles the U.S. Capitol in Washington, D.C.

State bird: Willow goldfinch or wild canary. A delicate little bird with a yellow body and black wings. Final designation in 1951.

State tree: Western hemlock. Designated in 1947.

State song: "Washington, My Home." Written by Helen Davis, arranged by Stuart Churchill. Adopted in 1959.

This is my country; God gave it to me;
I will protect it, ever keep it free.
Small towns and cities rest here in the sun,
filled with our laughter, thy will be done.

(refrain)
Washington my home;
wherever I may roam.
This is my land, my native land,
Washington my home.

Our verdant forest green,
caressed by silv'ry stream.
From mountain peak to fields of wheat,
Washington, my home.
There's peace you feel and understand in this,
our own beloved land.
We greet the day with head held high,
and forward ever is our cry.
We'll happy ever be as people always free.

For you and me a destiny,
Washington my home.
For you and me a destiny,
Washington my home.

State folk song: "Roll On, Columbia, Roll On." In the early 1940s, the federal Bonneville Power Administration produced a movie encouraging rural residents in the Pacific Northwest to electrify their homes and farms with the power being generated by the newly built Bonneville and Grand Coulee Dams on the Columbia River. As

The State Seal

Washington's state seal was the idea of an Olympia jeweler named Charles Talcott. Talcott had been asked by a design committee to create a seal for the meeting of the first state Legislature in 1889. The committee's design included the port of Tacoma, wheat fields, grazing sheep, and Mount Rainier. Talcott proposed a simpler design that wouldn't become dated. He drew two concentric circles using an ink bottle and a silver dollar. He pasted an image of George Washington from a postage stamp in the middle and lettered "The Seal of the State of Washington, 1889" between the inner and outer ring of the circle. The design was accepted and Talcott cut a die from a color drawing of George Washington on a packing box of "Dr. D. Jaynes Cure for Coughs & Colds" to create the official seal. Although there have been many variations of Talcott's design, including a new insignia created in 1967 based on a Gilbert Stuart portrait, the Secretary of State still uses the original die and press on official state documents. ✷

part of the project, the BPA hired folk singer Woody Guthrie at $270 for 30 days to tour the dam projects and the region and to write songs for the movie. Guthrie wrote 26 songs, the most popular of which was "Roll On, Columbia, Roll On," an ode to the harnessing of Washington's mightiest river. It was approved as the official Washington State folk fong by the Legislature in 1987.

State fish: Steelhead trout. A popular sport fish, the steelhead trout was adopted as the state fish in 1969.

State gem: Petrified wood. Adopted in 1975. The best place to see petrified wood is the Gingko Petrified Forest State Park, located on a bluff overlooking the Columbia River in Vantage.

State dance: Square dance, adopted in 1979.

State ship: *President Washington.* The designation of this 860-foot container ship as the state ship in 1983 symbolized the importance of international trade, especially trade throughout the Pacific Rim, to the state of Washington.

State fruit: Apple. Washington is the top apple-producing state in the country. The apple was named a state symbol in 1989.

State grass: Bluebunch wheatgrass. This grass is unique to eastern Washington. The symbol was adopted in 1989.

State tartan: The Washington State tartan was designed in 1989 as part of the state's centennial celebration, and adopted in 1991. The green background represents the rich forests of "The Evergreen State." Perpendicular bands of contrasting colors represent the following features: blue for the lakes, rivers, and ocean; white for the snowcapped mountains; red for the apple and cherry crops; yellow for the wheat and grain crops; and black for the eruption of Mount St. Helens. The Washington State tartan has been officially accredited by the Scottish Tartans Society.

State insect: Green darner dragonfly. The common green dragonfly was designated the state insect ir 1997, after a campaign by schoolchildren.

State fossil: Columbia mammoth. Newest state symbol, again the result of a schoolchildren's campaign. Fossils of the elephantlike Columbia mammoth have been found on the Olympic Peninsula.

Dragonfly. From *The Great Northwest Nature Factbook* by Ann Saling.

Tacoma

Tacoma Located in the shadow of Mount Rainier on the southern shore of Puget Sound, Tacoma (population 179,000) blossomed as early as 1873, when it became the Pacific terminus for the Northern Pacific Railroad. This remarkable city with deep historical roots has stood somewhat in Seattle's shadow. Today, however, it is a world-class container port. The downtown and waterfront have been rejuvenated with people-friendly projects. The cost of living in Tacoma remains affordable compared to its larger neighbor to the north, Seattle.

The renovated Union Station in Tacoma, which contains a spectacular display of works by world-renowned glass artist Dale Chihuly, a Tacoma native. Photo by Andrea Jarvela

Taxes

Taxes Washington voters have consistently rejected the notion of a state personal income tax, leaving retail sales taxes as the primary source of revenue, along with a tax on gross receipts on businesses and occupations (known as the B&O tax) and a pastiche of local and state excise, property, and use taxes. In 1997, the state ranked eighth nationally in the amount of taxes citizens pay. Washingtonians pay an average of $1,997 per person in state and local taxes. The state's total tax revenues for 1997 were $11.2 billion in taxes. Property taxes statewide totaled $1.9 billion; sales and gross receipts taxes amount to $8.2 billion.

Tax Rates.

Sales tax. Taxes on retail sales or on use of tangible personal property and selected services are 6.5 percent for the state, plus any varying local retail sales and use taxes.

Business taxes. The state B&O tax is based on gross income, sales, or value of products, and varies by business category; for example, the tax rate for manufacturing/wholesaling businesses is 0.484 percent, and for general services businesses it is 1.759 percent. Businesses may also have to pay municipal and county business taxes and licenses. These are generally also based on gross revenues or are flat fees based on factors such as class of business or number of employees. Local business taxes are generally about 0.05 percent to 0.2 percent.

Property taxes. The state assesses a tax on real or personal property for schools, based on assessed value: In 1997, the tax rate was $3.59 per $1,000 of assessed value. Local governments assess taxes on real and personal property, based on assessed value; while the rates vary statewide, in 1997 the average local regular and special levy rate was $10.34 per $1,000. The state assesses a leasehold excise tax, based on the rental value of leased, publicly owned property; the rate for this tax is 12.84 percent, less local taxes up to 6 percent. The state taxes sales of real property, amounting to 1.28 percent of the property's selling price.

Cars and gasoline. The vehicle excise tax (license tabs) is based on the depreciated value of a vehicle (to find out how much license tabs will cost for a given vehicle, check out the Vehicle Tab Calulator on the Department of Transportation's Web site at http://vs.dol.wa.gov/excisetax/ETFormZ. asp). In addition to vehicle license tabs, residents pay a state use tax for the use of automobiles (2.2 percent on the license tabs), campers/trailers (1.1 percent), and trucks and trailers (2.78 percent). Use taxes on aircraft are $20 to $125; on boats they are 0.5 percent. Also added to the cost of license tabs are local assessments of up to 1.5 percent for mass transit (0.725 percent), high-capacity transit (0.8 percent), and high-occupancy vehicle (HOV) lanes (0.3 percent). The tax on motor fuels is 23 cents per gallon (state). The tax on rental cars is 5.9 percent (state).

Energy and utility taxes. There is a tax on natural or manufactured gas (consumed within the state but not subject to public utility tax) of 3.852 percent. Gross operating revenues of public and privately owned utilities are taxed at the rate of 3.852 percent for gas and sewers; 5.029 percent for water; 0.642 percent for urban transportation; 1.926 percent for motor and railroad transportation; 3.873 percent for power; and 1.926 percent for all others. The state taxes public utility districts (PUDs) 2.14 percent of gross revenues plus 5.35 percent on the first 4 mills per kilowatt-hour. The state tax on refuse collection is 3.5 percent.

Beverage and tobacco taxes. These are sometimes known as "sin" taxes. In Washington, the wages of sin are assessed by volume or sales price:

State cigarette tax: sale, use, consumption, handling, or distribution of cigarettes, 82.5 cents per pack
State tobacco products tax: sale, use, etc., of other tobacco products, 74.9 percent of wholesale price
State liquor sales tax: sales of liquor and strong beer—consumers, 20.5 percent; Class H, 13.7 percent
State liquor liter tax: sales of hard liquor, $2.44 per liter
State beer excise tax: brewing or wholesaling of beer, $8.08 per 31-gallon barrel
State wine excise tax: wholesale sales of wine, 0.2292 cents per liter
Carbonated beverage "syrup" tax: wholesale or retail sales of syrup used to make carbonated beverages, $1.00 per gallon

Visitor taxes. Just passing through? The State Convention Center tax, assessed on accommodations in King County hotels with 60 or more units, is 7 percent in Seattle and 2.8 percent in the rest of King County. In addition, there are local hotel/motel taxes; transient rental income, 2.0 percent of state sales tax; special hotel/motel taxes; and 14 cities or counties levy additional taxes ranging from 2.0 percent to 3.0 percent.

Insurance premiums. The tax on gross premiums received by licensed insurers is 0.95 percent for ocean marine/trade insurers and 2.0 percent for all other insurers.

Timber excise tax. A tax on the stumpage value of timber at the time of harvest is assessed at 5.0 percent for public lands and 1.0 percent on private lands.

Pari-mutuel tax. Gross receipts of pari-mutuel machines are assessed 0.5 percent to 2.5 percent, depending on total receipts.

Boxing and wrestling tax. Ticket sales of boxing and wrestling matches are taxed at 5 percent of gross receipts.

Food fish and shellfish tax. These taxes are on the price paid by the first commercial processor of food fish or shellfish. The rates are: chinook salmon, 5.62 percent; sockeye salmon, 3.37 percent; oysters, 0.085 percent; and all others, 2.25 percent.

Hazardous substances. The value of certain chemicals and other products are taxed 0.7 percent at time of first possession in this state.

Oil spill tax. Crude oil and petroleum products delivered at marine terminals within the state are taxed 5 cents per 42-gallon barrel.

Licenses, Permits, and Fees. In addition to taxes, the state takes in more than $1 billion per year in fees for licensing occupations, uses, and privileges. These include accountants, banks, and savings and loans; sellers of real estate, travel, and insurance; health-care-related professionals—doctors, nurses, dentists, psychologists, pharmacists, therapists, and veterinarians; architects, builders, surveyors, and engineers; barbers and beauticians; safety inspectors; sewage treatment plant operators; and assessors of replacement tires.

Tides
The range of tidal movement is affected by a number of factors, including the shape and slope of the shoreline, the

Mud flats at low tide. Photo by John Marshall.

Budd Inlet: tidal range is 14 to 18 feet, with the highest tides over 16 feet and the lowest about minus 2 feet.

The National Oceanic and Atmospheric Administration's National Ocean Survey, which collects and archives tidal data, makes this tide information available on the World Wide Web at http://www.opsd.nos.noaa.gov/data_res.html. You can also consult tide tables published for specific areas, which are available at most sporting goods stores and book stores.

cycle of the moon, and storm conditions. Tides can vary wildly, from a range of only a few feet from high to low tide, to tens of feet; thus it is not possible to give just one average range for all of Washington's marine shoreline.

The most extreme tides—the highest high and lowest low tides—occur during the new and full moons; the least variation from low to high waters coincides with the quarter moons. Generally, the highest tides occur during winter months, and the greatest tidal ranges occur in the southernmost areas of Puget Sound. Below are some approximate ranges, along with some highest and lowest tides for several Washington tide stations.

Willapa Bay: tidal range is generally about 7 to 10.5 feet, with maximum high tides measured at well over 12 feet and the lowest tides at 2 feet below mean lower low water, or minus 2 feet.

Neah Bay: tidal range is generally about 8.5 to 9.5 feet, with the highest tides measuring over 10 feet and lowest at just under minus 3 feet.

Cherry Point: tidal range is about 7 to 9 feet, with the highest up to 10.5 feet and the lowest tides at minus 2.5 feet or more.

Bremerton: tidal range is about 11 to 14 feet, with the highest tides over 12 feet and the lowest at minus 2.5 feet.

Tourism
Tourism and travel dollars have become an increasingly important part of the economy of Washington State. Since 1991, travel spending has grown 4.7 percent per year, nearly double that of inflation. In 1998, travel spending in Washington totaled approximately $9.6 billion, generating $2.0 billion in payroll or directly supporting 124,680 jobs, according to a report prepared for the Washington State Community, Trade and Economic Development Department. **Washington State Community, Trade and Economic Development,** Tourism Development Office, 906 Columbia St. SW, P.O. Box 48300, Olympia, WA 98504-8300; (360) 753-7426, (360) 586-3582 . http://www.tourism.wa.gov.

Visitors to Washington include more than 600,000 overseas travelers, both for business and pleasure; international travelers in transit through the United States; and students. The Professional Convention Management Association estimates that the convention/meeting travel industry generates more than a third of the hotel and lodging industry's annual revenues. The State Convention and Trade Center in Seattle and the convention facilities at Spokane Center attract conventions and large trade shows year-round.

Among all the visitors, a number of the state's attractions stand out as favorites. Below are the most popular places and events that draw visitors in the state, according to the Washington State Department of Travel and Tourism.

Most Visited Sites.
Olympic Peninsula
Columbia River Gorge National Scenic Area
Wine Country
San Juan Islands
Long Beach Peninsula
Grand Coulee Dam
Mount Rainier and Mount St. Helens
Seattle
Spokane
Space Needle
Source: Washington State Tourism Division

The Space Needle in Seattle, one of the state's most popular sites for tourists. Photo by John Marshall.

Chambers of Commerce and Visitor Information Centers.
Most counties and many cities have a chamber of commerce, and many have visitor centers. To find a complete list and links to their Web sites, go to http://access.wa.gov/business/awcommerce.

Spokane Area Convention and Visitors Bureau, 801 W. Riverside, Suite 301, Spokane, WA 99201; (509) 624-1341. http://www.spokane-areacvb.org/spokane-center/index.htm.

Spokane Center, 334 W. Spokane Falls Blvd., Spokane, WA 99201.

Washington State Convention and Trade Center, 800 Convention Place, Seattle, WA 98101; (206) 694-5000. http://wsctc.com.

Favorite Festivals.
Skagit Valley Tulip Festival, March-April, Mount Vernon, (360) 428-5959.

Bloomsday Festival, May, Spokane, (509) 838-1579.

Mural in a Day, June, Toppenish, (509) 569-3982.

Salty Sea Days, June, Everett, (425) 339-1113.

Walla Walla Sweet Onion Festival, July, Walla Walla, (509) 525-0850.

International Kite Festival, August, Long Beach, (800) 451-2542.

Bumbershoot, September, Seattle, (206) 684-7200.

Ellensburg Rodeo, September, Ellensburg, (800) 637-2444.

Thanksgiving in Wine Country, November, Yakima, (509) 829-6027.

Zoo Lights, December, Tacoma, (253) 591-5337.

Trails
Hiking, walking, backpacking—at whatever level you wish to participate—are popular activities in Washington, and the state has many miles of trails, so many that there are libraries of guidebooks about them.

Asked to select its favorite trails for the state's centennial, the Washington Trails Association picked these:

Cape Alava Loop. One of the most popular hikes on the Olympic Peninsula—

3 easy miles between Lake Ozette and Cape Alava, the site of an ancient Makah Indian village that was covered by a landslide.

Elwha-Quinault. This 45-mile trail follows much of the route of the 1890 Press Expedition, a newspaper-sponsored group that was the first to cross the Olympic Mountains.

Hoh River. A 19-mile trail through one of only three temperate rain forests in the world.

Kettle Crest. Following the crest of the Kettle Range, this trail passes the state's oldest standing Forest Service lookout.

Klickitat Trail. This 16-mile trail was probably a trade route between the coastal and interior Indian tribes.

Naches Wagon Road. One of the torturous routes taken by pioneers crossing the Cascades to Puget Sound during the 1850s. Several ruts made by the iron-tired wagons still show along the crests of ridges. The road is reached by driving 20 miles east of Enumclaw on Highway 410 to FR 197, and following that road 8 miles to the Greenwater Trail sign.

Norway Pass. Views of Mount St. Helens' crater and lava dome and the remains of Spirit Lake can be seen on this hike.

Pacific Crest Trail. The 480-mile Washington section of this Canada-to-Mexico trail goes through or within sight of the Pasayten Wilderness, Alpine Lakes Wilderness, Mount Rainier National Park, Mount Adams Wilderness, Gifford Pinchot National Forest, and the Columbia River.

Shedroof Divide. This route, once used by Indians, is in the Salmo-Priest Wilderness in the Colville National Forest.

Spokane River. Spokane's Centennial Trail runs from the west side of Spokane along the Spokane River toward Idaho. The trail will eventually stretch to Lake Coeur d'Alene, Idaho.

Tucannon River. A 5-mile trail along another ancient Indian route, through the Blue Mountains.

Wonderland Trail. This 93-mile trail circumnavigates Mount Rainier. Campsites are placed about 10 miles apart on the main trail so that anyone who wishes to commit to hiking the whole thing can do it in about 10 days.

Yakima River Greenway. This is a popular riverside trail and urban greenway, along the Yakima River between Selah Loop and Union Gap.

For information about these and other trails, contact **Interagency Committee for Outdoor Recreation**, 4800 Capitol Blvd., KP-11, Tumwater, WA 98504-5611; (206) 753-7140. Another information source is **Outdoor Recreation Information Center**, 1018 First Ave., Seattle, WA 98104; (206) 441-0170.

Rail-Trails. Rail-trails are old railroad beds that have been converted to recreational trails for bicycling, running, walking, in-line skating, and horseback riding. The trails are built along abandoned rail beds or active railroad rights-of-way. Nationwide, there are more than 800 of these trails, running for more than 7,000 miles. Washington was among the first state to create rail-trails. The first was the Burke-Gilman Trail (along the west shore of Lake Washington), created in 1976. A nearly continuous series of rail-trails are gradually being connected, and rail-trail advocates hope to create a single cross-state trail from Seattle to Spokane. The trail segments include, from west to east, the Foothills Trail in Pierce County, the Snoqualmie Pass Trail, Iron Horse State Park, and the Milwaukee Road Corridor. For information, check out the Web site of **Rail-Trail Resource Center**, http://www.rail trail.org/fredwert/graphics/rtrcbanr.gif. Below are some popular rail-trails:

Burke-Gilman Trail, Seattle, 17 miles
Burlington Rail Trail, Burlington, 1 mile
Iron Horse State Park, Cedar Falls to
    Columbia River, 110 miles
King County Interurban Trail, Renton,
    20 miles
Snohomish-Arlington Centennial Trail,
    Snohomish, 8 miles
Snoqualmie Middle Fork Trail, North
    Bend, 4 miles

Water Trails. Western Washington's many protected inland waters and coastal bays have become the playground of avid sea kayakers. The sport's growing popularity motivated its devotees to form the Water Trails Association and lobby for water trails, in which sites along the shore are reserved for putting in and taking out human-powered craft. The first such trail is the 150-mile Cascadia Marine Trail, which runs from Olympia in south Puget Sound to the San Juan Islands, one of the few such paddling paths in the nation. In January 1993, the state Parks and Recreation Commission made the Cascadia Marine Trail official, and a short time later it was designated a national recreation trail by the National Park Service. The trail has 33 shore sites, but the Water Trails Association is aiming for 200 sites, extending the trail into Hood Canal and the Strait of Juan de Fuca. A water trail is being eyed for Willapa Bay also. **Washington Water Trails,** 4649 Sunnyside Ave. N., Suite 305, Seattle, WA 98103-6900; (206) 545-9161.

Transportation (See

also Airports; Ferries; Railroads; Roads and Highways) Washington's transportation system centers on the hubs of Seattle-Tacoma in the west and Spokane in the east, and includes the Interstate 5 north-south corridor, the I-90 and related east-west corridors, as well as the Columbia River corridor. Seattle is the terminus of transcontinental rail, air, and highway routes and the gateway to the Pacific Northwest, to and from Alaska, Hawaii, and Asia by air and by sea. Spokane is the chief city of the Inland Northwest and the center of a web of routes reaching out to Canada, the Northern Rocky Mountains, the Columbia Basin, and the Columbia Plateau and Great Basin country to the south. (See also Map, pages 198–99)

Tri-Cities (See also Hanford)

The cities of Pasco, Kennewick, and Richland, known collectively as the Tri-Cities and located near the confluence of the Columbia and Snake Rivers, sport enough nuclear energy visitor facilities for an atomic vacation. Kennewick (population 50,390) is the largest, Richland (population 36,860) is the second most populous, and Pasco the smallest (population 26,090). The nearby Hanford Reservation was the site of a major Cold War project for manufacturing plutonium, the essential ingredient of nuclear warheads. Richland's Atomic High School's sports teams are the Richland Bombers.

Lewis and Clark passed through the region in 1805. The first permanent western settlers raised cattle in the region after 1861. Railroad workers congregated in the area in the early 1870s as major bridges needed to be built to cross the rivers. Agriculture took off after the completion of initial irrigation projects in the 1890s. The massive Columbia dam-building and irrigation projects in the 1930s spurred growth even further, as about half a million acres are irrigated by these projects today.

Universities and Colleges Washington has an

extensive system of postsecondary institutions, including 29 community colleges, five technical schools, and six public and 18 private colleges and universities. Total full-time enrollment in higher education exceeds 180,000; however, total enrollment is nearly 300,000 students. There are more female students than males (164,000 versus 129,000) and more students enrolled in public institutions of higher learning (252,000) than in private schools (40,000). Minority enrollment statewide is 51,000 versus 232,000 white students and 9,000 nonresident aliens (foreign students).

State Universities.

Central Washington University, Ellensburg; (509) 963-3323. http://www.cwu.edu. Established in 1890 as Washington State *(Continued on page 200)*

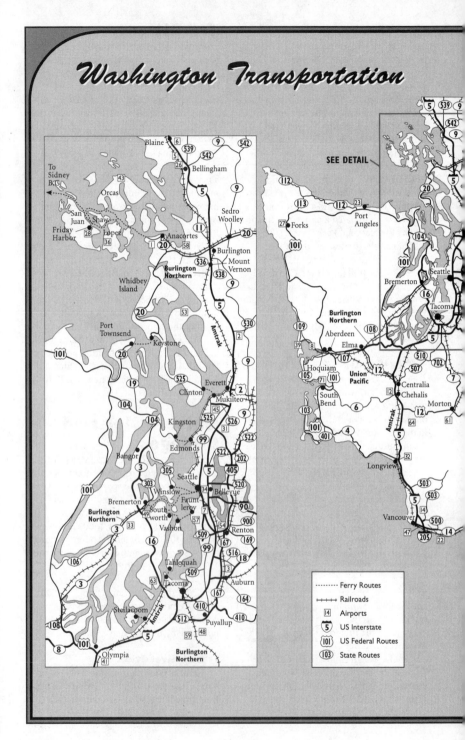

Washington Transportation

Legend:
- ·········· Ferry Routes
- ┼┼┼┼ Railroads
- 14 Airports
- 5 US Interstate
- 101 US Federal Routes
- 103 State Routes

SEE DETAIL

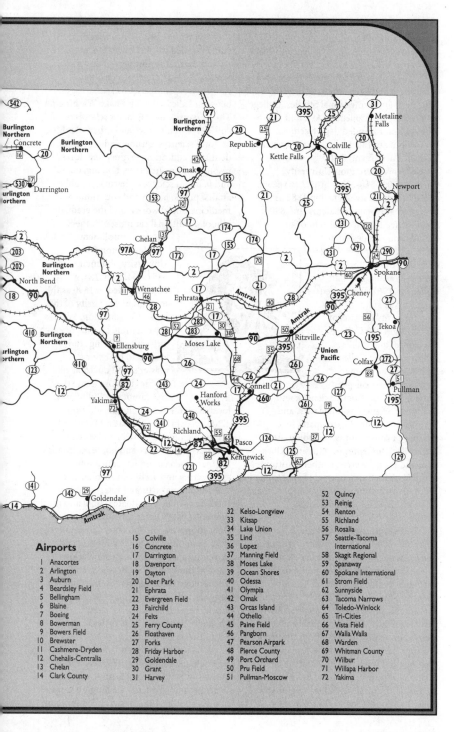

Airports

1 Anacortes	25 Ferry County	52 Quincy
2 Arlington	26 Floathaven	53 Reinig
3 Auburn	27 Forks	54 Renton
4 Beardsley Field	28 Friday Harbor	55 Richland
5 Bellingham	29 Goldendale	56 Rosalia
6 Blaine	30 Grant	57 Seattle-Tacoma
7 Boeing	31 Harvey	International
8 Bowerman	32 Kelso-Longview	58 Skagit Regional
9 Bowers Field	33 Kitsap	59 Spanaway
10 Brewster	34 Lake Union	60 Spokane International
11 Cashmere-Dryden	35 Lind	61 Strom Field
12 Chehalis-Centralia	36 Lopez	62 Sunnyside
13 Chelan	37 Manning Field	63 Tacoma Narrows
14 Clark County	38 Moses Lake	64 Toledo-Winlock
15 Colville	39 Ocean Shores	65 Tri-Cities
16 Concrete	40 Odessa	66 Vista Field
17 Darrington	41 Olympia	67 Walla Walla
18 Davenport	42 Omak	68 Warden
19 Dayton	43 Orcas Island	69 Whitman County
20 Deer Park	44 Othello	70 Wilbur
21 Ephrata	45 Paine Field	71 Willapa Harbor
22 Evergreen Field	46 Pangborn	72 Yakima
23 Fairchild	47 Pearson Airpark	
24 Felts	48 Pierce County	
	49 Port Orchard	
	50 Pru Field	
	51 Pullman-Moscow	

Normal School, then successively as Central Washington College of Education in 1937, Central Washington State College in 1961, and Central Washington University in 1977. The university comprises the School of Business and Economics, College of Education and Professional Studies, College of Sciences, and College of Arts and Humanities. Extended degree centers: Lynnwood, SeaTac, Steilacoom, Wenatchee, Yakima. Enrollment: 7,800.

Eastern Washington University, Cheney; (509) 358-6335. http://www.ewu. edu. The university opened in 1882 as the Benjamin P. Cheney Academy. In 1890 it became the State Normal School at Cheney and was designated Eastern Washington College of Education in 1937 and Eastern Washington State College in 1961. It achieved its university status in 1977. The university consists of four colleges: the College of Business and Public Administration; College of Education and Human Development; College of Letters, Arts, and Social Sciences; and College of Science, Mathematics, and Technology. Eastern participates in a number of consortiums, including the Intercollegiate Center for Nursing Education, and is one of five member institutions of the Spokane Intercollegiate Research and Technology Institute (see page 202). Other locations: EWU-Spokane Centers (2). Enrollment: 7,537.

The Evergreen State College, Olympia; (360) 866-6000. http://www.evergreen.edu. The Evergreen State College has earned a national reputation for providing innovative, high-quality programs in the arts and sciences. Students work closely with faculty in academic programs that are interdisciplinary, team taught, highly collaborative, and focused on real-world situations. It offers a full-time program, part-time studies in evenings and weekends, graduate programs in public administration and environmental studies, and a master's in teaching program. Other locations: Tacoma. Enrollment: 4,000.

University of Washington, Seattle; (206) 543-2100. http://www.washington. edu. Founded in 1861 on a 10-acre tract of wilderness that is now part of downtown Seattle, the University of Washington campus now comprises 694 acres located between Lake Union and Lake Washington. The university has 16 major schools or colleges—architecture and urban planning, arts and sciences, business administration, dentistry, education, engineering, forest resources, law, medicine, nursing, ocean and fisheries sciences, pharmacy, public affairs, public health and community medicine, social work—and the graduate school. Additional campuses: Bothell, Tacoma. Enrollment: 37,500.

Washington State University, Pullman; (509) 335-3564. http://www.wsu. edu. Founded in 1890 as the land-grant university of the state of Washington, WSU is today a multicampus research university offering study leading to bachelor's, master's, and doctoral degrees in more than 90 fields. The central campus in Pullman is located on 600 acres, plus an additional 4,200 acres in service area and farmland. The academic structure includes eight colleges—agriculture and home economics, business and economics, education, engineering and architecture, pharmacy, sciences, liberal arts, and veterinary medicine—plus a graduate school and the intercollegiate Center for Nursing Education based in Spokane, Cooperative Extension offices in all 39 counties, and agricultural research stations in various parts of the state. WSU Research and Technology Park, adjacent to the Pullman campus, aids technology transfer from faculty research. Additional campuses: Spokane, Vancouver, Tri-Cities. Enrollment: 20,500.

Western Washington University, Bellingham. Founded in 1893 as New Whatcom State Normal School, it successively became Western Washington College of Education in 1937, Western Washington

State College in 1961, and achieved university status in 1977. The university is organized as a graduate school and six colleges: arts and sciences, business and economics, Woodring College of Education, Fairhaven College, fine and performing arts, and the Huxley College of Environmental Studies. In addition to its Bellingham campus offerings, WWU offers a complete six- and nine-week summer session program, maintains a university extension center for continuing education, provides major conference facilities, and offers several education and human services programs through centers in Seattle, Everett, Bremerton, Oak Harbor, and Port Angeles. Enrollment: 11,476.

Private Colleges and Universities.

Antioch University, Seattle; (206) 441-3307. Enrollment: over 1,000.

Bastyr University, Bothell; (425) 823-1300. Degree programs: Undergraduate and graduate degrees in nutrition, oriental medicine, and naturopathic medicine. Enrollment: 1,049.

City University, Bellevue; (425) 643-1010. http://www.cityu.edu. Degree programs: undergraduate and graduate degree programs for working adults. Enrollment: 14,000.

Cornish College of the Arts, Seattle; (206) 323-1400. Degree programs: bachelor of fine arts degrees in art, dance, design, music, performance production, and theater. Enrollment: 230.

Gonzaga University, Spokane; (509) 328-4220. Degree programs: undergraduate and graduate degrees in arts and sciences, business, education, engineering, law, and professional studies. Affiliation: Independent Roman Catholic and Jesuit University. Enrollment: 4,632.

Heritage College, Toppenish; (509) 865-2244. Degree programs: undergraduate and graduate degrees in liberal arts. Other locations: Omak. Enrollment: 1,200.

Lutheran Bible Institute of Seattle, Issaquah; (425) 392-0400. Enrollment: 154.

Northwest College of the Assemblies of God, Kirkland; (425) 822-8266. Degree programs: associate and bachelor's degrees

in religious studies and professions, education, behavioral sciences, business, and interdisciplinary studies. Enrollment: 850.

Pacific Lutheran University, Tacoma; (253) 531-6900. http://www.plu.edu. Degree programs: undergraduate and graduate degrees in liberal arts, science, business, education, nursing, and physical education. Enrollment: 3,555.

Pacific Oaks College Northwest, Bellevue; (425) 889-0909. Degree programs: bachelor's and master's programs in early childhood education and human development, and a fifth-year teacher certificate program. Affiliation: Branch campus of Pacific Oak College of Pasadena, California. Enrollment: 150.

Puget Sound Christian College, Edmonds; (425) 775-8688. Enrollment: 120.

St. Martin's College, Lacey; (360) 491-4700. Degree programs: arts and sciences, social sciences, business, civil and mechanical engineering, computer sciences, nursing, and humanities. Affiliation: Independent Catholic college established by Order of St. Benedict. Enrollment: 1,033.

Seattle Pacific University, Seattle; (206) 281-2021. http://www.spu.edu. Degree programs: undergraduate degrees in liberal arts, science, and professional studies; graduate degrees in education and clinical family psychology. Affiliation: Christian university. Enrollment: 3,437.

Seattle University, Seattle; (206) 296-6000. http://www.seattleu.edu. Degree programs: undergraduate and graduate degrees in arts and sciences, education, nursing, engineering, theology and ministry, public service, and law. Affiliation: Independent Catholic university operated by the Jesuit Order. Other locations: School of Law, Tacoma. Enrollment: 6,000.

University of Puget Sound, Tacoma; (253) 756-3500. http://www.ups.edu. Degree programs: undergraduate degrees in liberal arts; selected graduate degree programs. Enrollment: 2,450.

Walla Walla College, College Place; (509) 527-2627. http://www.wwc.edu. Degree programs: pre-professional, two-year associate, certificate, and bachelor's programs in arts and sciences, engineering, computer science, education, nursing, social work, and religion; and selected graduate degrees in social work, biology, and education. Affiliation: Seventh-Day Adventist Church. Enrollment: 1,763.

Whitman College, Walla Walla; (509) 527-5111. http://www.whitman.edu. Degree programs: liberal arts. Whitman College is the oldest chartered institution of higher learning in the state of Washington. Enrollment: 1,260.

Whitworth College, Spokane; (509) 777-1000. http://www.whitworth.edu. Degree programs: undergraduate liberal arts degrees and master's degrees in education, international management, and nursing. Affiliation: Presbyterian Church. Enrollment: 2,000.

Other. Spokane Intercollegiate Research and Technology Institute; (509) 358-2000. The Spokane Intercollegiate Research and Technology Institute (SIRTI) fosters cooperative efforts in applied research and technology transfer between industry and Spokane's institutions of higher education. A collaborative project of five institutions, SIRTI's mission is to improve the economic vitality of the region by utilizing these collective resources to cultivate the development and commercialization of new technologies. The sponsoring institutions— Spokane's community colleges, Washington State University, Eastern Washington University, Gonzaga University, and Whitworth College—contribute instruction and research in high-technology disciplines such as engineering, technology, manufacturing, and computer science, as well as international management.

Community Colleges.
Bellevue Community College, Bellevue
Big Bend Community College, Moses Lake
Cascadia Community College, Bothell
Centralia College, Centralia
Clark College, Vancouver
Columbia Basin College, Pasco
Edmonds Community College, Lynnwood
Everett Community College, Everett
Grays Harbor College, Aberdeen
Green River Community College, Auburn
Highline Community College, Des Moines
Lower Columbia College, Longview
North Seattle Community College, Seattle
Olympic College, Bremerton
Peninsula College, Port Angeles
Pierce College, Lakewood
Seattle Central Community College, Seattle
Shoreline Community College, Shoreline
Skagit Valley College, Mount Vernon
South Puget Sound Community College, Olympia
South Seattle Community College, Seattle
Spokane Community College, Spokane
Spokane Falls Community College, Spokane
Tacoma Community College, Tacoma
Walla Walla Community College, Walla Walla
Wenatchee Valley College, Wenatchee
Whatcom Community College, Bellingham
Yakima Valley Community College, Yakima

Technical Colleges.
Bates Technical College, Yakima
Bellingham Technical College, Bellingham
Clover Park Technical College, Tacoma
Lake Washington Technical College, Kirkland
Seattle Vocational Institute, Seattle

Vehicle and Driver's Licenses
Washington has nearly 4 million licensed drivers driving 5.2 million cars and trucks—or 1.39 vehicles per driver. To be a duly authorized member of the traffic, new residents must apply for a drivers license within 30 days of becoming a Washington resident. You must notify the Department of Licensing within 10 days of

an address change or legal name change. A driver's license that is lost, stolen, or damaged may be replaced for a $5 fee. Military personnel may have a military designated expiration date on their license, which expires 90 days after discharge. Washington does not have a point system for license suspension or revocation; instead, the state counts the number of tickets on a driver's record (including those from other states). Driving privileges are suspended for four moving violations in one year or five violations in two years.

Except for farm, firefighting, and emergency vehicles, a commercial driver's license is required to operate a vehicle with a gross vehicle weight rating (GVWR) of more than 26,000 pounds; a trailer with a GVWR of more than 10,000 pounds (if the combined vehicle is more than 26,000 pounds); a vehicle designed to transport 16 or more persons (including the driver); and a vehicle that carries hazardous materials.

A motorcycle permit is required to operate a motorcycle on public roadways; you must have a motorcycle instruction endorsement.

Your vehicle license must be applied for within 30 days of your becoming a Washington resident. You may receive a $330 minimum traffic fine if you are a resident and do not license your vehicle in this state. If you bring your vehicle from another state, the Washington State Patrol must inspect your vehicle to verify the identification number.

In Clark, King, Pierce, Snohomish, and Spokane Counties, most vehicles manufactured since 1968 must pass a simple emissions test every two years. Other areas of the state may add that requirement in the near future.

Special License Plates. Applicants for disabled parking privilege must have a physician certify need. The privilege must

Looking Back

November 18, 1889

Elisha P. Ferry was inaugurated as the first governor of the one-week-old state of Washington.

be renewed every five years. Permanent placards need to be renewed every five years. A physician must recertify the need for the parking privilege. Knowingly providing false information to acquire a disabled permit is a gross misdemeanor that carries a penalty of up to one year in jail, a $5,000 fine, or both. Unauthorized use of the disabled permit carries a $250 penalty.

There are a number of specialized plates available to Washington vehicle owners. They include personalized plates, plates for antique cars, and plates that display the emblem of a square dancer or one's state college alma mater, amateur radio operators' call letters, or veteran status (including Medal of Honor and Purple Heart recipient and Pearl Harbor survivor). Some of the proceeds from specialized plates support designated programs, such as university scholarships and preservation of endangered species. **Department of Licensing,** 1125 Washington St. SE, Olympia, WA 98507-9020; (360) 902-3600. http://www.wa.gov/dol/.

Vital Statistics

According to the U.S. Census Bureau, there were 77,228 live births recorded in Washington in 1995 and 42,000 deaths, 39,200 marriages (or 7.7 per 1,000 population), and 25,500 divorces (5.5 per 1,000 population). Among the leading causes of death were heart disease (208.6 per 100,000 residents), cancer (183.0), cerebrovascular diseases (60.7), chronic pulmonary disease (39.7), and accidents (34.9). Infant mortality (1995) was 5.9 per 1,000 live births.

The Center for Health Statistics of the Washington Department of Health maintains all records of births, deaths, marriages, and divorces. Certified copies of birth or death certificates or records of marriage or divorce can be ordered from the department for a fee of $13. The department has birth and death records dating from July 1, 1907, and marriage and divorce records from January 1, 1968. Birth certificates for the years 1954 to present can also be requested from county health departments. Order forms for birth certificates, death certificates, and marriage or divorce records can be downloaded from the department's Web site or by mail. **Department of Health, Center for Health Statistics, P.O. Box 9709, Olympia, WA 98507-9709. http://www.doh. wa.gov/topics/chs-cert.html.**

Volcanoes and Volcanism

You don't have to look hard anywhere in Washington State to see evidence of its volcanic history. The rolling farmland and fertile soils of eastern Washington are ash deposits from prehistoric eruptions. North of the Columbia River, five volcanoes dominate the Cascade skyline: Glacier Peak, Mount St. Helens, Mount Adams, Mount Baker, and Mount Rainier, all dormant but technically active volcanoes. In an ancient eruption, Mount Rainier blew at least 2,000 feet off its summit. Steam continues to seep from vents in its crater.

On May 18, 1980, at 8:32 A.M, the top 1,313 feet and much more of the north face were blown off Mount St. Helens in a spectacular explosion that sent smoke and ash 80,000 feet into the air, released a mile-wide avalanche, and laid waste to forests as if they were matchsticks. This eruption was the first volcanic activity in the conterminous 48 states since Mount Lassen, another Cascade volcano, erupted in California between 1914 and 1921. The devastation zone, now a national volcanic monument, lies south of U.S. Highway 12 and can be toured by automobile.

The Cascade volcanoes exist because the floor of the Pacific Ocean sinks beneath the west coast of North America from southern British Columbia to northern California. As the sinking lithospheric slab reaches a depth of about 60 miles, red-hot steam rises and melts the overlying, already hot mantle,

forming basalt or andesite magma. The volcanoes occur along a line that marks where the sinking slab beneath gets hot enough to trigger rising steam and lava.

Other areas of the state formed by volcanic processes may be less apparent than the great peaks. More than 2,500 square miles of ancient lava flows underlie the vast, agricultural Columbia Plateau of central and eastern Washington. The ancient lava flows, which lie just below the surface, are exposed by ancient river cuts; for example, at the Grand Coulee, which is an archaic channel of the Columbia River. The Indian Heaven volcanic field, a 27-mile fissure between Mount St. Helens and Mount Adams, features smaller shield volcanoes and large lava flows. Big Lava Bed in southeast Skamania County covers 25 square miles and is about 10 miles long and 3 to 4 miles wide. It was created during a period of volcanic activity on Mount Adams.

The Cascades Volcano Observatory in Vancouver is a good source of information about volcanoes. The observatory also assesses potential hazards of the state's volcanoes and warns of potential eruptions, landslides, and debris flows. You can monitor the state's volcanic activity on the observatory's Web site. **Cascades Volcano Observatory, Vancouver. http://vulcan.wr. usgs.gov/home.html.**

Glacier Peak towers over Image Lake. From *Washington II* by John Marshall.

Voter Participation in Recent Presidential Elections

Year	Estimated Voting Age Population	Registered Voters	% of Voting Age Population Registered	Votes Cast	% of Registered Voters Voting	% of Voting Age Population Voting
1988	3,417,000	2,499,309	73.74	1,923,016	76.94	56.28
1992	3,818,000	2,814,680	73.72	2,324,907	82.60	60.90
1996	4,122,000	3,078,208	74.67	2,293,895	74.52	55.65

Source: U.S. Census Bureau

Voter Participation in Recent Mid-Term Elections

Year	Estimated Voting Age Population	Registered Voters	% of Voting Age Population Registered	Votes Cast	% of Registered Voters Voting	% of Voting Age Population Voting
1990	3,650,000	2,225,101	60.96	1,362,651	61.24	37.33
1994	4,000,000	2,896,519	72.40	1,733,471	59.85	43.34
1998	4,257,000	3,119,562	73.28	1,939,421	62.17	45.56

Source: U.S. Census Bureau

Voting

Residents of Washington who are U.S. citizens and 18 years of age are eligible to vote. Voters may register up to 30 days before an election to vote at a polling place, or 15 days before, provided they register at a specified location and vote by absentee ballot. Residents can register to vote at their county's elections or auditor's office, at their municipal clerk's office, when renewing their driver's licenses, or by mail. Most voters in the state register when they apply for or renew their driver's license (nearly 40 percent) or by mail. Voters who move to a different county must complete a new voter registration; voters who move within a county need only request a transfer of voter registration.

Increasing numbers of people are voting by absentee ballot, which may be obtained by applying to the county auditor from 45 days to one day before the election; the ballot must be postmarked or delivered on or before election day. Any registered voter may vote by absentee ballot. Disabled persons or those over age 65 may apply for status as an ongoing absentee voter and receive absentee ballots automatically. State and local election officials are required, wherever possible, to designate and use polling places that are accessible to all voters, including the disabled and the elderly (Washington State has one of the highest polling-place-accessibility rates in the nation). The Secretary of State and county auditors are required to provide assistance to elderly and disabled persons for federal elections, including letting them know which polling places are accessible and reassigning voters to accessible polling places upon request. Any voter unable to record his or her vote may request assistance from election officials or select someone to help them.

General elections are held the Tuesday after the first Monday in November; primary elections are held the third Tuesday in September. Washington's primary is an open election; voters do not have to declare a party affiliation and can cast their ballot for any candidate regardless of political party. Absentee ballots must be postmarked or received on or before election day.

Washington has a slightly higher percentage of the voting population registered to vote, 66.8 percent, than the United States as a whole, 62.0 percent. Likewise, the percent of the voting-age population who vote in the state is slightly higher than that for the rest of the country.

In the November 3, 1998, general election, more than 62 percent of the state's 3.1 million registered voters participated, the highest turnout in a mid-term election since 1982. A total of 1,939,421 ballots were cast in the general election. Compared to the state's estimated voting-age population, the turnout equals 45.5 percent—the highest since 1970. Nationwide, the turnout compared to the voting-age population has been estimated at 36 percent. The boost in turnout was attributed in part to the increasing use of absentee ballots. One-third of the state's registered voters are now signed up as permanent absentee voters, which means they automatically receive a mail ballot before each election. In the November 1998 election, 47.5 percent of the votes cast were by absentee ballot, a record high; in the September 1998 primary, 60 percent of the vote was by absentee.

Voter registrations reached an all-time high of 3,119, 562 in the November 1998 election. Currently, more than 73 percent of the state's voting-age population is registered, the highest level since 1978.

Elections are administered at the local level by county auditors (except King County, which has a Department of Records and Elections), and supervised by the Secretary of State. These county offices register voters, send out absentee ballots, and perform other elections-related services.

The Secretary of State's office publishes a voter information pamphlet for each election. Voter registration information and election information is also available at the Secretary's site on the World Wide Web. **Secretary of State Voter Information Hotline,** (800) 448-4881, TDD for hearing or speech impaired (800) 422-8683. http://www.wa.gov/sec/elections.htm.

Walla Walla
Walla Walla (population 29,440) is a refreshing green oasis in the great agricultural expanse of eastern Washington. Its ambience is enhanced by venerable Whitman College, shady streets, elegant old homes, and historic buildings. The adjacent countryside enjoys a long growing season, with wheat, potatoes, barley, asparagus, alfalfa, and the famous Walla Walla sweet onions the big money crops. Livestock and dairy products are also a significant part of the Walla Walla economy.

Water Sports
With its many rivers, lakes, and coastal waters, Washington offers many forms of recreation for water lovers.

Diving. Scuba diving may sound untenable in Washington's cold waters, but modern wet and dry suits have allowed cold to be a factor that deters only the dedicated wimp. Divers that do brave Washington's protected inland waters discover a large community of sea life. Not only are there varied and unusual fish species, but the world's largest octopus species—*Octopus dofleini*—is found here. This giant can grow

Inventing a New Water Sport

One summer day in 1928, Washingtonian Don Ibsen had the inspiration that he could ski on water as well as on snow. His first crude attempts involved a motorboat, boards from wooden crates, and Lake Washington. The earliest attempts were successful. Ibsen and his cronies became familiar sights during summers on Lake Washington, but commercial sales of the new product began slowly, and not until 1934. The Depression and World War II slowed even further the commercialization of the idea into a product. Not until after the war did water-skiing really take off as a sport, and it all started on Lake Washington. ✴

to 100 pounds with an arm span of up to 20 feet. Divers can also face off with the amazingly ugly, but harmless, wolf eel.

Among the more popular dive sites are the state's underwater parks. Edmonds Underwater Park, near the Edmonds ferry dock, has two sunken tugboats, an underwater "trail" divers can follow, and floats on the surface where divers can rest, providing that some cheeky sea lion hasn't already claimed them. In the southern Sound is another underwater park, Tolmie Underwater Park, on the south shore of the Nisqually Delta. The San Juan Islands also have numerous established diving sites.

Windsurfing. The Columbia River Gorge is to windsurfers what Yosemite is to rock climbers and Utah is to skiers. It is a mecca, a shrine, the ultimate challenge. With its dependable winds, easy access, and great local infrastructure, the Columbia River Gorge is one of the best locations in the world for windsurfers. The sport of windsurfing dates from the 1970s, and the Columbia River Gorge has been its epicenter from almost the beginning. This is because of the steady, strong winds and sheltered waters of the gorge. The difference in climate between the west and east ends of the gorge account for the steady winds. Each day, the sun heats the dry air on the east side, creating a pressure differential between east and west, which produces steady winds, often more than 30 miles per hour.

Another important feature of the gorge is the strong current of the mighty Columbia River. When the downstream current meets the opposing upstream-flowing wind, large swells result. These two forces cancel each other out. The expert windsurfer is able to balance current and wind, and never has to sail upriver to return to his or her starting point. Sailing the waves of the gorge is like skiing over moguls; it is especially exciting, but not for the novice.

Gorge sailing kicks in each year in March and continues through September. Wind and waves being what they are, the gorge sailor must travel each day to the ideal location, generally only a few miles

up- or downriver. Access is easy, as roads parallel both sides of the river.

Windsurfing is also popular on the state's large lakes and reservoirs and on Puget Sound.

Rafting and Kayaking. Washington's river terrain varies from wild white-water rapids to placid, slow-moving streams, with experiences ranging from white-water kayaking to relaxing float trips. River outfitters and guides can be found around most of the state's major rivers. Among the favorites are the Wenatchee and Yakima. The Skagit River is popular with eagle watchers.

Western Washington's many protected inland waters and coastal bays have become the playground of avid sea kayakers. The 150-mile Cascadia Marine Trail, from Olympia to the San Juan Islands, is one of the few such paddling paths in the nation and was the brainchild of the Washington Water Trails Association, a group of some 1,700 avid sea kayakers. One of the country's largest kayaking festivals, the annual West Coast Sea Kayak Symposium, is held in Port Townsend, and two national magazines, *Sea Kayaker* and *Canoe and Kayak,* are published in the Seattle area.

Boating. Protected marine waters, a long ocean coastline, large and small rivers, and numerous lakes and reservoirs all provide thousands of square miles of water for boating and yachting. Whether you own a boat or just want to be a passenger or observer, you can satisfy your nautical yearnings. Large luxury power yachts and sailboats ply the waters of Puget Sound and the San Juan Islands, jet boats tear through the Snake River canyon at breathtaking speeds, and picturesque wooden boats converge on Port Townsend at its annual Wooden Boat Festival.

The yachting and boating season opens on Puget Sound on about May 1, with a long procession of decorated sailboats, yachts, and pleasure cruisers—both new and elegant old classics. All pass through the Lake Washington Ship Canal in Seattle, so if you don't own a boat, you can still be part of the festivities. Just bring a picnic and sit on the banks of the ship canal and dream. If you get the urge to get on the water instead of just near it, you can check out the cost of owning at the annual Seattle and Tacoma boat shows, or you can rent or charter everything from a canoe to a luxury yacht. Marinas, boat landings, and state park campgrounds that are accessible only by boat can be found throughout the state.

Waterfalls (SEE ALSO DRY FALLS; RIVERS)

Washington's abundant water, basalt cliffs, cirques, and steep canyon walls provide ideal conditions for waterfalls. More than 700 waterfalls have been mapped, and there are many more yet to be discovered. Within or near Mount Rainier National Park, there are 122 waterfalls, two of them more than 300 feet high, the Clear Creek and Sluiskin Falls. Another, Comet Falls, plunges 320 feet from a hanging valley.

In eastern Washington near Washtucna, Palouse Falls drops 185 feet over a basalt rim of the Columbia Plateau. Like many waterfalls that crashed over the coulees and canyons of eastern Washington as the result of ice-age floods, the edge of the rim under Palouse Falls continuously crumbled under the silty torrent until the floodwater changed the course of the Palouse River. Prior to the ice-age torrent, it flowed directly into the Columbia; after the floods, it emptied into the Snake, as it does today.

The Columbia River was once the site of some of the West's most famous rapids and waterfalls. Celilo Falls, once an important fishing ground for Northwest Indian tribes, cascaded 20 feet down over a basalt cliff in the Columbia's main channel. Indians fished with spears and dip nets, and dried much of their salmon catch for eating and trading throughout the year. The Indian word Celilo means "floating sand cloud," which describes the sandstorms that occur when high winds sweep the Columbia Gorge. The falls were obliterated when The Dalles Dam was built across the river. Another important traditional Indian salmon-fishing site on the Columbia was Kettle Falls, which was flooded by the construction of Grand Coulee Dam.

A number of beautiful waterfalls are easily accessible to city dwellers. Spokane Falls is one of the most accessible in the state—in the center of the city of Spokane in Riverfront Park. The falls' total drop is about 150 feet, and the site has been used to generate power since 1871. Tumwater Falls, on the Deschutes River between the city of Tumwater and Budd Inlet on Puget Sound, can be seen from Interstate 5 in Olympia. Snoqualmie Falls, less than one hour east of Seattle on Interstate 90, is a popular tourist destination.

Weather and Climate (SEE ALSO CHART ON PAGES 212–213)

The crest of the Cascade Range divides Washington into two distinct climatic regions. The area west of the Cascades, which is exposed throughout the year to rain-bearing winds from the Pacific Ocean, has a temperate marine climate characterized by mild, wet winters and cool summers. The Cascades prevent the moist air blowing in off the Pacific from reaching eastern Washington. The Rocky Mountains on the eastern border also represent a climatic barrier. As a result, the severe winter storms that sweep the northern plains states do not reach Washington. Eastern Washington is much drier than western Washington, and its summers are hotter and its winters colder.

A wet marine West Coast climate predominates in western Washington. It is mild for its latitude due to the presence of the warm North Pacific Current offshore and the relatively warm maritime air masses. The region has frequent cloud cover, considerable fog, and long-lasting

The Cascade Mountains divide Washington into two distinct climate regions. West of the mountains, the wettest place is the rainy Olympic Peninsula, home to the only temperate rain forest in the continental United States. On the dry Columbia Plateau, average rainfall is measured in as little as fractions of an inch. Photos by John Marshall.

drizzles. Summer is the sunniest season.

The western side of the Olympic Peninsula receives as much as 160 inches of precipitation annually, making it the wettest area of the 48 conterminous states. Weeks or even months may pass without a clear day. Portions of the Puget Sound area, on the leeward side of the Olympic Mountains, are less wet, although still humid. The western slopes of the Cascade Range receive some of the heaviest annual snowfall in the country. Annual accumulations in excess of 200 inches occasionally occur. In the rain shadow east of the Cascades, the annual precipitation is only about 6 inches. Precipitation increases eastward toward the Rocky Mountains, however.

Because of the extreme climatic differences between eastern and western Washington, the growing season ranges from 100 days in some of the mountain areas to 280 days along parts of the Pacific shore. In eastern Washington, the growing season is 120 to 200 days. Around Puget Sound, the growing season is 160 to 240 days.

Weather Means and Extremes.

Temperature: The lowest recorded temperature in the state was minus 48°F at Mazama in 1968. The highest temperature was 118°F at Ice Harbor Dam in 1961. The average annual temperature ranges from 51°F on the Pacific coast to 40°F in the northeast.

Precipitation: The Olympic Mountains receive more precipitation than any other area in the mid-continental United States, often more than 140 inches yearly, much of it snow. The Cascades receive almost as much, and more than 300 inches have been known to fall on the mountain peaks in one year. Precipitation in Seattle averages about 36 inches per year, while the eastern slopes of the Cascades and much of eastern Washington receive only about 15 inches. In parts of the Columbia Plateau in south-central Washington, an average of only about 6 inches falls annually. The most rain recorded in one year in the Lower 48 reached a soggy 184.56 inches in 1933. It drenched *(Continued on page 212)*

State Weather and Climate Stations

1. Seattle (9 sites)
2. Tacoma (2 sites)
3. Walla Walla (3 sites)
4. Tatoosh Island
5. Neah Bay
6. Clallam Bay
7. Quillayute
8. Forks
9. Sappho
10. Spruce
11. Lake Sutherland

12. Elwa Ranger Station
13. Port Angeles
14. Sequim (2 sites)
15. Port Townsend
16. Coupeville
17. Chimacum
18. Quilcene
19. Anacortes
20. Olga
21. Blaine
22. Bellingham (2 sites)

23. Clearbrook
24. Sedro Woolley
25. Mount Vernon
26. Arlington
27. Everett
28. Glacier Ranger Station
29. Upper Baker Dam
30. Concrete
31. Darrington
32. Newhalem
33. Skagit Power Plant

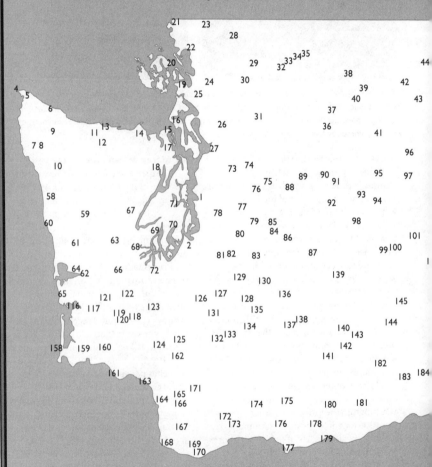

Average Temperatures, Precipitation, and Winds*

	January	February	March	April	May	June
Quillayute						
Max. temperature	46.2	49.6	51.9	55.2	60.6	64.2
Min. temperature	34.5	35.2	35.9	37.9	42.6	47
Precipitation	14.47	12	10.94	7.86	5.17	3.22
Snowfall	4.9	2.9	1.5	0.3	0	0
Mean wind speed	6.7	6.8	6.7	6.3	6	5.8
Prevailing wind direction	No data available, all months					
Seattle						
Max. temperature	44.6	49.1	52.3	57.5	64.3	69.4
Min. temperature	34.7	36.7	38.1	41.1	46.5	51.2
Precipitation	5.71	4.2	3.77	2.56	1.65	1.45
Snowfall	5.1	1.7	1.4	0.1	0	0
Mean wind speed	9.6	9.5	9.6	9.5	8.9	8.7
Prevailing wind direction	SSW	SW	SSW	SW	SW	SW
Spokane						
Max. temperature	32.9	39.1	48.2	58.3	67.1	74.3
Min. temperature	21.5	25.1	30.5	36.5	43.8	50.1
Precipitation	1.99	1.58	1.39	1.1	1.39	1.21
Snowfall	13	7.8	3.5	0.5	0	0
Mean wind speed	8.8	9.2	9.6	10	9.2	9.3
Prevailing wind direction	NE	SSW	SSW	SW	SSW	SSW
Yakima						
Max. temperature	36.9	45.8	55.3	63.8	72.8	69.7
Min. temperature	20.1	25.6	29.9	35	42.4	48.9
Precipitation	1.27	0.77	0.69	0.52	0.53	0.71
Snowfall	10.2	3.3	1.4	0	0	0
Mean wind speed	5.6	6.4	7.9	8.6	8.5	8.2
Prevailing wind direction	W	W	W	WNW	WNW	NW

*Temperatures: in degrees Fahrenheit; precipitation: in inches; winds: in miles per hour.

the community of Wynooche-Oxbow, located in a rain forest on the southwest flank of the Olympic Mountains. The nearby Quinault rain forest, which averages 134 inches per year, received a whopping 174.45 inches in 1968.

Snow: The most snow ever recorded in one spot in one year was 1,124 inches, which piled during the winter of 1998–99 on Mt. Baker. Paradise Ranger Station on Mount Rainier holds a world record for the greatest depth of snow in a single

month—25 feet, 5 inches in April 1972. Cold weather on Mount Rainier's upper slopes in winter can rival that of Mount Everest, with temperatures hitting minus 55°F and winds gusting at 80 to 100 miles per hour.

Worst storms: On February 1, 1916, 21.5 inches of snow buried Seattle, an all-time record for a 24-hour period in the city. It piled on top of 7 inches already on the ground from the day before. The total snowfall in Seattle in 1916 was

Average Temperatures, Precipitation, and Winds*

	July	August	September	October	November	Dec.
Quillayute						
Max. temperature	68.2	69.2	67.2	59	50.8	46.2
Min. temperature	49.8	50	46.6	41.4	37.5	34.5
Precipitation	2.26	2.71	4.7	10.31	14.4	14.99
Snowfall	0	0	0	0	1.1	2.7
Mean wind speed	5.5	5.1	4.9	5.4	9.3	9.6
Prevailing wind direction	no data available, all months					
Seattle						
Max. temperature	75.1	74.7	69.4	59.5	50.4	45.4
Min. temperature	54.5	54.7	51.2	45.3	39.6	35.7
Precipitation	0.79	1.1	1.82	3.51	5.98	5.94
Snowfall	0	0	0	0	0.8	2.6
Mean wind speed	8.3	8	8.1	5.5	9.3	9.6
Prevailing wind direction	SW	SW	N	S	S	SSW
Spokane						
Max. temperature	83.8	82.8	72.5	59.2	42.9	34.8
Min. temperature	55.8	54.5	46.7	37.6	30	24.3
Precipitation	0.57	0.63	0.82	1.18	2.12	2.18
Snowfall	0	0	0	0.2	5.4	11.2
Mean wind speed	8.6	8.3	8.2	8.2	8.7	8.7
Prevailing wind direction	SW	SW	NE	SSW	NE	NE
Yakima						
Max. temperature	87.4	86.1	77.8	64.2	48.2	38
Min. temperature	53.2	51.6	44.3	34.8	27.9	22.5
Precipitation	0.19	0.32	0.37	0.57	1.05	1.31
Snowfall	0	0	0	0.2	2.8	8.6
Mean wind speed	7.8	7.4	7.3	6.6	5.8	5.2
Prevailing wind direction	SW	SW	N	S	S	SSW

Source: National Oceanic and Atmospheric Administration

60.9 inches, still a city record.

Winds: The most savage windstorm in the state hit on Columbus Day, 1962. Typhoon Frieda blew off roofs along the Pacific coast, smashed windows, jerked power poles out of the ground, and separated log booms. Winds reached 160 miles per hour. Trees totaling 1.5 billion board feet blew down. A 10-car ferry sank at Lummi Island, and an ocean liner was ripped loose from its moorings in Seattle.

Weyerhaeuser

Weyerhaeuser Company, headquartered in Federal Way, is the world's largest private owner of merchantable softwood timber. Founded in 1900, the company's principal businesses are the growing and harvesting of trees; the manufacture, distribution, and sale of forest products, including logs, wood chips, building products, pulp, paper, and packaging products; and real estate construction and development.

Weyerhaeuser is the top forest-products

exporter in the United States. Its annual sales were $11.1 billion in 1996 ($1.8 billion were exports). Its North American workforce numbers about 39,700. The company manages approximately 5.5 million acres of private timberland in North America; 2.2 million acres are in the Pacific Northwest. It also owns and operates eight seedling nurseries and 17 tree farms. Weyerhaeuser harvests about 2 percent of its forests each year. Reforested sites will be harvested again in 40 to 50 years. Weyerhaeuser Company; www.weyerhaeuser.com.

Whales

Whales are among the largest and most intelligent of all mammals, and Washington's coastal and protected marine waters support both resident and migratory whales of several species. Whaling was an integral part of the life of Northwest Coast Indians, a tradition that Washington's Makah Indians were determined to pursue again after some 70 years of non-whaling. The Makahs were granted permission in 1998 to kill migrating gray whales off the Washington coast, and declared their intent to do so. The controversial decision was challenged by environmental groups, which attempted to halt the whale hunt.

The gray whale (*Eschrichtius robustus*) spends the summer feeding season in the Arctic and the winter breeding season in the lagoons of Baja California. Twice a year, they migrate past the Washington coast, often staying within a couple of miles of the shore. The gray whale is a baleen whale; it grazes along the bottom and strains its food, which consists mainly of shrimplike animals, from the water. Gray whales grow up to 50 feet and weigh up to 20 tons. Gray whales can be viewed from whale-watching expeditions, and sometimes even from a bluff along the ocean coast, in early and late winter. Occasionally, a gray whale will even stray into Puget Sound waters.

The other spectacular whale in Washington State is the killer whale or orca (*Orcinus orca*), which can be seen in Washington's inland waters. These waters are home to resident orca groups, called pods. Orcas are the largest of the toothed whales, reaching lengths of up to 25 feet and weighing up to six tons. They can swim at more than 30 miles per hour for brief periods. There are 89 whales in resident pods (named Pods J, K, and L), which are generally found in the San Juan Islands and around the south Vancouver Island area during the months of May through September. Researchers have identified each member of these pods by the shape and size of their dorsal fins and their gray and white markings. One of the best places to see orcas in summer is from Lime Kiln State Park on San Juan Island. Also on San Juan Island is the Whale Museum in Friday Harbor.

Migrating humpback and minke whales also move along the Washington coast and occasionally stray into the Strait of Juan de Fuca. Relatives of the orca, dolphins—particularly the Pacific white-sided dolphin—also make their way into the strait.

Organizations of Interest.

The Whale Museum, 62 First St. N., P.O. Box 945, Friday Harbor, WA 98250; (800) 946-7227. www.whale-museum.org.

Gray whale.

Wilderness (See also Map, pages 132–33)

Wilderness areas, managed by the U.S. Forest Service, are lands set aside by Congress as those places "untrammeled by man, where man himself is a visitor who does not remain." Generally this means that there are no commerical enterprises; no permanent roads; no use of motor vehicles, motorized equipment, or motorboats; no landing of aircraft; no other form of mechanical transport; and no structure or installation. So if it's nature you yearn for, head for Washington's wilderness areas. There are more than 2.5 million acres of wilderness, almost all of which lie within the boundaries of national forests.

Organizations of Interest.

The Wilderness Society, Pacific Northwest Region, 1424 Fourth Ave., Suite 816, Seattle, WA 98101-2217; (206) 624-6430. E-mail: info@twsnw.org. (See also Map, pages 128–29)

Wildflowers (See Plants)

Winds (See Weather and Climate)

Wine

Vineyards and wineries have become a fixture in Washington's agricultural and cultural life. The state has 102 wineries and more than 20,000 acres of planted vineyards, making it the

National Wilderness Areas

	National Forest	Acres
Alpine Lakes	Mount Baker-Snoqualmie National Forest	117,899
	Wenatchee National Forest	246,330
Boulder River	Mount Baker-Snoqualmie National Forest	48,674
Buckhorn	Olympic National Forest	44,474
Clearwater	Mount Baker-Snoqualmie National Forest	14,374
Colonel Bob	Olympic National Forest	11,961
Glacier Peak	Mount Baker-Snoqualmie National Forest	283,504
	Wenatchee National Forest	289,234
Glacier View	Mount Baker-Snoqualmie National Forest	3,123
Goat Rocks	Gifford Pinchot National Forest	71,203
	Mount Baker-Snoqualmie National Forest	37,236
Henry M. Jackson	Mount Baker-Snoqualmie National Forest	75,551
	Wenatchee National Forest	25,416
Indian Heaven	Gifford Pinchot National Forest	20,960
Lake Chelan-Sawtooth	Okanogan National Forest	95,108
	Wenatchee National Forest	56,456
Mount Adams	Gifford Pinchot National Forest	56,681
Mount Baker	Mount Baker-Snoqualmie Forest	117,848
Mount Skokomish	Olympic National Forest	13,015
Noisy-Diobsud	Mount Baker-Snoqualmie National Forest	14,133
Norse Peak	Mount Baker-Snoqualmie National Forest	52,180
Pasayten	Mount Baker-Snoqualmie National Forest	107,039
	Okanogan National Forest	422,992
Salmo-Priest	Colville National Forest	29,386
	Kaniksu National Forest	11,949
Tatoosh	Gifford Pinchot National Forest	5,970
Wenaha-Tucannon	Umatilla National Forest	111,048
William O. Douglas	Gifford Pinchot National Forest	15,469
	Mount Baker-Snoqualmie National Forest	152,688
Wonder Mountain	Olympic National Forest	2,349

Source: U.S. Department of the Interior

second-highest wine-producing state in the country. The state has four officially recognized viticultural appellations.

The **Columbia Valley** is the state's largest appellation. It extends from its northernmost boundary near the Okanogan wilderness, south into Oregon, east to the Idaho border, and west along the Cascade Mountains to the Columbia Gorge. Varietal grapes planted here include chardonnay, cabernet sauvignon, merlot, riesling, and pinot noir.

The **Yakima Valley** was the state's first approved viticultural area. Its boundaries are the foothills of the Cascades on the west and the Kiona Hills near Richland on the east. This region has the state's highest percentage of vineyard plantings per square mile.

The **Walla Walla Valley**, which includes areas in both Washington and Oregon, features cabernet sauvignon, merlot, riesling, and chardonnay grapes.

The **Puget Sound Basin**'s mild winters and long, warm summer growing season support early-ripening varieties such as pinot noir, chardonnay, Müller Thurgau, Madeline Angevine, and Siegerebbe grapes.

A number of sub-appellations are also emerging. They include Red Mountain and Benton County, vineyards sloping down from Red Mountain toward the Yakima River just above Benton City near Richland; Wahluke Slope, Royal Slope, and Cold Creek, on the high Columbia River plateau from Vantage to Othello; the Lower Snake

River, east of Pasco; Canoe Ridge, just above Crow Butte State Park on the Columbia River where a wide slope faces south-southeast toward the river; and Southwest Washington, along the Lewis River in the north part of Clark County.

Washington's Largest Wineries

	Number of Cases
Columbia Crest	1,136,000
Chateau Ste. Michelle	600,000
The Hogue Cellars	361,000
Domaine St. Michelle	251,000
Washington Hills	150,000
Paul Thomas	130,000
Columbia	125,000
Covey Run	100,000
Silver Lake	65,000
Hedges Cellars	63,000

Source: Puget Sound Business Journal Book of Lists 1999

Organizations and Events of Interest.

American Society of Enology and Viticulture, Northwest Chapter, (509) 786-9285.

The Tri-Cities Wineries Association, (509) 588-6716.

Washington Wine Commission, 206 667-9453. E-mail: WAWineCtr@aol.com. http://www.washingtonwine.org.

Yakima Valley Winegrowers Association, (800) 258-7270.

Barrel Tasting, June, Tri-Cities, (509) 826-0813.

Spring Barrel Tasting, June, Yakima Valley, (509) 829-6027. New release wine.

Wine and Food Fair, August, Prosser, (509) 786-3177.

Catch the Crush, September, Yakima-Tri-Cities, (509) 588-6716.

Grandview Grape Stomp, September, Grandview, (509) 882-2100.

Grape Stomp/Nooksack Harvest Festival, September, Deming, (360) 592-2300.

Tri-Cities Northwest Wine Festival, November, Pasco, (509) 375-3399.

Yakima
Early Western settlers in the Yakima region skirmished with the Yakama Indians, and early ranching efforts

The tasting room at Chateau Ste. Michelle Winery in Woodinville. Courtesy of Chateau Ste. Michelle Winery.

were not especially successful. Turnaround came in 1870, however, when the first irrigation canal was constructed. Orchards followed soon after, and the city of Yakima was incorporated in 1883. The Yakima Valley's volcanic soil is twice as productive as ordinary soil. Add 200 or more days a year of sunshine and abundant irrigated water from the Yakima River, and you have all the ingredients for a dynamic agricultural economy. Yakima (population 64,290) is the center of the tree fruit industry, which traditionally has employed a large seasonal labor force of workers from Mexico and Central American countries. Many of these workers stayed behind to raise their families and contribute to the community, and today the visitor can hear Spanish radio and experience Latin culture in the Yakima area.

Looking Back

December 12, 1905

The U.S. Department of the Interior approved the initial elements of the Yakima Project, which was planned to eventually irrigate some 350,000 acres.

Zip Codes

To find a zip code for a specific address, use the zip code finder at the Post Office Web site at http://www.usps.gov/ncsc/lookups/lookups.htm

Aberdeen   98520
Acme   8220
Addy   99101
Adna   98522
Airway Heights, Spokane   99001
Albion   99102
Algona (see Auburn)
Allyn   98524
Almira   99103
Amanda Park   98526
Amboy   98601
Anacortes   98221
Anderson Island   98303
Appleton   98602
Ardenvoir   98811
Ariel   98603
Arlington   98223
Ashford   98304

Asotin   99402
Auburn   98001-98003, 98023, 98047, 98063, 98071, 98092-98093
Bainbridge Island   98110
Baring   98224
Battle Ground   98604
Bay Center   98527
Beaux Arts   98004
Beaver   98305
Belfair   98528
Bellevue   98004–98009, 98015
Bellingham   98225–98228
Belmont   99104
Benge   99105
Benton City   99320
Beverly   99321
Bickleton   99322
Bingen   98605
Black Diamond   98010
Blaine   98230–98231
Blakely Island   98222
Bonney Lake (see Sumner)
Bothell   98011–98012, 98021, 98041, 98082
Bow   98232
Boyds   99107
Bremerton   98310–98312, 98314, 98337
Brewster   98812
Bridgeport   98813
Brier (see Lynnwood)
Brinnon   98320
Brownstown   98920
Brush Prairie   98606
Buckley   98321
Bucoda   98530
Buena   98921
Burbank   99323
Burien (see Seattle)
Burley   98322
Burlington   98233
Burton   98013
Camas   98607
Carbonado   98323
Carlsborg   98324
Carlton   98814
Carnation   98014
Carrolls   98609
Carson   98610
Cascade Park (see Vancouver)
Cashmere   98815

Malaga   98828
Malden   99149
Malo   99150
Malone   98559
Malott   98829
Manchester   98353
Mansfield   98830
Manson   98831
Maple Falls   98266
Maple Valley   98038
Marblemount   98267
Marcus   99151
Marlin   98832
Marshall   99020
Marysville   98270–98271
Matlock   98560
Mattawa   99349
Mazama   98833
McChord AFB (see Lakewood)
McCleary   98557
McKenna   98558
Mead   99021
Medical Lake   99022
Medina   98039
Menlo   98561
Mercer Island   98040
Mesa   99343
Metaline   99152
Metaline Falls   99153
Methow   98834
Mica   99023
Mill Creek (see Bothell)
Milton   98354
Mineral   98355
Moclips   98562
Mohler   99154
Monitor   98836
Monroe   98272
Montesano   98563
Morton   98356
Moses Lake   98837
Mossyrock   98564
Mount Vernon   98273–98274
Mountlake Terrace   98043
Moxee   98936
Mukilteo   98275
Naches   98937
Nahcotta   98637
Napavine   98565
Naselle   98638
Neah Bay   98357
Neilton   98566

Nespelem   99155
Newcastle (see Renton)
Newman Lake   99025
Newport   99156
Nine Mile Falls   99026
Nooksack   98276
Nordland   98358
Normandy Park (see Seattle)
North Bend   98045
North Bonneville   98639
Northport   99157
Oakbrook (see Lakewood)
Oakesdale   99158
Oak Harbor   98277
Oakville   98568
Ocean City   98569
Ocean Park   98640
Ocean Shores   98569
Odessa   99159
Okanogan   98840
Olalla   98359
Olga   98279
Olympia   98501–98509, 98512–98513,
   98516, 98599–99302
Omak   98841
Onalaska   98570
Orcas   98280
Orchards (see Vancouver)
Orient   99160
Orondo   98843
Oroville   98844
Orting   98360
Othello   99344
Otis Orchards   99027
Outlook   98938
Oysterville   98641
Pacific   98047
Pacific Beach   98571
Packwood   98361
Palisades   98845
Palouse   99161
Paradise Inn   98398
Parker   98939
Parkland (see Lakewood)
Pasco   99301–99302
Pateros   98846
Paterson   99345
Pe Ell   98572
Peshastin   98847
Plaza, Rosalia   99170
Plymouth   99346
Point Roberts   98281

Sumas   98295
Sumner   98390
Sunnyside   98944
Suquamish   98392
Tacoma   99401–98409, 98411, 99413,
    98415–98416, 98418, 98421–98422,
    98424, 98430-98431, 98433–98434,
    98438–98439, 98442–98447, 98450,
    98455, 98460, 98464–98467, 98471,
    98477, 98481, 98492–98494,
    98497–98499
Taholah   98587
Tahuya   98588
Tekoa   99033
Tenino   98589
Thornton   99176
Thorp   98946
Tieton   98947
Tillicum (see Tacoma)
Tokeland   98590
Toledo   98591
Tonasket   98855
Toppenish   98948
Touchet   99360
Toutle   98649
Tracyton   98393
Trout Lake   98650
Tukwila (see Seattle)
Tumtum   99034
Tumwater (see Olympia)
Twisp   98856
Underwood   98651
Union   98592
Union Gap (see Yakima)
Uniontown   99179
University Place   98467
Usk   99180
Vader   98593
Valley   98181
Valleyford   99036
Vancouver   98660–98668, 98682–98687
Vantage   98950
Vashon   98070
Vaughn   98394
Veradale   99037
Wahkiacus   98670
Waitsburg   99361
Waldron   98297
Walla Walla   99362
Wallula   99363
Wapato   98951
Warden   98857

Washougal   98671
Washtucna   99371
Waterville   98858
Wauconda   98859
Wauna   98395
Waverly   99039
Wellpinit   99040
Wenatchee   98801–98802, 98807
West Richland   99353
Westport   98595
White Salmon   98672
White Swan   98952
Wilbur   99185
Wilkeson   98396
Wilson Creek   98860
Winlock   98596
Winthrop   98862
Wishram   98673
Woodinville   98072
Woodland   98674
Woodway (see Edmonds)
Yacolt   98675
Yakima   98901–98904, 98907–98909
Yarrow Point (see Bellevue)
Yelm   98597
Zillah   98953

Zoos and Aquariums

There are a handful of zoos, wildlife parks, and aquariums in Washington that provide wildlife and sea-life viewing year-round. Exotic and endangered species can be found at the larger zoos, such as Woodland Park Zoo in Seattle and Point Defiance Zoo in Tacoma, and numerous Northwest species can be viewed at private wildlife parks such as Northwest Trek. The Seattle and Point Defiance aquariums offer close-up views of playful sea otters and seals, fish, and other curious-looking sea critters.

Cat Tales Endangered Species Conservation Park, 17020 N. Newport Hwy., Mead, WA 99021-9539; (509) 238-4126.

778-4295. http://northolympic.com/game-farm. A 180-acre preserve is home to exotic animals that have retired from show business.

Point Defiance Zoo and Aquarium, 5400 N. Pearl St., Tacoma, WA 98407-3218; (206) 591-5337. http://www.pdza.org. Polar bears, walruses, otters, and sea life can be seen here.

Seattle Aquarium, 1438 Alaskan Way, Pier 59, Waterfront Park, Seattle, WA 98101-2094; (206) 386-4320. http://www.seattleaquarium.org. Big fish, little fish, tide-pool critters, an underwater view of Puget Sound sea life, and lots of otters and seals are exhibited.

Wolf Haven International, 3111 Offut Lake Rd., Tenino, WA 98589; (800) 448-9635. http://www.wolfhaven.org. A 65-acre preserve is home to some two dozen gray wolves.

Woodland Park Zoo, 5500 Phinney N., Seattle, WA 98103-5897; (206) 684-4800. http://www.zoo.org. Outstanding natural exhibits, including a tropical rain forest and temperate forests, can be seen in the heart of Seattle.

http://www.cattales.org. More than two dozen big cats live in this preserve just north of Spokane.

Northwest Trek Wildlife Park, 11610 Trek Dr. E., Eatonville, WA 98328; (360) 832-7166, (800) 433-8735. www.nwtrek.org. Naturalist-guided tram tours take visitors near Northwest animals on 635 acres.

Olympic Game Farm, 1423 Ward Rd., Sequim, WA 98382; (360) 683-4295, (800)

News Highlights, 1998-99

The following is a collection of news events from mid-1998 to mid-1999. *The Washington Almanac* wishes to credit stories printed in *The Seattle Times, Spokane Spokesman-Review, Tri-City Herald,* and *Yakima Herald* as the primary sources of information for News Highlights.

Houses Slip-sliding Away in Kelso.

While landslides occur along Puget Sound's coastal bluffs nearly every winter, the unusually wet weather in the winter of 1997–98 triggered some especially destructive landslides. In Kelso, the entire neighborhood of Aldercrest began creeping downhill in March 1998 as the result of saturated and unstable sediments. Geologists concluded that an "ancient landslide" was reactivated by the heavy rains. Eighteen months later, an entire subdivision of 137 homes was already gone or at risk of total destruction.

Here No Mo.

During May and June 1998, the historic battleship USS *Missouri*—nicknamed "Mighty Mo"—a longtime sight on the Bremerton waterfront, was towed by a 7,200-horsepower tug, first to Astoria, Oregon, then across the Pacific to Honolulu. The trip to Hawaii took about 30 days. The ship was donated in August 1996 by the Navy to the USS *Missouri* Memorial Foundation, which moved her to Hawaii. She can now be seen at Pearl Harbor, near the sunken aircraft carrier *Arizona.* Nearly 200,000 visitors viewed the *Missouri* each year when she was in Bremerton, but that was not enough to keep her there. Built in 1944 at the height of World War II, Mighty Mo's 16-inch guns hurled shells as large as small cars as far as 20 miles. Her awesome firepower turned the tide at important battles in the Pacific. On September 2, 1945, General Douglas MacArthur accepted Japan's unconditional surrender on her decks. Mothballed at the naval shipyard in Bremerton in 1954, Mighty Mo returned to service during the Persian Gulf War in 1991. After launching missiles at the Iraqis, she was decommissioned in 1992.

Man versus Mountain—Paraplegic Reaches New Heights on Mount Rainier.

In June 1998 a paraplegic mountain climber from Pasco climbed to 12,600 feet on 14,411-foot Mount Rainier. He was turned back by a crevasse, which was uncrossable at the time. The climber, Pete Rieke, used a hand-cranked snowmobile or snow pod, which he invented. While many climbers like Pete are turned back by weather or ice and snow conditions, the climb was a great success in that it demonstrated to the world the capabilities of handicapped mountaineers.

A Great Growing Season for Fruit and Wine.

The hot summer of 1998 was ideal for fruit growers. While apple markets were in turmoil and much fruit was left in the orchards to rot, the growing season was fantastic. Washington produced an estimated 100 million boxes of apples in 1998, its largest apple crop ever. The wine grape harvest also was up. In 1998, Washington grape growers produced an estimated 77,000 tons of wine grapes on 14,500 acres. That's nearly double the wine grape acreage of 10 years ago.

Labor Dispute at Spokane Aluminum Plant.

Management and labor were locked in a bitter labor dispute at the Kaiser Aluminum plant in Spokane that began at the end of September 1998. Management was seeking productivity gains and reduction in costs. Labor was concerned about job security, wages, and other matters. The dispute led to a lockout and the hiring of replacement workers. The work stoppage, still nowhere near resolution by the end of summer 1999, has had an adverse effect on the economic health of the Spokane region.

Kennewick Man.

When some college students came upon partially buried human remains as they attempted to sneak in to watch hydroplane races in Kennewick in 1996, their discovery started a custody battle that would pit science against Native

Americans. The skeleton turned out to be 9,000 years old, one of the oldest, most complete human skeletons found to date in North America. Indian tribes wanted a proper burial for their ancestor; scientists sought to unearth the past. On October 29, 1998, Kennewick Man was sent to the Burke Museum at the University of Washington, where he remains, being scrutinized by a team of scientists.

A Ferry Nice Story. One of the first modern car ferries to ply Puget Sound, the *Kalakala* returned to Seattle in November 1998, after years of forgotten exile in Alaska. Built in 1927, the *Kalakala* ferried passengers and cars between Bremerton and Seattle from 1935 until she was retired from ferry service in 1967. The glam old dame was auctioned off and became a seafood processor vessel in Alaska, and then a shoreside cannery outside of Kodiak. By 1994, the *Kalakala* was abandoned and rusting away, out of sight and almost gone from local memory. But not quite. A local foundation purchased the *Kalakala* and successfully returned her in 1998 to Seattle, where she now sits on the shore of Lake Union, awaiting preservation and restoration to her glory days.

Radioactive Tumbleweeds and Other Oddities. A Department of Energy report released in November 1998 reported that scientists sampling flora and fauna on the Hanford Reservation since 1996 have found radioactive tumbleweeds scooting across the wheat fields and plains, and radioactive ants. That same month the Department admitted that there was new evidence that contamination is moving through the water table toward the Columbia River. An estimated 200 square miles of Hanford's groundwater are contaminated. The environmental cleanup of Hanford will be one of the largest in U.S. history.

Election Results. In November 1998, the 62 percent turnout of registered voters defied experts, who predicted a lower turnout. The interest in the elections was sparked by several major voter referendums:

A referendum to terminate affirmative action in the state passed with 58 percent of the vote.

Voters opted to raise the minimum hourly wage to $5.70 from $4.90, with 66 percent approval.

Medical use of marijuana was approved by 59 percent of the voters.

A ban on third-trimester, so-called late-term, abortions was defeated by a 59 percent majority.

A measure to fund transportation system improvements throughout the state passed with 57 percent of the vote.

The high voter turnout favored Democratic candidates. Republican candidates lost ground in part because they failed to connect with the middle-of-the-road voter. For example, Democratic incumbent Patty Murray soundly defeated conservative Republican Linda Smith for the U.S. Senate, with 58 percent of the vote.

No Mo II. The Sonics, the Seahawks, and the Huskies all said buh-bye to their old coaches and all hail to the new....

The Sonics fired Coach George Karl in May 1998 after six and a half seasons. He went to the Milwaukee Bucks, and took them to the 1999 play-offs. He was replaced by Paul Westphal, former coach of the Phoenix Suns. The Sonics didn't make the play-offs in 1999.

The Seahawks told Coach Dennis Erickson to take a hike after the '98 season in December 1998. He went to Oregon State University to coach the Beavers. He was replaced by Mike Holmgren, who had taken the Green Bay Packers to the Superbowl twice. He was hailed with all the pomp and superlatives of a new Caesar. The empirical data was not in as of press time, however.

The UW Huskies' longtime coach, Jim Lambright, was also axed in December 1998, and subsequently retired from coaching altogether. He was replaced by former Colorado coach Rick Neuheisel, whose salary was reported at $1 million per year.

Neuheisel promptly committed several serious recruiting violations, leaving the Huskies front office red-faced but hopeful.

Stormy Weather. Wet weather is nothing new to The Evergreen State, at least that portion of the state that lies west of the Cascade Mountains. It was clear that by March 1999, however, the winter of 1998–99 had broke all records for wetness. In a three month period, November through January, the Seattle region got soaked with 27.44 inches of rain. The rainfall broke the previous record, set in 1995-96. The rainfall was nearly double the previous year's, which was low on account of the El Niño phenomenon. Snowfalls in the mountains broke all records as well. Avalanches on Mount Baker forced closure of the ski area.

Drunk Driving Became Easier. Effective January 1, 1999, the legal limit for drunk driving was lowered from 0.10 percent blood alcohol to 0.08 percent. That new limit is the equivalent of up to three drinks in the average person.

Indian Slots. Slot machines and gambling casinos have become major sources of revenue on Indian lands in 23 states. A federal judge in Spokane, however, ruled in February 1999 that the slot machines at four casinos near Spokane are illegal. The ruling is a consequence of a conflict between two federal laws. The Johnson Act is 1950s anti-organized crime legislation that bans slot machines on Indian reservations. The 1988 federal Indian gaming regulatory act provides an exemption from the Johnson Act if states enter into compacts with Indian tribes to allow gaming, or if state laws permit such activity. Washington State law prohibits slot machines. This has led to the contested gaming activity on Indian lands.

Saving the Salmon. On March 16, 1999, nine separate runs of salmon were listed as threatened species by the federal government. The salmon listings added great impetus to efforts to protect, restore, and enhance salmon habitat, and promised far-reaching changes to land development and management practices throughout the region, as governments at every level sought to develop plans and responses and to restore the salmon.

Dams on rivers, which interfere with salmon runs, also came in for great scrutiny. On the Olympic Peninsula, the U.S. Congress authorized the removal of a dam on the Elwha River, the first instance of a dam being removed in order to restore the salmon. A study of dams on the Snake River, conducted by the National Marine Fisheries Service, concluded that breaching four dams on the lower Snake River would provide more than an 80 percent chance of restoring salmon runs.

Refinery Explosion in Anacortes. An explosion and fire took six lives and did great damage at an Anacortes oil refinery, the day before Thanksgiving, November 26, 1998. The state of Washington reached a settlement with the refinery company in May 1999. The company agreed to pay a $4.4 million fine and to make safety improvements. The refinery is one of the major employers in Anacortes.

From Permit to Potlatch. The Makah Indians of Neah Bay on the Olympic Peninsula hunted a gray whale for the first time in more than 70 years. The successful hunt was marked with a traditional potlatch in May 1999, which celebrated cultural renewal for the tiny tribe, for Native Americans, and for traditional peoples everywhere. The saga of the Makah whale hunt began with an 1855 treaty between the Makahs and the United States, which secured the tribe's whaling rights. The Makahs were granted permission by the International Whaling Commission to hunt up to five whales annually for cultural restoration. The hunt aroused the ire of the environmental protection and animal rights communities, who protested vigorously in the courts and on the water. The tribe's plans drew heated criticism as well, some of it with racist overtones. Nevertheless the tribe persevered. Young men of the tribe trained for many months for the significant event.

Spokane: Serial Killer Claims 10th Victim. A serial killer remained at large in the Spokane region throughout 1998 and was still at large in mid 1999. All 10 victims have been women with past involvement in drugs or prostitution. The killer shoots his victims in the head and dumps the bodies in isolated areas. The chain of evidence points to a single killer, perhaps a blond-haired man. Nine of the 10 murders occurred in Spokane. The 10th, similar in many respects but not proved conclusively to be the work of the same killer, occurred in Tacoma. A special task force of the local police and sheriff's departments and the Washington State Patrol has been established to crack the cases and nab the killer.

Term Limits Come A Cropper.
When George Nethercutt, Republican from Spokane, defeated longtime Representative Tom Foley, Speaker of the U.S. House of Representatives, in November 1994, term limits were an issue in the campaign. Nethercutt vowed that, if elected, he would step aside after serving the people for six years. Well, the six years are up, and guess what? Rep. Nethercutt realizes that his work in Washington, D.C., is too important for him to step aside at this time. He announced that he would run for a fourth term in Congress in 2000, despite his pledge to step aside after three terms.

Further Reading

Alt, David D., and Donald W. Hyndman. *Roadside Geology of Washington State.* Missoula, Mont.: Mountain Press Publishing, 1984.

Angell, Tony, and Kenneth C. Balcomb III. *Marine Birds and Mammals of Puget Sound.* Seattle: Washington Sea Grant Program, 1982.

Arno, Steven, and Romona Hammerly. *Northwest Trees.* Seattle, Wash.: The Mountaineers, 1984.

Blair, Karen J. *Women in Pacific Northwest History: An Anthology.* Seattle: University of Washington Press, 1988.

Brewster, David, and David M. Buerge, eds. *Washingtonians: A Biographical Portrait of the State.* Seattle, Wash.: Sasquatch Books, 1988.

Burns, Robert. *The Shape and Form of Puget Sound.* Seattle: Washington Sea Grant Program, 1985.

Canniff, Kiki. *Northwest Golfer: A Guide to Every Golf Course Where the Public Is Welcome in Oregon and Washington.* Portland, Ore.: Frank Amato Publications, 1996.

Chasan, Daniel Jack. *The Water Link: A History of Puget Sound as a Resource.* Seattle: Washington Sea Grant Program, 1981.

Cheney, Daniel P., and Thomas F. Mumford Jr. *Shellfish and Seaweed Harvests of Puget Sound.* Seattle: Washington Sea Grant Program, 1986.

Cox, Thomas R. *The Park Builders: A History of the State Parks in the Pacific Northwest.* Seattle: University of Washington Press, 1988.

Dietrich, William. *Northwest Passage: The Great Columbia River.* New York: Simon and Schuster, 1995.

Dorpat, Paul, and Genevieve McCoy. *Building Washington: A History of Washington State Public Works.* Seattle, Wash.: Tartu Publications, 1998.

Downing, John. *The Coast of Puget Sound: Its Process and Development.* Seattle: Washington Sea Grant Program, 1983.

Egan, Timothy. *The Good Rain: Across Time and Terrain in the Pacific Northwest.* New York: Vintage Books, A Division of Random House, 1990.

Ewing, Susan. *Going Wild: Seasonal Excursions to Wildlife Habitats.* Seattle, Wash.: Alaska Northwest Books, 1993.

Fahey, John. *The Inland Empire: Unfolding Years, 1879-1929.* Seattle: University of Washington Press, 1986.

Ficken, Robert E. *Rufus Woods, the Columbia River, and the Building of Modern Washington.* Pullman: Washington State University Press. 1995.

Ficken, Robert E., and Charles P. LeWarne. *Washington: A Centennial History.* Seattle: University of Washington Press, 1988.

Fobes, Natalie (photos), Brad Matsen and Tom Jay (text). *Reaching Home: Pacific Salmon, Pacific Peoples.* Seattle, Wash.: Alaska Northwest Books, 1994.

Foley, Tom, and Tish Steinfeld. *How to Rent a Fire Lookout in the Pacific Northwest.* Berkeley, Calif.: Wilderness Press, 1996.

Fox, James R. *1998 Washington State Almanac: An Economic and Demographic Overview of Counties and Cities, 12th Edition.* Eugene, Ore.: Public Sector Information, 1998.

Franklin, Jerry F., and C. T. Dyrness. *Natural Vegetation of Oregon and Washington.* Corvallis: Oregon State University Press, 1988.

Harris, Stephen L. *Fire and Ice: The Cascade Volcanoes, Revised Edition.* Seattle, Wash.: Pacific Search Press, 1980.

Holloway, James. *Columbia River Gorge.* Portland, Ore.: Graphic Arts Center Publishing Company, 1989.

Irvine, Ronald, with Walter J. Clore. *The Wine Project: Washington State's Winemaking History.* Vashon, Wash.: Sketch Publications, 1997.

Johnson, Charles Grier Jr. *Common Plants of the Inland Pacific Northwest.* Portland, Ore.: USDA Forest Service, Pacific Northwest Region, 1998.

Keyser, James D. *Indian Rock Art of the Columbia Plateau.* Seattle: University of Washington Press, 1992.

Kirk, Ruth, and Carmela Alexander.

Exploring Washington's Past: A Road Guide to History. Seattle: University of Washington Press, 1990.

Kruckeberg, Arthur R. *The Natural History of Puget Sound Country*. Seattle, Wash: University of Washington Press, 1991.

La Tourrette, Joe. *Washington Wildlife Viewing Guide*. Helena, Mont.: Falcon Press, 1992.

Laskin, David. *Rains All the Time: A Connoisseur's History of Weather in the Pacific Northwest*. Seattle, Wash.: Sasquatch Books, 1997.

Lee, W. Storrs, ed. *Washington State: A Literary Chronicle*. New York: Funk & Wagnalls. 1969.

Leonard, William P., Herbert A. Brown, Lawrence L. C. Jones, Kelly R. McAllister, and Robert M. Storm. *Amphibians of Washington and Oregon*. Seattle, Wash.: Seattle Audubon Society. 1993.

Lyons, Dianne Boulerice, and Archie Satterfield. *Washington Handbook*. Chico, Calif.: Moon Publications, 1992.

MacMillan, Daniel. *Golfing in Washington: The Complete Guide to Washington's Golf Facilities, 12th Edition*. Carnation, Wash.: Mac Productions. 1997.

Marshall, John. *Portrait of Washington*. Portland, Ore.: Graphic Arts Center Publishing Company, 1993

———. *Washington Apple Country*. Portland, Ore.: Graphic Arts Center Publishing Company, 1995.

———. *Washington II*. Portland, Ore.: Graphic Arts Center Publishing Company, 1999.

Mathews, Daniel. *Cascade-Olympic Natural History: A Trailside Reference*. Portland, Ore.: Raven Editions and Portland Audubon Society, 1988.

Molina, Randy, Thomas O'Dell, Daniel Luoma, Michael Amaranthus, Michael Castellano, and Kenelm Russell. *Biology, Ecology, and Social Aspects of Wild Edible Mushrooms in the Forests of the Pacific Northwest: A Preface to Managing Commercial Harvest*. Portland, Ore.: USDA, Forest Service, Pacific Northwest Research Station, 1993.

Morgan, Murray. *Skid Road: Seattle—Her First Hundred Years*. New York: The Viking Press, 1951.

———*The Dam*. New York: The Viking Press. 1954.

Nelson, Sharlene P., and Ted W. Nelson. *Umbrella Guide to Washington Lighthouses*. Friday Harbor, Wash.: Umbrella Books, 1990.

Nice, David C., John C. Pierce, and Charles H. Sheldon, eds. *Government and Politics in the Evergreen State*. Pullman: Washington State University Press, 1992.

North, Douglass A. *Washington Whitewater: The 34 Best Whitewater Rivers*. Seattle, Wash.: The Mountaineers, 1992.

Pandell, Karen, and Chris Stall. *Animal Tracks of the Pacific Northwest*. Seattle, Wash.: The Mountaineers, 1981.

Phillips, James W. *Washington State Place Names*. Seattle: University of Washington Press, 1971.

Pitzer, Paul C. *Grand Coulee: Harnessing a Dream*. Pullman: Washington State University Press, 1994.

Plumb, Gregory A. *A Waterfall Lover's Guide to the Pacific Northwest*. Seattle, Wash.: The Mountaineers, 1989.

Rockafellar, Nancy, and James W. Haviland. *Saddlebags to Scanners: The First 100 Years of Medicine in Washington State*. Seattle: Washington State Medical Association, 1989.

Sale, Roger. *Seattle Past to Present: An Interpretation of the History of the Foremost City in the Pacific Northwest*. Seattle: University of Washington Press, 1976.

Saling, Ann. *The Great Northwest Nature Factbook*. Seattle, Wash.: Alaska Northwest Books. 1999.

Scott, James W., and Roland L. DeLorme. *Historical Atlas of Washington*. Norman: University of Oklahoma Press, 1988.

Snively, Gloria. *Exploring the Seashore in British Columbia, Washington and Oregon*. Vancouver and London: Gordon Soules Book Publishers, 1978.

Steelquist, Robert U. *Washington's Coast*. Helena, Mont.: American Geographic Publishing, 1987.

———*Washington, Portrait of the Land*. Helena, Mont.: American Geographic

Publishing, 1988.

Stienstra, Tom. *Pacific Northwest Camping: The Complete Guide to More than 45,000 Campsites in Washington and Oregon.* San Francisco: Foghorn Press, 1996.

Sullivan, Barbara. *Seattle Picnics.* Seattle, Wash.: Alaska Northwest Books, 1991

Swanson, Diane. *The Emerald Sea.* Seattle, Wash.: Alaska Northwest Books, 1993.

Washington Atlas and Gazetteer. Freeport, Maine: DeLorme Mapping Company, 1988.

Washington State Office of Financial Management. *1997 Data Book, State of Washington.* Olympia, Wash.: Office of Financial Management, 1998.

Weis, Norman D. *Ghost Towns of the Northwest.* Caldwell, Idaho: The Caxton Printers, 1993.

Wert, Fred. *Washington's Rail-Trails: A Guide for Walkers, Bicyclists, Equestrians.* Seattle, Wash.: The Mountaineers, 1992.

Woodbridge, Sally B., and Roger Montgomery. *A Guide to Architecture in Washington State.* Seattle: University of Washington Press, 1980.

Yates, Richard, and Charity Yates. *Washington State Atlas and Databook, 5th Edition.* Eugene, Ore.: Public Sector Information, 1998.

Appendix: Washington State Constitution Preamble and Declaration of Rights

PREAMBLE

We, the people of the State of Washington, grateful to the Supreme Ruler of the Universe for our liberties, do ordain this constitution.

ARTICLE I DECLARATION OF RIGHTS

SECTION 1 POLITICAL POWER. All political power is inherent in the people, and governments derive their just powers from the consent of the governed, and are established to protect and maintain individual rights.

SECTION 2 SUPREME LAW OF THE LAND. The Constitution of the United States is the supreme law of the land.

SECTION 3 PERSONAL RIGHTS. No person shall be deprived of life, liberty, or property, without due process of law.

SECTION 4 RIGHT OF PETITION AND ASSEMBLAGE. The right of petition and of the people peaceably to assemble for the common good shall never be abridged.

SECTION 5 FREEDOM OF SPEECH. Every person may freely speak, write and publish on all subjects, being responsible for the abuse of that right.

SECTION 6 OATHS—MODE OF ADMINISTERING. The mode of administering an oath, or affirmation, shall be such as may be most consistent with and binding upon the conscience of the person to whom such oath, or affirmation, may be administered.

SECTION 7 INVASION OF PRIVATE AFFAIRS OR HOME PROHIBITED. No person shall be disturbed in his private affairs, or his home invaded, without authority of law.

SECTION 8 IRREVOCABLE PRIVILEGE, FRANCHISE OR IMMUNITY PROHIBITED. No law granting irrevocably any privilege, franchise or immunity, shall be passed by the legislature.

SECTION 9 RIGHTS OF ACCUSED PERSONS. No person shall be compelled in any criminal case to give evidence against himself, or be twice put in jeopardy for the same offense.

SECTION 10 ADMINISTRATION OF JUSTICE. Justice in all cases shall be administered openly, and without unnecessary delay.

SECTION 11 RELIGIOUS FREEDOM. Absolute freedom of conscience in all matters of religious sentiment, belief and worship, shall be guaranteed to every individual, and no one shall be molested or disturbed in person or property on account of religion; but the liberty of conscience hereby secured shall not be so construed as to excuse acts of licentiousness or justify practices inconsistent with the peace and safety of the state. No public money or property shall be appropriated for or applied to any religious worship, exercise or instruction, or the support of any religious establishment: PROVIDED,

HOWEVER, That this article shall not be so construed as to forbid the employment by the state of a chaplain for such of the state custodial, correctional, and mental institutions, or by a county's or public hospital district's hospital, health care facility, or hospice, as in the discretion of the legislature may seem justified. No religious qualification shall be required for any public office or employment, nor shall any person be incompetent as a witness or juror, in consequence of his opinion on matters of religion, nor be questioned in any court of justice touching his religious belief to affect the weight of his testimony. [AMENDMENT 88, 1993 House Joint Resolution No. 4200, p 3062. Approved November 2, 1993.]

Amendment 34 (1957)—Art. I Section 11 RELIGIOUS FREEDOM—Absolute freedom of conscience in all matters of religious sentiment, belief and worship, shall be guaranteed to every individual, and no one shall be molested or disturbed in person or property on account of religion; but the liberty of conscience hereby secured shall not be so construed as to excuse acts of licentiousness or justify practices inconsistent with the peace and safety of the state. No public money or property shall be appropriated for or applied to any religious worship, exercise or instruction, or the support of any religious establishment: Provided, however, That this article shall not be so construed as to forbid the employment by the state of a chaplain for such of the state custodial, correctional and mental institutions as in the discretion of the legislature may seem justified. No religious qualification shall be required for any public office or employment, nor shall any person be incompetent as a witness or juror, in consequence of his opinion on matters of religion, nor be questioned in any court of justice touching his religious belief to affect the weight of his testimony. [AMENDMENT 34, 1957 Senate Joint Resolution No. 14, p 1299. Approved November 4, 1958.]

Amendment 4 (1904)—Art. I Section 11 RELIGIOUS FREEDOM—Absolute freedom of conscience in all matters of religious sentiment, belief and worship, shall be guaranteed to every individual, and no one shall be molested or disturbed in person or property on account of religion; but the liberty of conscience hereby secured shall not be so construed as to excuse acts of licentiousness or justify practices inconsistent with the peace and safety of the state. No public money or property shall be appropriated for or applied to any religious worship, exercise or instruction, or the support of any religious establishment. Provided, however, That this article shall not be so construed as to forbid the employment by the state of a chaplain for the state penitentiary, and for such of the state reformatories as in the discretion of the legislature may seem justified. No religious qualification shall be required for any public office or employment, nor shall any person be incompetent as a witness or juror, in consequence of his opinion on matters of religion, nor be questioned in any court of justice touching his religious belief to affect the weight of his testimony. [AMENDMENT 4, 1903 p 283 Section 1. Approved November, 1904.]

Original text—Art. I Section 11 RELIGIOUS FREEDOM —Absolute freedom of conscience in all matters of religious sentiment, belief, and worship, shall be guaranteed to every individual, and no one shall be molested or disturbed in person, or property, on account of religion; but the liberty of conscience hereby secured shall not be so construed as to excuse acts of licentiousness, or justify practices inconsistent with the peace and safety of the state. No public money or property shall be appropriated for, or applied to any religious worship, exercise or instruction, or the support of any religious establishment. No religious qualification shall be required for any public office, or employment, nor shall any person be incompetent as a witness, or juror, in consequence of his opinion on matters of religion, nor be questioned in any court of justice touching his religious belief to affect the weight of his testimony.

SECTION 12 SPECIAL PRIVILEGES AND IMMUNITIES PROHIBITED. No law shall be passed granting to any citizen, class of citizens, or corporation other than municipal, privileges or immunities which upon the same terms shall not equally belong to all citizens, or corporations.

SECTION 13 HABEAS CORPUS. The privilege of the writ of habeas corpus shall not be suspended, unless in case of rebellion or invasion the public safety requires it.

SECTION 14 EXCESSIVE BAIL, FINES AND PUNISHMENTS. Excessive bail shall not be required, excessive fines imposed, nor cruel punishment inflicted.

SECTION 15 CONVICTIONS, EFFECT OF. No conviction shall work corruption of blood, nor forfeiture of estate.

SECTION 16 EMINENT DOMAIN. Private property shall not be taken for private use, except for private ways of necessity, and for drains, flumes, or ditches on or across the lands of others for agricultural, domestic, or sanitary purposes. No private property shall be taken or damaged for public or private use without just compensation having been first made, or paid into court for the owner, and no right-of-way shall be appropriated to the use of any corporation other than municipal until full compensation therefor be first made in money, or ascertained and paid into court for the owner, irrespective of any benefit from any improvement proposed by such corporation, which compensation shall be ascertained by a jury, unless a jury be waived, as in other civil cases in courts of record, in the manner prescribed by law. Whenever an attempt is made to take private property for a use alleged to be public, the question whether the contemplated use be really public shall be a judicial question, and determined as such, without regard to any legislative assertion that the use is public: Provided, That the taking of private property by the state for land reclamation and settlement purposes is hereby declared to be for public use.[AMENDMENT 9, 1919 p 385 Section 1. Approved November, 1920.]

Original text—Art. I Section 16 EMINENT DOMAIN— Private property shall not be taken for private use, except for private ways of necessity, and for drains, flumes or ditches on or across the lands of others for agricultural, domestic or sanitary purposes. No private property shall be taken or damaged for public or private use without just compensation having first been made, or paid into court for the owner, and no right of way shall be appropriated to the use of any corporation other than municipal, until full compensation therefor be first made in money, or ascertained and paid into the court for the owner, irrespective of any benefit from any improvement proposed by such corporation, which compensation shall be ascertained by a jury, unless a jury be waived as in other civil cases in courts of record, in the manner prescribed by law. Whenever an attempt is made to take private property for a use alleged to be public, the question whether the contemplated use be really public shall be a judicial question, and determined as such without regard to any legislative assertion that the use is public.

SECTION 17 IMPRISONMENT FOR DEBT. There shall be no imprisonment for debt, except in cases of absconding debtors.

SECTION 18 MILITARY POWER, LIMITATION OF. The military shall be in strict subordination to the civil power.

SECTION 19 FREEDOM OF ELECTIONS. All Elections shall be free and equal, and no power, civil or military, shall at any time interfere to prevent the free exercise of the right of suffrage.

SECTION 20 BAIL, WHEN AUTHORIZED. All persons charged with crime shall be bailable by sufficient sureties, except for capital offenses when the proof is evident, or the presumption great.

SECTION 21 TRIAL BY JURY. The right of trial by jury shall remain inviolate, but the legislature may provide for a jury of any number less than twelve in courts not of record, and for a verdict by nine or more jurors in civil cases in any court of record, and for waiving of the jury in civil cases where the consent of the parties interested is given thereto.

SECTION 22 RIGHTS OF THE ACCUSED. In criminal prosecutions the accused shall have the right to appear and defend in person, or by counsel, to demand the nature and cause of the accusation against him, to have a copy thereof, to testify in his own behalf, to meet the witnesses against him face to face, to have compulsory process to compel the attendance of witnesses in his own behalf, to have a speedy public trial by an impartial jury of the county in which theoffense is charged to have been committed and the right to appeal in all cases: Provided, The route traversed by any railway coach, train or public conveyance, and the water traversed by any boat shall be criminal districts; and thejurisdiction of all public offenses committed on any such railway car, coach, train, boat or other public conveyance, or at any station or depot upon such route, shall be in any county through which the said car, coach, train, boat or other public conveyance may pass during the trip or voyage, or in which the trip or voyage may begin or terminate. In no instance shall any accused person before final judgment be compelled to advance money or fees to secure the rights herein guaranteed. [AMENDMENT 10, 1921 p 79 Section 1. Approved November, 1922.]

Original text—Art. I Section 22 RIGHTS OF
ACCUSED PERSONS— In criminal prosecution, the
accused shall have the right to appear and defend in
person, and by counsel, to demand the nature and cause
of the accusation against him, to have a copy thereof, to
testify in his own behalf, to meet the witnesses against
him face to face, to have compulsory process to compel
the attendance of witnesses in his own behalf, to have a
speedy public trial by an impartial jury of the county in
which the offense is alleged to have been committed,
and the right to appeal in all cases; and, in no instance,
shall any accused person before final judgment be compelled to advance money or fees to secure the rights
herein guaranteed.

SECTION 23 BILL OF ATTAINDER, EX POST FACTO
LAW, ETC. No bill of attainder, ex post facto law, or
law impairing the obligations of contracts shall ever be
passed.

SECTION 24 RIGHT TO BEAR ARMS. The right of the
individual citizen to bear arms in defense of himself, or
the state, shall not be impaired, but nothing in this section shall be construed as authorizing individuals or
corporations to organize, maintain or employ an armed
body of men.

SECTION 25 PROSECUTION BY INFORMATION.
Offenses heretofore required to be prosecuted by
indictment may be prosecuted by information, or by
indictment, as shall be prescribed by law.

SECTION 26 GRAND JURY. No grand jury shall be
drawn or summoned in any county, except the superior
judge thereof shall so order.

SECTION 27 TREASON, DEFINED, ETC. Treason
against the state shall consist only in levying war against
the state, or adhering to its enemies, or in giving them
aid and comfort. No person shall be convicted of treason unless on the testimony of two witnesses to the
same overt act, or confession in open court.

SECTION 28 HEREDITARY PRIVILEGES ABOLISHED.
No hereditary emoluments, privileges, or powers, shall
be granted or conferred in this state.

SECTION 29 CONSTITUTION MANDATORY. The
provisions of this Constitution are mandatory, unless by
express words they are declared to be otherwise.

SECTION 30 RIGHTS RESERVED. The enumeration in
this Constitution of certain rights shall not be construed
to deny others retained by the people.

SECTION 31 STANDING ARMY. No standing army
shall be kept up by this state in time of peace, and no
soldier shall in time of peace be quartered in any house
without the consent of its owner, nor in time of war
except in the manner prescribed by law.

SECTION 32 FUNDAMENTAL PRINCIPLES. A frequent recurrence to fundamental principles is essential
to the security of individual right and the perpetuity of
free government.

SECTION 33 RECALL OF ELECTIVE OFFICERS. Every
elective public officer of the state of Washington expect

[except] judges of courts of record is subject to recall
and discharge by the legal voters of the state, or of the
political subdivision of the state, from which he was
elected whenever a petition demanding his recall, recit-
ing that such officer has committed some act or acts of
malfeasance or misfeasance while in office, or who has
violated his oath of office, stating the matters com-
plained of, signed by the percentages of the qualified
electors thereof, hereinafter provided, the percentage
required to be computed from the total number of
votes cast for all candidates for his said office to which
he was elected at the preceding election, is filed with the
officer with whom a petition for nomination, or certificate for nomination, to such office must be filed under
the laws of this state, and the same officer shall call a
special election as provided by the general election laws
of this state, and the result determined as therein provided. [AMENDMENT 8, 1911 p 504 Section 1.
Approved November, 1912.]

SECTION 34 SAME. The legislature shall pass the necessary laws to carry out the provisions of section
thirty-three (33) of this article, and to facilitate its operation and effect without delay: Provided, That the
authority hereby conferred upon the legislature shall not
be construed to grant to the legislature any exclusive
power of lawmaking nor in any way limit the initiative
and referendum powers reserved by the people. The
percentages required shall be, state officers, other than
judges, senators and representatives, city officers of
cities of the first class, school district boards in cities of
the first class; county officers of counties of the first,
second and third classes, twenty-five per cent. Officers
of all other political subdivisions, cities, towns, town-
ships, precincts and school districts not herein
mentioned, and state senators and representatives,
thirty-five per cent. [AMENDMENT 8, 1911 p 504 Section 1. Approved November, 1912.]

SECTION 35 VICTIMS OF CRIMES—RIGHTS. Effective
law enforcement depends on cooperation from victims
of crime. To ensure victims a meaningful role in the
criminal justice system and to accord them due dignity
and respect, victims of crime are hereby granted the following basic and fundamental rights.

Upon notifying the prosecuting attorney, a victim of a
crime charged as a felony shall have the right to be
informed of and, subject to the discretion of the individual presiding over the trial or court proceedings, attend
trial and all other court proceedings the defendant has
the right to attend, and to make a statement at sentencing and at any proceeding where the defendant's release
is considered, subject to the same rules of procedure
which govern the defendant's rights. In the event the
victim is deceased, incompetent, a minor, or otherwise
unavailable, the prosecuting attorney may identify a representative to appear to exercise the victim's rights.
This provision shall not constitute a basis for error in
favor of a defendant in a criminal proceeding nor a basis
for providing a victim or the victim's representative with
court appointed counsel. [AMENDMENT 84, 1989
Senate Joint Resolution No. 8200, p 2999. Approved
November 7, 1989.]

Index